THE KOL TRIBE OF CENTRAL INDIA

THE KOL TRIBE OF CENTRAL INDIA

BY

WALTER G. GRIFFITHS

GYAN

ISBN : 978-81-212-1816-0 (HB)

First Published, 1946

Published, 2018

Published by

Gyan Publishing House
5, Ansari Road
Daryaganj, New Delhi-110002
Phone: 011-47034999, 9811692060
www.gyanbooks.com
E-mail: books@gyanbooks.com

Printed at: G. Print Process, Delhi.

FOREWORD

It is with great pleasure I am presenting to the scholarly world the first reprint of the monograph, "The Kol Tribe of Central India", written by W. G. Griffiths which was published by the Asiatic Society in 1946. The very name of the book is sufficiently indicative of the subject matter that it deals with. This monograph is based on the first hand experience of the author who has spent about 15 years in Jabbalpur of the then Central Province during late 30's and 40's.

The Monograph extensively deals with the Kol Tribe of Central India. The coverage of the monograph is very wide and the first authentic document on the subject. It includes distribution and strength of the tribes, their origin, historical data, inferential Hindu scriptures, their beliefs, their material culture, social structure, their birth, childhood and puberty, their marriage cycle, family and the social unit, their death and its attendant ceremonies, religion and attendant festivals, magic and witchcraft, folklore and fables, music, songs, dance and art. It also includes some life stories of living and their economic life. A concluding chapter is also there which deals with the Kol tribe in transition. This has added a new dimension to the subject.

The monograph is illustrated with drawings and well-chosen photographs taken by the author. There are certain drawbacks also. Nevertheless, the merit of the book is overwhelming. It fills in ethnographic map of India, as supplying for the first time a dependable account of the life and customs of a large and well-known primitive tribe of Central India.

The United Nation's declaration of the present year as international year of indigeneous people, has drawn the attention of all of us, academics, in particular, to the persistent need for caring for such people. The first step towards that is to know and understand them better.

The present reprint is, therefore, our humble response to this cause. We hope, that this response would be reciprocated by the scholarly world.

CHANDAN ROY CHAUDHURI
General Secretary

22nd March 1993

INTRODUCTION

By

DR. B. S. GUHA, A.M., Ph.D., F.N.I., F.R.A.S.B.,

DIRECTOR,

ANTHROPOLOGICAL SURVEY OF INDIA

During the past century and more Christian missionaries have made numerous contributions to the anthropological literature of India. One of the first of these was the Abbé Dubois, whose account of the manners and customs of the people of India, though written in a witty style and from one who was a genuine lover of the Country, was nevertheless very superficial and gave a completely distorted picture. Later the Rev. G. U. Pope, a very fine scholar who retired in due time to Balliol, and the Rev. Mateer studied the customs and folk-literature of Southern India, and their books may still be read with profit. In the recording of folk-tales, missionaries have always taken a leading part. The Rev. Lal Behari Day's account of the Folk Tales of Bengal is still regarded as classic; the Rev. J. H. Knowles' collection of stories from Kashmir is extremely fascinating and the Rev. C. Swynnerton devoted a quarter of a century to the compilation and study of tales from the Punjab. The Rev. (later, Bishop) A. Wood's anthology, *In and Out of Chanda*, however, is hardly on this level, and the author has even been accused by an American scholar (W. N. Brown) of doctoring his sources. The same may be said of Bishop Eyre Chatterton's *The Story of Gondwana*, which borrows much of its material from the *Papers* of the Rev. S. Hislop, who was the first to record the Gond legend of Lingo, and whose admirable collections were edited after his death by Sir R. Temple in 1860.

In modern times valuable contributions have been made by missionaries in Chota Nagpur, and I need only mention the names of the distinguished authors of the *Encyclopædia Mundarica*—Fathers Hoffman and Van Emelen, the work of Father Hahn and the books of Father Grignard. In recent years under Father Koppers, editor of

Anthropos and one of the leaders of the Kulturkreise school of Vienna, other missionaries in Central India—Father S. Fuchs, for example and the Father Jungleblutt—have done some good work. Above them all stand however, the work of the Rev. P. O. Bodding of the Scandinavian Mission, who as a result of over half a century's work in the Santal Parganas, published the most authentic and detailed accounts of the beliefs, practices of the Santals, and a dictionary of the Santal language—contributions without parallel on any primitive tribe so far made by any one in India. It had been my privilege as Hony. General Secretary of the Royal Asiatic Society of Bengal to publish Part III of his Memoir on "How the Santals Live". Unfortunately the other parts of the series could not be published due to the author's sudden death in Denmark during the war. But it is to be hoped that in the MSS removed by his widow to Oslo after his death, there are still preserved some of the notes and papers on the Santals which the Royal Asiatic Society of Bengal may yet find it possible to publish.

In these works, three different attitudes, each characteristic of the temper of the times, may be distinguished. The earliest writers, though enchanted in spite of themselves by the interest and beauty of the things they saw, could not escape the belief that every thing outside those approved by the Christian Church was wrong, and would have to disappear before the spread of their teaching. This accounts for the somewhat astringent comments of the Abbé Dubois, which have very rightly offended Indian readers. During the present century, however, the spread of scientific knowledge and a more intensive study of comparative religion, together with a vast amount of scholarly research on the origin of civilization, compelled many to take a more liberal view and this was not without some wholesome influence on missionary anthropologists, such as, for example, Briggs' book on the Chamars (a book quoted several times by Dr. Griffiths), Mrs. Sinclair Stevenson's carefully compiled *Rites of the Twice-Born*. The third trend of thought revealing a type more acceptable to the scientific anthropologist, keeps its theological predelictions behind and approaches its subject in a spirit of detached and objective enquiry as exemplified in the Rev. Dr. W. C. Smith's work on the Ao Nagas and the Karen People of Burma by the Rev. H. I. Marshall of the American Baptist Mission, both of whom were trained anthropologists and had taken courses under recognised specialists on the subject. This was also the attitude of Hoffman and Bodding, as well as of Dr. W. G. Griffiths.

Hitherto, not much information was available on the Kols, excepting a few short papers and the accounts given by Crooke, Dalton, Risley, Russell and Hiralal. Although they are one of the most widely spread and well known tribes of the Central Uplands extending from Kolhan in the district of Singhbhum and as far west as the Chitor Hills. Contact with them was from the earliest as shown by the name "Kolarian", still used by many in a generic sense for the languages and people of the Munda group. Dr. Griffiths' account of the Kols in a readable handy form is expected to remove much of this want. As a missionary of the Methodist Church, who spent many years in Jubbulpore, Dr. Griffiths had great opportunity of intimate acquaintance with the Kols of this part and his account, therefore, is based on deep personal knowledge. The Kols described by him, however, are greatly acculturated with Hindu ideas and beliefs and do not retain their original practices in the same form and extent as those living in the interior of Rewa. Nevertheless, Dr. Griffiths has succeeded in discovering traces of many interesting customs not hitherto described. Such for example is the practice of local or village exogamy (pp. 69-70) although clan-Kurhi (or Got from Sans Gotra) exogamy is no longer prevalent (p. 52). The author considers that totemism has lost its significance among the Kols (p. 54), but Russell and Hiralal mention (The Tribes and Castes of the Central Provinces, Vol. III, pp. 510-11) the names of several totemistic septs among the Mandla Kols, *e.g.*, the Bargaiyan Kols, the Kathotia, the Katharia, and the Kumhra, who show special reverence to the Banyan tree, the Tiger, the Mattress and the Gourd respectively. Other apparently totemistic septs are the Mudia or Mudrundia, the Bhuwar, Nathunia and the Karpatia. Some of them such as Kathautia and Kathariya, Kurha, Bhumiya, Mudia (Murha) find place in the list of 22 clans given by the author (pp. 32-33). The possibility of a totemistic basis of their social organization is strongly suspected, but may perhaps be investigated with greater chances of success among the wilder Kols of Kaimur Hills, and those living in the interior of the Rewa State. Another interesting feature noted by the author is the use of bangles, specially made from metals like copper and iron, as effective protection against evil spirits, and of beads as defensive ornaments against the evil eye in children (p. 180).

The book is illustrated with drawings and well chosen photographs taken by the author, but there are unfortunately several printing errors and certain inconsistencies in the writing of the names of works cited, *e.g.*, W. Crooke's work is cited as "The Tribes and Castes of the North Western Provinces and Oudh" on p. 4, but on p. 33, the same work is written as—"Tribes and Castes of *North-West* Provinces and Oudh." Similarly Dr. Verrier Elwin's "The Baiga" is written incorrectly as *The Baigas*.

These small blemishes, however, do not detract from the real merit of the work and the blank it fills in the ethnographic map of India, as supplying for the first time a dependable account of the life and customs of a large and well known primitive tribe of Central India.

Dr. Griffiths is to be congratulated for doing so in the midst of his other works.

PREFACE

The writer of this monograph on the Kols of Central India spent fifteen years in Jubbulpore, Central Provinces, and during the latter half of that period was in frequent contact with the Kol group. The materials used in the preparation of this work were collected during this period, and in pursuing the investigations numerous tours were made through areas where Kols are found and the materials and information obtained elsewhere were checked and supplemented. Careful notes were kept and many photographs taken, some of which appear in this volume.

The author must thank a large number of friends and helpers, who, by their kind and persistent pressure, have encouraged him to finish this task when many unexpected responsibilities seemed to make it an impossibility. I am especially grateful to Professor George Weston Briggs of Drew University who on a visit to India took valuable time to read the first draft of the manuscript. I am also grateful to the late Professor Oscar MacMillan Buck of the same University for his help in putting the material in final form. To the Reverend Albert Austin Parker, Principal-Emeritus of the Leonard Theological College, I am thankful for encouragement and for a generous measure of the financial help needed for the extensive field work. I am also grateful to those who assisted me in the field work : Nathaniel Peters, Theodore Tirkey and Eleazar Pershadi. Mention must be made of help in translating poetry and I am indebted to Pandit Kanade, Masihdas Wany and the Rev. A. G. Atkins for their assistance. My mother Mrs. Elizabeth R. Griffiths, has given me invaluable help in the preparation of the final copy of the manuscript. To my wife, Mabelle Elwood Griffiths, I am deeply indebted, not only for the sketches found in this book, but also for her consistent encouragement. I have had advice and encouragement from the Late Rai Bahadur Sarat Chandra Roy well-known for his studies of aboriginal groups in Chota Nagpur. I am especially indebted to Dr. B.S. Guha of the Anthropological Survey of India, for reading the first draft of the manuscript and for valuable suggestions in connection with the final form, and for the latter's interest and cooperation in the anthropometric measurements which were made on the Kols by Dr. B. K. Chatterji of his Laboratory, whose detailed report will be published separately later on. Dr. Bani Prasad also gave me valuable advice when it was expected that these materials would appear as a Memoir of the Zoological Survey. The outbreak of the war with Japan stopped all publications. As the war dragged on and it appeared that Government Publications would be unduly delayed the Council of the Royal Asiatic Society of Bengal accepted the manuscript for this series. I am deeply grateful to all concerned.

Of course thanks and acknowledgement are due to a host of Kols who graciously allowed themselves to be questioned and probed, measured and photographed. They have admitted us into their houses and into their counsels. They have shared with us many of their joys, troubles and difficulties. They are a very human folk, and as one sat and talked with them, his heart went out to them, and we felt as one. They have been pleased and touched as we have attempted to understand their life and thought. What is here offered of that, however, is but a drop in the great ocean of Kol experience, and the author is conscious of all its limitations.

It is also necessary to make clear the terminology of this book, for there has been a change in the meaning of terms. The word 'Kol' was once used in a generic sense to describe 'Munda-speaking' tribes and the term 'Kolarian' is still frequently found, especially in older textbooks of Ethnology. The word was originally used by Max Muller in a linguistic sense, but has now been generally abandoned in favour of 'Munda'. The Munda-speaking people, as distinguished from the Dravidian, delineate the large majority of the aboriginal people living in Chota Nagpur and in the highlands of Central India. The word 'Kol' as it will appear in these pages denotes a particular branch of the 'Munda-speaking' stock settled in Central India.

There are various theories held today as to the racial composition of present-day India. The first inhabitants of India are thought to have been a Negroid people akin to the Negritos of today. This strain is at present largely submerged. In the course of time another race of people became dominant in the land. Dr. Guha has called them Proto-Australoids. They apparently displaced the Negritos and probably absorbed some of their blood. The Proto-Australoids of India show marked resemblances to the Veddas of Ceylon and to the aborigines of Australia. Practically the whole of the Central Indian and South Indian tribes, though speaking different tongues, belong to this group. If anything, these people may be called the true autochtones of the Indian Peninsula. This same racial stratum persists today (though probably modified by contacts with other groups) in the Oraons, Santals, Mundas and Kharias of Bihar; in the Kols, Bhils, Gonds, Korkus, Baigas, etc., of Central India; in upper India among some of the lower castes such as the Chamars and Doms; and in South India in the Chenchus, Kurambas and Yeruvas.

The aim of attempting to present as accurately and completely as possible what the Kol is, does and thinks, has been constantly kept in mind. This is a study of a primitive tribe living in contact with Hindu influences. No attempt has been made to exclude any materials which Kols have in common with other village people, and to present those things peculiar to Kols alone. One would in that case not get an accurate picture of the Kol as he is, for much of what he considers his own is also the possession of many groups among whom he lives. Uniformity of belief and practice is nowhere characteristic of India, nor of this tribe, but the general picture as here presented has been found remarkably consistent through the areas we have toured. It is the author's hope that this book will encourage further studies in primitive groups, and also help to preserve the memory of these children of Sheori.

W. G. G.

TABLE OF CONTENTS

LIST OF ILLUSTRATIONS

FIGURES

CHAPTER I

THE KOL TRIBE OF CENTRAL INDIA

DISTRIBUTION AND STRENGTH OF THE TRIBE. The Kol tribe, with which this monograph deals, is one of the primitive tribes of Central India. The Central India area, in which they are found, may be described as a triangle with the Nerbudda and the Son rivers for its hypotenuse, having for one of its sides the valley of the Ganges and, for the other, the Chambal river and the Chitor hills. The Kol tribe occupies the north-eastern part of this area. While individual members may be considerably scattered the bulk of the Kols is found in the north of the Central Provinces; in Rewa State, which is included in the Central India Agency; and in the southern portions of the United Provinces adjoining Rewa State. The main centre of distribution for the Kols is Rewa State and the Kols of Central Provinces look back to Rewa as their homeland. The accompanying map of India shows the distribution of the Kols[1]. It will be seen that they belong to the highlands at the northern end of the peninsula. They live among the Vindhya mountains and in the Kaimur hills. These mountains have played an important part in the cultural and ethnological history of India. In early days, before the forests were denuded and the roads cut through, they were an effective barrier to the movements of people. They have been traditionally associated with the southernmost limits of Aryan influence. There is good evidence that they have sheltered some of the oldest races in India since the dawn of history.

The tribe itself should be carefully distinguished from the Munda tribes of Chota Nagpur which are frequently called Kols in the generic sense. There is no specific Kol tribe in that area, although there is a group called the Larka Kols, or Hos, famous for an insurrection in the year 1832, and a part of the district of Singhbhum is called the Kolhan after them. Mention of the specific Kol tribe is made only in the Census Reports of the Central India Agency and that for the Central Provinces. In the United Provinces the Kols are classed as an exterior caste.

The Kols stand second in strength among the Munda tribes of the Central Provinces. According to the 1931 Census the Korkus are first with 176,616 and the Kols follow with 91,556. Among all the tribes in the province the Kols stand eighth in numerical strength. In the Central Provinces as a whole the Census Reports give the following figures for the Kol tribe :

1 Figure 1, p. 2.

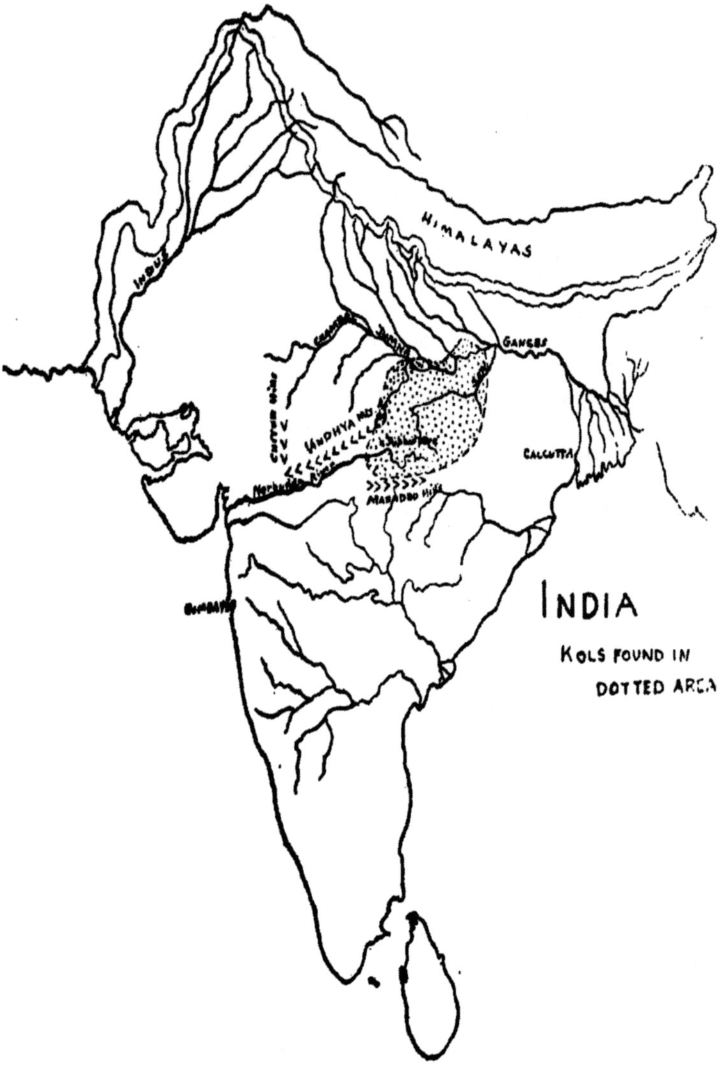
HIMALAYAS
INDUS
GANGES
CALCUTTA
INDIA
KOLS FOUND IN
DOTTED AREA

Fig. I.

Year			Total	"Hindus"	"Animists"
1891	..	..	87,000	No record	No record
1901	..	..	65,043	Do.	Do.
1911	..	..	82,598	58,679	23,819
1921	..	..	96,593	92,117	4,476
1931	..	..	91,556	75,757	15,799
1941	..	..	93,944	No record	No record

According to the 1931 Census Report the majority of the Kols found in the Central Provinces is living in the Jubbulpore division, and numbers 57,827, of which only 84 persons returned themselves as adhering to Tribal Religions.

In the Central India Agency the Census Report of the Kol population is as follows. The figures from earlier Census Reports are incomplete :

Year			Total	"Hindus"	"Animists"
1921	..	..	163,000	..	..
1931	..	..	200,249	193,526	6,723
1941	..	..	32,076	..	..

The Rewa State in the Central India Agency is the home of the Kols according to their own belief. Of the 200,000 Kols in the Central India Agency, the 1931 report showed that 175,391 were found in Rewa State, and of this number only 861 returned themselves as other than Hindu. The report for Central India in 1931 says that there had been a tendency in the past to classify all aboriginal tribes as 'Gonds,' but that this tendency was carefully checked and adjusted in this report.[1]

In the United Provinces bordering Rewa State, Kols are found in considerable numbers. The figures are as follows, and in the Report no distinction is made in regard to tribal religions : all were returned as Hindu and the group treated as an exterior caste :

Year	Total	Year	Total
1891	68,556	1921	68,941
1901	49,653	1931	76,848
1911	65,647	1941	76,737

These are limited practically to three districts : Mirzapur, with some 38,000 ; Allahabad with 26,000 and Banda with 11,000. The increase over 1921, which amounts to 11.5% is ascribed to immigration from Rewa State. In the United Provinces Report the Kols are treated as an external or depressed class ; elsewhere they are uniformly treated as a forest tribe.

1 *Census of India*, 1931, xx:1, p. 217. But the 1941 figures show that a new method of classification was followed. At the time of printing the explanation was not available.

Considering India as a whole the Census Reports give the following figures for the Kols :

Year		Total			
1881 ..	..	57,420			
1891 ..	..	143,551			
1901 ..	..	105,474			
1911 ..	..	148,245	(Including	23,819	'Animists')
1921 ..	..	328,245	Do.	9,944	Do.
1931 ..	..	368,653	Do.	22,522	Do.[1]
1941 ..	..	202,757	..	..	..

ORIGIN OF THE KOLS : GENERAL : HISTORICAL DATA. In recent years there has been an active interest in the study of the origin of tribe and race in India. There are still vast fields to be explored, since much mystery surrounds the movements of races in India. This is just as true of the Munda group to which the Kols belong. Mr. Sarat Chandra Roy in his book *The Mundas and Their Country* published in 1912, was one of the first to make a serious study of the traditions of the tribes of Chota Nagpur concerning their origins. He does not find that their oral traditions throw much light upon the name or location of their original home.

One of the legends collected by Roy suggests the place of origin as *Seva Sandi Bir*—'the vast desolate forest.' This vague terminology makes it difficult, if not impossible, to identify any specific locality. It may refer in general to the Highlands of Central India, or even to the dense jungle that is said to have covered parts of the Gangetic Valley. Roy also points out that the Cosmogonic legend of the Munda tribe names a place called *Ajabgarh*—a place first raised out of the primeval ocean, where Sing Bonga, the Supreme deity of the Munda group in Chota Nagpur, created the first parents of the Munda tribe. Roy holds that this idea was probably borrowed from the Hindus and then mixed up with some of the current Munda legends[2]. The Kols of Central India seem to know nothing, or have heard nothing, about Sing Bonga.

Sir William Crooke, in his article on the Kol tribe, gives us the following legendary information[3]. A certain King, Yayati, fifth King of the Lunar race, divided his empire among his five sons. According to the Harivansa, the children of Yayati's son Turuvasu settled in the south. The tenth generation (from, and including

1 *Ibid.*, 1:2, pp. 522, 523.
2 Roy, Sarat Chandra, *The Mundas and Their Country*, p. 12.
3 Crooke, W., *The Tribes and Castes of the North-Western Provinces and Oudh*, Vol. III, pp. 295, 296.

Turuvasu), consisted of four brothers: Pandya, Korala, Chola and Kola. These divided the kingdom amongst themselves and the descendants of the last son, Kola, became the ancestors of the present Kols.

There is another legend recorded by Colonel Tickell[1] which tells of two self-existent primeval deities called Ote Boram and Sing Bonga. These deities created a boy and a girl and put them together in a cave expecting them to people the earth. However they were found to be too innocent to give hope of progeny and were therefore instructed by these deities in the art of making rice beer which inflames the passions. This was done, and in the course of time they had twelve sons and twelve daughters. These were divided into pairs in order to form the races to people the world. The choice was made on the basis of the kind of food they chose to eat. Sing Bonga set various kinds of food before them, with results which may be summarized thus:

1st	pair chose	bullock flesh	and became	Kols.
2nd	"	buffalo	,,	Bhumiyas
3rd	"	vegetables only	,,	Brahmins.
4th	"	Do.	,,	Chhatris.
5th & 6th	,,	goat	,,	Sudras.
7th & 8th	,,	fish	,,	Sudras.
9th	,,	shell fish	,,	Bhuiyas.
10th & 11th	,,	pork	,,	Santhals.
12th		nothing	,,	Ghasis.

As the last pair had nothing the first pair was sorry for them and gave them some of their food and ever since they have been dependent on the Kols for food.

Crooke also records how the Kols of Mirzapur relate that they are emigrants from a place called Kiutali, in the territory of the then Bardi *Raja* in Rewa State. They name one Nanhu as their ancestor and had a tribal temple at Pipri near Chunar on the East Indian Railway, in which they installed Birmha *devi*. "Like many of the kindred tribes, they have legends of a kingdom in the Gangetic valley, whence they were expelled by the Savaras and returned to the hill country of the south."[2]

Russell and Hiralal in *Tribes and Castes of the Central Provinces* have nothing to add to Crooke's account in connection with traditions of origin. Apparently they did not put much emphasis on this subject.

1 *Ibid.*, p. 296.
2 Crooke, W., *Op. Cit.*, p. 296.

INFERENTIAL: HINDU SCRIPTURES. A study of the sacred books of the Hindus indicates that in the Rigveda two distinct classes of people are recognized from the earliest times. There seems to be constant antagonism between the fair-skinned Aryans (R. V. I:100:18) or Devas on the one hand, and the black-skinned groups (I:100:1) which were termed *dasyus* and *dasas*.[1]

A survey of later Hindu Scriptures such as the Puranas, Upanishads, the Mahabharata and Ramayana seems to indicate that Hindu Scriptures give no really satisfactory account of the origin of the Munda people, nor therefore of the Kols which we are studying. It is not unlikely that in the references to the Nishadas, Chandalas, Paulkasas and the like, we may find truer examples of the savage races who from ancient time occupied upper India. It can be argued that these ancient writings really do not say anything that is of Munda or Kol significance, yet nevertheless they do show the presence of an aboriginal group which very likely included the Munda peoples, and that this group was in possession of the land and was not easily displaced. They also show that the aborigines were different physically, socially and linguistically; that there were religious differences and that they were looked down upon and despised. But whether the tribes which the Aryans had to overcome were Mundas or Dravidians, or both, is very difficult to say. One of the writers in *Encyclopaedia Mundarica*[2] (Article on *Horo*) believes that it may be universally admitted that the first contact of the invaders with the Dravidians proper did not take place before the expeditions described in the Ramayana, and that in Vedic times and earlier, north India was inhabited by the Munda Tribes which, however, never seem to have reached the shores of the seas.

The discoveries in the excavations of Harappa and Mohenjodaro have led to a radical revision of earlier pictures of the condition of northern India before the coming of the Aryans. Further search of the Sind valley in northwestern India has revealed scores of settlements of the Indus valley civilization and some probably even preceding it known as the 'Amri' culture.[3] The whole area, apparently, was one of thriving activity long before the Aryans moved southwards.

The earlier interpretations of the pre-history of India were based largely on the Rigvedic descriptions and it was taken for granted that they recorded actual conditions. From these evidences the assertion was made that the peoples of India—the pre-Aryans—were on a much

1 See Appendix vi. Glossary of Vernacular Terms.
2 Hoffman, J., and Van Emelen, A., *Encyclopedia Mundarica*,
3 Mackay, Ernest, *The Indus Civilization*, p. 3, 4.

lower level of civilization than the Aryans and were so degraded as to be called *dasas*. The mention of the *dasas* being wealthy in cattle and goods, as being good fighters and living in forts was discounted as an exaggeration. Their inferiority was tacitly taken for granted and Marshall comments : "Never for a moment was it imagined that five thousand years ago, before even the Aryans were heard of, the Punjab and Sind, if not other parts of India as well, were enjoying an advanced and singularly uniform civilization of their own, closely akin, but in some respects even superior to that of contemporary Mesopotamia and Egypt."[1] Marshall goes on to sketch the main outlines of their culture and shows that it was "not an incipient civilization, but one already age-old and stereotyped on Indian soil, with many millennia of human endeavour behind it."[2]

Whether the Rigvedic descriptions represent the clash of the "Aryans" and the Indus valley peoples is an open question and waits for further light. Whomsoever they met, as they moved over the plains of northern India, gave them much opposition and it took a long time to overcome and definitely subjugate them. And whether this relatively advanced type of culture succumbed so low before the "Aryans," that its peoples became their servants and slaves is also problematical. Possibly the groups which have become the lower castes in northern India and Bengal belong to an ethnological stream other than that represented by the Mohenjo-daro peoples, and were really a primitive jungle people occupying the highlands of Central India and finding support in the more menial tasks which accompany a higher culture. Those that preferred the jungle ways have as a whole maintained their identity in their forest isolation. More than once they had to retreat before the encroaching "Aryans," and by a series of migrations, now dimly enshrined in their traditions, reached the central parts of India where they now reside.

PARTICULAR : BELIEFS OF THE KOLS IN CENTRAL INDIA. Kols questioned by us in our investigations do not seem to have many definite myths of the place or time of their origin. Those who live in Jubbulpore district almost without exception say that Rewa is their native land, their *desh*, the place of their origin. In Rewa itself two informants, in giving us stories of the origin of the Kols, said that the place of origin was Sheori Narayan, a town in the eastern part of Central Provinces, near the city of Raipur. Another town to the east mentioned by a Rewa Kol is called Pharenda, which, he said, was five or

1 Marshall, John, *Mohenjo-daro and the Indus Civilization*, Vol. I, p. v.

2 *Ibid.*, p. v.

six *kos* east of Rewa city. One of the Kol sub-divisions is called the Binj *kurhi*, and it seems to be generally considered the highest of all their divisions. This group does not seem to exist now-a-days, or at least they do not know where its members may be found, but the implication is that this is the highest group and so perhaps the first group, and that it had its origin in the Binj mountains, the modern Vindhya range of Central India. These mountains lie, generally speaking, to the west of the centre of the Kol population of the present time. The inference might be drawn from these facts that they are from the country to the west. Other informants said that the Kols came into Rewa from the north. It would thus appear that their traditions are very uncertain on this point. Other of their traditions look back to Chitrakot, in the Banda district, which is to the north-west of the present population centre.

A story is told by Kols that the *devatas* or gods were very happy at the birth of Rama and that they desired to celebrate it properly. What was the best form in which to enter the world, was the question they had to decide. They considered that part of the praise should be by song and drum—the *dholak*—so they conceived the idea that the best they could do would be to take the form of Kols. This they did and built a great temple at Chitrakot, sang songs and played the *dholak* there in honour of Rama. When asked further just why the *devatas* took the form of Kols the answer was a bit fuller than intimated at first. They said that the Kols were both the best labourers and the best singers in the world. No one could build the temple so efficiently and so speedily as they and also none like them could praise so acceptably. Therefore the gods came in the guise of Kols.

Quite consistently the Kols to whom we talked trace their origin back to a certain Sheori or Savari or Shivari, calling her 'The Mother of all Kols.' The name may possibly go back to the Savaras of the *Mahabharata*, although it seems more likely that it is based on a certain Ramayana story. The stories vary considerably but their main purport is as follows : There once lived a certain woman named Sheori. She is called by some Kolni (hence Kols) and by others Bhilni.[1] The latter term links the Kols and the Bhils together : this is quite a common, and significant occurrence in their stories. She was a faithful devotee of Bhagawan. Sometimes those who relate the stories call him Siva and at other times Krishna. She followed her lord always and it was her greatest desire to serve him in any way she could.

1 '*Ni*' is the feminine sign : thus 'Kolni' means a Kol woman. In the same manner 'Bhilni' means a Bhil woman.

PLATE I.

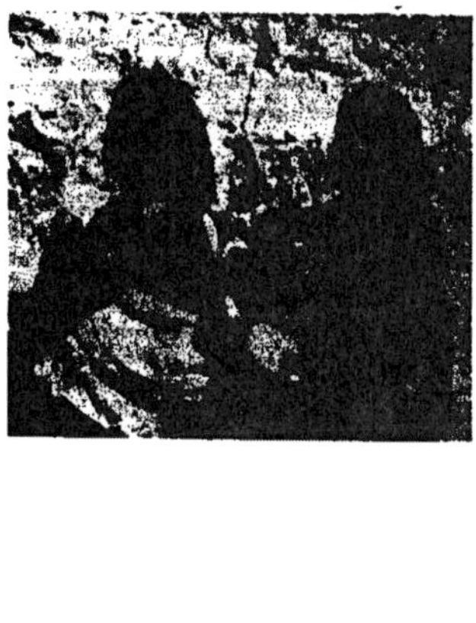

PLATE II.

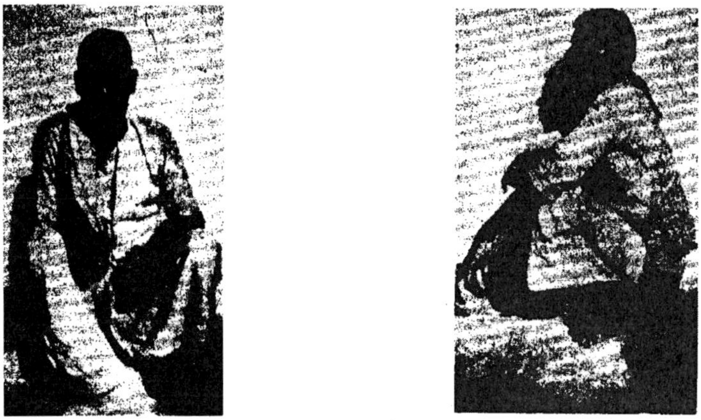

Raja Kol of Garha- -a Rautiya.

Now it appears that the god was very fond of jungle plums or *bers* (*Zizyphus jujuba*), which she made a habit of gathering for him, and she also gathered large leaves for his couch in the forest. The story goes that for some reason, (unknown at least to the Kols telling the story), Sheori was driven out of some unknown habitation and in her flight to the forest came upon a colony of *rishis*, *munis* and *devatas*. Each devotee had his own little hut and in front of each hut was burning the sacred fire kept alive by cow dung cakes, and beside each fire was the place of meditation. When she arrived she found the colony deserted, as the devotees had all gone for a walk, and to take their bath in a near-by sacred tank. Sheori noticed that the places where the devotees sat for meditation were not very clean, for ashes and other refuse lay scattered about. She was moved to clean all this up while they were still away and this she set out to do and accomplished it before the *ashram* members returned. She swept it all clean, straightened up things, and plastered the place of meditation with cow dung in the most approved way. She then seated herself at one side and awaited their return. When they arrived and saw the woman seated near the sacred fires and realized what she had done they were very angry for they considered that she had defiled the place by her presence. They addressed her harshly and gave her a good scolding which she received meekly and without a word. Hearing this, Bhagawan, or as some said, Rama who is frequently addressed as Bhagawan, was greatly angered and in punishment for their rude behaviour caused their sacred tank to become putrid and full of loathsome insects and worms. At first the devotees did not connect this with their treatment of Sheori, and they were greatly amazed. Then Bhagawan broke in on the astonished group and said : "Unless you take this woman to the tank and cause her to bathe therein, your tank will remain vile and unclean." They were very much surprised, but obeyed Bhagawan and taking Sheori to the tank allowed her to bathe therein. The moment her feet descended the *ghat*, and touched the waters, the tank was transformed and again became pure and wholesome, and all the vile insects vanished.

Later on, as she continued to serve Bhagawan, she gathered jungle plums, keeping the sweet ones for him and eating the others herself. Bhagawan was pleased with her devotion and one day asked her if she would like a boon. He offered her a *raj* or a *barti*—a kingdom or a family, and she chose the latter. Five sons were born to her and ever since the Kols believe that they have been outstanding for the size of their families. "Children are God's gift to us," they say. Yet there are many who find fault with this choice and say that

2

Sheori was foolish and has brought the Kols into great economic difficulties with her choice of children. However, when asked who the father of these children was they looked rather startled and could give no answer. They were but the gift of Bhagawan. The first five brothers so born eventually scattered and founded various subdivisions: Binj, Thakuriya and Kathautiya being mentioned. The first brother went to the Binj mountains and thus the Binj *kurhi* was formed. Bhagawan's boon was granted to Sheori in the jungles near the modern Sheori-Narayana, not far from Raipur, and today there is a great temple there to which all castes may go and worship.

Such traditions as the above are significant as folklore, but indicate that the Kol accounts cannot be very old and certainly not pre-historic, nor can they give us much real information concerning the place of their origin nor their migrations. They are too much diluted with Hindu mythologies and were undoubtedly drawn from Ramayana stories and coloured by their own imagination. They do indicate, however, a definite movement of thought. Even though the Kols possessing a primitive animistic outlook have come into contact with Hinduism and have accepted certain Hindu deities, nevertheless the acculturation has not been complete: the tribal god (Sheori, a goddess in this case), is even yet given preference over Hindu gods, and this in spite of possibly some 3,000 years of contact.

Up till now but little information has been available about this interesting group, and there is still much that should be done. This study is mainly of the Kols who are in contact with Hinduism, and no attempt is made to isolate the primitive Kol. Further detailed and systematic fieldwork will undoubtedly supplement and may even correct some of the statements found here, and it is not claimed that this should be taken as the last word on the Kols of Central India.

Chapter II

THE MATERIAL CULTURE OF THE KOLS

There is considerable variation in the material culture of the Kols. This is due to the economic changes which rapidly occur when these primitive people come into contact with cities and their industrial order. The Kols make excellent workers, and in many of the industrial centres of Central India the majority of the cheap labour is supplied by them. This group, however, is not typical of the Kols; and the following description of their material culture is based upon the village Kol, who, while having considerable contact with modern influences, still clings mostly to the older ways known to his people for centuries.

The Village. While this study is particularly of the Kols who are in contact with Hindu culture, nevertheless a few words should be written about the more primitive Kols who live in villages tucked away in some rather inaccessible spot. Such villages are usually not found among the trees of the forest, but in an open space. The form which the village takes depends on the terrain and also upon the general custom of the area. The Gonds generally build their houses in separate enclosures, each an individual unit. We have found a few Kol villages of this type. Sometimes there have been two or three houses within a thorny stockade.

It is more usual, however, to find the Kols grouped together as a single unit. The form of the primitive village varies, but the shoestring type predominates. The village has but the one central pathway which winds between small courts plastered with mud and cow dung situated immediately in front of the house. The court is usually clean, the pathway seldom so.

Primitive villages do not show many signs of permanency. The huts are of a type that can be destroyed over night if it should seem wise to shift the village. In actual practice, however, the Kol does not make a move quickly. Most of these villages though very temporary in their make-up have nevertheless been in existence for years.

The cattle sheds, where they exist, form a part of the hut and may only be distinguished from human habitations by the fact that they are more open. The Kols do not keep pigs, nor do they have gardens about their huts. Sometimes a form of pumpkin may be allowed to grow by the wall and climb over the roof. A *nim* tree (*Melia azadirachta*) will usually be found on the central pathway and under it a raised platform of mud where most of the village worship is observed. There are, generally speaking, no well defined village boundaries. Such boundaries exist in theory, but are not always marked out. The religious ceremonies which are supposed to take them into account just go round the outskirts of the village, paying no particular attention to supposed boundary points.

The ordinary Kol village is not a pretentious affair. There will be one or two central paths, three to ten feet wide and up to 200 yards long, which are the main streets and which the houses face. If the terrain permits, these paths usually run in a northerly-southerly direction and are often winding. Between the houses there are little lanes through which one may squeeze to get to the back of the village where the trash is thrown. The houses are made of *chatai* walls plastered with mud, or possibly of thick mud walls. The roof is usually of grass, but cheap country tiles are frequently employed. A two-storied house is unknown except in the larger towns where brick is used and some wealthy person resides. There is no street in the ordinary sense of the word and the lanes which provide the outlets for the various houses are narrow, dirty and tortuous. The individual group may have two small buildings, one of which houses the cattle, though it is not unusual to find the cattle kept on the veranda. It is from such a village that the labourers go out to their fields which not infrequently lie from two to three miles distant from the village. On the edge of most villages are seen a few meaner huts grouped together and in these one usually finds the depressed and the untouchables. The fact is at once known by the pigs which are all about such houses. Where Kols do not have their own village and are attached to some larger village or hamlet the two groups usually live on the edge; but the Kol, generally speaking, is more cleanly than the lower groups whose houses occasionally adjoin his dwelling place. When questioned why they live apart the answer has usually taken a three-fold form: It is claimed first that Hindus do not like to have Kols living near them because they (the Kols) eat meat and especially pork, which is consumed at the time of sacrifice. The next reason is an economic one: Kols are too poor to rent lands or pay the house rent required in the villages. One rupee a year is the maximum paid outside the village and sometimes nothing is required save a bit of help to the *malguzar* or landlord when he needs labourers in his fields. Kols also claim that if they live in close proximity to the higher castes they would not be free to sing and play the drum the whole night through, a thing which they consider necessary at certain times of worship.

Living Conditions. There is a good deal of variation in the conditions under which the Kols live. In places where tenancy is assured, they build houses which may favourably be compared even with those of the poorer Brahmins. Such well-built houses are of mud walls about two feet thick, a tiled roof laid out on bamboo poles and a fairly large courtyard. We found the houses and courtyards in Barela scrupulously clean. Refuse, however, was thrown into the manure pits right alongside the houses. In Kharara Ghat the houses were not of the same standard of cleanliness as in Barela. There seemed to be no particular direction which the houses must face. Enquiries revealed that there was no particular objection to having the door face toward the south. To some Hindus this is the direction of the dwelling place of the God of Death, *Yama*, and there should be no door that way. Most houses seemed to have no central courtyard, such as is common in Santali villages. If two houses face each other, both houses have a courtyard and there is a common pathway between. The mud walls, inside and outside, the floors and the courtyard are plastered with a mixture of cow dung and clay. There is generally but one room in the average house, and it is littered up with many things. There is found somewhere a large sun-dried mud urn, large enough for a man to get into, and in this is stored the grain so that it may not be destroyed by rats and moisture.[1] There are baskets and tools in the corners ; on bamboo poles stretched just across the top of the mud walls, not much higher than the head, hang clothes, rags and tattered bedding. In one corner, the view of which is generally hidden as one enters the low door, is the cooking department with its stone mill and *chulhas* and a few pots for cooking purposes. There will be a few bottles for oil, and a few tins, usually old tins once thrown away by some city dweller, in which are kept such things as salt and spices used in the preparation of the meal. This is a description of the better type of house. In summer it is dark and cool. There are no windows and all the light comes through the door leading to a small veranda.

On the other hand, there is the meaner type of house. At Barela there were numbers of these alongside of other better houses. The pictures show the differences.[2] These ruder huts have no veranda space, though usually there is an attempt at a small courtyard. The doors are so low that one has to get on his hands and knees to enter. The roof is of grass, and usually this type of house does not furnish much protection from rain. The walls are merely bamboo *tati* or just branches woven together and protected by thorns. This type of house is airy compared to the others, but the door can never be locked. In-

1 See Plate vii.
2 See Plate v.

side are the few poor possessions of the inmates. The clothes are nearly always on their bodies, and one finds only a few rags, some cooking utensils, and the like. The floor is damp and poorly plastered. At Kymore we saw a few houses that even a dog would not consider worthy of entering, which sheltered families. One wonders how in the heat and the rain and the cold a human being can live in such places.

A number of the better grade houses have two rooms. These houses have some veranda space, and here are examples of outside measurements of some of the better types:

26′×7′; 35′×18′; 40′×20′; 39′×23′;
12′×16′; 15′×16′; 15′×12′; 10′×15′.

In one of the above houses that had two rooms one measured 10′×5′ and the other 10′×15′ In these better houses the height of the mud wall is six to seven feet above the level of the floor. Some of the meaner huts measured 5′×10′ and 6′×12′, with walls about three feet high. In one of these measuring 6′×12′ we found five people living, in another of a similar size four. At Kymore the huts were about seven feet long and three feet wide.

See figures 2 and 3 showing diagrams of typical Kol houses.

GROUND PLANS OF KOL HOUSES

1. KATNI

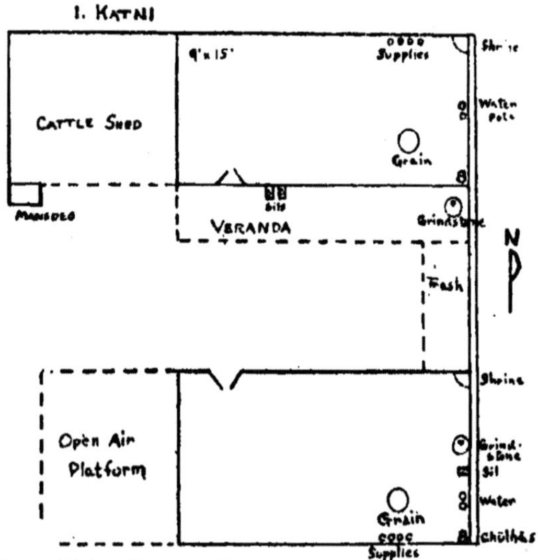

House for two families: nine persons, all related.
Walls are of mud; roof grass thatched.

Fig. 2.

A View of the Kol Mahalla, Jubbulpore.

Primitive Kol Dwellings at Barela. See Fig. 3

The Home of an Influential Kol in Barela.

Panagar Kol Dwellings. Note Granary left centre.

Primitive type of House at Barela.

Primitive Huts in the Kaimer Hills.

Those who own cattle usually provide for them in a place separate from their own dwellings. They are occasionally given a place on the veranda, but usually a rude hut is erected to one side of the house where the cattle are housed during the night and afforded some measure of protection. In some of the more jungly sections back in the Kaimur hills, we found that a group of houses usually had a thorny stockade built around it.[1] There was one entrance for all, cattle and men. This is for protection from wild animals and an occasional outlaw. In the industrial sections attached to cities like Jubbulpore the Kols are sometimes put in the regular workers' lines; or are at other times

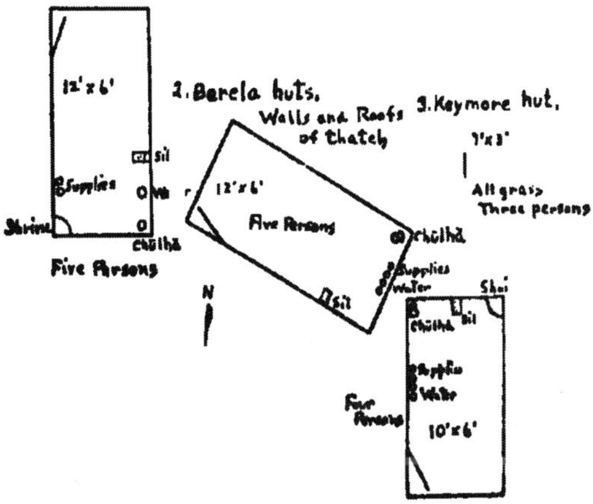

Fig. 3

given a plot of ground and certain materials for building purposes (mostly tiles) and allowed to construct their own village. Some fairly decent houses result, but usually there is no system to the narrow winding paths that lead one amongst the village houses. In Kymore the Cement company is building brick accommodations for their Kol workers. Recently one of the grass huts caught fire while the parents were away at work, and before it could be checked, it had spread to other huts and a number of small children were burned to death.

The problems of sanitation are the same with the Kols as they are all over village India. Filth of all varieties is thrown on the manure pits right alongside the houses, and flies and other insects breed prolifically.

1 See Plate IV.

BUILDING CUSTOMS. Like their village neighbours about them, Kols have numerous superstitions relating to houses and certain customs in connection with their construction. In India, it has been said, "a house should face north or east and not south or west, as the south is the region of Yama, the God of Death, who lives in Ceylon, and the west is the quarter of the setting sun."[1] Kols are not quite so particular in this respect although due to Hindu influences there is a general tendency to follow this plan. The Kols observe a general rule which is that if the house is to be longer than it is wide, the greatest length should be parallel to the north-south line.

When a new house is about to be built in a village, its actual position is generally determined in relation to the other houses about it. If the position of the house is not limited by other houses, and if there is doubt as to the location, a Hindu *pandit* is sometimes called to help decide the exact place. The *pandit* consults astrological factors as from these he is said to be able to determine whether the place is suitable or not, or if an evil spirit lives on that spot or nearby. If the report should be unfavourable, another spot is selected and the process repeated. When satisfactory, the *pandit* will also fix the day on which work should begin on the construction of the building. For this service he is paid two annas to a rupee according to the ability of the builder to pay.

If the house is not to be permanent little or no ceremony is observed in connection with its building, as it is considered a temporary structure which can be broken up in a few minutes.

If, however, the house is one with mud walls and is of a more permanent nature, there are certain customs which are quite generally observed. The foundation trench is first dug although this may be hardly more than a levelling of the ground on which the walls will stand. A "foundation stone" is usually placed somewhere in the trench, and beneath it are put two pice, some rice coloured yellow with turmeric and an areca nut (*Areca catechu*). The walls are constructed of mud with a certain amount of cow dung and straw mixed in to insure its stability.

One of the pictures[2] shows a Kol house in the process of construction. This particular house was being built on the site of another house. In this case, which was observed for some time, the following customs were noted, and found also to apply to other cases of building.

Just within the threshold of the single entrance to the house there

1 Russell and Hiralal, *The Tribes and Castes of Central Provinces*, Vol. III, p. 88.
2 See Plate VIII.

Makkhi of Barela.

Three Kols with a Brahmin who officiates at certain social ceremonies. Taken near Deori.

Stockaded House in the Kaimer Hills. See also Fig. 4.

Village Scenes in Rewa State. Two views of the Dwelling of a Prosperous Kol Farmer.

is put a charm to protect it from the demons. In this case pieces of iron were found scattered about : bolts, nuts and scraps from the railway

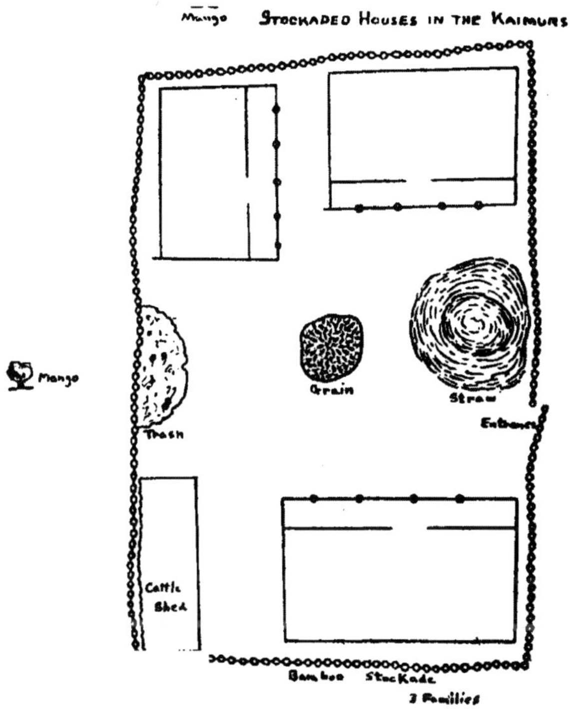

Fig. 4.

line. There were also rather large pieces of stone scattered here and there under what would be the floor of the house. If obtainable, the best kind of stone to use is said to be the *sil* or grindstone for preparing condiments. At least one should be under the floor of every house, and should be under the section where the cooking is to be done. The *sil* is a symbol of fertility as well as a protector. Another protective device is old leather, and in this case an old shoe was utilized. In the picture such a shoe can be seen to the right, placed on the end of a stick stuck into the wall. As the wall is made higher, this too is raised. An old shoe is also generally found along with the iron and stones under the floor. Occasionally bits of dried *tulasi* plant (*Ocymum sanctum*) are also scattered about the floor or again a bunch of *tulasi*. may be tied at the base of the central pole. This pole stuck in the centre of the house being built is not a part of the permanent construction, but is a device to render the building work satisfactory and protect the home from demons taking possession of it while in the process of construction. On the pole can be seen hanging a basket and in this basket were found pieces of iron and tin, and bits of the outer *lepoed*[1] covering of another house. It may be taken from the walls of a house in which a happily married and prosperous family lived. In an earthen pot placed on the floor there was a yellowish liquid. The builder told us that this was water, but it had the appearance of cow's urine, although this could not be confirmed. Occasionally there is a sign of a little shrine about the construction somewhere, which shows signs of the presentation of the *hom* offering.

The inner floor of the house will be filled in and packed down after the walls are up. In dwellings of good construction the floor of the interior of the house should be higher than the veranda floor, and the veranda floor should, in turn, be higher than that of the courtyard. Kol houses have no windows, and the door-ways are low. On entering one must bow, or even get down on hands and knees. Bowing as one enters is said to be a method of showing respect to the household deities. Windows might let in evil forces, hence none is included.

Women may aid in building the house, but their work is limited to assisting in building the walls and floor of the house by bringing the earth or water, mixing them and helping to place the mud in the proper place. They take no part, however, in the construction of the roof. This is not a woman's job, and for a woman to get upon a roof is taboo—a thing that requires punishment or a fine.

Kols are able to construct the whole house. If the roof is to be of grass, the grass is brought from the forests, and *kusa* (*Poa cynosuroides*) and *duba* (*Agrestis tinearis*) are generally used. If tiles are utilized, cheap country tiles are obtained from the village potter. The Kol puts the tiles on the roof himself. The only thing which he cannot make is the door and frame, but these may be bought quite cheaply in the markets or may be made for him by the village carpenter. They are set in the opening left for the door, and the mud is packed in about them. There is usually but one door to a house. The more primitive types of houses so common among

1 See Glossary, Appendix VI, for meanings of Vernacular terms.

PLATE VII.

Interior Views of a Kol House. Bedding and Clothes in Centre ; Dewahar to far left.

Closer View of the Dewahar showing evidences of Worship.

A Jar used for the storing of Grain inside the House.

PLATE VIII.

A house in the process of Construction. See text, p. 16.

Kumhars preparing tiles at Barela.

Kols have neither mud walls nor wooden doors. When they leave the house, a bit of thorny brush is put in front of the doorway. This will keep out dogs and also any dangerous spirit which may be seeking admission.

When the building of a house is completed, there is usually a dedicatory ceremony consisting of installing and worshipping the household god or goddess or both, and a small niche in a corner or in the side wall is reserved for this purpose. The place is marked with *sendur* and the *hom* sacrifice is made. An offering of a chicken or young goat may also be made at the village shrine. A *tulasi* plant should also be planted somewhere in the courtyard.

DAILY LIFE. The daily life of the village and forest Kol centres mainly about the problem of daily bread. Before daybreak the women are up and are the first to be seen about the village. They sweep the house, the veranda and the courtyard; fetch water from a nearby stream, well or tank and grind the wheat for the morning meal. The sound of the grindstone is one of the earliest to be heard in a Kol village. The men are also up early, but do not have much to do in the way of household duties unless it is to chop a bit of wood. They wash their faces and rinse out their mouths with water which the women have brought, and, if they have bullocks, these are fed and got ready for the work in the fields; or if this is not to be done, they sit around in the sun in the courtyard and wait for some hot tea, or more probably for rice and *chapati* remaining from the meal of the night before. During the season when the work is heavy, they are in the field not long after the day has dawned, and the village is inhabited only by the women, children and older men. The bullocks for ploughing are driven before them; some of the older boys may assist in this, and the men carry the iron-pointed wooden plough. If some of the men-folk have no work in the fields, they may go into the forest for wood and grass; or, if there is plenty of food in the house and there is no pressing need for money, they sit around in groups and smoke cheap country cigarettes (*biris*) and gossip.

In the meantime the women are preparing the morning meal. It is not usual for men and women to eat together. The women and children usually eat about the same time, though when the boys get in their teens, they like to eat with the men. During the middle of the morning, after the meal is nearly ready the women go for their daily bath to a nearby stream or tank. Women bathe every day throughout the year. The men bathe daily in the hot weather, but not so frequently in winter. The women do not remove their clothes when they bathe, though men usually remove all but a loincloth. The women stand in the stream up to their hips with their *saris* still draped around them, and if there is a possibility of men in the vicinity, also cover their heads. Water is poured over them or they may immerse themselves. Ordinarily no soap is used, in fact the use of soap is not common to village people, though it is not unknown. After the bath the women come to the shore and by first draping a fresh *sari* about them slip off the wet one without exposing themselves. They do not dry themselves with any towel, though the hair may be rubbed dry with some cloth. Oil is sometimes applied to the body. They next wash the *sari* they have removed, which is done by beating it with a stick on a flat stone. After being wrung out it is taken home to be hung up somewhere about the house to dry and be ready for use the next day. The *sari* put on at the time of the morning bath is constantly worn until the next bath. The bather may now take a bit to eat, or occasionally she may have her morning meal, though it is more usual for her to wait until the men have been fed or she takes what is left. The husband usually returns from work about mid-day and gets his meal; but if the work is heavy and he must be there, she will take it out to the fields to him, where he will eat it and, after a short rest, resume his work. If the work is pressing, she may remain to assist him, though she should never touch the plough. She may reap, weed, and thresh, and she carries home the rice and wheat which has been threshed. During the hotter months field work begins before daylight, and the men are back by ten o'clock. In the threshing season the work continues steadily throughout the day, for that is the time when the hot winds are active and the chaff is easily separated. The men may bathe on their way back at noon, or in the evening before their evening meal. If they return from the fields at dusk, the evening meal is usually not taken till after eight o'clock. Unless there is some social event such as preparations for a wedding or a tribal feast, or, perhaps a religious ceremony, the Kols are asleep by about nine at night. On religious and social occasions, however, the whole night may be spent in singing, watching the women dance and chatting. The social events occur usually in the slack season and work is not interfered with; but under industrial conditions there is a limit to night operations, and the singing is usually over by midnight.

The children have their tasks too. The boys, as soon as they are old enough, herd cattle and goats in the forest, gather sticks, leaves and roots, and run errands for their mothers. The girls assist their mothers in the home, gather cow-dung for use as fuel and as plaster for the walls and floor.

The main variations of this routine are occasioned by social requirements or by religious observances. They do much to break the monotony and to provide a change.

HOUSEHOLD ARTICLES AND UTENSILS. Beds and cots are seldom, if ever, found in Kol houses. Those who dwell near cities, or work in the industrial centres sometimes own a cheap rope cot called a *khatiya*. The head man of the village may own a cot or two, and when one visits a village, this is often brought for the European guest to sit upon. The usual place for sleep is the mud floor of the dwelling. A blanket or mat may be all that is underneath, while in the hot weather not even this is availed of. Pillows are not used, but if it should be desired that the head be raised, it is probable that a small wooden stool a few inches high will be employed.

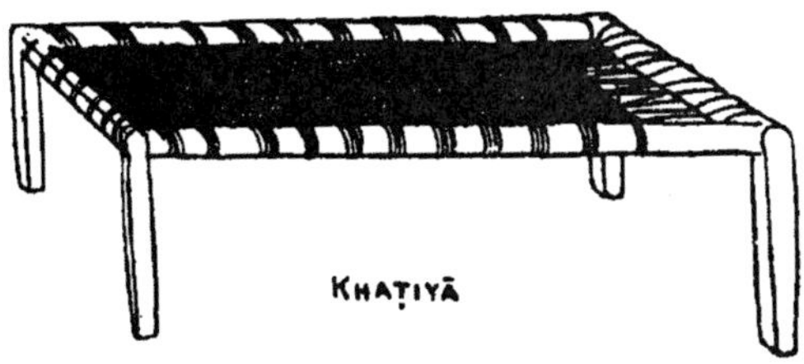

Fig. 5

Chairs, tables and the like, are never found. Anything that must be put away and cannot be hung over the rafters or the bamboo poles stretched across the walls is placed in a wooden chest. One usually finds some kind of a small box about the place which is locked. Valuables, however, are usually buried in a hole in the floor and the same completely *lepoed* to hide all trace of the spot.

The main articles in the house are those connected with food and drink. Gourd vessels are occasionally used as receptacles for storing water, but more commonly such vessels are made of earthenware or brass. Kols do not make either of these. The earthen vessels may be purchased cheaply in the bazaar from people of the Kumhar caste—the traditional potters. Food is also stored in them and in one of the Kol sub-divisions, the *Kurhas*, food should only be taken from a particular type of black earthenware dish. As a rule the various kinds of earthenware vessels are being replaced all over village India by those made of brass and aluminium.

The stone implements are the grindstone and the *sil*. The former consists usually of two pieces of round stone, although the bottom stone may be squarish. The upper stone, which is slightly smaller, is about 16" in diameter. It has a peg for a handle by which it is rotated. There is also a hole into which the grain is poured, though often the stone is simply lifted and the grain spread out over the lower stone. In the centre there is a pivot around which the upper stone rotates. The *sil* is essentially a grindstone but is used mostly to grind spices, and mix together ingredients on the mortar-and-pestle

Grindstone for Wheat

Fig. 6.

The Sil - where Spices are ground

Fig. 7.

system. The *sil* has two parts: an oblong stone 18″×12″ the surface of which is roughened by being chipped; the roller, a piece of stone which is rounded and which is used something as a rolling pin, only the stone grinds and does not revolve.

An iron knife which is attached to a piece of wood and on which all the cutting of vegetables is done is usually found about the house. The user sits on the floor and cuts the vegetables or meat on the knife. In the process the knife is steadied by pressing the feet on the wooden attachment and thus both hands are free for work.

Vegetable Cutter

Fig. 8

A few baskets will always be found lying about the house. These also are not manufactured by Kols. They are used for transporting things to and from the bazaar, for gathering leaves, sticks and cow-dung for fuel or plaster. Vegetables and the like may be stored in them. The winnowing basket (*supa*) is always found near the granary. This is used to clean the grains and also has its work in certain magical ceremonies which will be described further on. A sort of broom made of bamboo and grass will be found somewhere about the place.

Typical Basket

Fig. 9

In one corner of the room is located the *chulha*. This is a low mud hearth with one or two fireplaces. The smoke goes into the room. Here the meals for the family are cooked. Nearby are the cooking vessels and an iron spoon or two for stirring the food and some tongs for the fire. Somewhere will be found the large sun-dried mud urn in which the wheat or rice is stored. This is rat proof and is arranged so that it may be watched for termites which do much damage in villages. Some piles of fuel will be seen: dried cow-dung cakes or bits of wood which have been chopped by the men of the family,

USE OF FIRE. Matches are fast finding their way into the villages of India and as a result primitive ways of making fire are disappearing. Enquiries among Kols in sections where matches are not generally in use showed that they have two primitive methods of making fire. Even here it is not often necessary to prepare fire afresh, as it is usually

Fig. 10

kept in ignited lumps of cow-dung, which burn slowly and are not easily extinguished. It is not infrequent to see, in such villages, a woman going from one house to another taking with her a smoking piece of cow-dung to start her own fire.

The most usual method is to strike a stone against iron. The spark is directed into a bit of cotton from the *semal* tree (*Bombax malabaricum*) which is very easily ignited. Kols collect and preserve the cotton for this purpose. The second method often practised is that of rubbing together two well-dried sticks of the *pipal* tree (*Ficus religiosa*). One stick is notched. A sawing method is used, and a bit of *semal* cotton dropped into and around the notch, where the heat generated by friction ignites it. This is carefully nursed and transferred to dry leaves and grass.

FOODS AND THEIR PREPARATION. Like most village and common folk in India the Kols have two meals a day : one about noon and the other late at night. Early in the morning something is usually taken before going out to work. This may consist of a *chapati* or a bit of rice left over from the night before. The two main meals are almost similar and there is usually no variation in the menu. In the season when rice is cheapest, it will form the main part of the meal ; or when wheat is the cheaper, this is eaten in the form of *chapatis*. In Rewa millet is frequently used. Along with these main articles a little vegetable curry and some pulse is usually eaten. Meats are not taken regularly as they are too expensive, but Kols eat most meats except beef. These include, fish, goat, chicken, hare, mutton, buck, and even pork. Apparently carrion is never eaten. The flesh of the deer may be eaten but not that of the tiger. The villager is an adept at preparing vegetables for his curries, and throughout the year depends largely upon the following according to the seasons: *sags* of various kinds; egg plants; pumpkins and gourds; okra; potatoes, both ordinary and sweet; onions; roots of various plants; and corn on the cob roasted until it is brown.

The community feast, or feasts, given to a relatively large group on special occasions, are things which help to break the monotony of diet. Community feasts are usually paid for out of the proceeds of fines levied by the *panch*. An individual also may give a feast as a thank-offering, or at child-birth, at the time of a wedding, or at death. One of the favourite foods is said to be a preparation described below known as *bara*, and is served at every feast. If some social event should make a feast obligatory, and if the person concerned should fail to provide the expected meal, the *panch* brings pressure upon him to do so. If he still fails, the person is boycotted for a period. The usual menu at such a feast includes rice and *chapatis*, pulse, vegetable curry, *chatni*, *bara* and if they can be afforded, meats of various kinds. Kols drink milk when it is available and apparently do not feel that all milk should be kept for the calf, as some Munda tribes believe. Milk is also used in the preparation of certain special foods, such as *khir*, which is used for the child's first feeding. See below.

Foods are usually divided into two classes: *pakka* and *kachha*. The former kind is cooked in *ghi* or *ghi* is used in its preparation, and the latter is simply cooked with water. *Ghi*, like other products from the sacred cow, protects from impurity. While caste Hindus have numerous restrictions in connection with this classification, the Kols do not seem to be particular in this regard. They will take food cooked by "clean" Hindu castes, but never from those castes which they consider below them, such as Chamars, Mahars, Dhobis, Basors, and Doms. Nowhere Kols seemed to be starved nor emaciated. Apparently, they have enough to keep them in fairly good health, though not in abundance. We did not find stout people among them.

The main food-stuffs are listed below. In an average Kol house all of these are probably not found at any one time, but they are those used when available:

Grains: Wheat, rice, millet (in northern areas).

Pulses: Black pulse (*Phaseolus radiatus*). Red and yellow types (*Cajanus indicus* and *Dolichos lablab*).

Oils: Mustard oil usually from *Guisotia abyssinica*. Sweet oil or *til tel* from (*Sesamum indicum*). Occasionally *kusum tel* from *Sleichera trijuga*.

Vegetables, in season and according to price: Greens of various types called *sags*. These are cooked like spinach and similar greens. Egg plant; pumpkin; potato; yams; onion; corn; okra; jungle roots and leaves. These are usually cut into bits and cooked together in water to make a thick soup, which is flavoured with spices and poured over the rice, or eaten with the *chapatis*.

Fruits in season: The common fruits such as mango, custard apple, guava, jack-fruit. The forest fruits such as those belonging to the fig types: *Jitia Pipar* (*Ficus religiosa*); *Bar* (*Ficus Bengalensis*); *Dumbar* (*Ficus glomerata*). Also the *Jamun* (*Eugenia jambolana*); *Kusum* (*Sleichera trijuga*); the *Bel* (*Aegle marmelos*); the *Khajur*, the fruit of the wild date palm (*Phoenix sylvestris*); the *Ber* (*Zizyphus jujuba*).

Dairy Products: Milk, clarified butter (*ghi*), milk curds.

Meats: Chicken, goat, mutton, buck, hare, pork, fish.

Condiments include salt, *chatnies* made from fruits such as the mango or the tamarind, and the "seven spices," which include *khaskhas*, from poppy heads; *jira*, cummin seed; *haldi*, turmeric; *rai*, mustard; *nariyal*, cocoanut; *gol mirch*, pepper; *lahasun*, garlic; *lal mirch*, red chilis.

Sweet spices used include *ilachi*, cardamom; *long*, clove; *darchini*, cinnamon.

The general preparation of the chief dishes used by Kols may be briefly described as follows. They are arranged according to ingredients. Certain of them have been borrowed from their Hindu neighbours.

Chapatis. Whole wheat flour is used together with a little salt. The whole is moistened with hot water and made into a dough which must be well mixed before it is rolled or patted into a pancake. This is cooked on a hot fry-pan until well browned. It must often be turned in the process.

Puris are a very special dish and are often offered to the deity at the time of religious worship. There are many kinds of *puris* possible. A *puri* is essentially a *chapati* fried in clarified butter. Usually white flour is used, and occasionally some *dal* or shortening is mixed in.

Rice (*Chawal*). The cheaper rice is simply boiled with water until the grains are well done. Indian rice, when properly cooked does not stick, but the grains are flaky. The rice water is poured off and is often used as a gruel.

Pulses or dals are cooked separately, having been first soaked in water for a period. They are cooked into a thick soup, and a portion of this is either mixed with the rice and curry or is put to one side of the plate and eaten with the rice.

Khichri. This is a preparation of rice, pulse and spices. Meat may also be used with it. Clarified butter is also used. The rice and pulse are mixed and soaked for a few hours. The spices are next mixed and made ready to put in and some onions are fried in clarified butter and are put on top after the *khichri* has been prepared. The rice, *dal* and spices are cooked together until ready. There are usually about three parts of rice to one part of *dal.* The new bride when first coming to her husband's home is required to demonstrate her ability to cook by preparing *khichri.*

Curries may be either purely vegetable or they may have meat in them as well. Among the vegetables used in a typical curry would be onion, ginger, *haldi*, and potato. Salt and spices will be added. These will be fried together and later water will be added to make a gravy. When meat is used it is cut into small lumps and both fried and boiled.

Meats are usually boiled in fat in large vessels. Fish is sometimes wrapped in dry grass and the grass burnt, and the fish is ready.

Fruits are usually eaten raw.

Some of the special dishes commonly found among the Kols are the following :

Lai is much like puffed rice. Unhusked rice is warmed in a pan until the husks come off and only the grain is left. The rice in turn is put into an iron vessel in which sand has been heated over a hot fire. The heat expands the rice and when the whole has been puffed, the sand is shaken out and the *lai* remains. Sometimes this is sweetened by being sprinkled with syrup.

Lawa is another name for *lai.* But it is not sweetened and sometimes parched corn or millet is mixed with it.

Laddu is essentially a mixture of wheat flour and sugar. White flour is taken and to it is added enough clarified butter to make it into a dough. This is browned over a fire. Sugar is added as well as more *ghi*, and the whole is moulded into balls. If available, nuts and raisins may be mixed in. Sometimes the whole is soaked in a syrup made from sugar.

Bara. Black pulse is the main ingredient. This is husked and cleaned and soaked from eight to twelve hours in order that it may become quite soft. This is next ground on a grindstone (*sil*) with the stone roller until it becomes a fine smooth dough. While being ground on the *sil* salt and some spices are usually added. The dough is then moulded by hand into cakes of various sizes which are fried in sweet (*til*) oil or in clarified butter. *Bara* is usually eaten in this form though occasionally, if curd is available, it is soaked in that until soft.

Dahi is a form of sour milk, though a particular strain of bacteria seems to be required. A bit of old *dahi* is put into the new milk which has been sweetened and to which possibly a little sliced green chili has been added. This is set aside until the *dahi* is formed.

Khir. This is made by boiling rice in milk over a slow fire. Sugar is added to sweeten. When the mixture becomes creamy, chopped cocoanut, pistachio, and *ilachi* seeds are added to taste.

Batasa. Sugar is boiled with water until there is a very thick syrup. This is poured into a cocoanut shell which has a small hole in the bottom through which the syrup may drip. This is allowed to drip on cloth or paper forming small balls of various sizes. The product turns out to be a small whitish ball, spongy and very sweet.

FOOD TABOOS. There are certain things which Kols never eat. The use of beef and carrion is universally tabooed. The latter is eaten only by outcastes, and beef is not taken in deference to their Hindu neighbours. It was noted that pork is among the foods used. In Hinduized centres it is no longer eaten as a regular dish, but it is still partaken of at festival times when a young pig may be offered to the goddess and ceremonially eaten. Nothing that creeps on the ground should be eaten.

Among other animals which they never kill nor eat are found the names of the parrot, sparrow, crow, kite and *galgal* (*Acridotheres tristis*).

INTOXICANTS. There is evidence to show that the Kols are not so addicted to the use of intoxicants as they were in previous years. At times of religious ceremonies liquor is still used quite freely and no penalty is attached. In one centre we were informed that the *panchayat* fines any man who is caught drinking liquor, and that they had totally abolished its use in that village. In other places they were not so successful, and yet there was a standard penalty of Rs. 10 or a community feast, when, in the judgment of the *panch* the circumstances warranted it.

Contact with city life seems to increase the use of liquor; and Kol dwellers in Jubbulpore have distinctly less feeling against it and more often indulge in its use than do the people living in the village.

As far as we could learn there was no record of the Kols resorting to the illicit distillation of intoxicants. When they need liquor for their feasts or religious observances they go to the toddy shops. Here they may secure the following types of intoxicants: From Indian sources liquors from the Mahua tree (*Bassia latifolia*); the toddy palm (*Borassus flabellifer*); the date palm (*Phoenix sylvestris*) and the sago palm (*Caryota urens*). Cheap "foreign" liquors may be bought too, and a bottle of cheap wine may be used at the time of worship; but as a rule they do not resort to these on account of their being relatively more expensive.

PERSONAL DECORATION. Kol men do not wear much in the way of decoration. In their case most ornaments are purely amulets. The Thakuriya Kol often wears a bit of gold about its person, usually in the form of an ear-ring.

Kol women are fond of decorations and there are many kinds of cheap jewellery available with which they often bedeck themselves. There is usually found a gold nose decoration fitted into the left side of the nostril which had been pierced when the woman was quite young. The text figure shows one of these, which is said to have cost Rs. 4-3-0. There are generally some ear decorations as well. These take various forms and are of both silver and gold or sometimes of cheaper materials. On the arms above the elbow one may find a silver bangle, and below the elbow several silver bangles, between them, however, being yellow and red lac bangles. The lac bracelets are bright and pretty, and they also serve the purpose of keeping the silver bracelets apart, for the rubbing wears down the silver. Often between the silver and the lac bracelet there is a silver bracelet entirely wrapped with thread or string in order to keep the silver bangle next to it from rubbing against anything.

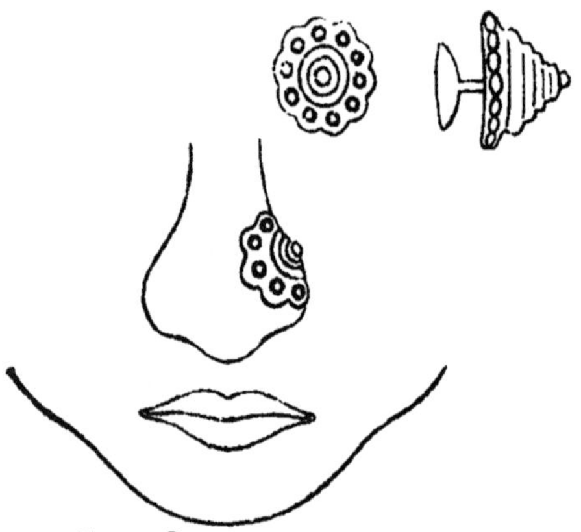

NOSE DECORATION

Fig. 11

The head is decorated with hair chains, and sometimes the ear-rings have a string of coins attached to them. Around the neck is often a plain silver ring.

For the legs there are anklets or ankle bracelets. These are sometimes silver, or again may be of cheaper metals. These are allowed to rub one against the other and make a tinkling sound as they move. There are ten toe-rings, one for each toe. It is not to be thought that these things are all worn continually. A few are always worn, and when some opportunity arises to wear the others, they are put on.

A lac *tika* is stuck on the forehead of young married women. This is put on by the husband in order that all may see that she is married and also to protect both of them.

TATTOOING. Every woman should have tattoo marks (*godna*) upon her body. Men are not tattooed. The time for this varies. Among more Hinduized sections it is said that it should be done at puberty, that is, at the ages of ten to twelve. Again, and it seems to be the more common custom among the Kols, the *godna* is done shortly before the marriage. In certain cases which we came across, it was said to have been done after marriage. Kols do not do the tattooing themselves, but it is done by the regular tattooer called *bajigar* or *godnari*.

On the accompanying text figures tattoo designs copied from Kol women are shown. There is generally a purpose for each position. Design 1 is placed on various parts of the body. It is found over the right kidney region to take away pain. It is also put on the breasts to ensure a good supply of milk. On the palms of the hands it is believed to help in making *chapatis* light and palatable; on the arms it is supposed to benefit the husband, while on the face it is purely decorative.

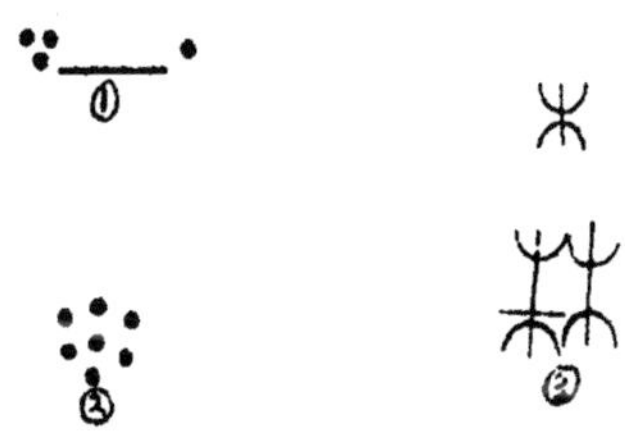

Fig. 12

Design 2 was found inside the left wrist.

Design 3 was on the right leg and takes away pain.

Design 4 was on the outside of the upper left arm. It was mainly decorative, but a protective significance was also suggested. It was said that in this case it took two hours to tattoo the design and that it was a very painful process. (See figure 13.)

Design 5 was found on the same woman on the outside of the left forearm. Another Kol woman had design 6 on the inside of the left forearm. This same woman had design 7 on the outside of the upper left arm. (See figures 14, 15, 16.)

There are certain traditions connected with tattooing. We were once told that when a Kolin is cremated Bhagawan catches the hand which has the *godna* and conducts her to *Baikuntha*. Therefore, it is exceedingly important that the hands and the arms should be tattooed. In case the body is buried, the tattoos, as another group told us, save the body; for when *Baimatā*, a female demon, comes to devour it she cannot eat any of the tattooed portions, and thus much more is left to go to Bhagawan.[1]

Fig. 13

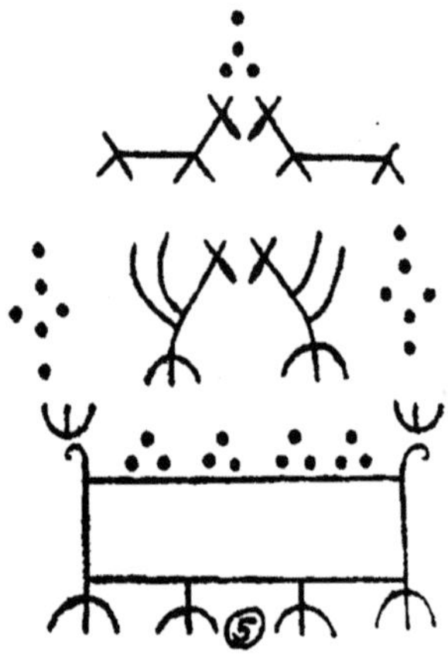

Fig. 14

Tattooing also wards off the evil eye, to which women, especially when with child, are very susceptible. As stated above, it has also a medical significance, in that it keeps the organs healthy and functioning properly. The tattooings about the ankle are a protection against snake bite.

The art of tattooing is probably of Polynesian origin and its widespread practice among Munda tribes may be due to their common racial affinities.

It was noted above that Kols say that *Bajigars* do their tattooing. *Bajigar* literally means a 'juggler', 'actor'. Russell and Hiralal know nothing of this group unless it be the same as *Bajgari*, a subcaste of *Gandas*. The latter are wandering musicians and are considered unclean. It is not unlikely that Kols make use of other groups for tattooing but the available information is not conclusive on this point. The term *godnari* means simply "one who tattoos." The colours usually used are blue and black, and the operation is often a painful one. The

1 See Briggs, G. W., *The Chamars*, p. 145.

basis of the black colour is soot. Sometimes this is obtained by burning certain kinds of wood and cocoanut shells. It is finely powdered and mixed with water. Sometimes milk from the breast is said to be a desirable solvent. After pricking, the parts are oiled with a mixture of *haldi* and *til* oil, which soothes the affected parts and removes any impurity from the touch of the tattooer.

Fig. 15

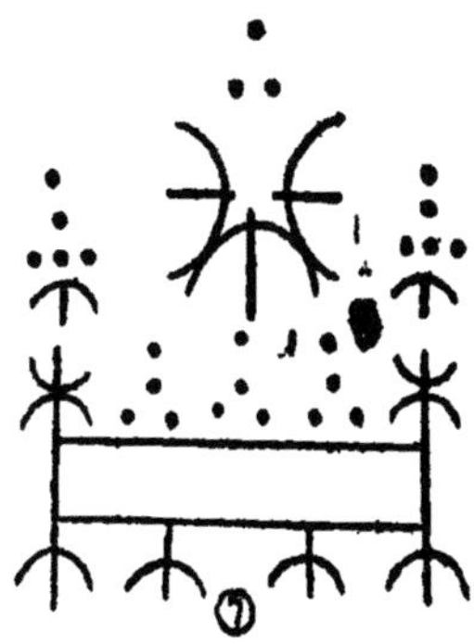

Fig. 16

AGRICULTURE. Kols mostly work as labourers in the fields of others, and even where they rent their fields, there is nothing in their methods which is not characteristic of the whole countryside. February to April is the usual slack season, although during the latter part of this period the wheat crop is harvested in Central India, and the threshing season is on. Before the rains at the end of June the ground is made ready for the first showers, and is roughly scratched with rude ploughs. Just before the rains the seed is broadcast in a prepared plot and is transplanted in the mud after the monsoon has broken. Only men sow the seed. From July to September the rice is growing and must be weeded and looked after. The weeding is generally done by women, but men also help. In October the rice is cut and threshed and stored. The soil, still moist from the monsoon rains, is now prepared for the wheat crop which is sown about the end of October or early in November. The wheat also requires weeding and care, and is ready for the harvest in late March and April. Religious observances in connection with agriculture are described in a later chapter.

Chapter III

SOCIAL STRUCTURE OF THE KOLS

Within the Kol tribe there are numerous subdivisions which are generally called *kurhis*, and occasionally *gotras*, though there is no trace of any exogamous clans. On the whole these groups are endogamous although hypergamy is sometimes practised, especially when no suitable mate from the same *kurhi* is available. There are certain restrictions in connection with food, and members of one *kurhi* will usually not take food with those of another.

When questioned about *kurhis* and their number the answer has invariably been, seven; but when asked to list the seven there has been a great variety of answers and no two sets have ever agreed.[1] There seems to be considerable confusion in the minds of the Kols themselves and there is apparently no standard list.

THE MAIN DIVISIONS OR KURHIS. Investigations as to the number, kinds and nature of the *kurhis* were carried out in a number of centres. In general the procedure was to get a group of Kols together and during the talks ask them about the *kurhis* and their names. The findings have been tabulated in the order of frequency. Twenty-one groups were consulted and the number following the name is the number of times a particular group was given. It will be noted that only the Rautiya *kurhi* occurs in all cases.

Rautiya	21	Kulmangan	5
Thakuriya	18	Swasaha	4
Rautel	11	Bhumiya	4
Kurha	11	Murha	3
Binj	9	Gunj	2
Garhvariya	8	Kabiriya	2
Khangar	8	Narchhila	2
Kathautiya	7	Bhariya	1
Mawasi	6	Borowar	1
Kathariya	5	Maubhaiya	1
Khairwar	5	Pawai	1

In the light of these investigations a considerable boiling down

1 This same seven-fold classification occurs among other groups which actually have many more divisions. See for example G. W. Briggs' *The Chamars*, pp. 21, 22.

of this list is possible. When the list as a whole was presented to a large and representative Kol group it was asserted that certain of the names on this list were not true Kols; Khangar, Murha, Kabiriya, Khairwar and Narchhila were mentioned, but they did not know what to say about Binj and Gunj, and professed to have never heard about them. It was claimed that Rautel, Kurha, Kathautiya, Kathariya and Kulmangan were all forms of the Rautiya *kurhi*; they had heard of most of them, but had never actually seen all of them. Narchhila was said to be a group of Chamars. This confusion is no doubt due to the fact that other groups have been absorbed into the Kol community and have perpetuated names which are still current in spite of the mixture.

Of the twenty-two names collected from the Kols, Russell and Hiralal have only seven of their thirteen in common with ours. It is not unlikely that some of the names mentioned above are not actual Kols and in the following pages comments on each of the so-called *kurhis* will indicate certain conclusions. Rautiya Kols usually consider themselves the highest of the *kurhis*, although it was frequently noted that individuals from other groups also made the same claim.

William Crooke gives the following list of "endogamous septs", a list based on investigations in southern United Provinces and representing conditions about 1890, over fifty years ago.

1. Rautiya or Rautele
   Dahait or villagers
   Mahtiyan or leader (These are subdivisions)
2. Thakuriya .. "a lord"
3. Banaj ..
4. Pahariya .. "mountaineer"
5. Barwar .. "descendant from the fig (bar) tree"
6. Bin .. (or Binds ?)
7. Harwariya .. "ploughman"
8. Rajwariya .. (from Bengal Rajwars ?)
9. Hanriyanwa .. "people of the cooking pot"[1]

An examination of this list and its comparison with the one which we obtained shows that there are some common divisions, while some of the others may also be identical. There is exact agreement in the case of the Rautiya and Thakuriya *kurhis*, though the subdivisions of the Rautiyas do not bear much resemblance. Barwar is probably the

[1] Crooke, W., *Tribes and Castes of the North West Provinces and Oudh*, Vol. III., Article Kol.

same as Borowar on our list; Bin and Binj are probably the same, and Harwariya may have become Garhvariya: the ploughman becoming the fortress-dweller.

Russell and Hiralal[1] state that they found the subcastes noted below, but their results appear to be based on materials gathered from the eastern edge of the Central Provinces. It will be noted that there are points of agreement and disagreement between their list and ours: Rautia, Rautele, Thakuriya, Kagwaria, Desaha, Bharia, Savar and Khairwar. They also include as "totemistic septs" the following: Bargaiyan, Kathotia, Katharia, Kumhra and Bhuwar.

1. *Rautiya.* This designation is believed to be derived from the word Rawat meaning "a prince," and as such may be traced to some ancient landholding or warrior group among the Kols in centuries past. This group claims to be the highest of the Kol *kurhis* and such assertions were usually not disputed by either Thakuriyas or others in joint group discussions; although on one or two occasions it was controverted as recorded under the Thakuriya (*vide p.* 41). Almost without exception the Rautiyas make use of the Brahmin priest at the time of wedding, and of the Hindu *nai* or barber, and the *dhobi* or washerman in certain ceremonies connected with birth and death. Not to do this would be to sin against social conventions; yet in one or two cases we were told that if a Rautiya is too poor to employ a Brahmin he might make other arrangements. This probably means that far back in their history they attended to such matters themselves, but have now become Hinduized and feel unable to act for themselves. Rautiyas made the claim that they move freely among Hindus and are recognized by them in a manner that other Kol *kurhis* are not. While the group is theoretically endogamous, hypergamy is occasionally practised with the Thakuriyas. This is probably a relic from the time when intermarriage was common, but the process of Hinduization has now stabilized the *kurhis*. They admit that if necessary Thakuriya girls may be married to Rautiya boys, but deny that they ever give their girls in marriages to Thakuriyas. If a *swasaha* Rautiya—those whom perform marriage without the help of a Brahmin—has an eligible son they would give their daughter to him in marriage only if it is agreed that the Brahmin priest and the *nai*, will officiate in the regular way.

Rautiyas have a very definite taboo in the case of the horse. Horse manure is absolutely forbidden to be touched. There are several curious stories that came to our attention. One of them is that in the dim ages past Bhagawan gave the Kols the gift of a horse. In a few

1 Russell and Hiralal, *Op. Cit.*, Vol. III, Article Kol.

days it grew to be so tall that no Kol could mount it. They did not know what to do, and the only thing that they could think of (being jungle people) was to take an axe and shorten its legs. This they were about to do when the horse disappeared. A variant story of the above is that the horse given by Bhagawan had a peculiar power which made it impossible for Kols to ride upon it. At one moment it would be so small that it would run right out from under the man who was riding it, leaving him standing in the way ; on other occasions it became so tall that no one could climb upon it. Once, when it was in the latter form, a Kol in desperation took his axe and started to cut short the legs of the horse, but before he could actually do this it was snatched away by Bhagawan. Since then Kols have never used horses, for they were "deceived" by Bhagawan. They claim that they will never touch the dung of the horse, "not even if we are beaten." They have no taboos in the case of cow dung.

The Bharias, a tribe of cultivators, probably Mundas, found mostly in Jubbulpore district have a similar story which is recorded by Russell and Hiralal as follows :

> They have an aversion for the horse and will not remove its dung. To account for this they tell a story to the effect that in the beginning God gave them a horse to ride and fight upon. But they did not know how to mount the horse because it was so high. The wisest man among them proposed to cut notches in the side of the animal by which they could climb up, and this they did. But God, when he saw it, was very angry with them, and ordered that they should never be soldiers, but should be given a winnowing fan and broom to sweep the grain out of the grass and make their livelihood in that way.[1]

Some Rautiyas also have a taboo against the use of mattresses or quilts made from pieces of old clothes. They also seem to have a very definite taboo against the use of gold as an ornament, although it was often stated that this custom is passing away. It is not that they cannot *touch* gold, for this they may do, but they should not wear it on their persons. The reason for this goes back to Sheori the mother of Kols who would never touch gold. They now consider that this was probably a mistake on her part and that Bhagawan does not mean that Kols should avoid its use. This taboo is not observed by most of this Rautiya women, who use gold if they can afford it.

In the course of our investigations it became apparent that other

1 Russell and Hiralal, *Op. Cit.*, Vol. II, p. 250.

sub-groups are recognised within the Rautiya *kurhi*. These are often listed as entirely separate from Rautiyas, but when those conversant with such matters were pressed, it was found that these are really sub-groups of the Rautiya. The sub-groups are .

1a. *Rautel.* This group appears in eleven of the twenty-one lists as a genuine Kol *kurhi*. Further study has revealed that this name is used rather loosely and that there is really very little difference between the Rautels and the Rautiyas. In Maihar State groups calling themselves Rautel claimed that they practise hypergamy with Rautiyas and Thakuriyas; but this occurs only if suitable Rautel girls are not available for marriage. The groups in Maihar State claimed that they are the highest class of Kols, as a Brahmin priest always officiates in their wedding ceremonies, while the Rautiyas do not always observe this essential. It came out in the same discussions that Rautels eat off an earthen dish known as the *kurha*, and that they are thus probably identical with the sub-group of Rautiyas known as Kurhas. A Kathautiya Kol later confirmed this interpretation. This same informant said that his group used to practise hypergamy with Kurhas, but that now there are no restrictions, and in most places either can take or give their girls in marriage without hindrance. This opinion, however, was found to be inconsistent with enquiries in other centres.

1b. *Kurha.* The Kurha is definitely a Rautiya of a particular kind, and might be considered a "totemistic sept". This group is expected to do all its eating off black earthenware vessels known as *kurhas*. These are not made by Kols themselves, but are bought from members of the potter caste, the Kumhars. The following stories were noted in regard to their origin.

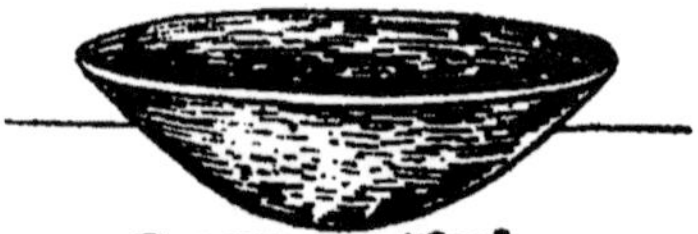

The EARTHENWARE KŪṚHĀ
This is the dish from which the Kūṛhās should eat.

Fig. 17

Once upon a time there were two brothers who were orphaned of their father and brought up by their mother. After a time the old mother died and the two sons were forced to go out into the world and earn their own living. Following quite a long period of separation they happened to meet, and each enquired after the work and welfare of the other. The younger related how he was working for a certain master and how this master had fed him from a *kurha* made by a Kumhar. Then after becoming independent of his master he told how he had continued to use that type of dish. The elder brother was much annoyed at this and told his younger brother that they could no longer associate nor eat together because of this practice.

This led to a separation between the brothers and they formed two divisions of the same family. The elder brother was the head of the family of Rautiya Kols and the younger of the Kurha Kols.

Another story relates that there were once five brothers of the same *kurhi*. Due to lack of food they were forced to separate : one went to the Binj mountains and founded the Binj *kurhi* ; another went to a Thakuriya house, found shelter there, and from him are descended the Thakuriya Kols ; another who took refuge with the Kumhars, the potters, was the ancestor of the Kurha sept. It is not unlikely that these stories contain the truth that this *kurhi* may have arisen from some marriage with Kumhars or perhaps miscegenation with them, or it may have reference to some occupational adventure on the part of some Kols.

Apparently the use of an earthen vessel by one sub-group does not prevent marriage within the whole group, nor does it limit it to that group, for marriages are possible between them and the Kathautiya Rautiyas who use wooden vessels from which to eat. There is the restriction, though, that Kurhas and Kathautiyas should not eat together unless they are related by marriage, and when this is the case they may compromise by the use of the ordinary brass plate. In a certain centre we were told that the only "pure Rautiyas" were those who used the *kurha* and that there were also definite marriage restrictions between them and the users of the wooden bowl. This, if ever true, is disappearing.

1c. *Kathautiya*. Evidence goes to show that this *kurhi* is also a sub-group of the Rautiyas and differs from the Kurhas in that its members eat from a wooden bowl, called *kathauta* or *kathota*. The women folk, and occasionally the men, wear bits of wood in the lobes of their ears. During childhood the hole in the lobe is enlarged by the insertion of fibres from weeds, and from time to time a new bit is inserted in the attempt to enlarge the hole. We did not find that the Kathautiya Kols were consistent in the use of the wooden dish. At Sihora they told us that while they were Kathautiyas they had nevertheless given up the use of the *kathauta* and had adopted the ordinary brass plate. In other centres, notably one near Katni, they still use the bowl and cling to the custom tenaciously. As far as possible, they declared, all food should be prepared in wooden vessels, and it is expected that they should eat their food from such vessels. They do not manufacture their own *kathautas*, nor is any particular kind of wood used, but the dishes are made by Hindu carpenters from such wood as is available. At the time of death or eclipse of sun or moon the Kurha Kols must throw out all their earthenware dishes ; the

Kathautiyas also throw out their earthenware vessels, but not the wooden ones which are considered to be unaffected by these occurrences. This may be due to Hindu influences.

It was intimated that hypergamy is occasionally practised with the Thakuriyas but in such cases it appears that the girls are "kept" rather than "married" One group of Kathautiyas asserted their superiority over the Thakuriyas and claimed that if a Thakuriya girl came to live with a Kathautiya boy, the Thakuriyas could take her back; but that they would never take back one of their girls who went to live with the Thakuriyas.

Some Kols stated that Binj, Kathariya and Kulmangans are types of Rautiya Kols, but the best evidence appears to be otherwise and these groups are treated separately below.

The use of the word "Rautiya" is not confined to the Kols. There is a Munda tribe in Chota Nagpur called Rautiyas and a few members of this tribe are found in the Jashpur State of the Central Provinces. It is also the name of a subcaste of Dahait, a mixed caste of village watchmen of the Jubbulpore and Mandla districts, and several of their subcaste names bear a close resemblance to those of the Kols. It is also a sub-caste of the Kawars and of a section of the Chamars and Rawats (Ahir).[1] The other subgroups of Rautiyas as noted above were not in use elsewhere except that among the Darzis, or tailors there is a Kathautiya subdivision.[2]

2. *Thakuriyas*. Russell and Hiralal[3] are of the opinion that this word is derived from *thakur* meaning "a lord", and they trace this *kurhi* to the intermarriage of Rajput males with Kol females. Such intermarriage probably followed the gradual penetration of the Rajputs into the regions occupied by the Kols. The stories given below concerning the origin of the Thakuriyas probably reflect a long period in which there was a considerable mixture of blood.

According to one story a certain Rautiya Kol had two wives who often quarrelled and the husband saw fit to scold the elder of the two. As a result she left the protection of the Kol and in anger went to the house of the *malguzar* of the village who happened to be a Thakur. She began to live on the veranda of his house, and earned her food with her own hands in any way she could. After some months she gave birth to a son and the Thakur sent word to this effect to her husband, with the request that he should come and take the mother and child

1 Russell and Hiralal, *Op. Cit.*, Vol. I, p. 402.
2 *Ibid.*, Vol. I, p. 376.
3 *Ibid.*, Vol. III, p. 509.

PLATE XIII.

Dhunka of Garha - a Rautiya Kol.

A Kathauta Rautiya with the wooden bowl from which they must eat. Near Katni.

PLATE XIV.

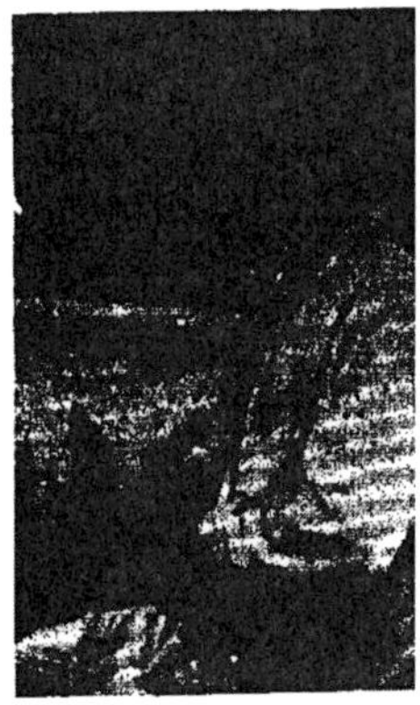

Jagdeo - a Thakuriya Kol.

Bharosa and Nunhu - Thakuriya Kols.

back to his home. When the Kol received the news he denied that the son was his and claimed that the Thakur was the real father. In the end the Thakur kept the child and when he grew up the boy was married, and his descendants make up the Thakuriya Kols.

Another story is that there were once two sisters Shivari and Sudama. Shivari was the elder. Sudama entered the house of a Thakur and conceived a child by him and her descendants are called the Thakuriyas. Shivari's children became the Rautiyas.

There is also a much longer story current which involves a battle with the Ahirs.[1] Once there lived at Pipari, south of the Ganges river near the river Belam, an old Kol named Makhara Dudjh. He had a very beautiful wife named Chandwa. They had five daughters, four of whom were married without difficulty. Many Ahirs lived some distance from the Kols in a village called Gaura, and the two groups were on good terms and often ate together. This gave the opportunity to an Ahir named Loharik to elope with Chandwa. The Kols were much angered at this breach of hospitality and a group of three hundred and sixty of them armed with guns, swords and spears set out after the Ahirs and defeated them, but could not locate Chandwa. In the course of time Loharik Ahir and Chandwa Kol had a son called Bhorik. After a few years Loharik remarked to his brother Samar that the Kols were getting too powerful and should be destroyed, and that they had better play a trick and thus eliminate them. A marriage was arranged between Bhorik and an Ahir girl and the Kols were invited. The Ahirs had five or six great jars of liquor ready for the wedding feast. The three hundred and sixty Kols came with all their arms to the village of Gaura. Loharik Ahir stood before Makhara Dudjh with folded hands and respectfully asked him to have all the implements of warfare put into a room and locked so that at the time of drinking no incidents might occur. The Kols foolishly trusted him and their weapons were locked away. The Ahirs had been warned not to take a second drink, but rather to feign drunkenness after the first drink. Before long the Kols were too drunk to fight and the Ahirs quickly killed all of them.

Now Makhara Dudjh had a younger brother named Devasi who was blind and hence had to live by begging. His sister cared for him

1 In the *Census of India*, 1931 1:3 p. B 64, it is related that "The Abhiras, from whom the modern Ahirs are said to have descended were a widespread people....The Abhiras ware in the North-west Frontier Province before the Christian era. In the third century A.D. they were in lower Sind and North Gujarat and next they appear to have passed down the Tapti valley into Khandesh." Possibly these Kol stories go back to 250 A.D. and to the struggles with the Abhiras for the possession of the land. Later material is mixed up, as the Thakuriyas are also brought into the story.

and led him wherever he went. He always had a bow and some arrows with him, as he was also a mighty shooter. As they were out begging they met a Brahmin female beggar who had just been to Gaura, the Ahir village, and had learned of the slaughter of the Kols. When the blind Devasi heard of this he said to his sister: "Sister, why should we live any longer when all our friends are dead? Let us now go to Gaura village and as we approach it tell me carefully where the two Ahir leaders are sitting so that I may shoot them." When they were within a mile of the village she spied them standing before the village and ready to give battle. The two halted and the sister carefully observed all that was going on. At last the two brothers turned their faces toward the blind archer and his sister. She told him that all was ready and handed him two arrows and then set his face toward the brothers. His aim was so exact that he shot the arrows right into the eyes of the two brothers and both fell down dead. Devasi's strength was so great that the bow almost broke when it was bent. The Ahirs were astounded at this mighty feat and wondered who did this. In their estimation Devasi was a mighty Kol and in terror they deserted the village. The blind Kol and his sister then took possession of the village and drove the 360 head of cattle therein back to their own village. They found some children whom they brought along, and when they grew up they intermarried with the Kols and the offspring of this union were called Thakuriyas.

The last part of the story does not seem to fit into the tale as a whole and the Ahir story may refer to some event other than that of the formation of the Thakuriyas. There is a section of the Ahirs called Thakurs and there may be some connection at this point. Russell and Hiralal also cite the belief that the Abhiras, the ancestors in part of the modern Ahirs, came into India from Central Asia about the time of Christ.[1] To-day they are a much mixed race.

It was ascertained that the Thakuriyas do not have the Rautiya taboo against the horse; that they can make mattresses and can even sit on those made by Kathariyas, and that they have no feeling against the use of gold as ornaments. In fact it is believed that a Thakuriya cannot carry out a wedding without the use of gold and that the parents of the bride should at least see some gold about the bridegroom's neck. If the bride can also wear it, so much the better.

One informant said that Thakuriya men occasionally eat chicken and pork, but that their women-folk never eat them. They do not object to eating with other *kurhis*, and while they cannot take Rautiya girls in marriage, they can marry their daughters to them.

1 *Ibid*, Vol. II, p. 10.

When a number of Thakuriyas were asked which *kurhi* is the highest they responded as follows : "Judge for yourselves, the Rautiyas both eat and keep chickens and pigs, but we never touch them. Should a pig stray into one of our houses we have to clean and purify everything and also ourselves. We may eat pork, but always *outside* of our houses and before we can enter them again we must bathe. Our women never eat such meat. So judge for yourselves which is the better group."

3. *Binj.* This name is derived from the Binj hills, the modern Vindhyan range which cuts across the Indian peninsula. At Sihora we were assured that Rautiya and Binj were identical, but apart from this dissenting view this division was generally accepted as a separate *kurhi*. The Binj were usually said to be the highest of all the Kol groups yet no one that we interviewed had actually seen a Binj Kol. They had heard that there was a Binj *Raja* in Rajputana to the northwest, but where he lived now they did not know. They may be related to a Binjhwar tribe in the Central Provinces called "a comparatively civilized Dravidian tribe, or caste formed from a tribe."[1] It is now established that they are one of the subdivisions of the Baigas.[2] They also trace their ancestry back to the Vindhya hills.

The following account was given to us of the Binj Kols : A Thakur or Rajput, fell in love with a Kol woman and the couple ran away together and sought refuge in the Binj mountains. A son was born to them who was named "Binj" after the mountains ; this boy stayed in the hills and was the forefather of the Binj *kurhi*. Other children born to the couple returned with their parents to their old home and gave rise to the Thakuriyas. The Binjes and the Thakuriyas are thus closely linked.

Another story is that a Kol woman became pregnant and gave birth to a son far away in the jungles. Being unable to care for the child she was forced to leave it there. Before long a tiger came across the hapless infant and took it to his den and looked after it. The child grew and lived in the jungle with the tiger and was called Binjhwar. The lad was very intelligent and proved to be a fine hunter and brought the tiger his daily food. When he was old enough to be married the tiger decided that he ought to find the boy a wife, but he was unable to decide how to manage it. One day by chance a Raja's wedding party accompanying the bride-to-be was passing through that very jungle. The tiger saw his chance and frightened the men

1 *Ibid.*, Vol. ii, p. 329.
2 Elwin, V., *The Baigas*, p. 5 ff.

so badly that they dropped the *palki* in which the girl was being carried, and ran away as fast as they could. The poor girl was at the mercy of the tiger, who brought her to the boy, and gave her to him to be his wife. The tiger then released the boy from his forest life and together the new couple left the jungle and went to Sheori who was the boy's relative, as his mother belonged to Sheori's family. The offspring of this couple became the Binj Kols.

These two stories do not even make the same point but both probably preserve certain traditions: one of a connection with the Binj mountains and the other of some inter-marriage with jungle Baigas or Binjhwars.

4. *Khangar.* There is a distinct group of village watchmen and field labourers of low caste called by this name and found mostly in northern central India and in the United Provinces. The name is said to be derived from the words *khand*, a pit, and *gar*, a maker or digger; because the Khangar digs holes in other peoples' houses for the purpose of theft. According to another account the name is derived from *khadgahar* meaning a Kshatriya or warrior, who earns his livelihood by means of a *khadga*, or sword.

With regard to Kol Khangars we were told that they were *swasahas*, not making use of Brahmins or other Hindus in social events, such as marriage. They are considered low on the social scale and Rautiyas always avoid them. If a Rautiya girl elopes with a Khangar she can never be received back, and the offspring are Khangars. In Chota Nagpur there is a Khangar tribe which is a branch of the Munda group. The following story is told of their origin:

> Two Munda brothers were travelling with their wives from one place to another. One of the brothers and his wife preceded the other brother in the country. On the way, the former brother's wife was brought to bed of a child. While leaving the place the Munda couple buried the placenta etc., in the hearth which they had improvised at their temporary lodging. Soon afterwards, the other brother came up there with his wife. On opening up the hearth he discovered the placenta etc., buried there and thought that his brother had bagged some game and left a portion of the meat for him to cook and eat. And so the couple unsuspectingly ate the unclean meat. When the brothers met, and the truth was known, the brother who had eaten the unclean meat was excommunicated and his descendants became Khangars.[1]

1 Roy, S. C., *The Mundas and Their Country*, p. 401.

The Khangars of Central India have a tradition akin to the one related of the Thakuriyas, of a slaughter by a Bundela Rajput after they were made drunk.[1] This may be an altogether different story but probably belongs to the same period when the Rajputs came into Bundelkhand. No first-hand accounts were obtained by us which would shed any light on the origin of this *kurhi*.

5. *Garhvariya*. While this name occurs eight times in the list of Kol subdivisions nevertheless we found only one living specimen in spite of the fact that there were said to be many of this group around Jubbulpore. This particular Garhvariya came to us in a group of Thakuriyas and Rautiyas and was the butt of their jokes. He was short and dark and had a very flat nose, much broader than is usual with Kols. The other *kurhis* said to his face that they would have nothing to do with him socially. When asked about himself he said that he was a Rautiya who had the misfortune to be born out of Rewa State and hence was called a Garhvariya. The other Kols present would not agree that this was the real situation. Garhvariyas are considered unclean and no other sept will take their girls or give them their own daughters in marriage. They are mainly employed as field labourers. It is not unlikely that we met others, but they would not admit that they were Garhvariyas.

6. *Mawasi*. Very little was to be ascertained from the Kols about this group. They seem to be a very "low" *kurhi*, and do not even call in a Chamarin to act as midwife and cut the cord of the newly born infant, doing such work with their own hands. They are so low that no social intercourse is possible with Kols like Rautiyas and Thakuriyas. They are considered the most despised of all the Kols and "live just like Basors who are outcastes and make baskets and keep pigs."

The Munda tribe known as the Korkus and found in the Satpura hills of south central India are sometimes called Mowasis.[2] Regarding Korkus Russell and Hiralal state that the sept names of the Korkus are in many cases identical with those of the Kols and Korwas, which may mean that they are an offshoot of "the great Kol or Munda" tribe. The word "Mowasi" has reference to the largest of their subdivisions but its derivation is uncertain. The Census Report for the Central India Agency says : "The Mawasis were reputed to be a fighting section of the Kols."[3]

7. *Kathariya*. This *kurhi* takes its name from *kathri*, a mattress

1 Russell and Hiralal, *Op. Cit.*, Vol. iii, p. 439.
2 *Ibid.* Vol. iii, p. 550.
3 *Census of India*, 1931, xx: 1, p. 237,

or quilt which they make from their own worn-out clothes or even from the cast-off clothes of others. These quilts and mattresses are used in place of blankets and other forms of bedding usually found in villages, and present a ragged sight when taken out in the sun to air. The Rautiya Kols have a taboo for the Kathariya mattress. Rautiya Kols generally despise this *kurhi* because they do menial work, but this cannot be the main reason.

All the evidence that we were able to collect indicates that Russell and Hiralal are incorrect in their conclusions regarding the Kathariyas having the mattress as their totem. They say: "A member of this sept (Katharia) must never have a mattress in his house nor wear clothes sewn in cross-pieces as mattresses are sewn. The word *kathri* should never be mentioned before him as he thinks some great misfortune would thereby happen to his family, but this belief is falling into abeyance."[1] The actual facts which we have carefully checked seem to be the exact opposite.

8. *Khairwar.* This is probably the same as a group in Chota Nagpur known under the slightly different name of Kharias. In the year 1937 Sarat Chandra Roy[2] published in two volumes a complete and comprehensive study of this important group. The Khairwars in the Central Provinces seem to be a mixture of jungle tribes and are often confused with the Gonds. Russell and Hiralal say that the most probable derivation of the name is from the *khair* or catechu tree (*Acacia catechu*) from which catechu, "any one of the several dry, earthy, or resinlike, astringent substances got from certain tropical plants and used in tanning and dyeing" is manufactured. We were given this same information: this group is called Khairwars because its members make *khair*. They are also said to be a low type of Kol and this work is despised as a profession for now-a-days it is done only by primitive jungle dwellers. It is not unlikely that a group of Kols at one time were active in preparing *khair* and so received this name, but it is more probable that they are somehow related to the Kharias of Chota Nagpur.

9. *Kulmangan.* This is another of the so-called lower types of Kols, the name being derived from *mangna*, "to ask." It appears that during the time of birth, marriage, death, or special religious functions, members of this *kurhi*, if such it may be called, make it a practice to ask alms from Kols. On certain occasions they are said to play the *sarangi*—a one-stringed musical instrument. There is no

1 Russell and Hiralal, *Op. Cit.*, Vol. III. p. 510, see also Vol. 1, p. 91.
2 *The Kharias.*

possibility of marriage with higher Kol groups. It is not at all unlikely that the name is not the title of a *kurhi*, but rather of a type of Kol who, though he may belong to any *kurhi*, uses the above occasions for making a little extra money. One informant assured us that Kulmangans were really Rautiyas.

10. *Swasaha*. The word probably is a corruption of *swastha*, meaning self-reliant, independent. When the word is applied to Kols the inference is that they do not follow the Hinduized customs of most of their tribe in regard to the calling in of the Brahmin priest, the *nai*, and the *dhobi*. All these matters are cared for by some member of their own community, usually one of the elderly persons. We came across one who claimed to be a Swasaha, but as a group they were never found. Some evidence was found which would indicate that this is not a distinct *kurhi*, but is rather something remaining from earlier times. If any family or group is independent of the *pandit*, *nai* or *dhobi* in weddings and the like, they may be called Swasahas. We found evidence which leads us to believe that there are Swasaha Rautiyas. The lower *kurhis* are probably mostly of the *swasaha* type. Nevertheless most of the Kols believe and claim that this is a distinct *kurhi*.

11. *Bhumiya*. The word literally means 'born from the land' or 'aboriginal.' It is also a title of the Bharias, a Munda tribe residing in large numbers in the Jubbulpore district. At present the Bharias are usually associated with the Gonds and are probably very much intermixed with them as the number of names and sub-divisions would indicate. We were unable to elicit any definite information from the Kols about this *kurhi* save that Bhumiyas may sleep either on beds or on the ground. This same title is also found among the Baigas and the Korkus, and the Gonds have a subdivision of this name. Bhumiya and Bhuiya are synonyms.

In connection with the Kols the name may have arisen as a nickname, or a title given to Kols who held land. Certain tribes and some Hindus are said to employ the term Bhuiya as the equivalent for *Zamindar*.[1] There are thus Bhumiyas by tribe and also by title. Roy has written a book on the Hill Bhuiyas of Orissa.[2] They are also Mundas and in view of this fact it is not strange that some Kols should either bear the title of Bhumiya or belong to the Bhumiya *kurhi*. A Bhuiya subcaste bears the name of Rautadi, which is not far removed from Rautiya.

12. *Murha*. Russell and Hiralal state that this is a caste of

1 *Ibid*. Vol. II, p. 306.
2 Roy, S. C., *The Hill Bhuiyas of Orissa*, 1935.

navvies and labourers found in Jubbulpore and adjoining districts and numbering about 1,500 persons only. They are connected by some writers with the Bind tribe of northern India and Bengal, but it is more likely that in Central India they are recruited largely from the Kol group. "In Mandla some Murhas seem to be Kols."[1] This caste is employed in all kinds of earthwork, such as building walls, excavating trenches and making embankments for large tanks or for the rice fields. We found that similar work is being done by Kols all over Central India. At Barela there is a large tank covering several acres and called 'Murhai.' Local Kols told us that it was so named because it was dug by Murha Kols many years ago.

13. *Gunj*. Russell and Hiralal not mentioned any group of this name. The 1931 Census has a "Gunjwar" in a long list of tribes and castes, but calls it "Unclassified." It was claimed that the Gunj *kurhi* originally lived in the west and came from thence into Central India. No one interrogated concerning this matter had even met a member of this *kurhi*. It is not unlikely that the name may be a variant of Binj, although one group included both in their list of Kol *kurhis*.

14. *Kabiriya*. The word means 'follower of Kabir' and is probably basically a religious group. Kabir was brought up in the home of a Mohammedan weaver (*Julaha*), but through Ramananda came into touch with the theistic and *bhakti* type of faith proclaimed by Ramanuja. He was half-Hindu and half-Moslem and is revered by both. George Weston Briggs notes: "The real importance of Kabir rests in the enormous influence which he has exercised upon subsequent religious thinking, especially as it has affected the masses, because of his use of the vernacular. His attitude toward caste drew to himself a large following from the lower levels of society."[2] This designation on the part of the Kols shows that Kabir's influence had reached them, but the name may have some occupational significance. Kabir was a weaver and two weaver groups in Central Provinces, the Koris and the Koshtis have Kabiriya subgroups.

15. *Narchhila*. The name means literally "a cord cutter" and refers to the cutting of the umbilical cord at childbirth. It was stated that the *kurhi* is given the name because it does not call in a midwife from a low-Hindu caste to cut the umbilical cord (*nara*) of the new-born child. It seems more likely that this is a general term, as in the case of the Swasahas, for a family in any one of the groups who for

1 Russell and Hiralal, *Op. Cit.*, Vol. IV, p. 253.
2 Briggs, G. W., *The Chamars*, p. 204.

some reason or other do not call in a low caste midwife. It was also reported that this group does not make any use of the Hindu priest and is very low in the social scale. Some claimed that this is really a group of Chamars—leather workers in the traditional sense, but Russell and Hiralal do not mention it in their glossary of caste divisions nor does Briggs report it. It is probably of minor significance.

16. *Bhariya* is the same as Bhuniya, see above.

17. *Borowar* does not appear in Russell and Hiralal nor in the list of tribe and caste responses in the 1931 Census. Nor is Barwar found there. Barwar, said to mean "disciple of the *bar* or banyan tree' (*Ficus indica*), is listed among the septs of the Kols in the north by Crooke as was seen in the previous note[1] on his findings. In a later book Crooke speaks of Barwars as a criminal tribe of Oudh.[2]

18. *Pawai*. One group gave the information that this *kurhi* lived in the south, 'Chawhan Khand'. In Singhbhum, Bengal, the Bhuiyas call themselves *Pawan-bans* meaning 'children of the wind'. The Bhuiya highlands are called Pawri Desh.[3] This may indicate a memory of a connection now long lost.

19. *Maubhaiya*. No trace nor information concerning this group could be found. It was reported only once.

The Census of 1891 attempted to record the names of subdivisions of castes in some detail, and the resultant list contained thousands of names of every kind. The Ahir alone had over 1,700 entries. The subdivisions of the Kols manifest the same tendency and show that the groups have absorbed into themselves members from higher and lower castes. The Thakuriyas probably contain a Rajput element and at the other end we find Kols mixed with Khangars, Murhas, Khairwars and Chamars. The Kols of today are probably pretty well mixed with other groups.

MAINTENANCE OF THE SOCIAL STRUCTURE. Kols who live in close contact with city life have frequently lost the sense of social solidarity which characterizes the Kols living under more primitive conditions. Various factors in city life, or near-city life, tend to make the same rigid social order impossible, and yet even under these conditions there is an attempt to maintain something of the older traditions.

Almost every village has an elderly man who may be considered in a sense the head-man of the community. He is usually called *Mahata* or literally, the leader. This man is the natural head of the

1 See page 33.
2 Crooke, W., *Religion and Folklore of Northern India*, p. 166.
3 Russell and Hiralal, *Op. Cit.*, Vol. II, p. 315.

community and has come to be recognized as such largely by his personal worth, wisdom and character. There is no formal election of the head-men; they were recognized as such by a kind of social gravitation. Usually the *Mahata* has an assistant known as the *Chharibardar*, who does most of the necessary running around. The *Mahata* is not the sole authority and is not empowered to act or even to make decisions of any importance without first consulting the more influential heads of the community. But he usually takes the initiative in calling together the leaders of the local group if factors requiring a meeting come to his knowledge, or if a definite request for it is made.

The ultimate authority of the local group rests with the village *panch* or *panchayat*, literally 'the council of five'. The *panch*, however, is not to be thought of as limited to five members only, for it is usually composed of all the influential adult males of the community. They must possess, in the words of the Kols, "*dharam aur dhan*"—piety and property —if they are to be regarded worthy of a place in the *panchayat*. There are however, no elections to the Kol *panchayats*. The leader may or may not recognize one as a member of the group, and while others may attend and even take part in the discussions, they have no right to decide on the ultimate issue.

Practically all major and minor issues affecting the life of the community are decided by the *panch* which thus forms a council for the arbitration of matters pertaining to the community. Its power is really remarkable and the decisions of the *panchayat* are rigidly respected. It is dangerous for a member of the community to go against its advice or decision, for in most cases the *panch* can bring to bear upon the recalcitrant such strong social pressure that he is practically cut off from his community, which means that he is a man without a country or a caste. Personally he may be cut off from all social intercourse, from the use of the well and other village amenities; he is not invited to any functions and is treated as an outcaste. But worse yet, he can neither get his children married, nor admitted into the tribe.

Some of the matters which a Kol *panchayat* deals with include the following:

1. Eating and drinking with other castes if such has been forbidden or is against custom.
2. Sexual abberations not approved by the usual Kol practices.
3. Marriage matters: selecting the bride or the bridegroom if there is any difficulty or dispute; arbitration of disputes over financial aspects of the marriage. Irregular unions dealt with and suitable penalties determined.

PLATE XI.

Kol Elders in Rewa State.

Elders in Panagar discussing Kol Customs.

PLATE XII.

A Demonstration of the Kol Salutation.

4. Divorce and the care of the children.
5. Failure to provide adequately for members of the household.
6. Debt, drink, betting and quarrels.
7. Injury to, or the killing of animals which are considered sacred.
8. Defying the Kol social traditions, not listed above.
9. Deciding upon contributions of money or supplies for group religious observances.
10. Property and inheritance when there is a dispute or doubt.

Should the decision of the *panch* not be accepted in some serious dispute, particularly where real property is involved, the matter may be taken to the civil courts. While this method is open and often threatened, it is seldom resorted to. Kols are not often found in the courts, for there is always the chance that they will lose the case and also have to face social boycott of the *panch* for not heeding its decision and advice. In some matters the *panch* itself may advise going to court. If there is a grave offense, such as murder or theft, the police step in and the matter is taken entirely out of the hands of the community. Nevertheless the Kols boast that they are law abiding and that most sections of them have had no police record whatsoever. Enquiry from the police confirmed this claim; in this respect Kols give no anxiety and the police seldom trouble them when some crime has been committed in the larger villages of which Kols form a part.

When a penalty is decided upon the *panch* sees that it is enforced. If the person to be disciplined is amenable to the *panch* the penalty is usually either a fine or a feast. If the latter, the person must feed the leaders of the community and thus express regret for his act; or if a fine is imposed, such, if realized, is usually used for a feast. In the past it is said that the fines were used for the purchase of alcoholic liquors and drinks, and in some places still are; but now-a-days this seems to be largely abandoned. The fine in some cases might even amount to fifty rupees, but for a Kol this is an excessive amount and it is unlikely that so much is ever declared under ordinary circumstances. Five rupees or so is the usual amount for ordinary violations.

INTER-VILLAGE COUNCILS. The general social solidarity of the Kols is further shown by the fact that under the more stable conditions of village life, no single village stands alone in making an important decision affecting one of its members, for there are inter-village federations. Sarat Chandra Roy also reports this among the Kharias.[1] In several

1 *The Kharias*, p. 172.

centres we found evidence of this inter-village organization. In Maihar there was a *panchayat* composed, theoretically, from members of seven castes ; but Kols have inter-village councils of their own and the leaders of each village, along with a few other leading men, occasionally come together when important matters are under consideration. Such a meeting is called only for something which seems vitally important and affects the total life of the community. Their sense of social solidarity is so acute that a matter affecting one is regarded as affecting all. Near Katni there is an inter-village organization which includes twenty to thirty Kol communities, and this federation is said to be very active in matters pertaining to the life of the Kols of that area.

Sometimes the heads of the villages in a federation are consulted by sending around a sort of circular, giving information about the case and instructing them to think over the decision which should be eventually reached. Occasionally they are then and there asked to pronounce their opinion. In Barela we were in a house to which had just come a communication, originating in Barela, and which was being circularized among the villages of the federation to which Barela belonged. It was written for the Kols by the village writer of the Kayasth caste and we were able to secure a copy of it. The circular affords a good example of the way in which certain matters are settled, and shows that the matter of eating is serious enough to be called to the attention of the larger group. The translation of the document is as follows :

From Barela *Panch*.

Sri,

To

All the kings (members) of the various *panchayats*, we (the members of the local *panchayats*) send our very respectful greetings. We would respectfully make this complaint that people under your jurisdiction (*i.e.* Kols) eat the flesh of swine cooked by the Kumhars (potters). If this is so why should we not start the pipe with them (have social intercourse with them). You get the animal killed by the Kumhars and then wash it with water that has already been touched by them (and so polluted), and if a girl becomes pregnant you punish the family by the imposition of a fine or a caste dinner.

If these are facts please admit them or if things are otherwise, say so and make your mark (signature). Also give your opinion whether you are agreeable to social intercourse with the Kumhars.

This letter should be circulated in the following villages :

1. Kharara Ghat : the whole *panch*, Sahmat, Dhannu, Sunnu.
2. Bargaon : the whole *panch*.
3. Matawar Do.
4. Bharda Do.
5. Panagar Do.
6. Usmer Mohniya.
7. Jatma.

This letter, without naming the offenders, is a complaint that somewhere in this particular Kol community social intercourse with the potter caste has been allowed without penalty. The Kumhars are among the lowest untouchables and no Kol should eat or drink with them. The *panch* of that particular village was so lax that the matter even went as far as a Kol girl becoming pregnant, due, presumably, to this association. They did not watch over the welfare of the group and began to check it only after it had gone as far as that. To the minds of the complainants the association with the Kumhars should never have been permitted and the rhetorical question is asked, if Kols should not have full intercourse with them, implying that to do so would be to degrade the Kols to the level of the Kumhars. This, of course, would be absurd, but is just what the other *panch* is allowing and so it should be checked. The letter attempts to put a stop to this and gives an example of the way such matters are sometimes handled.

Totemistic Elements in the Social Organization. The phenomenon of totemism is widespread among the Munda tribes of India, and in many cases it still forms a fundamental feature of the social organization particularly in connection with marriage, kinship, and sexual relations. In certain cases, as with the Oraons,[1] there is a definitely intermediate stage, and endogamy is becoming the rule, but the clans among the more primitive tribes are still exogamous. Among some of the latter type, the Korwas and Birhors[2], for example, the totemistic organization is still quite intact; in contrast, the Hill Bhuiyas of Orissa and the Juangs of Keonjhar, both Munda tribes, have at the present day no totemistic organization.[3] Although

1 Roy, S. C., *The Oraons of Chota Nagpur*, p. 324 ff.
2 Roy, S. C., *The Birhors*, Chapter IV.
3 Roy, S C., *The Kharias*, pp. 145, 146.

in the case of the Hill Kharias the clan organization is based on totemistic principles, there is still no exogamy connected with it.[1] Roy remarks about another section of the Hill Kharias: "There is strong evidence to indicate that this section of the tribe has probably lost its clan organization as they have lost their aboriginal language, unless it may be that they never evolved any such organization."[2] Other Kharias, notably the Hill Kharias of Singhbhum and Manbhum districts have recorded of them that "the division into exogamous clans is recognized for the purpose of marriage."[3]

An examination of the clan organization of the Mundas, which might quite readily be worked out from existing materials, would be an interesting study. From our study of the Kols of Central India it is clear that they, like some of the Munda tribes noted above, have at the present day no totemistic clan organization as the basis of their social organization; exogamy is practically unknown, marriage being regulated within the group and even sub-groups on the basis of genealogical relationships. Fifty years ago Crooke wrote of the Kols of the Southern United Provinces that they have "shed off the elaborate system of totemistic septs which are found among the Mundas of Bengal."[4] On being asked questions dealing with a totem or an emblem of a clan the Kols said that they have clans which they term *gots*. Asked further how these differed from *kurhis* the answer given was that *gots* and *kurhis* are essentially the same. They said that on a tribal basis exogamy is unknown amongst them, and that marriage is always among the same *gots* or *kurhis*. There seems therefore to be no difference at the present time in marriage regulations between members of septs within the clan.

Some of the Kol *kurhis* which have no totems or clan emblems may be called *gots* in the same sense as are the three *kurhis*: Kurhas, Kathautiyas and Kathariyas, which apparently have as clan emblems the earthen vessel, the wooden bowl and the mattress, respectively. No rites are observed in connection with these totems, either for their multiplication or for their preservation. As far as could be ascertained there are now no taboos in connection with them. In the cases of those who strictly use one or the other of these dishes the taking of food in the wrong kind of dish is taboo, that is, the Kurha should eat off earthen vessels; yet there are Kurhas who do not observe

1 *Ibid.*, pp. 123, 124, 125 *etc.*
2 *Ibid.*, p. 122.
3 *Ibid.*, p. 125.
4 Crooke, W., *Tribes and Castes of the Northwest Provinces and Oudh*, Vol. III, Art. Kol.
5 See pages 36, 37, 44.

this in a strict way, and when certain situations arise they may eat from a brass dish without offence. The same applies in the case of the Kathautiyas.

Russell and Hiralal[1] are supposed to have found traces of totemism among the Kols, but as previously noted it is clear that they have made a mistake in the case of the Kathariyas. They list certain "totemistic septs" in Mandla. They note that the Bargaiyan sept is really named after the village of Bargaon, that the sept connects its name with the *bar* or banyan tree (*Ficus indica*) and is said to revere it. This tree, however, is generally revered by Kols. Some of the sept's uses and taboos of the tree are mentioned in their article. The second sept, the Kathautia has the explanation that we have given, except it is reported that the sept reveres the tiger and keeps Bagheshwar Deo,[2] the tiger god, on a little platform on the veranda. We found no trace of this among the Kathautiyas interviewed. The third is the Kathariya sept, of which we have already spoken and where we believe the authors have gone astray. Fourthly, "The name of the Mudia or Mudrundia sept is said to mean shaven head, but they apparently revere the white *kumhra* or gourd, perhaps because it has some relation to the shaven head. They give the white gourd to a woman on the third day after she has borne a child, and her family do not eat this vegetable for three years."[3] Fifthly, the Kumraya sept is said to revere the brown *kumhra*. Again, the Bhuwar sept is named after *bhu* or *bhumi* and its members must never sleep on cots, always on the ground. We found no trace of this belief. "Other septs are Nathunia, a nose ring; Karpatia, a kind of grass; and Binjhwar, from a tribe of that name."[4] Russell and Hiralal do not state whether there are exogamic tendencies in connection with these septs or not. Totemism however, is a very complex phenomenon and differs widely even among the Mundas. There is apparently no single criterion. "Exogamy may or may not be coupled with the other features, totemistic taboos may be dissociated from a totemistic name for the group practising them; descent from the totem may or may not be postulated; and so forth."[5] Lowie goes on to discuss Goldenweiser's and Fraser's theories of totemism and finds them inadequate to explain the totemistic phenomena. "Only confusion can result from envisaging what is disparate under a single head."[6] The

1 Russell and Hiralal, *Op. Cit.*, Vol, III, p. 510, 511.
2 See index : Tiger.
3 *Ibid.*, p. 510.
4 *Ibid.*, p. 511.
5 Lowie, R. H., *Primitive Society*, p. 140.
6 *Ibid.*, p. 145.

Rautiya Kols have a strong taboo in relation to the horse, but repeated enquiries have failed to establish any totemistic connection, although it may exist. In view of these facts and in the light of these investigations it seems that totemism as such is apparently a negligible factor in the lives of the Kols of Central India. There are, it may be, certain traces of it kept alive by tradition, but its real significance has been lost. The unit of social organization turns out to be the family within the endogamous *kurhi*.

CHAPTER IV

BIRTH, CHILDHOOD, PUBERTY

For the Kols there are certain very obvious turning points of life and at such times Kols believe that evil is present, ready to render the outcome of events unfavourable. To Kols the anxiety is not merely one born of a physical crisis but goes deeper into their consciousness, for at such times favourable supernatural aid must be secured or the evil spirits will triumph over them. Hence at these turning points there are certain rites and ceremonies which must be observed and recourse should not be had to some newer unknown and untried method. Kols are unable to give a rational account of why they perform these rites; as far as they are concerned it is just the custom. Though in many cases the customs may have been adopted from Hinduism, it was so long ago that Kols are now altogether unconscious of it. It should be remembered, therefore, that many of the things described in this connection will also be found true of the village folk all over this part of Central India. An attempt has been made by long and patient enquiry to find out what the Kols themselves do on these important occasions, but we have not sought to compare them with other groups in this regard.

BIRTH CUSTOMS. *Pregnancy.* The pregnant mother is not considered unclean and there are no particular taboos placed upon her. She is allowed to go about her regular work and do all cooking and household duties without restriction. She may eat what she likes and there are no foods which she must avoid other than those a Kol never uses. She should be careful, however, not to go near places where *bhuts* and other evil spirits are known to lurk, they might attack her and as a result cause a miscarriage. When the woman comes to know that she is pregnant the matter is taken to the family goddess—*devi*—who is usually resident in one corner of the house and she is promised that she will receive an offering if she protects the mother and the unborn babe for the full time of pregnancy. After delivery, or often shortly before if all has gone well, the family will present to the *devi* the particular things that they had promised her. This may be an animal such as a goat, pig or chicken, or just a cocoanut. Again, the simple *hom* offering or fire sacrifice is common. This consists of an oblation of clarified butter (*ghi*) placed in the fire burning before the *devi*, the anointing of the wall with vermilion (*sendur*) and the presentation of a piece of a broken cocoanut. Occasionally, particularly when the woman is in severe pain before the time her birth-pangs are expected and normal, there may be a special sacrifice of one of the animals noted above. Hindus also observe similar ceremonies.

There are certain charms which are believed to be useful to the expectant mother to ward off evil. A small metal box for the protecting *devi* is worn on a cotton thread round the neck, while a copper necklace is regarded as an especially effective protection. Sometimes the leaves of the *tulasi* plant (*Ocymum sanctum*) are useful. Such leaves may be laid on the mother's abdomen with a prayer that she may be safeguarded through this dangerous period. These various means help in the prevention of miscarriage which, if it does occur, is believed to be due to the influence of some evil force. But even should a demon trip the woman up and cause her to fall heavily to the ground, no harm will result if these precautions have been attended to. When there is a case of miscarriage the foetus is taken away to the burial ground and put into a hole without any ceremony.

Labour. Among the more primitive Kols difficult labour is ascribed to evil spirits; the more advanced ones speak of it as a punishment due from Bhagawan for some bad *karma*. In case the delivery proves difficult there are certain things that should be done. Some Kols definitely averred that nothing can alter the difficulties of labour, but questions have been answered in such a way by others that it appears to be established that there are magical practices in this connection. If things are not going well the first thing to be done is to make a suitable offering to a *devi* or *deva*, or both. Then one should go carefully about the house and open the mouth of each covered earthen pot; the knots on every bundle should be carefully untied and strings or pieces of ropes untwisted. As far as possible every closed thing in the house should be opened up. This, it is believed, will make the delivery easier. Often five handfuls of rice are taken out of the opened rice jar and Bhagawan is challenged to divide the grains into two equal parts without making an error. They imply that if he can do such a thing and do it right he will surely be able to see the child safely through delivery.

Another magical use of grain is also made at this critical hour. Prayers are first offered for a safe delivery, then a handful of grain is taken out of the pot by a male member of the family. This is carefully counted. If it happens that the number of grains is even, then all will be well, for it is a good omen, and the delivery will be easy. If the number is an odd one, it is a warning of the likelihood of pain and danger.

Kols generally believe that the soul of the child enters and possesses its new body before the child is born. The more general opinion is that the movements of the child in the womb, which first occur about the sixth month, are the signs that the body has received its soul and is already a person. The soul is a gift to the child by Paramatma, and it enters the child's body through the mouth, nose or ears. The Kols' idea of the state and nature of the soul before entering the child's body is very vague and it is unusual to find any clear idea of transmigration and previous existence in another body.

Delivery. There is no uncleanness attached to the woman up to the time of the birth of her baby, but for six days thereafter she is considered unclean. The actual delivery of the child always occurs at home for no use is made of hospitals or the like.

When the time of birth is near the female relatives who have come for the occasion take charge of her. No male members of the family are allowed in the delivery room and men are kept out for the six days following. In a few places however we learned that they might enter after three days. Her mother-in-law and her sister are the ones to make the arrangements and do the actual work, although other female members of the two families may stand ready to assist. The woman awaits her time in a darkened room protected as far as possible from the entry of evil spirits. A few hours before (and sometimes just at the time) birth is expected a mid-wife—*dai*—is summoned. The Kols usually summon a Chamarin, or if she is not available, a Basorin. Sometimes, particularly around Jubbulpore, the Basorin seems to be preferred. If the birth should occur before the *dai* arrives the women in the house can do everything except the cutting of the umbilical cord. In one place we asked what would happen if the *dai* did not arrive and they replied that before a Kolin would cut the cord they would have to let the mother and baby die! Some Kols are said to do it themselves, but we did not find any who admitted that they do so. If the child should be born in a field the mother gathers up the child and the after-birth in her *sari* and carries it home and then the *dai* is called to cut the cord and care for the infant.

The birth usually occurs with the mother squatted on the floor seated on her heels and bending over a large basket placed upside down on the floor, her head meanwhile resting on her hands. The female relatives support her and give encouragement. The *dai* is the one to receive the child. No one in the family should touch the child until it has first been purified by the *dai*. This applies to the mother as well. The *dai* cuts the umbilical cord with an iron instrument which she has brought with her and takes charge of the child. The female relatives may move the mother to another part of the room. The first thing to be done to the baby when it is certain that it has begun to breathe, which is learned by the crying of the infant, is to sprinkle it lightly from head to foot with wood ashes. This, it is claimed, prevents skin trouble, a possible chill, and wards off evil spirits. Ashes are also sprinkled about the floor where the mother squatted. The ashes on the child are then removed with a soft cloth and the baby is bathed in luke-warm water. It is then dried and is usually gently massaged with the sweet *til* oil from *Sesamum indicum*. The child should now be given a smoke bath. There has been a fire burning in the lying-in room and into this is sprinkled some *ajwayan* or dill seed (*Anethum graveolens*), which gives a smoke with a pleasant odour. The child is waved through this several times and the smoke and warmth are said to help in removing the moisture from the body and give it protection from evil. Some old pieces of cloth are now ready and in these the child is wrapped by the *dai* who places it on a *supa* (winnowing fan).

The *dai* now turns her attention to the mother who is probably lying on some dirty rags in the corner. The mother is cleaned by the *dai* and is massaged with sweet oil. Usually *karowar*, sometimes called *sarson* oil (mustard oil from *Brassica juncea*), is mixed in with the *til* oil. The *dai* should also clean up and dispose off all the dirty cloths and the placenta. We found some differences as to the method of the disposal of these things. In most places it appears that they are never taken out of the house lest evil spirits work through them, but that they are buried with clarified butter (*ghi*) in a hole in the earthen floor and a fire kept burning over the spot for six days. Sometimes, though rarely, the placenta and soiled cloths are collected in an earthen vessel (or sometimes placed upon a large-sized earthen tile) and are taken outside the house. These things are usually placed somewhere at the back of the house in a place which may not be visited, or are thrown on the manure pile, or sometimes they are buried there. At other times all is burned in the fire which is alight in the lying-in room and the ashes are later thrown into some stream. Again, it was said that it is all wrapped up in a dirty cloth and thrown into a secluded spot. These customs seem to vary, but the first is the most usual.

Roy in *The Birhors* says that this group buries the after-birth just outside the door—the deeper it is buried the longer is the interval before the birth of the next child. No animal should be able to get at it and eat it, or the mother will sicken and die. In the case of the umbilical cord the child will die if this is eaten; if it is buried deeply the child's teeth will appear late and if shallow they come early.[1]

No traces of corresponding beliefs were found among the Kols, but they have the conviction, common to village India, that, should wrong persons get possession of the placenta and the umbilical cord they are likely to be used in magical practices dangerous to the mother and the infant. They should therefore be well-guarded and no outsider should have access to them; this is why they usually are not taken out of the house and are buried beneath the floor. A childless woman, by eating a portion of either the placenta or the umbilical cord may dispel the influences which keep her barren, but in so doing there is every chance that it will result in injury and even death in the family from which she received by stealth the required parts.

The work of the *dai* ordinarily lasts for six days, that is, during the full period of the uncleanness. Sometimes however, this is dispensed with as far as the full period is concerned, but during the time the *dai* is in the house it is her duty to care for the mother and child. For the first three days the mother is not supposed to take anything except a little milk but after that period is over she eats a bit of food after the first bath. If the child is a male the *dai* is usually paid one rupee for her work, and if the child be of the other sex, half that amount. During the period of her work the *dai* is given food from the household and when she leaves certain other presents and clothes are likely to be forthcoming. No difference in the period of uncleanness is made on account of sex—in either case it lasts for six days. In some places there is a relaxation of the strictness after the third day. A special drink said to be made of "ginger root (*Cleome viseosa*), raw sugar (*gur*) and certain jungle roots boiled together" is given to her three times a day until she is stronger.

During this period the mother is confined to her room. She should not touch anything and should spend the time lying down. Certain measures should now be taken to protect the mother and the young child from evil influences. These influences are particularly malignant during the first six days, but may be overcome by certain methods. A small fire should constantly burn in the lying-in room and should be kept alive by wood from the *bel* tree (*Aegle marmelos*). *Bel* is the wood of the gods and they are attracted by its smoke and no evil spirits dare be present at the same time. Sometimes twigs of *bel* wood are placed beside the infant or a twig of the same may be imbedded in the floor. The wood of the *nim* tree (*Melia azadirachta*)

1 *The Birhors*, p. 223.

is also a valuable charm against evil spirits and is often used. Ashes from the fire burning within the room are also taken and sprinkled around the cot or around the spot where the newborn infant is lying on the floor. No spirit will dare cross this line of ashes. Ashes are also placed on the door sill to bar access to the house from that direction. Iron is similarly used ; bits of nails being driven into the frame about the door, or a piece of iron hung just over it. Sometimes wine may be sprinkled around the delivery room after the *dai* has cleaned up. This attracts the beneficent deities and as a result the evil ones will have to flee. During those six critical nights an elderly man should sleep just outside the doorway. Every form of protection known should be attempted, for there is no telling where *bhuts* may enter as they can come into the house as air does.

There is a night bird belonging to a class of owls which the Kols greatly fear. This is the night-jar (*Caprimulgus asiaticus*), called by them the *kurset* bird and often known as the goatsucker. As it is particularly fond of human milk this bird is said to watch for the women nursing babies. During the night, when the mother and child are sound asleep, this bird is very active and may slip into the house and draw the milk from the mother's breast. The mother is not aware of this, or if she is dimly conscious of something, she believes that the baby is feeding. For lack of milk the child does not grow, gets thinner and thinner and soon dies. Its constant crying is a sure sign that the *kurset* bird is stealing away its milk. The mother is also affected and may die. The best possible protection against this bird is the closed door (there being no windows), with branches of the *nim* tree hanging over it. He may also be frightened away by ill-sounding noises. These birds, commonly seen in Central India, have a peculiar way of looking at one, as if they were staring and searching for something.

The stump of the umbilical cord, called the *nara*, has usually fallen off by the sixth day and this is invariably buried in the floor of the house, and fire kept burning over the place of its burial for six days more. Several things are buried with the cord, although reports vary. Occasionally some *bel* leaves are put with it and it is thus interred; again a few copper pice, some turmeric (*haldi—Curcuma longa*) and *supari* nut (*Areca catechu*) are also buried with it. At other times some grains of rice may be coloured yellow with *haldi* and then dropped one by one into the hole prepared for the cord. As each grain is dropped the name of some relative is called. In the future the child should hold these names in great respect and never call such persons directly by name. This dropping of rice, however, is not usually observed. The burial of the *nara* or cord is said to be very important. It is really a part of one, and if another person should get it he would have power over the child. Its burial is also, strangely, a proof of birth. If a Kol is asked where he was born he replies : "My *nara* is buried in...." and names the village. In a real sense a part of him is buried there and he is a part of that village. The spot is plastered over with a mixture of cow dung, earth and water, and the fire lit over it. The *hom* sacrifice may also be offered.

Any extraordinary happening at birth or anything unusual is generally considered a bad sign. For example, a child born with teeth already in its mouth is much feared, for it signifies bad luck and a member of the family, probably one of the parents, will be sure to die within a short time. They say the child has come to destroy a member of the family. An extra finger, though, is considered as a good omen. Twins seem to have no special significance attached to them and their occurrence appears to be infrequent among the Kols.

The Sixth Day Ceremony : *Chhatthi*. After six days it is believed that the greatest period of danger is over and the woman can begin to make preparations to take up her normal life. This period corresponds with the time of greatest physical danger, for by the sixth day after birth, the dreaded septicaemia, if it is to come, will make its appearance. When day has come and all is well the *dhobi* and the *nai* are usually sent for. The former takes all the soiled clothes. The wife, after a preliminary bath and anointing by the *dai*, puts on fresh clothes. The barber trims the nails of her hands and feet and puts vermilion on both her feet and the feet of her child so that no evil spirit may harm them as they make their way to the place of the ceremonial bath. Her head has been oiled with *til* oil and occasionally the child has been pricked on the stomach with a hot iron, so that "the waters may be digested". All the earthen vessels in the house should be thrown out and new ones purchased from the Kumhar, and the house should be cleaned and plastered. The *nai* also gives the male members of the family a good shave, both of the face and the head.

The mother is now ready for the ceremonial bath at the village bathing place. The women of the household go there in a group accompanied by a Basor beating a drum. This is done just at sundown. The mother carries a brass vessel (*lota*) on the top of which burns an earthenware lamp (*diya*). At the place of bathing offerings are made : cocoanut, *haldi*, *supari*. Incense may be sprinkled in the fire in the lamp. Mustard seed (*rai*) is often scattered about in order to frighten off any evil spirits which may be at the place ready to injure the mother and the child. There is then a formal sort of bath, the water being poured over the mother who is now considered as perfectly clean—able to take her full place in society again. That night there is a feast for the women folk only, called *bilui*. Special foods prepared with *haldi* and *ghi* are partaken of, there is singing and dancing following the feast and the whole ceremony usually lasts all night. If a feast is impossible raw sugar (*gur*) is distributed among the singers. The whole procedure

Fig. 18

is usually called *chhatthi*, or sixth day ceremony and signifies the removal of uncleanness. In Rewa we were told that at this time Dulha Baba, who is often regarded as a household god, should be worshipped. Certain drawings are put upon the walls of the houses at this time. They vary considerably, but the accompanying text figure 18, shows a form that was found by us.

During the time the woman is confined to the house the man goes about his work just the same and no trace of the couvade has been found. If it can be managed, on the twelfth day after birth there is further rejoicing with a family feast.

CHILDHOOD RITES. *Naming the Child.* Amongst the Kols of Central India the giving of the name, so important in some primitive cultures, does not seem to hold a place of any great significance. Of course certain things as noted below are done, but no trace was found of any magical rites used in the selection of names, such as Roy describes in the case of the Oraons and the Kharias.[1] There is no fixed time within which the name must be given. Under more primitive conditions we have found that often no ceremony whatsoever was in use, and when a name was given the Brahmin priest was not called in. While there is no set time for the giving of the name it is generally preferred that it be given from ten to fifteen days after birth. The proposed name may be discussed in the family before hand, and actually given to the child by one of its parents or near relatives, a friend, or even a stranger. In the latter instance we were told on two occasions that should a *chaudhari* Chamar happen to pass through the village at a propitious time he might be requested to name the child. At the time of the bestowal of the name, in the case where the family selects the name itself, the child is taken into the arms of the person giving the name who then formally announces it to those present. Until such a name is given the child is called by a pet name, *dadu* for the boy and *butu* for the girl. In Kotmi, near the borders of Rewa State, the village priest, the Kol *panda*, gives the child a name and receives four pice for this act. At the same time, being the official vaccinator, he vaccinates the child against small pox: it is a crude vaccination, but in this way the Government is able to provide some protection from the disease.

Among the more Hinduized Kols use is made of the Brahmin priest. He is called upon to select the child's name and does this from a list of names in his possession which are considered auspicious for children born at certain seasons. He is paid from one to four annas for this performance. It is common to find names derived from days of the week, and Monday and Tuesday, *Somvara* and *Mangalbara* are said to be the best; the child is never named after Saturday. Again, the name of the month may be used, as in the case of the name Phagu,

1 Roy, S. C., *Oraon Religion and Customs*, p. 129; *The Kharias*, pp. 209 ff.

derived from the month of *Phagun* (February-March), or the town or village of his birth may be selected. More often though, the name of some Hindu deity or hero is given: combinations of Ram being common as Ram Prasad, Ram Avatar and the like. In Appendix II is given a list of Kol names.

It is common though, to find that the name thus officially given to the child is seldom used in actual life and a pet name or *alias* is used. This name is often a coarse one, or one considered inauspicious. The real name is kept secret and often forgotten and the child becomes known by his alias. A name is really part of one's personality and can be misused if obtained possession of by an unfriendly person or spirit. So the child may be called *Makkhi* (fly), *Ghatita* and *Ghasu* (pulled up, useless), *Pagal* (crazy), *Langra* (lame), *Ghuruwa* (filth) or *Kana* (one-eyed). When directly asked why such names as these are given two answers were commonly given: the first is that high caste people did not like to hear low caste people called by high-sounding names. This is probably a rationalization, though there may be truth in it. The second answer was the frank avowal that some malicious person or *bhut* might come to know of the real name and through it work some mischief on the person concerned.

Hair Cutting: *Mundan*. Occasionally this also becomes an opportunity for a ceremony of a special kind, but like name-giving a great deal is not made of it, particularly among the more primitive Kols. If the family is somewhat Hinduized they may have the hair cut on the banks of the sacred Nerbudda River; or the ceremony may be performed in the house by calling the Hindu *nai*, who shaves the head, leaving but a small top-knot called the *choti*. Adult Kols, however, do not always keep the *choti*. If they can afford it a young kid or pig is sacrificed at this time and the blood sprinkled over a fire placed before some *devi* such as Shardamai. The animal is then cooked and is feasted upon by all. The *nai* may be paid one rupee for his services. The time of hair cutting is not fixed, but it is generally done between the time of the close of the mother's impurity and the first anniversary of the child's birth. Yet there are exceptions to this, even if it be the regular procedure, for we have often seen Kol boys with uncut and unkempt hair. When the older folks have been asked why this is allowed they have given various answers. One family said that they would not cut their child's hair until they returned to their native land of Rewa when it would be "properly" cut. Another said that until there was a marriage in the family they would not cut the child's hair. It is also held that it is left uncut so that the demons will believe that the child is a girl and let him alone, for it is boys that they really try to get hold of.

Hair from the first cutting should never be thoughtlessly thrown out on the ground. The best thing to do is to wrap it in a small piece of cloth and take it to the Nerbudda River where it is thrown in as an offering. No special trip to the river is required and the hair may be kept in the house until some convenient season or until some friend or relative happens to be going that way. The belief that magic may be worked with hair is prevalent in India, but Kols do not seem to fear this danger, nor do they believe that another may work harm by possessing it.

FIRST FEEDING: *Pasni.* Most Kols attach considerable importance to the child's first feeding with solid food. This should be done when the child is about six months old. One group said that the feeding should be done at five months in the case of a girl and six months for a boy. This indicates Hindu influences.

The family invites as many of the child's relatives as they can afford to feed for a general feast following the ceremony. The child is to be fed with sweetened *khir*—rice boiled in milk—which has been specially prepared for this occasion. A portion of *khir* is placed in a small cup made from the leaves of the mango tree (*Mangifera indica*). As the ceremony begins, the friends and relatives wash their hands with water specially brought for them; the child's teeth, if in, are cleaned by being lightly brushed with a mango twig. The person who breaks the child's "fast", and this may be one of a number of relatives, among whom we find mentioned the name of the father, mother and father's sister (*phuphu*), first dips the index finger of the right hand into the *khir* and brings a portion up to the child's mouth but does not actually touch its lips, for the finger is immediately withdrawn. This movement is made six times, but on the seventh occasion the finger is put into the child's mouth and with it a bit of the *khir* is inserted. Others present follow in the same way until all have fed the infant. Each one who thus feeds the child is supposed to drop into a dish beside it some money, the amount varying according to circumstances: it ought not to be less than four pice and may be as much as eight annas. The money thus collected is used to buy silver bangles for the child.

Sometimes the child is fed with a silver coin rather than by the plain finger. This may be an influence of Hinduism. One group said the silver coin must be either a four or eight anna piece. The coin used is dipped into the *khir* and the baby fed on the seventh approach as in the above description. The *phuphu* receives the coins by which the child is fed and the money is used to buy an ornament. When groups using the finger were asked about using the coin, they said that it should not be done as the coin was not clean. Another group used a mango leaf instead of the finger. In Rewa State one group stated that just before the feeding of the child the mother should take it before the household deity, naming Bhanmati in this case, and bowing down before her ask the *devi* to protect the child, the household, and the children yet to come.

NOSE AND EAR PIERCING. The piercing of the nose and ears is usually done by a *sonar* (goldsmith), although Kols may do it themselves. The hole is generally made by simply forcing the ends of the ring through the lobe in the ear, but for the nose a bronze instrument is used. As far as could be ascertained no ceremony is performed at the time nor does the *sonar* repeat any *mantras*. The best time to have piercing done is at the time of some large *mela* (religious gathering) in the vicinity, for then there are plenty of *sonars* on hand awaiting work. When the nose is pierced a small plug of wood is first inserted, but the earrings are allowed from the beginning. The wound has onion and turmeric rubbed into it, which help it to heal. The *sonar* is given a seer of rice, some chillis and a little salt, or may be paid four pice for the piercing and paid extra for the rings according to their value. It has already been noted that the Kathautiyas use woodpith to enlarge the holes in their ears and as a result their lobes have larger holes. Kols about Jubbulpore claimed that in Rewa every Kol woman should have a ring of gold and silver on her ears or nose. Our observations however did not confirm this claim.

Earrings help to protect the child from evil. Other things as well ward off evil influences and we found that the *retha* nut (*Sapindus mukorossi*) and half a *ghata* nut (*Ziziphyus xylopyrus* (?)) are put into a strip of cloth, tied in a knot and worn round the neck. This is considered a good protection from *nazar*, the evil eye, but it does not help in the case of *bhuts*. Black bangles on the wrists and a white *pot* (dab) just in front of the ears also protect from the evil eye. A copper ring may be put on one of the ankles for any evil spirit attacking the child will become imprisoned in this. Good spirits live in amulets about the neck and drive off *bhuts*. At other times a piece of a broken or discarded human tooth, tied on a string about the wrist, is considered an effective protection. A strip of coloured cloth, red and yellow being preferred, may also be tied somewhere about the child's person. These are some of the measures which may be taken to protect the young child during the early months and years of life. Other instances

PLATE XV.

Kol Women and Children in Barela.

Another group in Panagar.

PLATE XVI.

A Group of Kol Children at Barela.

Children in the Kol Mahalla, Jubbulpore.

Children of Factory Workers.

of charms used are discussed in the chapter on Magic and Witchcraft.

PUBERTY. From the above mentioned ceremonies until the Kol child reaches puberty, there is little of importance to note. When the first milk tooth falls out the child is told to take it outside near the house, to shut his eyes and to throw it on the roof, never looking to see where it has gone. This will aid in the coming in of the new tooth.

The girl is tattooed when between the ages of ten and twelve and just before her marriage may be given further tattooing. In the Kaimur hills it was said that a woman must be tattooed, for without it Bhagawan would not know how to grasp her and take her spirit on its way to the heavens. No ceremonies occur at the time of tattooing, and apart from saying that it is the custom Kols could give us almost no information on the matter. The designs are usually similar to those of their Hindu neighbours and the actual tattooing is done by the same man who does it for other castes. See the description on pages 28-31.

No particular rites are observed in connection with the girl's first menstruation. At such a time she is asked to stay in the house and if there is a second room into which she can go she retires there. She is not put out into a menstruation hut as is common among some Munda tribes. During the four to six days that the menses last she is considered unclean and should not cook, bring water for the family, nor touch men's clothes. When the menses have ceased she has to go to the village shrine and offer a cocoanut.

Nowhere among the Kols were we able to find any definite trace of puberty rites which are common elsewhere. We were told that a boy of the Kol tribe could only be considered a Kol when he reached the age of twelve to thirteen. In the full sense he becomes of age when he is sixteen. A girl is considered to be of age when she goes to live for good in the house of her husband. No traces were discovered of any ordeal that either sex had to undergo; no scars are made on the body nor were any hair tying ceremonies observed among the groups studied.

Bachelors' Quarters. No trace was found of bachelors' quarters nor of segregated dormitories for boys and girls, which are well-known among the Mundas and allied tribes of Chota Nagpur. The Gonds of Bastar and elsewhere also have them. They have been considered as a place for sex instruction but the system has been widely criticised by the more advanced Mundas and is being abandoned in many places. Other writers have attributed no social or religious importance to these quarters. One writes: "The thing is that the poor people in a village cannot afford to build big houses for themselves containing many rooms and consequently they cannot maintain strict decency in living with their wives when the children grow up."[1] But the phenomenon is too widespread and is linked with too many factors to really bear this explanation. The house for the boys is as a rule the village guest house as well and at its centre there is a pole which is sometimes carved and differs in this respect only from other homes. The girls usually sleep with an elderly widow in another portion of the village. In some places it is reported that the boys and girls sleep together huddled "higgledy-piggledy."[2] We found no trace of these conditions among the Kols, though they may exist among those who live in close contact with other tribes who practice such customs. When Kols were asked how they managed to get along with one room and many children they replied that somehow they could tuck them all in. The absence of separate quarters strengthens the family tie and helps to make it a more stable and important unit. There was also no trace of sexual segregation, such as the separating of the husband and the wife, which would also tend to weaken the family.

1 Majumdar, B. C., *The Aborigines of Central India*, p. 80.
2 *Census of India*, 1931, xii: i, p. 415.

CHAPTER V

THE MARRIAGE CYCLE

Marriage is a necessity to Kols and the ceremonies that accompany it are the most complicated of all their social rites. It is of the utmost importance that Kols be married and the bachelor or spinster life is altogether foreign to the Kol way of thinking.

ENDOGAMY WITH HYPERGAMY. During the discussion of the Kol *kurhis* the principle of endogamy was established. It was shown, however, that along with endogamy hypergamy is occasionally practised, possibly due to Hindu and Rajput influences. Several instances of this were observed and one case may be mentioned in which there were two sons in a Rautiya family; one had married a Rautiya wife and the other a Thakuriya. Their respective children considered themselves full and equal Rautiyas. But Rautiyas never give their daughters to Thakuriyas. Hypergamy is probably a relic of the time when there was a good deal of mixing between men of higher castes and women of lower castes. In the case of the Kols this study indicates that hypergamy is practised only in connection with the *kurhi* that is considered immediately below it in the social ladder. This social ladder, however, is not absolutely fixed, though about Jubbulpore Rautiyas are generally considered the highest *kurhi*; yet it was sometimes stated that the Binj *kurhi* practise hypergamy with the Rautiyas and would take their daughters, but not give theirs to them. Russell and Hiralal, in discussing hypergamy in the Central Provinces say: "This custom prevails largely among the higher castes of the Panjab, as the Rajput and Khatris, and among the Brahmins of Bengal."[1] The stories in connection with the origin of the Thakuriyas may imply a form of hypergamy, except that the offspring do not rise to the level of the father.

TRACES OF EXOGAMY. While the principle of endogamy is strictly enforced and the thought of any other union is repugnant, there are nevertheless certain traces of an exogamous tendency which is not a *kurhi* or *got* exogamy but rather village exogamy. It is not the rule for a Kol to arrange a marriage with someone in his own village. This is occasionally done, but as the last resort, after failing to find a mate in another village. Roy notes the same tendency toward village exogamy among the Kharias. He remarks: "The probable reason

1 Russell and Hiralal, *Op. Cit.*, Vol. 1, p. 28.

for this village exogamy is that originally members of one and the same clan (*gotra* or *gotar*) lived together, as the traditions of the Dudh and Dhelki sections definitely testify, and as is still the case in many Hill Kharia settlements."[1] The Kols themselves offer other explanations for this type of exogamy, but the idea of the oneness of the village lies at the back of certain of their reasons. Some said that the children of a village living, as they do, like brothers and sisters makes any thought of such unions repugnant. A similar reason was implied in the response that the boys and girls know each other too well and such a condition would not be conducive to the future marriage relationships. It was also asserted that the presence of parents-in-law was not desirable in the same village, for if the bride was ever beaten by her husband (and it was thought that this was inevitable) her parents might be very angry and a serious quarrel with much trouble between the families was sure to result. Therefore it was considered best to get a girl from another village, and the further the village, the better the chances of avoiding such parent-in-law conflicts. Near Katni they claimed that they often got their girls from the Jubbulpore section, and that they sometimes had gone as far as Assam, where Kols have gone to work in the tea gardens.

As remarked earlier, no trace of a clan exogamy could be found among the Kols of to-day, nor an exogamy based on god-septs as among the Gonds,[2] where marriage is not possible between clans with the same number of gods. A family having three gods may marry into another with the same gods or into another with other and a different number of gods.

MARRIAGE LIMITATIONS. There is, however, a clear line limiting the choice of either the bride or the bridegroom. It is based on kinship, for as long as relationship is remembered no marriage should take place. No trace was found of the cross-cousin marriage nor of the ancient Munda custom of marrying a grandfather to a granddaughter.[3] No distinctions are made between cousins. The Kols also possess that which Lowie calls the "incest horror."[4] Children of siblings are brothers and sisters and between them marriage is considered impossible. The levirate, in which the younger brother may be expected to take the wife of a deceased elder brother, is acknowledged. There is, however, no necessity for his doing this, and public opinion does not enforce it; yet in a real sense he is responsible for her welfare and

1 Roy, S. C., *The Kharias*, p. 224.
2 Grigson, W. V., *The Maria Gonds of Bastar*, pp. 194, 195, 239.
3 Ghurye, G. S., *Caste and Race in India*, p. 117.
4 Lowie, R. H., *Primitive Society*, pp. 15, 16.

occasionally she is taken as his wife if he is unmarried or is able to support another wife. No trace of the sororate was found among the Kols.

BARS TO MARRIAGE. Before marriage is possible there are a few other matters that must be carefully checked. That the younger child must never be married before the elder, is a custom quite commonly observed all over India; the proper and the correct thing is to marry the children in the order of their ages. There is another interesting limitation; the eldest boy of a family (*Jetha*) must never marry the eldest girl (*Jetha* or *Jethi*) in the month of *Jetha* (May-June). If this be done it is bound to result in a very unhappy and quarrelsome match.

Physical or mental defects are also bars to marriage, or at least to satisfactory marriages. A person who is half-witted or deformed has very little chance of making a favourable marriage. Often such children do not survive, not through any deliberate action on the part of the parents, but being so helpless, or unable to take care of themselves as the children of the poor must do, they are simply not able to survive. Blind girls generally remain unmarried, but a blind boy who knows some kind of hand work which he may use to help support his wife may be married. If deformed children survive and do not get married they remain at home where their parents support them.

If a Kol bachelor should "keep" a woman he is not allowed to contract a real marriage until such time as this woman is renounced; the *panch* sees to this. It is not unknown that a bachelor may keep a young widow, give her up for marriage with another girl, and then after those formalities are over and forgotten, bring her back into his house as a kept woman. He will have to pay a fine or give a feast as the *panch* decides, but he is not forced to drive her out.

Sometimes a man feels that he cannot stand the expense and obligations that go with a *pakka* or real marriage. He desires to marry, say, a certain girl, or his parents want him to do so, and there can be found no valid objection to such a match, nor is there any element in it which would force an elopement. In such a case the matter is put up to the *panchayat* and if it is ascertained that the woman in question has not been married before and that there are no other valid bars to the marriage the permission may be given. Instead of the wedding formalities the only expense involved is that of feeding the proper persons—the *panch*, the relatives, or perhaps the whole community. This decision usually rests with the *panch* itself. The formal ceremonies consist in the putting of ten black bangles on the arms of the woman, the smearing of a little *sendur* on her forehead, and the distribution of something to eat.

The Age for Marriage. Because of the influence of Hinduism adult marriage among the Kols is not so much the rule as it is amongst certain more isolated Munda groups. The Kols generally recommend a fairly young age as the best for marriage. They told us that a boy should be married when between the ages of seven and ten and a girl when six or eight. Of course the young folks do not live together as man and wife at these ages; the actual consummation of the marriage occurs at the *gauna* time when the boy is twelve to fifteen and the girl ten to twelve. The practice of early marriage is deeply ingrained in the social thought of India in general for it has been the tradition and India is tenacious in its observances of this tradition handed down from ancient times. The usual reason advanced is that it protects both parties from promiscuous sexual relations. From their own reports the Kols give the impression that early marriages are very common among them, yet an examination of Census Reports does not seem to indicate that Kols are particularly addicted to early marriages. The report for 1931[1] lists eighty castes, tribes and races in the order of the incidence of child marriage. The Kols stand sixty-third on the list with only 3.4% of their married females being under thirteen years of age. At the head of the list are found the Golars, a nomadic shepherd group with 21.9% of their married females being under thirteen. They are a relatively small group. But the Telis, a "clean" Hindu caste of oil makers which has a large number of members in the Central Provinces, report 13.8%. The Brahmins in the same Province have 3.5% and thus the Kols come just below them. From this evidence it would appear that the Kols are not extreme in their practice of early marriage. However, the definition of marriage may be different and may refer to the time of actual consummation and the living together of the couple as man and wife.

Kinds of Marriage. For the Kols there is but one approved and genuine form though, as we have noted, there are cases where people are living together and recognized as man and wife without the performance of a marriage ceremony in the accepted sense. Among the Birhors Roy reports ten different kinds of marriages which are recognized as valid.[2] Among the Dudh and Dhelki Kharias he lists five types of recognized marriages: (1) Regular, (2) Elopement,

1 *Census of India*, 1931, xii:i, p. 180.

2 Roy, S. C., *The Birhors*, pp. 144 ff.

(3) Marriage by forcible application of vermilion, (4) Intrusion, (5) Widow.[1]

In discussing marriage with the Kols of Central India it was generally found that they recognized only one type of marriage. When asked about the remarriage of widows, they would say "yes", but indicated that while widows could remarry this was nevertheless a concession. A woman, they say, may be truly married but once; a man may be married several times. They know of the intrusion marriage (*Ghar baita*), and one of the stories in connection with the *kurhis* illustrated that form;[2] but it occurs very seldom. A Kolin may go and live as a servant in the house of a man she wants to marry. The man may take her to be his wife, but there is in this case no formal marriage ceremony; nevertheless he must feast the *panchayat* as a penalty. Kols claim that while they have heard of the *sendur* marriage, where the red mark is forcibly applied to the girl's head by her lover in some public place where it can be witnessed, they do not know that it has ever happened among the Kols. At least they professed ignorance of such an occurrence. The known types of marriage, including the elopement marriage which frequently occurs, are dealt with below.

FORMS OF MARRIAGE PRACTISED BY KOLS: I. *The Elopement Marriage* (*Bhagal*). This type of marriage may take two forms with variations in each. The first type is the least binding and has no recognized standing. If there should be a love match between a couple in the same village or a nearby village, who, because of parental opposition cannot easily be married, and no commitments have been made by the parents on either side to any other arrangement, the couple may decide to go off secretly together. They may go to some friendly relative's home in another village or perhaps will put up a grass hut in which they begin to live and thus start life as man and wife. The young man puts ten black bangles on the girl's wrists, some *sendur* on her forehead, and she is reckoned as his wife. Later on, should the young couple want to return to the village they may be allowed to live there provided that they give a feast as directed by the *panch*. It is unusual, however, that they get off so easily. However, if the young couple who elope are within prohibited degrees of relationship or if they are not of the same *kurhi* they cannot be received back into the community and must become virtual outcastes from those who know them. They will probably be forced to

1 Roy, S. C., *The Kharias*, p. 239.

2 See pages 38, 39

migrate to a place where nothing is known of their history, for if they should try to remain they cannot enter into the life of any community of that area unless they cast their lot with the lowest of the low.

The above form of the elopement marriage does not have the same standing as the regular forms. If such a union should break up, and the woman go to live with another man, the first man has no right to make a formal complaint to the *panch*, nor can he claim her nor any compensation for her. The *panch* takes no responsibility for irregular unions and this fact is a real deterrent. Marriage would thus seem to have the marks of a contract; it binds the two persons and gives certain proprietory rights which are enforced by the community.

The second type of elopement marriage attempts to regularize the procedure after a couple has eloped. In this manner a control over such cases is exercised, and certain obligations must be met or there is a severe social penalty. If a boy runs off with a girl already married, who has also been through the *gauna*[1] part of the total cycle, but who has not become the actual property of her husband, he is required by the *panch* to refund to the party to whom the girl was first married all the expenses in connection with the *lagan*, the *sadi* and the *gauna*. This is a very heavy burden which few would undertake to face, for it may amount to as much as a hundred rupees. And even if he is able to pay he still has to feast the *panch*, and they see that he does it well. Following all this the regular marriage ceremony must be performed with its additional costs and obligations, before the couple are allowed to live together. This makes such an elopement a very costly affair, and the *panch* is in the position absolutely to enforce these penalties.

If the *gauna* has not yet occurred and the girl elopes with another boy, all he has to do is to pay a penalty to the *panch*, but before they are allowed to live together the regular *sadi* must be performed. No *gauna* is thereafter necessary and they begin to cohabit. The regulations are thus much more severe if the *gauna* is passed than if the elopement occurred before it. There are variations in procedure, but this seems to be the custom.

2. *The Recognized Form of Marriage* (*Biwah*, *Biyah*). The description which follows is one compiled from investigations made in many places. When we first learned of the marriage customs of the Kols who lived close to Jubbulpore, we thought that the customs

1 See page 93.

among the Kols living out in the jungles and away from larger centres would be simpler. We were therefore surprised by how consistently various groups gave us similar information. It should be noted that it is not claimed that these customs are peculiar to the Kols. Investigation among the simple village people of Hindu background will probably show that all over this area there is a great similarity in the marriage customs, the details may vary, but not the main outlines.

(1) *Selection of the Girl.* When a father considers it time to arrange a marriage for his son it is he who should take the initiative. The first thing he should do is to make some private preliminary enquiries. It is against the custom for the parents of the girl to make any direct advances. In this type of marriage neither the boy nor the girl has anything to say concerning his or her future mate. It is entirely in the hands of the elders. The boy's father may ask some relatives in another village to be on the lookout for a suitable girl, and he will consult the *panch* of his own village to see if any one of them knows of a girl who would make a suitable match for his son. As a result two or three names are suggested as possibilities. The next thing that is ordinarily done is to try to catch a glimpse of the girl without her parents knowing about it. It is best if this can be done by the boy's father, but he may send some trusted member of the *panch* to carry out the investigations for him. If the results are satisfactory, the boy's father reports to his *panch* and asks them if there is any objection to such a marriage. This is done to guard against a marriage which would be objectionable from any angle. The *panch* is usually pretty well posted on matters of relationship, and its opinion, in the absence of written records (for such are never kept by Kols), is authoritative. The father of the boy then arranges to see the girl's father privately, and when he goes he usually takes three or four of his friends from his village with him. In the interview that follows he does not come to the point immediately, but may talk about general matters for some time before bringing up the main question. Mutual enquiries are made concerning the status of the two families, the health of the children, etc. The friends of the father vouch for the accuracy and truth of his statements. If both parties find themselves in accord and if the girl's father is willing to give his daughter, the matter is then with the girl's father and it is he who now consults his *panch* and makes any private enquiries that he sees fit. Up till this time the matter is considered as strictly private and if either of the parties is not satisfied with any of the details and does not wish to follow it up the matter may be dropped without prejudice.

(*a*) *Negotiations.* If the girl's father, after enquiries, is fully satisfied the matter becomes one of real concern. The boy's father is informed of this and a day is set for him and his party of men (the boy and the women do not go and have no formal part) to go to the girl's house and start actual negotiations for the wedding since the matter is now no longer a secret. On the way to the girl's house this party must be sure to take note of good or bad omens. If the latter are frequent they may turn back and decide on a new start at a later hour or even on another day, if the omens have been particularly bad. To pass four people seated together is a good omen and to meet a Hindu *pandit* is another. But to meet a person with an empty vessel is a bad omen, as is also a meeting with a *teli* (oilman). A jackal about to cross the road is a dangerous omen and one should make every attempt to head him off and to stop him from actually crossing the road. If it should occur, the best thing to do under the circumstances is to take a thorny branch, place it in the centre of the road at the point where the jackal crossed, put a heavy stone on top of the branch, and with one foot planted on this stone roundly curse the beast. This will ward off the evil and save the person concerned from disaster.

It was noted that the groom-to-be does not accompany this party nor does any female member of his family go to see the girl. The party of men must take with them certain things, among them *dahi* (curds) kept in a new *marki* (earthenware vessel) which has been nicely whitewashed on the outside and has yellow symbols superimposed. The top is sealed with leaves and securely tied for it is eventually to be presented to the girl's father. They should also take *haldi* (turmeric, *Curcuma longa*) and *sendur* (vermilion). When the party arrives at the girl's village they are warmly greeted and brought to the house where the matter is formally discussed and much of the ground previously gone over privately is now publicly repeated. After a formal agreement has been reached by both parties the girl's father should ceremonially wash the feet of the boy's father, but another may do this if the father is unable to do so or is dead. This is a witness to the fact that the matter is now settled and that the match is arranged. The boy's father should at this time make payment of the first instalment of the price agreed upon in their discussions. The figure differs according to locality and is not uniform. It is divided into two parts, the first is paid on this visit and the balance just before the *sadi*. The following figures are typical, the first figure being the first payment: Rs. 8 and 4; 10-8-0 and 5-4-0; 9 and 4-8-0. The larger amount is paid first and half of it later. At Benda village it was claimed that there was no bargaining and that the price was fixed at twelve rupees, payable in two equal instalments. Two *saris* are often presented at this time—one for the girl and another for her mother. The washing of the feet and the payment of the bride price are definite expressions of the acceptance of the proposal. Nevertheless, the engagement thus sealed may be broken if either party is dissatisfied. If the girl's side breaks the engagement they must return the bride price and the presents. If the boy's side breaks it they are not entitled to any refund and the money may be kept by the girl's family.

(*b*) *Betrothal and Lagan.* The *lagan* is a letter given by the bride's father to the bridegroom's father, appointing the day of the marriage and ceremonies connected therewith and thus providing an outline for this part of the wedding cycle. The *lagan* should be prepared by the *pandit* of the girl's village or one selected by her family. When the time is ripe for the boy and girl to be formally married the Brahmin priest is called to the house or is informed of the proposal and is asked to write up the *lagan*. The *lagan* should have the complete programme for the *sadi* worked out after consulting horoscopes and taking into account auspicious or inauspicious seasons and circumstances. The best days for weddings are, in order, Monday, Saturday, Thursday and Tuesday, and the *lagan* will take this into account. The luckiest months are *Chaita* (March-April), *Magh* (January-February) and *Phagun* (February-March). After the *lagan* is written the paper is sprinkled with *haldi* water. Here is an actual example of a Kol *lagan* :

SHRI

> Shri—may god Ganesh help us. Hari the lord was worshipped with *gur* (raw sugar) and *sendur* (vermilion). The son of Sail named Matukdhari has been selected as the bridegroom. May the lord make the marriage time auspicious.
>
> On Wednesday, the sixth day of the bright fortnight of Magh, the marriage bower will be constructed ; on Thursday, the seventh day, the anointing ceremony will take place ; on Friday, the eighth, the bridegroom's marriage party will come and on Saturday, the ninth, the circumambulation of the marriage post will take place.

Written by Radha kunji
on the second day of the bright fortnight of Magh.
May all be auspicious !

For a *lagan* such as the above the *pandit* is paid an amount which varies according to the section of the country. Near Jubbulpore he is said to receive Rs. 1-4-0; in Rewa State it was from Re. 1 to Rs. 1-8-0; in the Kaimur hills annas eight. This is paid by the boy's father who takes the *lagan* to his village where it is read to all who are interested so that they may come to know about the arrangements. It is common to promise the *pandit* a fee for the performing of the ceremonies in connection with the forthcoming wedding. This fee is generally said to be about three rupees and must be paid before the Brahmin will come and begin his work at the expected time. Occasionally there is bargaining between the two, and if the *pandit* thinks that the boy's father can pay more he holds out or compromises for a larger sum. We were told that should the two disagree no marriage is possible until a settlement has been reached, as they cannot ask a Brahmin other than the one who has jurisdiction over the girl's village to perform the ceremonies. A settlement is usually reached before long and the rest of the night is spent in eating, singing and dancing, the women of the girl's house providing for this entertainment. During the meal time the *marki* containing the curds is opened by the girl's father and is shared by both the parties.

In the morning the *pandit* is expected to deliver the *lagan*, which he has prepared the night before. He had to make certain enquiries and consult his books in order to prepare a proper one. Before he arrives with it, preparations are made to receive him. The place where he will sit to read the *lagan* is plastered and in the centre is placed a brass *lota* filled with water, into which two-pice coins have been dropped, and on top of which is set an earthenware *dip* or lamp. The Brahmin may come with the *lagan* already prepared, or he may write it off from memory then and there in their presence. He then reads it to the two parties and gives them any other advice he thinks necessary.

The boy's party usually stays the rest of the day and another night, leaving for their village on the third morning.

The priest is ordinarily used in the later *sadi* which will be performed according to the time set in the *lagan*, but in Maihar State we were informed that after the writing of the *lagan* by the Brahmin he may be dispensed with and the work which he ordinarily would do may be performed by the *bahnoi* (a sister's husband) or the *phupha* (father's sister's husband).

On the third morning preparations are made by the bridegroom's party to return to their own village. The girl's mother, with other female members of the family or relatives in the village, prepares the yellow *haldi* water and keeps it in a number of *lotas*. As the guests are about to depart the women appear with the *haldi* water and *kajra* (lamp-black), the latter being in the form of a paste. The yellow water is sprinkled over the departing guests and the lamp-black is applied just below the eyes. This is considered auspicious and both are believed to have a protective significance. In jest the *kajra* is sometimes applied to other parts of the face and hearty laughs and ridicule result, all of which the party must bear cheerfully. The girl's mother should sprinkle the *haldi* water on the boy's father and after she has done this and put the colour below his eyes she holds her brass *lota* before him and he is expected to drop some money into it—at least one rupee. The rest of the men are then sprinkled by the other women and are also asked to give a gift, but not as much as the father gave. The women then courteously salute and go off taking with them the *lotas* containing the coins.

For a brief time the men of the two parties remain seated together, eat *pan supari* and pass around the *hukka* for a smoke. Finally the boy's party gets up and all go to the edge of the village together where they embrace and separate. This ends the first part of the wedding cycle.

(2) *Domestic Preparations.* The time that is to elapse between the writing of the *lagan* and the *sadi* is fixed by the *lagan* itself and depends on several factors of an astrological nature. Usually there is less than a month between them. During this period there are active preparations in both houses as certain important things must be accomplished.

In the girl's village some uncooked rice coloured with *haldi* is taken around by members of the family and given to those who are to be invited to the ceremonies. With the rice the time and place of the ceremonies are made known. There should be plenty of supplies of food on hand and among the things listed there should be *sendur*, a *dauri* (small basket), new clothes, cash for small gifts and payments, rice, pulse, especially *urad* pulse (*Phaseolus radiatus*) and wheat.

(*a*) *Mangarmati.* The *mangarmati* or *magarmati* is a ceremony whereby a certain amount of earth is obtained from which *chulhas*, or earthen fireplaces, are to be constructed. This ceremony, which is performed at both homes and on the same night, is essentially alike in both the houses and must be performed after sunset. Only the women take part in the gathering of the sacred earth, but we were allowed to watch a *mangarmati* ceremony in the Kaimur hills. It was found that a portion of the courtyard just in front of the house had been plastered and marked somewhat according to the accompanying diagram. About eight o'clock in the evening, as we waited nearby with a group of men, the beat of the drum was heard and we went up to the thornfenced enclosure. Only women were allowed within the

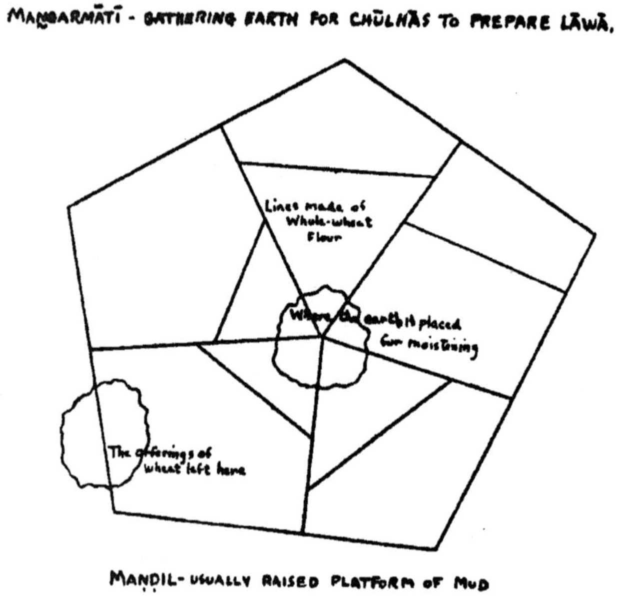

Fig. 19

courtyard, and the men had to remain outside, but a good view was had of the proceedings. The drum was played by a Chamar male, hired for this occasion, who was the only man taking any part in the ceremony. The women and children formed a procession within the courtyard. There were a number of baskets (there should be seven) carried on the heads of unmarried girls, while others carried a pick (*gainti*) and a mattock (*kodali*). The leader and the first in line of the procession should either be the sister of the bride or her *phuphi*, her father's sister. On her head was an earthen jar like a brass *lota* (sometimes the latter may be used) which was filled with water and into which were inserted mango twigs with the leaves attached. On the top of this rested an earthen lamp, *dip*. Figure 20 shows how this was carried. With this light on her head she led the way to the place where the earth was dug up and they sang as they proceeded. Some of the songs which were sung at Deosori in the Kaimurs are as follows :

THE LEADER OF THE MANGARMĀTĪ PROCESSION

Fig. 20

1. *Lanka gaye Hanuman,*
   Rama Lakshman ghar aye.

   To Lanka far went Hanuman,
   Then Ram and Lakshman came home.

2. *Mati khodain gai,*
   Bichhi marisa haya daiya haya;
   Mati khodain gai, bisa le bahu.
   Ho daiya ho, Ho daiya ho, Ho daiya ho.

   The clay was dug,
   I was bitten by a scorpion—
   Alas, Alas!

The clay was dug,
It poisoned me much—
Alas, Alas, Alas!

3. *Pate par bi jhiliya,*
Jhilmiliya pan.
Char Char bandra,
Ghi, roti, dei.

She stands on a rock by the lake
Her lips are shining with *pan*.
(And she says) "Come along monkey
I shall give you buttered bread."

4. *Sari dekh ke gaya sasurar,*
Aur sarhaj dekh ke lubhaya

Sari dekh ke gaya sasuriya
Dhan dekh ke lubhaya.

He went to his father-in-law's abode,
Drawn by the beauty of the bride's own sister.
But there he fell in love with the wife of the bride's brother.

Again he journeyed to his father-in-law's abode
Tempted by the beauty of the bride's own sister.
But this time he fell for the wealth of his father-in-law.

All but the first song are really directed at the bride to be, and there are certain implications not always easy to understand. In the second one the idea comes out that the girl even at the *mangarmati* time is liable to be smitten by love enroute to her digging. The third refers to the plight of a young girl caught alone, perhaps, with a tempting mouth, and a vague promise for the future. In the last song the bride is taunted with a song which implies that her lover has not really come because of her. In fact, she has no attraction for him, for it is her married sister, or her sister-in-law or the father-in-law's wealth that really draws him.

As these songs were sung the party moved slowly forward to the spot where they were to dig; in this case it happened to be not more than seventy-five feet from the house. Upon reaching the spot they formed a circle and all the time sang and beat time with their hands, the Chamar accompanying them with his drum. Several of the women took part in the digging of the earth and each girl was allowed but one blow with the pick. The earth thus displaced was gathered up with the mattock and put into the baskets. It was estimated that about thirty pounds were actually brought. The group then returned to the courtyard as slowly as they went but in the reverse order, with the lamp at the rear. The earth was then thrown in the centre of a small raised platform called the *mandil*, though occasionally the *mandil* is made later on from the earth brought in at this time. After the baskets were emptied the women brought water in small earthenware vessels and each threw water on the pile of earth until it was thoroughly soaked. The women then went to another part of the courtyard where each had left a bit of wheat which they brought from their homes when they first came. This was piled at another point and as each presented her wheat the mother dipped a bit of sweet oil from her household oil-jug and gave it to the other women. After this a small cone of cowdung, which is worshipped by unmarried girls, was set up on the *mandil*. See Figure 19.

This earth should be sufficient to make either five or seven *chulhas* and they should be prepared sometime during that night. In Deosori they said that it would be done in the morning, and as it is done only by the women of the household it is likely that it was done after the people had departed. The party broke up at this point and from twenty to twenty-five women and young girls departed. This happened at 9 P.M. Occasionally there is a feast following the *mangarmati*, but there was none in this particular case.

The next day the *chulhas* constructed from this earth should be ready for the preparation of the *lawa*, a mixture of parched paddy and millet, which is considered an indispensable part of the wedding preparations. During the time of its preparation there is joking and fooling. Before they can start to parch the rice one of the male members brings a young chicken and thrusts it into the lighted *chulha*. If the chicken does not catch fire and die (that is, if the *chulha* is not hot enough) it becomes the property of the male relative, but if it dies the women take it and make it into a curry. If the chicken catches fire no effort is made to save it. The parching of rice may now begin and this should be initiated by the man who brought the chicken. The same *chulha* which was used for the burning of the chicken should not be used for the subsequent parching. As the man commences his work some of his female relatives approach him and do all they can to disturb his work and irritate him. They may throw mud at him, abuse him verbally (give *gali*), take all kinds of liberties with him and try their best to make him lose his temper. He is supposed to take no notice of this but to remain calmly at his work. After the *lawa* is prepared (the man does not prepare all that is required) it is put into a new *ghara* decorated with pictures representing females. Sometimes other articles are also put into the *ghara* –uncooked rice, bits of *supari* nut, *haldi* and two-pice coins. When prepared at the bride-groom's house the *lawa* is kept to be taken with the boy's party on their trip to the girl's village for the *sadi* and is there mixed with the *lawa* prepared in the girl's house for use at the time of the wedding. The preparation of the *lawa*, which is made a day or two before the group leaves for the wedding, is made the occasion for the reconciliation of estranged relatives within the village and the consequent restoration of friendship. This reconciliation may also be extended to any member of the *kurhi* with whom there have been unhappy relations.

(*b*) *Marriage Booth: Marhwa*. In the meantime there has been far more to do at the girl's house where the actual wedding is to take place, for the wedding booth (*marhwa* or *mandap*) must be constructed there. This is usually set up in the courtyard immediately in front of the girl's house. In this booth the essentials of the marriage ceremony are performed and the sacred pole is fixed at its centre. Male relatives of the bridegroom help to build it, but women must have nothing to do with its construction. Before the men who come to work can actually start operations the bridegroom must have his body rubbed with *til* oil mixed with *haldi*. The anointing should be done by his sister or another close female relative and he should then be dressed in clothes which have been dipped in *haldi* water. The construction of the *marhwa* may now begin.

The *marhwa* is constructed of prescribed kinds of wood. Its size varies, but is usually about eight feet square and six to seven feet high. Nine poles are used in its construction, including the central post, called the *magrohan*, which however does not reach up to the roof. *Saleh* (*Boswellia serrata*) is the most favoured kind of wood and if procurable is preferred, both for the framework of the booth and for the sacred pole at its centre. The eight remaining poles are arranged so that there are three on a side. Text figure 21 will make this clear. If *saleh* wood is not available, *gular* (*Ficus glomerata*), *sal* (*Sheora robusta*), *char* (*Buchanania latifola*) or even bamboo are permissible. The central post, however, must be of *saleh* wood and they search far and wide until they have found it. The leaves of the banana plant are tied to each of the eight poles and over the top. The roof is formed by bamboo branches covered with banana leaves. Around the upper edge of the *marhwa* is hung a frieze of mango twigs. Mango leaves are always found in connection with Kol weddings; they do not wither easily and are a symbol of everlastingness and stability. Strips of paper, usually coloured red, are used for decoration. The ground under the *marhwa* is carefully levelled and plastered with cowdung and in the very centre a hole twelve to eighteen inches deep is dug. This is where the central pole will be placed. Before the pole is lowered into position a *supari* nut (*Areca catechu*), some pieces of *haldi* (usually five) and two-pice coins are placed in the pit, and according to some accounts, rice coloured with *haldi* is also thrown in. The *magrohan* is a piece of wood three to four feet in length and two to four inches in diameter. It should preferably be green wood, though a dry pole is used if a fresh one is not available. It is coloured red with *sendur* or yellow with *haldi* and has some thread, coloured either white or yellow, wrapped about it seven times from the top to the bottom. Along with the *magrohan* a short green bamboo stick is fixed together with a green *gular* branch and the iron bar used in digging the holes for the booth. If the central post should be of *gular* or other wood a bit of *saleh* must be inserted with it. The *saleh* is a symbol of fertility, being an evergreen tree which never withers and takes root easily and quickly; even an apparently dry stick will sprout. After the *magrohan* has been put in place it is reverently circuited by the builders seven times in a clockwise direction and then *sendur* and cowdung are applied. The sacred pole stands at the centre of the wedding observances and at that time is surrounded by the articles now to be mentioned. Their position is indicated in figure 21 on the next page.

1. The *magrohan*.
2. A *kalsa* (earthenware pot) filled with water. In the water there are mango leaves which are allowed to protrude at the top and over the top is placed a *dip* or earthenware lamp.
3. A *sil* (grinding stone) on which are placed the following articles noted in the sub-heads :
    a. A *lorha* (stone roller)—which the bridegroom will use to roll over the pice and disturb their arrangement.
    b. Husked rice, which is sprinkled over the surface of the *sil*.
    c. Seven pice coins which are laid in a row on top of the rice.
    d. Seven bits of wood, each a different kind.
    e. A whole *supari* nut.
    f. *Haldi* water is sprinkled over the whole.
4. A branch of *gular* or *palasa* (*Butea frondosa*) buried near the *magrohan*. In a crotch of the same will be inserted a small earthen pot containing *haldi*, *supari* nut and two pice.

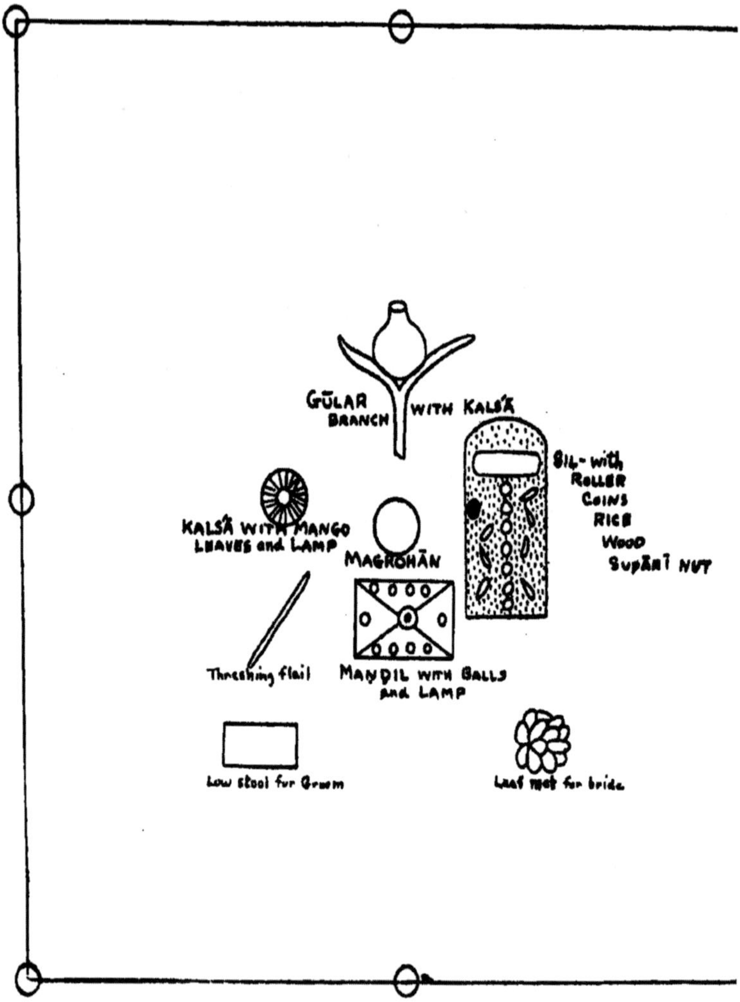

Fig. 21

5. A flat cone of earth (*mandil*) about one foot high and a foot in diameter on which are placed around its edge eight to ten small round balls of earth. Over the whole four arches of earth are constructed and in the centre another *dip* is set.

6. A *pira* (low stool) on which the bridegroom will be seated.

7. A small mat of large leaves on which the bride will sit.

8. A *musar* (threshing flail).

(3) *The Wedding Ceremony. The Sadi.* The actual wedding is divided into three parts, each occurring on a different day and the whole lasting three days. There is first the arrival of the *barat*—the party which brings the bridegroom and which reaches the girl's village on the evening of the first day. The next part occurs on the following night and is the wedding proper, the *sadi*; and finally the bridegroom departs for his own home on the third day and this is called the *bida* or farewell.

(*a*) *Barat.* A day or two after the parching of the *lawa* there are preparations at the bridegroom's house for the departure from thence for the house of the bride. The *barat* is usually so planned that it arrives at the girl's village just after dusk. The *barat* is made up entirely of men, and women are not permitted to accompany the procession. Before the *barat* can leave there is a feast given to its members by the women of the family. Following this the bridegroom is put into a *palki* or litter. The party also takes with it various things needed for the *sadi* including the *lawa*, a *barain* (small whitish-coloured earthenware pot decorated with yellow figures and in which are carried a *seer* of rice and, if in season, two mangoes), seven *dips* (earthenware lamps), and a *dahingar* (a decorated earthen pot like the *barain* in which *dahi*—curds—are kept). These things are carried by the party in baskets on their heads, but in the *palki* will be put the *sendur*, *kankan* (black and red beads strung on a thin iron wire), some toys and *gobar* (cowdung). Some one to beat the drum should accompany the party which leaves the boy's village amid music and singing. The women who remain behind are busy preparing for the return of the bridegroom and his party three days later.

The procession should not arrive in the village until night has fallen. Upon its arrival it does not at once enter the village, but stops some distance away and with drums and singing announces its presence. The girl's party which has been waiting the arrival of the *barat* is now summoned by her father. The women of the bride's party accompany the men in greeting the *barat* and the group proceeds to the edge of the village with lights, the person carrying the leading light being either the girl's sister or a female cousin. This light is carried on top of an earthen jar resting on the head in a manner similar to the way the light is carried at the *mangarmati* time. The men of the party bring a *chhattari*, or an umbrella made of bamboo branches and leaves from the *palasa* tree. Like the crown in Europe, the umbrella in village India is essentially a symbol of sovereignty. A *mashal*, or torch on the end of a pole is also brought and waved about in imitation of a battle. The men of the two parties now meet and greet one another. In more Hinduized communities they may set off fireworks at this time if they can afford them. The arrangement for these is made by a Basor. In the midst of this din the girl's father speaks to the boy's father and tells him that they are glad that they have come, that they will expect them to tarry for some days in their village, and that everything possible will be done for their comfort. As the best wedding months are usually dry and pleasant, the boy's party may be accommodated under a large tree. Wherever they are put, the place is called the *janmasa*. If there is an available house so much the better.

THE WEDDING PALKI - BRIDEGROOM

Fig. 22

On entering the village the two parties repair to the bride's house, led by the woman with the lamp on her head. Upon reaching the house the rice is taken out of the *barain*, pipes are passed around for a smoke, and even drinks may be offered. During this time the bridegroom has remained seated in his *palki* which is now brought close to the marriage booth. He reaches out and shakes the booth, to test, as it were, its strength and workmanship. The girl's mother comes to the *palki* and with the thumb and little finger of her right hand dabs a bit of vermilion on the forehead of her future son-in-law and then pours out the water which was in the *kalsa* with the light that brought them into the village. Members of each group should bring *gular* or *semal* twigs, as the case may be, which have been plastered with *gobar* and which have some *tikas* (dabs) of *sendur* on them. These are laid in the centre of the booth next to the *magrohan*. The *ghara* of *lawa* is taken by a member of the boy's group, who walks round the *palki* seven times with it. After the seventh round the boy's *maur* or wedding crown (made up usually, of peacock feathers, bamboo and palm leaves) is removed and the party retires to the place prepared for them, the *janmasa*.

Arriving at the *janmasa* they settle themselves and are again supplied with smokes by members of the bride's household. Preparations are then made for the bridegroom to eat *lahakaur*, the food prepared especially for the occasion. This may be of several types. It is sometimes said to consist of rice, pulse, *puris* and *bara* ; and again of milk, rice and sugar. This is brought by a female member of the family, the *sarhaj* (bride's brother's wife) being preferred. Before the boy is asked to eat the *lahakaur* two women dressed in dancing garments make their appearance; they sing and dance and are accompanied by some men with their drums. This party advances towards the *janmasa* singing songs which contain many questionable allusions and are considered as *gali* (abuse). They carry the emptied *kalsa* with the lighted lamp still on top of it, and place it before the boy who is asked to go around it seven times and sit down. When he has done this the *sarhaj* tries to make him eat the *lahakaur* ; she brings it up to his mouth five times in her right hand and after smelling it as many times he refuses to eat. She is paid four annas for this by the boy's father. There is more singing and the giving of *gali* by both sides. Finally the *sarhaj* brings a *lota* of water and washes the feet of the members of the boy's party and at the same time openly counts them so that they may know how many will need food. Much of this food has already been cooked but it is not served till midnight or later. In the meantime, during the meal, and even for the rest of the night, there are songs and the *dadra* dance.

About eleven o'clock the next morning the members of the bridegroom's party take their morning meal at the bride's house, but the groom stays by himself in the *janmasa* where his food is brought to him. When the others arrive their feet are washed as before and each member is given a *lota* of water so that he may wash his hands. The male members of the two parties always eat together first and the meal is usually served on leaf-plates, or, if they are available, brass ones. The men then go for a chat and rest and sometime later the women take their food. At no time do the men and women eat together.

(*b*) *Sadi*. The Actual Ceremony. The evening of the second day sees the performance of the marriage proper, the *sadi*. The premises of the girl's house are again plastered and all made clean and ready. The Brahmin priest who wrote the *lagan* is expected to arrive after nightfall. If the family should decide to dispense with his services the part of the priest may be taken by the *phupha* (father's sister's husband). The priest first marks out a square, called the *chauk*, on the plastered portion of the courtyard not far from the wedding booth, using whole wheat flour to mark the lines. A *kalsa* is then placed at its centre into which will be thrown the gifts for the couple. The bridegroom soon arrives dressed in his wedding garments, being brought thence in the *palki*. In the *palki* there is some *sendur* and a pair of shoes which are for the bride, and which his father removes and gives to the girl's representative for use later on. The *sendur* is used during the ceremony to mark her forehead. The bridegroom is now helped out of his *palki* and is asked by the priest to worship certain deities and as he does so he gives each a small offering of money.

The bride now makes her appearance for the first time; up till now she has been secluded in the house and none of the male members of either party has seen her. So now the bridegroom sees her for the first time, but only her form, as her face is covered with a part of her *sari*. She sits beside her future husband on the *chauk* and the priest repeats some Sanskrit formulas, but what they were we were unable to ascertain.

The time is now ready for the offerings to be presented to the persons about to be married. (At one place this was said to come later). This is called *chari* and comes from the groom's side. As they come forward with their gifts they first touch the feet of those about to be married and then cast their gifts into the *kalsa* in the centre of the *chauk*. The usual gifts are money, clothes and brass vessels, and as far as possible these are thrown into the *kalsa*. But if one wishes to give a chicken, a goat, or even a cow he says, "I give a chicken" and makes a motion as if he were throwing it into the waiting vessel. This gift will be given later on. In reality this is a worshipping of the couple. If the girl has a brother he now appears with a small *lota* of water and a *thali* (tray). The girl is asked to stretch out her hands before her, the tray is placed beneath them and the water poured over her hands and into it.

The *lawa* is now served. It will be recalled that this was prepared at both houses after the *mangarmati* ceremony and the two portions are now brought and mixed together. Some *batasas* (small sugar-like wafers) are also added, the whole being mixed by the girl's brother. When he is satisfied that this has been well done he takes out seven handfuls, one at a time, which he places one by one into the washed hands of his sister which are still stretched before her. She receives each handful and places it on another *thali* set before her. This is called the *lawa parsana* (or *parosna*), and the bridegroom's party pays the boy four annas for it. The mixture, now called *bran*, is placed near the *magrohan* in the centre of the wedding booth. Some incense is put into the fire burning there and some of the *bran* is used to make a magic circle about it.

The bride and the bridegroom are now conducted to the *marhwa*, and the latter is seated on the low wooden stool while the former sits either on a small mat of *palasa* leaves or on a low square made of mud and cow dung on his left. The *pandit* reads some sacred words, (supposedly from the Vedas) and as he does so the couple is instructed to throw *ghi* and rice coloured with *haldi* into the sacred fire. Each time the fire blazes up the priest utters the words *swaha, swaha*, meaning 'accepted', 'accepted'. This is really a *hom* offering. The *lagan* is sometimes read again at this stage.

The couple are asked to stand together, the girl being on the left of the boy. Some of the *sendur* is passed to him which he, with a silver coin, applies to the girl's forehead. As they stand there the *pandit* makes them promise to forgive each other at least seven times during their married life. After the promise the ends of their clothes are tied together, usually by the girl's sister. Into the knot that joins the two should be put a *takka* (a two-pice coin), some *haldi* and bits of a *supari* nut. Then begins the *bhanwar* or circumambulation of the bride and bridegroom about the sacred pole. If the couple are too young to live together and the marriage is not to be immediately consummated by her going to his house, there will be but five rounds of the *magrohan* For four of the five rounds the boy walks ahead, and the wife, the ends of the clothes still tied, follows, but on the fifth round the girl precedes the boy. The fire and pole are always kept to their right and they move round them in a clockwise direction. After the completion of each round they stop and the girl puts her right foot on the *sil* (the flat stone used for grinding spices). While she stands thus her brother or a representative makes a round of the pole with the *barain* containing the remainder of the *lawa*.

After the five rounds are completed (there would have been seven had the couple been old enough to live together) the two, still tied together, retire into the house, the girl leading the way. The women in a jesting manner attempt to bar their entrance and the pair have to force their way through. Rude songs and jokes of a sexual nature are now in order. Members of both parties have been given some of the seven handfuls of *lawa* kept in the booth and this is thrown upon the couple. Inside the house a lamp (*dip*) has been left under a basket, thus giving but little light to the room. The girl's mother asks the boy to take up the basket and blow out the light. He does not consent to do this until he receives a gift from his mother-in-law. Sometimes the challenge is for him to light a second lamp from the first. When he gets the desired gift he takes off the basket, but does not blow out the light. When this is done the knot is untied and his *maur* (wedding crown) is removed. He then turns to his bride and takes off a portion of the *sari* covering her head and sees her features for the first time. She immediately covers her head again. This is repeated seven times but after the seventh he does not again remove the covering, and it is said that henceforth her head is to remain covered to the day of her death if he outlives her, and to the day of his death if she becomes a widow. A *sari* cloth is now brought and is wrapped about the boy and girl; in the seclusion of this the boy puts some *sendur*, with the little finger of his right hand, on the girl's forehead indicating that she is now a married woman. The first three fingers should on no account be used. The Brahmin now takes his leave, for his work is done, and he is paid a fee usually amounting to Rs. 1-4-0.

The boy soon comes out of the house and greets his friends and tells his party that it is time for them to retire to the *janmasa*. Before they are allowed to depart, however, they are invited to a feast close to the *marhwa*. Their feet are again washed and a feast, as lavish as can be managed, is given them. At least the following should be provided: rice, pulse, *bara*, *puris*, curds, spices and sweets. Sometimes there is drinking but the Kols are not much addicted to this. The bridegroom begins the feast by taking the first mouthful; then the others may start. Usually they eat seated in a circle on the ground and are entertained at the time by singing and dancing. The bridegroom is paid four annas for starting things off and the rest of the night is spent in this manner.

(*c*) *Bida* (or *bidai*): The Return of the Bridegroom to his House. The returning party leaves the girl's village on the third day. About noon on that day there is another feast, the final one, which is only for the members of the departing company, except that the bridegroom's *sar* (brother-in-law) also eats with them. The groom refuses to eat until his mother-in-law promises him a gift such as a goat or a cow. The bridegroom is also presented with the gifts which were made to the couple and these are handed over to his *swasa* to keep for him. The men of both parties embrace and put a *tika* of *sendur* on one another, each man waving a pice over the head of another and then presenting it to him. *Ilachi* (cardamom), *pan* and *supari* are distributed.

The women now appear in a group and the mother-in-law puts lamp black under the eyes of the boy's father and also sprinkles a bit of *haldi* water over him. The other women do the same to the remaining members of the bridegroom's party. A bit of lac on a string is sometimes tied about their necks. The boy's father drops a rupee into the *lota* belonging to the girl's mother and the others drop as much as they can afford into the *lotas* of the other women. During this time neither the bride nor the groom is present.

The *marhwa* must now be untied for it has served its purpose and both the bride and the groom are called for this, the groom being seated in his *palki* ready for his departure. There is singing and dancing around the *marhwa*. The boy leaves his *palki* and enters the girl's house and the two are again tied together and the boy crowned. They come out side by side and both get into the *palki* which is to carry the bridegroom to his home. The women of the house take a pice in their right hand and waving it over the couple give it to the bearers of the *palki*. The women perform the wave ceremony yet once again, but this time do not use money but instead a *supa* (winnowing fan), and all the time the drummer beats the drum vigorously. The *palki*, however, does not move off, as the knot must be untied and the girl gets out, for she is not yet ready to go to her husband. The girl disappears into her house and the women go in with her. The two groups of men move out toward the edge of the village and a short distance beyond they bid each other farewell; thus comes the end of the second part of the wedding cycle.

The *marhwa* is taken down four to eight days after the *sadi*. It is torn down by the *swasa* who is helped by four or five men. The eight supporting poles are of no particular significance now and are usually thrown somewhere near the house where they are eventually used for fuel. The *magrohan* must be treated differently. Sometimes it is just left in the ground and grows into a tree, or if it should fail to do this it rots away. If it is removed, as is the usual procedure, it should not be carelessly thrown aside. Sometimes it is kept in the house, but more frequently is carried by the women, who sing and chant as they go, to a near-by stream or tank where it is ceremonially thrown into the water. Afterwards the area is plastered with cow dung to make the whole spick and span.

(4) *Gauna:* The Return of the Groom for his Bride. The third part of the marriage cycle is called the *gauna*, literally the going or moving. On this occasion the girl goes for the first time to the boy's home. Up till now she has not been alone with him, nor even talked to him in any confidential way. She knows nothing of the womenfolk in the boy's house with whom she has to live for a time until she has a home of her own. The time lapsing between the *sadi* and the *gauna* depends upon the ages of the couple; in certain cases where both have reached the age of puberty the *gauna* may immediately

follow the *sadi*, but more often a period of several years separates the two. The girl should be between ten and twelve and the boy between twelve and fifteen before the *gauna* ceremony can be performed. The exact time depends upon the *pandit* and upon auspicious days and seasons.

When the time for the *gauna* has come a large party carrying the bridegroom in a *palki* leaves the boy's home much in the same manner as they departed for the *sadi*. The boy's party is once more welcomed but the ceremony is not quite so elaborate as it was before. On the second night the Brahmin may be called in, though not always, and the remaining two circumambulations (*bhanwars*) of the fire are made. This time, however, there is no *marhwa* nor *magrohan*. The place where the final ceremony is performed is simply plastered and in the centre of the spot is set up a low mound made of cow dung; beside it is placed a *kachha kalsa* (an earthen pot not yet fired), on top of which is a brass plate containing (1) a *dip* burning with *ghi*, (2) *sendur* paste, and (3) a whole cocoanut. The couple are tied together as before and go round the fire twice, thus completing the seven rounds in all. This makes the marriage *pakka* and the final ceremony is followed by feasting, singing and dancing which last the rest of the night.

Sometime during the next day the couple depart for the boy's home. They are tied together and seat themselves in the same *palki* which the bearers carry a few yards and then set down while the knot is untied and the bridegroom gets out leaving the *palki* for the bride. He either gets into another one or joins the party on foot. Just before this party, which now consists of the group that went with him, reinforced by men from the girl's home, arrives at the boy's house the *palki* is set down, the boy again gets into it, and the knot is once more tied. *Haldi* water is sprinkled over them and pice are waved over the bearers who are again presented with the coins. Upon arriving at the house the couple find a new cloth five yards long and a yard wide spread on the ground leading from the path to the door of the groom's house and at one end of this the *palki* is put down. As the bride is about to get out she is presented with a tray of balls made of water and whole wheat flour. At each step she must deposit one on the cloth at her feet. Her husband follows, for he is still tied to her and as he comes he must pick up the balls and put them into a small *thali* (tray). Inside the house the knot is untied for the last time. From the *palki* the women bring a seer or two of uncooked rice along with a few other supplies including pulse, which the bride had brought with her in order that she might prepare a dish known as *khichri*, a food made by boiling the pulse and the rice together. When this is prepared she offers each of the male guests a portion of it and they in turn give her from two to four annas which she is allowed to keep for her own use. Following this there is a big feast at the boy's house and the night is spent in chatting, singing and dancing.

(5) *Raman* or *Rauna:* Final Break with her Family. There now remains one more thing, which is the simplest of all to do: to bring the bride back for good. The *raman* is the last part of the cycle and is the taking possession of the girl and the bringing her for the last time to the bridegroom's house. The time for this is set by the *pandit* and there is said to be very little ceremony or no ceremony at all. The bridegroom simply goes with one or two male friends and the girl is brought back to his home in a *palki* and "they live happily ever after." She is now a member of the new household but may come and go at will between the two places.

3. WIDOW REMARRIAGE: (*Kaṛi hui*; *Path*). It is nevertheless well recognized that a widow may be married again though for the Kols such unions are not marriages in the strict sense. We were often told that while a man may be married more than once, a woman can be married not more than once.

The Kols recognize two possible forms of widow marriage: a widower marrying a widow and a bachelor taking a widow as his wife. The latter form is the least common. Some say that a union like this should never be dignified by the term marriage, for while a Kol bachelor may "keep" a widow he may never marry her and the union has no legal standing. Others call it but half a marriage. Such a liason is never allowed if the Kol bachelor is living in his parents' home; it is only after he leaves the home that such a thing is possible. As long as this widow is kept by him the *panch* sees that he does not contract a real marriage with anyone else.

There are, however, traces of a sort of legalization of this procedure, but this really consists in first making the Kol a widower! If he wishes to marry the widow he must first consult the *panch*. They will usually do their best to try to dissuade him, but if he persists they tell him what he will have to do in the way of penalties. If he is willing it has to be ascertained whether the girl also is agreeable. If she is not, the thing is off, but the Kol youth would probably not have made the request without being sure of her consent. The *panch* then arranges a mock wedding for him, and he is "married" to some inanimate thing. There are several forms possible; one is that the bachelor should be made to perform the *bhanwar* (circumambulation) seven times about a silver or a gold ring fastened to a *magrohan* stick smeared with *sendur*. This marries him to the ring. Immediately after this procedure he should be anointed with sweet oil mixed with *haldi*—a sign that the "wife" has died and that he is now a widower. He may then put black glass bangles on the widow, and after giving a feast as directed by the *panch* he may take the widow into his home without shame and as if with the permission of the community. Roy has noted a similar custom, only that the bachelor is married to a brass *lota* or a flower.[1] He however, says nothing of the bachelor being made a widower.

This type of marriage is very unusual, the more common type of widow marriage being between a real widower and a widow. It may be said in passing that a Kol widower may marry a virgin, and that if this is done the regular form of marriage is resorted to in full.

When a Kol widower wishes to marry a certain widow he should first take the matter up with his *panch*. They look into the matter of relationships and the like, and deal with it on its merits. If it is agreed upon, some one from the *panch* is commissioned to go to the place where the widow is living (probably with her relatives), and through her female relatives make enquiry to see if she would welcome this match. If she is willing and her *panch* has no objection, the way is clear. The widower is told by the *panch* what he will have to do by way of a feast, and this he must do before he is allowed to proceed further. A *barat* is made up and the widower and his party go to the village of the widow where they stay for three days and go through the general procedure as in the case of the regular marriage, without, however, building a *marhwa* or the like, and the general festivities are limited to dancing, singing and eating. The widower must bear all the expenses, none being borne by the widow or her relatives. On the third day the *panch* of her village is called together and certain questions are asked as to their intentions. Upon satisfactory answers they are made to sit together and often they are anointed with oil and vermilion is put on their foreheads. The man is asked to put five black glass bangles on each wrist of the widow and they are considered married. The party leaves soon after this and there is no ceremony that would correspond to the *gauna* nor *raman*. They go to the man's village where they must feed the community before they are considered to be in good standing.

Marriage Costs. The cost of a Kol wedding is a great financial strain on the parties. Both groups have to pay a part of the costs.

1 Roy, S. C., *Oraon Religion and Customs*, p. 170.

Usually the girl's party pays the costs of all the ceremonies in her village, while the boy's party pays at his village. Possibly, though we were never actually able to determine the proportion, the costs in the end are about the same for both parties. The boy's father has to pay out more in actual cash, but has to bear a lesser expense in the home in connection with the preparations. In reply to our enquiries, we were given various estimates, but probably no one knows exactly just what the costs are. Sometimes there may have been an exaggeration, but in the light of their economic level the costs are staggering. The cost of a regular marriage is hardly ever less than thirty rupees per family and it ranges from this anywhere up to one hundred rupees per family. In the latter case the people must have originally greater resources and feel that they must do things more lavishly. As the Kol almost never has any money saved or in hand, most money for such expenses must be borrowed; and with the economic level as it is the repayment of such loans is practically impossible. The debtor becomes a virtual slave to the *malguzar* from whom he borrows the money.

The marriages described above bear many marks of, and resemblances to, Hindu marriages. It is believed that in the main the above is a fairly consistent account of the Kol types of alliances. Enquiry from other places show certain variations in practice and order. There are still many details to be filled in, and there are many variant practices yet to be noted and compiled. The process is a complicated one, and without doubt there is considerable variation between village and village in the matter of details.

POLYGYNY. If the husband can afford the added expense it is not uncommon for him to have two wives. In a case where there are two wives, it is usually discovered that the second "wife" has not been married with all the ceremonies as was the first, and that in reality she is just "kept." This arrangement however is considered legal and binding and a feast to the local group usually atones for the irregularity of the procedure. In our survey of Barela we found that there were three households in which more than one wife was found. In one of these instances a quarrel was then in progress between the wives and twice within the period of two weeks the aggrieved wife had run away and the man had to go out and search for her. In Panagar one Kol was found to have five wives, one of whom boasted to us that it was a sign of strength on the part of the husband. But a man standing by slyly remarked: "But look at their clothes and their condition." Kols expect their wives to work and so they are often looked upon as an economic asset. If there should be two or more women in the family, one of whom is married and the other just kept, their respective rights were said to depend solely upon the will of the husband and it was not admitted that any of them had greater rights than the others. Their children have equal rights and no discrimination is made between them. If the wife is barren and the other has sons, the property upon his death reverts to the sons. If both "wives" have sons it is divided at death according to the husband's expressed wish or by a decision of the *panchayat*.

We did not find much sexual laxity among the Kols; but the Hindus assert, whether from knowledge or prejudice it is hard to say, that the sexual relations of the Kols are very loose. A Malguzar reported that in some villages under his jurisdiction where Kols happened to be in the majority he knew of at least one case of a Kol woman having several husbands, a sort of polyandry, and that the men frequently exchanged wives.

DIVORCE. It is not uncommon for a man and his wife to separate but as long as this separation is not sanctioned by the *panchayat* it involves certain disabilities. The *panchayat* never takes the initiative nor does it advise or suggest divorce—rather the opposite—but it has to act if the separation is to have official sanction. The usual grounds for separation and divorce are:

1. Sterility of the wife
2. Sexual unchastity of either
3. Quarrelsomeness in the home
4. Laziness resulting in the neglect of household duties and support of the family
5. Any tendencies such as thievery, frequent absences from home without apparent reasons, and the like

There are numerous variations in the process of securing this separation. It is usually considered more difficult for a man to get rid of his wife than it is for the wife to get rid of her husband. The matter is first officially brought to the attention of the local *panchayat* by either of the aggrieved parties. In some cases the local *panch* has full authority, but in Maihar State we found that if, after investigation, the local *panch* thought there was a good case for divorce, the matter is referred to an intercaste *panchayat*; one which should include members from seven different groups or castes. This seems to be an exception, and when asked what castes could act together they mentioned only three: Kol, Kurmi and Chamar.

If the husband is the complainant he tells the *panch* his grievances, and brings specific charges against his wife. Others present may confirm his charges if they believe them to be true. He states his desire and his particular intention in this case. It should be noted that the decision of the *panchayat* is not absolutely binding on the parties. If the *panch* decides that the man is in the right and if he gets his hoped-for decision everything is satisfactory for him; if not he may go against their decision, but it will not be without a fine or a feast of some kind to atone for it. If the woman is also present and if she wishes she may make her own defence, although if another defends her it must be done by a male member of her family. If the charges are admitted either by the woman or her representative the matter is easily settled, for the *panchayat* will allow him to divorce her without any penalty. If the woman is present she is then brought to the centre of the circle and a member of the *panch* orders her husband to go to her and remove seven times the portion of the *sari* covering her head; this is the sign of the dissolution of the marriage. She is not required to remove her glass bangles which are the real signs of marriage. These are broken, however, by the man with whom she goes to live (as most of the cases seem to involve a man), and he gives her new bangles in their place.

If the woman brings the charge against her husband, or if she is favoured in case he brings it against her, and the husband does not accept the *panch's* ruling, he may still dismiss her from his house and keep, but he must pay a penalty. In Maihar and Rewa we were informed that the decision was not final until the matter had been presented to an officer called *Mahata*, who is paid Rs. 1-4-0 for his judgment and must give the final assent. He is looked upon as a government servant, but his post was said to be hereditary.

If the woman should leave her husband and go to another man, the *panchayat* insists that the man taking her must pay a fine, while the former husband has no blame attached to him. Nevertheless if the wife was regularly married to her first husband, the man who takes her not only has to pay the fine but also must return to her former husband the amount of money that the latter paid as the bride price when first they were married. One group told us that if the wife wanted to go away for other reasons than to marry a man, she is free to do so and the *panchayat* does not interfere, nor is any fine involved. The complications begin, however, if she should want to marry again; it is then that the *panchayat* steps in. If the woman refuses to recognize this and if she should try to run away with another man, the *panchayat* advises that the matter be taken to the civil courts where the claim may be made that the woman is stolen. Judgment has been secured on this basis, and so most Kols prefer to pay the fine and not take chances in the court. This also tends to prevent a too easy divorce.

In regard to the children it was said that should the *panchayat* agree in favour of the husband, the children must go to him, with the exception that a mother may keep a nursing child. But when the nursing period is over and the child is weaned it must be handed over to the father. If she should begin to live with another man it must be given up at once. On the other hand should the man be proved a renegade and the *panch* decide that the woman is in the right she is allowed to keep the children, the property and the possessions. He is "driven out" with nothing but his personal effects. She is not required to uncover her head and nothing of a similar nature is required of him for he is simply told to *jao*—go! The woman however, should publicly say that she renounces him.

Such is a brief survey of the marriage customs of the Kols. Through these observances it is possible to trace a strong sense of social solidarity, and of the care exercised by both *panchayats* in adjudging the suitability of the matches. By the imposition of penalties which seek to discourage irregular unions the *panch* attempts to steady things. At the time of weddings there is a feeling of brotherhood and good fellowship, and in certain respects the wedding is the most important of all the social rites. Apart from its attendant ceremonies there is little of interest and excitement in the life of the average Kol. While there may be many instances of conscious or unconscious borrowing from Hindu sources, nevertheless this is not of recent occurrence, and probably goes back for hundreds of years, so far, indeed, that the Kols believe it to be their very own and assert: "These are the things we do, we do not know why we do them, but they are done by us."

CHAPTER VI

THE SOCIAL UNIT: THE FAMILY

THE KOL FAMILY. The basis of Kol society is found in the family. This family is patrilinear and patrilocal, with a recognition of the bilateral kinship group because important social relations are observed with the kin on both sides. Nevertheless the household usually contains only dependent members from the father's side, but there are no taboos for the other side of the family and visiting is allowed back and forth freely and without hindrance. No trace was found of a rupture in the parent-in-law relationship and no restrictions either in talking or associating were traced. In all, however, the family stands out as a distinct unit separate from the wider life of the community.

In a typical Kol family under the one roof will usually be found the husband, the wife (or wives), unmarried children, and occasionally some dependent member or members of the father's family, such as a widowed grandparent. Soon after marriage the Kol son usually sets up a home for himself. In the more primitive sections it is unusual to find a married son and his wife living with his parents. In the more Hinduized communities, where the Kols are better off and can afford more elaborate houses, married sons and their wives were frequently found living with the boy's parents. In one such home in Barela, for example, there were two married sons and their wives living with the boys' parents. This seems though to be an imitation of the Hindu family system, rather than a true Kol institution. The older dependents are found in the house only if their own homes are broken up by death. One occasionally finds an old couple living together in a little hut, and when one or the other dies the surviving member goes to live in a son's or another relative's house. In one centre, however, four such persons were found, each living alone in a little hut. They were either not wanted or had no relatives with whom they could reside.

In Barela and Kharara Ghat a survey was made of the number of people in each home or sheltered under one roof. The average number of people per house, excluding four houses where there was one each who was somehow *persona non grata* with relatives, was 3.9. In Kharara Ghat the average came to 4.8 persons per house. The 1931 Central Provinces Census Report reveals that primitive tribes average 3.8 children per family. The distribution of people was as follows:

1. *Barela* : *Persons reported* : *Houses reporting* : *Total for class.*

Persons reported		Houses reporting		Total for class
9	..	1	..	9
8	..	2	..	16
7	..	1	..	7
6	..	5	..	30
5	..	10	..	50
4	..	8	..	32
3	..	16	..	48
2	..	12	..	24
1	..	4	..	4
		59	..	220

2. *Kharara Ghat* :

Persons reported		Houses reporting		Total for class
9	..	2	..	18
8	..	..	..	..
7	..	2	..	14
6	..	5	..	30
5	..	6	..	30
4	..	6	..	24
3	..	4	..	12
2	..	4	..	8
		29	..	136

In the case of the Barela Kols the lower average is due to two causes : the first is that the town is near the main road and as the Kols are much more Hinduized as a community there is a natural loss of household members who leave home for work in Jubbulpore. The second is that the health of the Barela Kols is far less satisfactory than of those in Kharara Ghat, for the town is much more open to infection, and illnesses are more numerous.

THE POSITION OF WOMEN. The place of women among the Kols can be said to be fairly high. There is a wholesome sense of equality among the sexes. The women do not keep themselves in seclusion (*parda*), and are generally free to go about on any errand. In Hinduized sections they cover their heads in the presence of men or when they are outside their houses, but under primitive conditions they are not so particular. In a general sense the husband is the main authority in the family, but the wife is in no sense his slave and plays a large part in its control and management. All affairs are brought before the family for discussion and decision before final action is taken. If one party is not agreeable to a certain proposition the other tries by coaxing or by some other means to win his or her consent. Nevertheless this picture, given by the men, may be over bright, for it appears from close observation that the rights of the wives are much less than those of the men. She is not as free as the men are and it is not the custom for her to go here or there without hindrance. The woman has a certain amount of what might be called "personal property" and is not debarred from possessing it, though this is limited to her ornaments, her clothes and anything that she may make or acquire for her personal use. When the husband dies his property goes to the sons, but as long as she is living she must be supported by the sons. If there is no son, the property remains with her as long as she lives, but passes to the husband's male relatives at her death.

The Kol widow is not subjected to the same disabilities as are found among certain classes of Hindus. She is not required to shave her head, nor discard her metal bangles and ornaments, nor wear a white *sari*. If young she may marry again, usually not less than a year after her husband's death, and if she is elderly she may go to live with her son or relatives. Widows are expected to make some contribution for their keep and are often found searching for fuel or roots and leaves.

PLACE OF THE WIFE. After marriage the chief duties of the wife are to care for the house, prepare the meals and be a mother to her children. In between it is generally expected that she will find some means to supplement the family income, either by directly engaging in remunerative work, or by gathering roots and tubers from the jungle, cow dung from the roads and paths, or wood for the kitchen fire. Dried cow dung cakes are most generally used for the fire. She does the washing of clothes for herself and her children. Men wash their own clothes.

During her monthly courses there is some interruption of her regular work. During that time she may prepare her own food, but is not permitted to prepare food for another. The man must do his own cooking or make some other arrangements for the time being. There are other taboos at this time; she must never touch men's clothes nor should milk of any kind be touched by her. She may bring water from the well for her own use, but such water is taboo to any other member of the family.

There are at least two other things which a Kol woman must never do: she may not plough, nor climb up on the roof of a house. Such matters are looked upon as serious breaches of custom and deserve a penalty from the *panch*. Repeated enquiries elicited no recent violations of these taboos, and there was no definite statement as to what would be done in case they occurred. This latter taboo, however, probably has its exceptions, as we knew of a Kol woman helping to repair a roof on the mission house in Barela.

It is the rule that wives should never utter their husband's name and the same is true of the husband who should never call his wife by her name. They are addressed, rather, as the mother or father of the children. For example if the child's name is Makkhi the husband will address his wife as Makkhi's mother. There is another general prohibition to the effect that a woman should never speak the name of a man older than herself; he should be addressed in some indirect way.

PARENTS AND CHILDREN. Kols say that children are Bhagawan's gifts to them in answer to Sheori's prayer. Both sexes are welcome in the home and there is no evidence that they favour one above the other. Abortion is all but unknown and it is considered an evil thing to attempt it. Apparently they know of no herb or plant growing in the jungle which would cause it.

When children are old enough they are assigned tasks about the house (there is no school besides this)—the girls learn cooking and other household duties, gather wood and cow dung, while the boys help herd goats or cattle, if any, or accompany their fathers to the fields where they play about and help to bring back its produce or the wood cut in the forest.

Almost no moral training, as such, is imparted, nor are the children severely punished when discipline is called for. A slap over the ear is usually all that is attempted and more often than not this is adroitly dodged. On the whole Kol parents are over indulgent with their children. The sum of moral training was said to be "Don't steal, don't lie, don't hurt anyone." When they were asked about the type of religious instruction given to children they said: "We neither know, nor can we tell." What children learn is largely by observation and practice rather than by direct instruction. Among the more literate people of Northern India moral teaching is given through the reading of such literature as the Ramayana of Tulsi Das. The Kols, though, do not have even this, unless it so happens that a mendicant reads to them, nevertheless it would not appear that their morals are any worse than those who have considerable more light to guide them.

ORPHANS. Concerning treatment of orphans and provision for their care, there seems to be different practices according to locality. In most centres the matter resolves about the question whether the orphan or orphans concerned have relatives or not.

1. Where there are relatives it is the father's brother who is the responsible party. He is the one to arrange for the orphans of either sex. If there be a girl of marriageable age and no arrangement has been made for her, the paternal uncle will at once try to find a suitable match for her. Other relatives, and members of the *panch* are called in to help decide the question. If the children are still young, the uncle will attempt to provide for them. It may be, if he is able, that he will take the children into his own home; or they may be divided up among relatives who are able and willing to care for them. Any property belonging to the family is divided among the children and goes with them wherever they are placed.

2. If there are no relatives, it falls to the *panch* to provide for the orphaned children. Before actual provision is made, a thorough search for relatives is undertaken, and if any are located, the children are turned over to them. If not, the *panch* must decide how to care for the orphans and to whom they should be given. A certain family may be appointed as guardians of the children, and to help this family, the *panch* may order a collection to be taken from the Kol community.

The child taken into the home of a family, which is not related to the adopted child, is nevertheless considered as one of the family and the other children, if any, as his or her brothers and sisters. If the child be a boy, he cannot marry a female member of the family adopting him. Adoption generally occurs only within the limits of the *kurhi*. Records have been found of occasions that have arisen which necessitated the adoption of Thakuriyas into Rautiya families. This is unusual, but if the adopted child be a girl, the problem is relatively simple: when she becomes of marriageable age, she can be married to a Rautiya under the rule of hypergamy. If the child be a boy, the problem of his marriage is much more complicated as he cannot be married within the Rautiya *kurhi* The family must search for a Thakuriya girl. One might think that a Thakuriya boy brought up in a Rautiya family might pass for a Rautiya, but close watch is kept by all concerned on the history of people, and it would practically be impossible to pass off the child as a Rautiya. Kols claim that they very rarely take a member of another *kurhi* into the family, while a non-Kol is never taken into a Kol family as an adopted member.

Division of Labour. There is a distinct division of labour amongst the Kols and the following table, used as a basis for investigation, gives the main results. There has not always been complete agreement, but the following summary pretty well represents the views of the Kols on the matter of labour. The exceptions are noted. The following list of occupations includes practically everything that the village Kol is called upon to do.

Occupation.	*How Divided.*
Gathering wood in the forests.	Both men and women.
Gathering *biri* leaves.	Do.
Carrying wood to the bazaar.	Do.
Carrying grass to the bazaar.	Do.
Cutting grass in the fields.	Do.
Grazing cattle.	Usually men, women only under certain conditions as when the grazing is close to home.
Ploughing fields.	Men only.
Sowing of seed.	Men only.
Transplanting rice.	Both men and women.
Winnowing wheat.	Do.
Repairs to the house :	Do.
Walls and floors.	Do.
Roofs.	Men only.
Plastering floors and walls.	Women only, except that a bachelor may do so to his own quarters.
Grinding wheat.	Women and bachelors.
Buying in the bazaar.	Both may purchase, but the women are restricted.
Cooking in the home.	Women and bachelors.
Bathing children.	Women only.
Mending clothes	Both, but men always mend men's clothes and women women's clothes.
Cleaning up cattle sheds.	Usually women, but men may do so occasionally.
Collecting eggs.	Women, though some Rautiyas state that they do not touch eggs.
Feeding the children.	Women.
Breaking rocks for the roads.	Both men and women.
Day labourers in the fields.	Do.

Occupation	*How Divided.*
Playing musical instruments.	Men only.
Dancing.	Women only.
Sacrificing an animal.	Men only.
Hom sacrifice.	Usually men, but women may.
Making blankets, clothes and gourd vessels.	Neither ever make these except Kathariyas make mattresses.
Making *lathis* of bamboo.	Men only.
Weaving mats and making leaf plates.	Neither makes these : are purchased as needed.
Counting *biri* leaves.	Both men and women.
Keeping watch over crops :	Do, but generally men.
By day.	Do, but generally men.
By night.	Men only.
Bringing water from the well.	Both men and women.
Cleaning up the toilet of children.	Women only.
Husking of paddy.	In charge of men.
Cutting wood for home use.	Usually men, but women may do.
Gathering cow dung.	Women only, and children.
Weeding the paddy field.	Both men and women.
Reaping the paddy or wheat.	Do.
Washing plates after meals.	Women.
Washing clothes.	Each wash their own, except that women wash the children's.
Making fireplaces.	Women only.
Bringing fruits from the forest.	Both men and women.
Gathering roots for eating.	Do.
Care of chickens.	Usually women, but there are exceptions.
Care of goats.	Both men and women.
Weaving of cloth.	Neither does this work.
Selling of excess grain.	Men in charge of this.
Construction of houses.	Men, with the help of women who must stay on the ground.
Milking of cows.	Usually men, but women may assist.
Milking of goats.	Do.
Sweeping of houses and open courtyards.	Women only. Bachelors.
Throwing out of trash.	Do.
Bringing mud to repair walls.	Both men and women.

Occupation.	*How Divided.*
Care of small house garden.	Both men and women.
Moral training of children.	Do.
Punishment of naughty boy.	Both, but usually the father.
Punishment of naughty girl.	Both, but usually the mother.
Purchase of clothing :	
For children.	Both may do this.
For wives.	Men usually.
For men.	Men only.

From the above statement it would appear that the following general observations may be made :

1. There are certain occupations which are usually, if not always performed by the men of the family. Among these may be listed the following :

Ploughing.
Sowing seed.
Repairs to house and always of the roof.
Playing musical instruments.
Sacrificing before the deity.
Watching crops at night.
Threshing.
Purchasing clothes.
Washing own clothes.

2. Women are usually expected to :

Plaster floors and walls of the houses.
Grind the wheat for *chapatis.*
Cook the meals.
Clean the cattle shed.
Feed and care for the children.
Clean up the toilet of the children.
Gather cow dung for plastering and for use as fuel.
Wash plates and cooking vessels.
Wash children's and own clothes.
Make fire-places.
Sweep houses, courtyards and dispose of trash.
Dance.

3. A bachelor must perform. certain of the duties in the home usually done by the women.

4. In some things the men take the leading part, but the women assist in certain occupations, such as:

Grazing cattle.
Purchasing supplies in the bazaar.
Watching crops by day.
Cutting wood for the house.
Construction of houses.
Milking of cows and goats.

5. There are some things that are absolutely taboo to the women such as:

Ploughing.
Getting up on a roof.

6. There is one thing that a man should never do: wash the clothes of a woman.

7. There are a number of things neither a man nor a woman does, some of them have been listed and others have not. These tasks are the particular work of certain castes and occupational groups, and Kols leave such work to them.

Among Kols working in industrial centres the wife and husband often work side by side at the same task, such as digging stone, carrying baskets of stone for the lime kiln, and the like.

GUESTS AND HOSPITALITY. On account of the smallness of Kol houses it is not possible for Kols to do much in the way of entertaining. Nevertheless hospitality is extended as far as is possible under the circumstances. A visiting relative is given a place within the family. On his arrival, he is met by the men of the house and greeted. The salutation takes the form of an embrace. The two put the arms around each other and touch first the left shoulder to the left shoulder, then the right to right. The next thing is to touch each others' knees, first the left, then the right, both hands generally being used. The final part is the grasping of the right hand.[1] Provision is made for the relative so that he or she may sleep comfortably during the night. This often entails hardship on the members of the family particularly if the house is crowded. A relative takes food with the other members of the family: men sitting with men and women with women. If the visitor should be a friend but not a relative, it is usual for him to be given a place to sleep, but he does not take his food with the family. He is expected to cook his own food, although the materials for the same are supplied free to him by the family with whom he is stopping.

1 See plate XII.

There is no claim of hospitality by a Kol on another Kol if he is unknown to the latter. Even though he be of the same *kurhi* and knows relatives of the persons in the family and is in need of hospitality, he can expect none; any kindness shown him is an act of mercy. For this reason it is unusual for a Kol to ask hospitality at the hands of strangers. He asks for hospitality and shelter for the night only where he is known.

PROPERTY AND INHERITANCE. The average Kol does not own a great deal of property, but like most people he is interested in acquiring goods. Even marriage is commonly looked upon as the acquiring of a piece of property in the person of the wife. Almost nowhere are Kols found to own land in the full sense of the term. Even the land upon which their houses and rude huts are built is rented, the usual rent being one rupee a year. This is paid to the *malguzar* who does not disturb them further if the payments are regular. Away from the larger towns where land so often lies waste, it is usually found that no charges are made whatsoever.

The personal property held by Kols includes clothes, cooking utensils, tools and a few ornaments if there is money to buy such. Animals are also considered their own property. Apart from the clothes a person wears, the rest of the goods held by the Kols are considered as held by the family as a unit, and the head of the family can sell or exchange only after consultation with the others. Upon the approach of his death the head of the family is expected to make a statement concerning the disposition and division of the property. However if he should suddenly die without making such provision, it does not follow that the elder son, or next in line, inherits the rights of the father concerning the disposition of the goods, and any division or exchange must be decided upon by the family as a whole with the help of someone from the *panch*. While it appears that any member of the family might purchase any article required, either for themselves or for the family, yet after purchase the article becomes the property of the family as a whole, and the purchaser has no right to resell or dispose of it without permission of the head of the family in consultation with the other members.

Upon the break-up of the family by death the sons are generally supposed to have equal rights to the property. If, prior to his death, the deceased requested that the elder son should get the larger share, this is accepted. No distinction is said to be made between the children of the "married" wife and the "kept" woman if there are both in the family.

Should a dispute arise over the division of the property the matter must be settled by the *panch*. They will probably distribute it as equally as possible among the sons. Should this not be satisfactory to all concerned the sons have the right to appeal to the law courts of the land and have the matter settled there. Among Kols this is seldom, if ever, done.

The female members of the family do not enjoy equal rights with the males. A girl, when married, loses her membership in her family, and becomes a member of the new home. When she goes to live with her husband she takes nothing with her apart from her clothes and some personal adornments. It was noted by Russell and Hiralal that:

> Succession among the Mundas passes to sons only. Failing there, the property goes to the father or brother if any........ Daughters get no share in the inheritance and are allotted among the sons just like livestock. Thus if a man dies leaving three sons and three daughters and thirty head of cattle, on a division each son would get ten head of cattle and one sister; but should there be only one sister, they wait until she marries and divide the bride price.[1]

This quotation, from their article on the Kols, does not apply to the specific Kol tribe, but nevertheless we found instances of this tendency.

There is a difference of opinion as to the disposition of the property if there are no sons and only girls in the family. In many places it was affirmed that property could pass to the daughters if there were no sons. This was always her own property and nothing could alienate it from her, not even her marriage. When such a girl is married she takes her property with her and such property is considered her own and does not become a portion of her husband's wealth. If she should ever leave his home due either to divorce or quarrel she still remains its owner. Keeping it thus in her name and under her control is a protection to her in case of need. At her death, such property, if still existing, is supposed to revert to her father's family, his brothers or their heirs. When a wife dies her clothes are disposed of as noted in Chapter VII. Her metal jewellery is kept and may be worn by a new wife or passed on to the sons.

1 Russell and Hiralal, *Op. Cit.*, Vol. III, p. 515.

CHAPTER VII

DEATH AND ITS ATTENDANT CEREMONIES

Death is an event which every Kol knows must be faced relatively early in life. One does not find a high proportion of aged Kols.[1] Among many primitive people death is usually ascribed to evil influences, but among the Kols this does not seem to be the common belief. While they believe that some deaths may be ascribed to evil influences they do not believe that all are caused that way. On the whole they take quite a natural view of the phenomenon. What the gods will that they do. Death also may be due only to natural causes or carelessness and no hidden malevolent cause is assumed. Death is usually deserved, for as one sows he also reaps. Hence an early death may be justly merited and caused by corrupt living. The Kols do not seem to be as superstition ridden as many groups are, yet we found indications that they hold the general local village point of view. On the whole there is a wholesome attitude toward the supernatural—the world is not altogether evil.

THE APPROACH OF DEATH. When it is clear that a person is about to die there are certain things which ought to be done. It was found that the custom of bringing a cow to the bedside of the dying man is known and is occasionally practiced. The dying man is asked to take hold of her tail. This will help him to get to heaven, for the cow is now considered an offering to God, and it is held that by holding the tail the dying man makes this offering. If available, he is also made to drink a little Ganges water which is regarded as the very best of drinks to give him at that hour. Failing this, a sip of water in which gold has been washed is efficacious. Gold is considered an incarnation of God and a symbol of purity. Again, some ordinary water into which some ground up leaves of the *tulasi* plant (*Ocymum sanctum*) have been thrown is advantageous. Such drinks are said to purify the dying person and prepare the soul for its flight to other worlds. Hindu influences are apparent.

Usually the person who is dying is placed on the ground to expire. The body is placed on the ground so that there may be close contact with Mother Earth. In some places it is said that a man may just as well die

[1] This holds for primitive tribes in general, although any statement of age is unreliable. The 1931 census figures show that among the Kols there were only 100 men and 99 women per mile over forty. Other tribes show the following: Gond 154 men and 155 women; Maria 106 and 97; Baiga 143 and 146. Hindus rank higher—171 and 173 for Brahmins and 196 and 183 for Kunbis. *Census of India*, 1931, xii : 1, p. 131.

on a bed, if he is on one, as on the ground, but it is mostly affirmed that the ground is the place for the dying person. The body should be put there only when it is certain that the person is about to expire. The place where the body is laid should be first plastered with cow dung if that is possible. The head should be toward the north, that is, pointing towards the sacred Ganges, and the feet to the south, for it is in that direction that the soul has to go to the land of death. Most of the graveyards are to the south of Kol villages.

As soon as it is ascertained that the person is dead the fact of death is publicly proclaimed by loud lamentations set up by members of the family. The lamentations do not seem to be linked up with the frightening away of evil spirits but are essentially a natural expression of grief; although to an outsider they may seem to be overdone. The body should not remain within the house, but should be immediately removed to a place made ready for it on the veranda or the small courtyard in front of the house. There the body is laid upon the ground and is covered with a new white cloth. Nothing is done to the body in the way of measuring its length or the tying of its toes.[1]

PREPARATIONS FOR THE FUNERAL. Immediate preparations are now begun for the funeral, which, under favourable circumstances should be underway within an hour or two. Friends prepare a bamboo sling (*tatari*), made of two long bamboo poles with a few crossbars. On this the body is placed and fastened. A wooden *charpai* (rope cot) may serve just as well, and if the death occurred on one, this is used. Such a *charpai* has to be discarded anyhow, and in this case it is abandoned at the place of disposal. It is, however, immediately taken possession of by a low caste Hindu—a Basor or a Domar.

Occasionally the body is washed with a bit of cold water at the house before being transported to the place of burial or cremation. The most common procedure, though, is that the body is not washed till the funeral grounds are reached.

If the person has died in the evening, too late for immediate disposal, the body may be kept upon the earth outside the house during the whole of the night. Friends and relatives sit round the body which is regarded with awe and sometimes fear. A lamp is kept burning so that no evil spirit may get possession of the corpse and enter it in the darkness. Nevertheless no efforts are made to tie the corpse

1 As soon as the body is laid out, some non-Kol groups measure its length and tie its big toes together in order to determine whether or not a live spirit has gained entrance to the body during the period between death and its removal to the cemetery. If a spirit has entered, the body will elongate and the thread about the toes will be broken.

nor measure it to see whether a spirit has gotten within and caused the body to swell. Other groups, such as the Chamars,[1] are said to do this. In Rewa it was reported that they should not wait till daylight, but should make immediate arrangements even though the work has to be done at night. They said that if a man died about 9 p.m., they would have the corpse buried by 3 a.m. This, though, seems to be the exception and not the rule; other groups have denied this, saying that no burial ever occurs at night.

Transportation of the Corpse. The body is transported to the burial or cremation grounds on the *tatari* as noted above. The corpse is always carried by men. Among the Oraons it is said that the custom once was that the women always carried the corpse.[2] Four men at a time act as pall bearers. The men are frequently changed so that as many as possible may assist. Even a man's "enemies" should come and help and if such a person does there will be no further enmity between him and the rest of the family. This will also appease the spirit of the deceased. The body is usually carried so that the feet go first. There is a division of opinion on this matter though, as some Kols claim that the head should always be kept in the direction of the Ganges; hence in cases where the graveyard happens to be in the north of the village the head is carried forward. That the feet go first is generally true in other groups, in order, it is said, that the spirit of the deceased may not find its way back. But the Kol has no objection to the spirit's return, and in fact expects it back; actually food is put out near the house for it. If the body is set down for a time the head should point north and the feet south.

On the way to the *masan* or *marghat* (burial place) or the *ghat* or *chita* (burning place) there should be no chanting nor singing nor music of any kind. Lamentation and weeping is all that is in order. The party goes in two groups, first the men with the bier, and, following a short distance behind, the women and the children. The women bring the water for washing the body as well as the oil and turmeric for anointing. As the party proceeds it is customary to drop some mustard seeds along the way, and *laddu* balls made with sweetened *lai* (puffed rice) are also dropped at intervals. On the way back they try to see if these have been picked up, and form an opinion as to whether the omens are good or bad. Some say that if the spirit of the deceased returns he will pick them up. The *rai* seeds will keep the evil spirits

1 Briggs, G. W., *The Chamars*, pp. 100—101.
2 Roy, S. C., *Oraon Religion and Customs*, p. 173.

PLATE XVII

A Kol burial ground near Barela. The two mounds represent recent interments.

busy and they will not bother the sweets. Often it is said that no particular ceremonies are observed as the body is being carried toward the burial place. Nothing is done at the time of the crossing of small streams.

Up to this time no work has been done at the funeral ground, and no one has gone ahead to prepare the grave, or pyre; all is done after the arrival with the body. The funeral ground is always near some stream or *nala* (dried up water-course). Kols practice both cremation and burial and it is usual that the dead are cremated only a few feet away from the place where the burials take place. The introduction of cremation may be due to Hindu influences. On the whole burials are far more common than cremations because, Kols suggest, they are much cheaper, and the subsequent formalities of gathering the ashes and taking them to a river are not necessary. Burial is much the simpler process, and is first described.

BURIAL (*Garna.*) The funeral party arrives at the *masan* where the body is put down, head north and feet south. Some of the men in the party have brought implements for digging and go to seek a suitable place to dig the grave. Others remain with the body and prepare it for burial.

Preparation of the Body. Up till this time it is usual to find that the person has on the clothes in which he died. As he was transported to the burial place a white cloth was thrown over him. Now this and the clothes are removed. In the case of a male corpse the men attend to the changing of the garments, the washing and anointing. If the corpse be of the opposite sex the women attend to everything connected with its preparation. The body is first washed with water brought by the women from the village tank or well in new *gharas*. No pregnant woman should carry water, nor should she accompany the procession to the funeral place. Some of the water may be retained for a ceremonial sprinkling when the people get back to the village. After the body has been washed and dried it is anointed with a mixture of *til* or *karwa* oil and *haldi*. Sometimes *ghi* is also rubbed on. The corpse is now ready to wrap in new clothes which have just been purchased. If the family is not able to afford new clothes old ones which have been carefully washed will do. The grave clothes must always be white no matter the sex or the age. No coloured cloth should be used. The old clothes are taken away by the Basor. The hair is oiled and combed and the body is made as attractive as possible. Sometimes, in more Hinduized situations, the *nai* is called to shave the body and to prepare the hair, but he is not usually called for a woman. If the body is that of a woman her glass bangles are broken and her metallic jewellery removed. The breaking of the glass bangles is a symbol of the dissolution of her marriage. From many enquiries it appears that neither food, coins or iron is put into the mouth of the deceased.

Up to this point it seems that the bodies of men and women are treated alike, except that persons of corresponding sex make them ready. Only in rare cases a trace was found which indicated that there is the belief that the soul of the pregnant woman might become an evil spirit called a *churel*; preparations for burial of such women seemed to be uniformly the same as when the woman is not with child. Only once in scores of burials was there any indication that the pregnant woman was cut open after her death and the fœtus removed and buried with her. This, if ever done among the Kols, is now a rare thing with them.

Digging the Grave. In the meantime the grave is being made ready. The spot where it is to be dug must first be "purchased." This is done by one of the relatives who, when the place has been decided on, strikes the ground five times with his *phaora* or mattock. Two pice are then laid down on the ground and the digging proceeds. It is proper for the chief male mourner to break the first earth at the spot agreed upon. He may take out five or seven clods and thereafter relatives or friends lend a hand and complete the task. The grave is dug in a north-south line, and is about six feet long, three feet wide and four feet deep. "Chest deep" is the rule. No special implements are used in digging nor are the ones used considered unclean afterwards. When the grave has been dug there are still things which must be done before the body can be laid in it. One of the relatives sprinkles a little salt on the bottom of the grave. Usually, though, a cloth is laid in first, using the one which was thrown over the body after death, or the blanket on which he died, and the salt is sprinkled over this. The body is now lowered into the grave. One or two men enter the grave, the body is passed down to them and they place it in its proper position.

In the case of a woman she is buried flat on her back, face upwards, having her arms stretched by her side with the palms up. Male corpses are laid face downwards with the hands folded behind over the buttocks, palms upwards. In both cases the head is to the north.[1] After the body is properly placed it is covered with another

[1] The direction in which the body is placed in the grave varies considerably among primitive tribes. The Murhas have the head to the south; the Birhors likewise. The Hill Bhuiyas are laid on the left side with the head to the south and face to the west. The Munda tribes, Kharias, Hos and Santals bury their dead with the head north. Bodding states that the Santals burn with the head south. (*Census of India*, 1931; I: 3, p. 102). Elwin finds that the Baigas bury with the head south. (*The Baigas*, p. 296).

new white cloth and is ready to be interred. Nothing in the way of money, implements, or the like is buried with the deceased.

The grave is now ready to be filled. Some words of farewell may be spoken. If the person be an adult, words like this are said by the chief mourner: "*Aj se tumhara hamara ho chuka. Jo ham se banta tha wuh main kar chuka. Aj se tum ham alag ho gaye.*" "From this day our connection is severed. I did whatever was possible. From this day we are separated." Then all say "*Jao, tum baikunth dham sudharo.*" "Go now, go to your dwelling place in paradise."

For children and young people, who seem to have been cut off untimely, these words are spoken: "*Jao, ab kisi ke ghar ana to pura din leke ana.*" "Go, and if you are born in another's house, come with a full life."

While the chief mourner speaks he throws in his handfuls of earth—five or seven. When he has completed the others may throw in some handfuls of earth and all join in doing so. After the body is fairly well covered a layer of thorns and stones is put in. Then more earth and at least another layer of thorns and stones and maybe a third, before the grave is filled. The remaining earth is piled in a small mound over the grave and last of all some flattened stones may be laid on top of it. When asked why the thorns and stones are laid the answer has uniformly been that it is to prevent the body being disturbed by flesh-eating animals, which probably would release the spirit. In view of other common beliefs, it may be that this explanation is a rationalization, as it is quite commonly believed that the stones and thorns may bar the return of the spirit to life and keep any other spirit from gaining possession of the body.

Circumambulation of the Grave. Before the burial is actually completed there is generally a circumambulation of the grave. This does not always occur and there are variations in the procedure. Sometimes it takes the form of a horseshoe-like movement, never making a complete circle, but retracing the steps. The first move in this case is made by the chief male mourner, who goes to the east of the head, walks around the feet to the west of the head and returns. This is done seven times, after which he moves away. Others may follow suit, but usually they do it but once and follow the chief mourner. Another method is that of walking round the grave in a clock-wise direction, keeping the grave always on the right. This is done seven times by the chief mourner. Sometimes the movement about the grave is dispensed with altogether Except when finally leaving the place, one should never during the formalities turn the back toward the body or the grave. After that he should not look back but go straight on towards the village.

Before the mourners depart there are certain other things that should be done. The two pice previously mentioned should be laid at the northern end of the grave. These the Basor or some other low caste Hindu present will remove shortly afterwards. Some salt and some mustard seeds are also scattered over the grave. Salt is generally regarded as a protective and devil-scarer, while the mustard protects from evil spirits who are kept so busy picking up the tiny seeds that they have no time to think of evil. Sometimes a little milk and some millet seed are also scattered over the grave. Milk is an offering to Mother Earth.

It is not unusual to keep a fire burning over the place where the head is resting, though this is not the general custom. Such a fire should burn at least two days. This is managed by starting a fire and placing upon it two logs which keep on burning slowly for the next few days. Ordinarily the Kol puts no definite marker on the grave. The stones laid on top help to keep him from digging a new grave where an old was dug; yet it has been reported that in digging a new grave they have often come upon bones. Such a place is covered up and a new start made.

CREMATION. It was noted previously that the question whether a body should be burned or buried is, according to Kols, largely an economic one. Under modern conditions, especially near cities, where wood is scarce and expensive a cremation costs at least Rs. 5 and can hardly be afforded. Even then cremation is considered the most satisfactory method as it gives a greater freedom to the spirit. As long as the skeleton remains undecomposed in the grave, the spirit, if reborn into this world, will have to take some form like his previous one. If, however, the body is burnt and the bones largely consumed, the spirit is free to be reborn into anything else. There are other considerations in the mind of the Kol: children and unmarried young folk should always be buried, as should people dying from diseases such as leprosy, plague and smallpox. One dying of smallpox should on no condition be burned.

If the method of cremation is decided upon, the making ready of the body for this type of disposal is essentially the same as described above in the preparation for burial. Upon arrival at the *ghat*, the funeral pyre, rather than the grave, is prepared. In most cases the wood is purchased, although it is the custom for friends and relatives to bring bits of wood. Cow dung cakes may also be added. Ordinarily any kind of wood may be used, but some more Hinduized groups say that *chandan* (sandalwood—*Santalum album*) is preferred. They may buy seven small bits of it which they place over the seven important points of the body, which may be then considered as covered with *chandan* wood. In building the pyre no trench is usually constructed, but a good base is built up and the body laid on the pyre in the same manner as in the grave, head north, feet south; in the case of a man face downwards and for a woman face upwards. More wood is piled on top and the pyre is ready for ignition.

Lighting the Pyre. The fire is brought in an earthen vessel from the home of the deceased and is usually preserved by the use of burning cow dung cakes. It is the duty of the chief mourner to light the funeral pyre. If the deceased is a father or mother the eldest son, if he is of age, lights the fire. If the deceased is a son or daughter the father lights the pyre. If there is no parent, the eldest and closest male relative lights it. The chief mourner takes a torch lighted from the cow dung cakes and keeping the body to his right walks about the pyre seven times. At each round he touches the head with the burning torch. After the seventh time the torch is thrown into the pyre. After that others may also light various parts of the pyre.

It will be noted that so far the Hindu priest has not been called upon. Ordinarily he has no place in Kol funeral ceremonies. He is only utilized on the fairly rare occasions when Kols take the ashes to the river where they are thrown in ceremonially. In due course there follows a description of such ceremonies. But there is always a low caste Hindu present, usually from the Basor or Domar group in the case of the Kols, who collects the cast-off things—*charpai*, clothes, and the pice that may be left at the burning place or grave. Later he is given gifts at the house and has his part in the funeral feast.

Gathering the Ashes—Khari or *Rakhi.* Moving ahead, in order to keep the cremation account intact, it is found that on the third day after the cremation a party should return to the *murdyaghat* to collect the ashes. Some milk is first sprinkled, then the bones which are unburnt are collected. The chief mourner picks up the first pieces. This is done with the left hand and the pieces deposited in either a new cloth bag or a new *ghara*. Usually only the men pick up the bits of bones, but on occasions the women may assist. The pieces are kept in a suitable place for later disposal. The sooner this can be done the better; but as quick disposal is not always possible they are brought back from the *ghat* to the village. The ashes are never brought within the house, and preferably they should not be brought into the village, but this is not avoidable in all cases. It is usually the custom to hang the *ghara* in a tree at some distance from the house and village, although at times the *ghara* is buried after being sealed and the place above it is marked for later exhumation.

It is preferable that the bones be taken direct from the burning *ghat* to the place of disposal, a sacred river being the most suitable place. The Ganges and the Nerbudda are the best for this purpose; but if there is no immediate hope of being able to go to one of these all the bones and ashes except a mere fraction are thrown into a tank or a stream nearby and the residue is kept for a future trip to one of them. It may be two or three years before this can be done, and if a relative cannot take it a friend may do so.

After the ashes have been collected the place where the body was burned must be treated. It is first plastered, this being done by the women of the house, though the chief mourner may begin it. Over the plastered portion is now scattered the following, or some of the following: rice, rock salt, mustard seed, millet seed, and a little milk. A two-pice piece (*takka*) should also be deposited. These things have a dual purpose: they serve the spirit of the departed and also protect it from the encroachment of evil spirits. The growth of the mustard plant, should it sprout, is said to be something in memory of the departed. Sometimes a little sugar "for the ants" is also scattered over the plastered place.

Throwing the Ashes in the River. We were told at a centre about ten miles from the Nerbudda river, how the ashes should be dealt with if taken to the river. In this place following the more Hinduized types of behaviour, they make use of a Brahmin priest. He performs a ceremony which is called *sirana,* meaning the "head side"; probably signifying the resting place of the head. The ashes are brought to him in the bag or *ghara* and he reads some sacred words from his books and makes a prayer to Yama, the god of death, to accept the spirit of the deceased. This is followed by a prayer addressed to the sacred river, Nerbudda *Mai*. She is implored to accept the ashes and to give peace to the departed spirit. The ashes are then cast into the river. The Brahmin receives a fee in cash or offerings.

Further north the Kols look to the Ganges as the river into which the ashes should go if that is possible. The Kols in the south insist that the Nerbudda is just as sacred and as good as the Ganges. One man claimed that occasionally the ashes are divided, half being taken to the Nerbudda and the other half to the Ganges. The place where the ashes are thrown is called the *Kharighat* and the ceremony described as *khari thanda karna*—"the cooling of the ashes."

THE RETURN TO THE DWELLING PLACE. Whether the body has been buried or burned, the return from that place to the house is essentially the same. The party moves off one by one after encircling the spot, but presently the men linger and group themselves together, and the women do likewise in another group in the rear. Having once completed the round of the grave or cremation place, they should not look backwards lest the movement be interpreted by the spirit as an invitation to come along; or lest they be attacked. The women bring back with them any of the sweets that remained after placing them along the pathway as they went toward the funeral place, also some of the water left after washing the body. The sweets are cast into the tank or river in which they bathe, and the water is kept till they reach the house after the ceremonial bath, when a bit of it may be mixed with *haldi* and scattered on the chief mourner or others, and the rest used to put out any fires in the house.

Bathing. The ceremonial bath should be taken in a tank or a stream, and if necessary a detour is made to include one in their return trip. If neither is available water from a well may be used, but the actual bathing must be at some distance from the well and the water should be drawn by some one who was not at the burial ground. Whether the bath is taken at a tank or stream, the men should bathe first. The bathers should line up and if possible should all go under the water together. After being submerged once or twice they step back to the bank and proceed home in their wet clothes. The women then bathe following much the same procedure, and go home in wet clothes. Reaching there fresh water must be used to wash their feet and now they may enter the house.

Cleaning the House. During the next few hours after the return home there is much to do. All clothes have to be changed and the dirty ones washed, preferably by a Hindu *dhobi*. All the pots and vessels made of earthenware must be thrown out upon the refuse pile. Sometimes they are broken and at other times are set out and the Domar or Basor comes and takes them away. The floors and walls of the house have to be plastered and thoroughly cleaned. The chief male mourner must have his head and face shaved, but a little tuft of hair, the sacred scalp lock or *chutiya*, is generally left. Usually a Hindu *nai* is called in for this, although the work may also be done by a Kol. Often all male members of the family are shaved in this manner. Nothing is done to the female mourners to correspond with this. Unkempt hair and dirty clothes are the signs of their mourning.

MOURNING FOR THE DEAD (*Daswi*). This may also be considered as the period of uncleanness, although many Kols do not recognize it as such. The number of days that the dead should be mourned, and certain taboos observed, varies according to sex and age. For a man or for a married youth the period is ten days, hence "*daswi*";—for a woman or a married maiden nine days; for a child it varies according to age: five days, three days, or, if it is a very small child there is no period of mourning at all. All over the area the customs are uniform in the cases of men and women, but for children there seems to be a considerable variation of custom.

During the period of mourning certain foods are taboo and certain kinds of cooking vessels must not be used in the preparation of food. Only simple food should be eaten: nothing should therefore be cooked in *ghi* or oils. No salt or flesh of any kind should be taken. The cooking vessels which are taboo are those in which rich foods are prepared and cooked in oils and *ghi*, such as a frying pan. This rules out the cooking of *puris*. The food during that period must always be eaten at home, and on no account should one accept food cooked in another's house or by someone who is not a member of the family, even if it is cooked in his own house. Violators of these regulations are dealt with by the *panch*. One should also stay pretty close to home, and should not freely enter others' houses, especially at the time they are eating.

FEEDING THE DEAD. The Kols have a custom of feeding the dead which they generally call *dona*, or *dauna rakhna*. The dead should be fed twice daily during the period of mourning if one can afford it, and if not, once in the evening. This is discontinued after the funeral feast. The chief mourner is generally expected to prepare this food, or it may be prepared along with the ordinary household food. Such food is placed on a *dona*, leaf-plate, and is taken out from the house to a distance of from thirty to forty yards, in the direction of the graveyard. This is placed in the crotch of a tree or it may be set down on the ground. Other things may also be placed there, things the

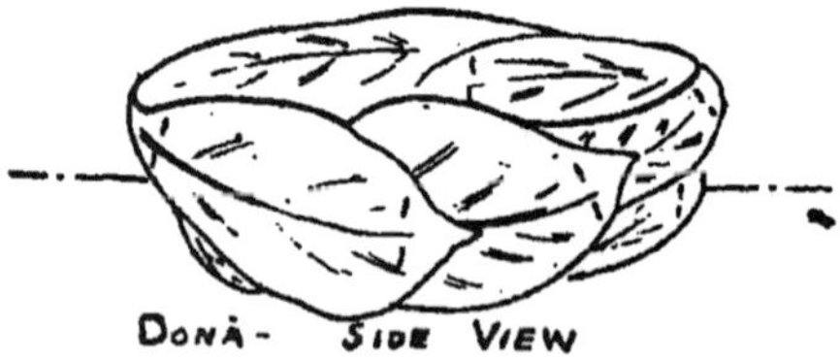

Fig. 23

departed liked best in life : sweets, tobacco, and the like. A little water is generally left too. They assert that liquor is never put out. As soon as the food is set out they quickly turn and do not look back lest they should disturb the eater. If the *masan* is not too far away the food may

DONÂ - LEAF PLATE ON WHICH THE DEAD ARE FED

Fig. 24

be placed on the grave. The usual procedure, though, is to place it near the old home. The belief is that the spirit of the deceased wanders about for ten days and frequents his old haunts. After ten days *dutas*, corresponding to angels, come for the soul and conduct it to another realm. The Kols seem to have no great fear of the spirits of their departed. Nothing is done to appease their anger, and they are thought to be in general kindly disposed toward their loved ones. There was some evidence of fear in a few cases where, they said, if the ashes are not deposited in the river the spirits might come and trouble them ; but this may be a part of another outlook. On the whole Kols regard their dead as kindly. The food, which they set out day by day, is consumed by birds or other animals. There is no special kind of food placed out, merely that used by them in the house during the time of mourning.

FUNERAL FEAST (*Din Pani*). If the deceased was a male the funeral feast occurs on the tenth day after the death, and if a female on the ninth day. The time of the feast after a child's death is not so uniform. Unless the child is grown up and rather important, it is not usual to have a feast ; or if there is one it is a private one within the home. But in the case of adults such a feast must always be given, otherwise the honour of the tribe would be tainted, and the family rebuked by the *panch*. On the morning of the feast preparations for it are made in the house.

The home is plastered, the barber is called and the faces are shaved and the nails of both hands and feet are pared. A special bath is taken and clean clothes put on. The people who are invited to such a feast are usually only relatives, though occasionally a larger group of the deceased's tribal friends may be invited. Others, who do not actually eat, are there to watch and talk, making quite a crowd. Special food has been prepared, and the things tabooed during the period of mourning are freely made use of and eaten at the feast. Hereafter all the members of the household, except the chief mourner, may freely partake of any food and there are no restrictions. The chief mourner eats this food at the feast, but for a year following must continue to observe the food taboos of the first ten days as noted above. There are no dishes or food peculiar to the funeral feast; it and the wedding feast may be much alike as far as the kinds of foods are concerned—rice, pulse, curries, of either vegetables or meats, *puris*, *bara*, *dahi*, *chapatis*, and the like. The presence of a large group is considered desirable and is a sign of solidarity.

The first morsel consumed at the funeral feast should not be taken by a Kol. It is usually the custom to call in a Hindu lower caste man, a Basor, who eats this. At this time he is called *Mahabrahmin*—great priest.[1] He is summoned only in the case of adults. Certain of the deceased's possessions are also his right and he is given things such as the axe, knife, sickle, *khurpi*, etc. In Maihar the general report was that a Basor is never called in for any funeral feast. When called in it is the duty of the Basor to take the first morsel of food. He also has a right to take away with him the vessels from which he has eaten, should they be of brass. If he is fed on a leaf plate he has the right to certain brass vessels used in serving. At any rate he gets something. No one can begin to eat till he has begun, and often he delays it, asking for a boon or gift of some kind. The Kols have been able to give no explanation of why he must be called. A Basor was also asked, and he said that it is because Kols fear to take the first bite, as it must be offered to the deceased and in his name. He might therefore come and possess the person who takes the first bite, and to avoid this possibility they call some one who is not of their family. Is not the Basor afraid? we enquired. No, he is not. The word *Mahabrahmin* is usually applied to the funeral priest, who is himself a Brahmin. Crooke[2] has given an account of his duties: the Basor seems to perform his duties for the Kols and they in return call him *Mahabrahmin*.

1 Dr. Guha suggests that the importance attached to the Basor may indicate that these observances were borrowed from the Hindus and that the Basor is the symbol of the Hindus.

2 Crooke, William, *Religion and Folklore of Northern India*, p. 144.

After the Basor begins the others may start and all set out to enjoy themselves. Liquor is sometimes freely consumed on such occasions.

Another feast, a family one called *barkhi* (H. *Barsi*), is given after a year, and after this the chief mourner can eat as he likes; it also marks his entry into the society once again. During the year of mourning it is sometimes his custom to eat normal foods at home, but never to go to a feast elsewhere.

MISCELLANEOUS DEATH CUSTOMS. After the return from the graveyard there is no formal visiting of the spot unless it be for the purpose of putting food upon the grave. After three or four days someone from the household may pay the graveyard an informal visit to see if everything is all right and that the grave has not been disturbed by animals. No flowers are put on the grave at any time, and the bones are never dug up and buried again at some other place. Kols also say that they never throw bodies into the streams, although we were informed by one of them that it is sometimes done. At Satna in Rewa State it was related that some times a male corpse may be taken to a river, where the head is shaven by the Hindu *nai* whom they pay two to four annas. As the body is about to be cast into the river the mourners announce that they are ready to give the river a gift, naming a certain sum of money, which they will pay to the Brahmin presiding over that part of the river. The usual amount is Rs. 1-4. This is called *gaunda*—alms. As the body floats away they shout "Go and get salvation" and also the words, "we've been so long together, but from now on we are separated, you from us and we from you, and we shall now have nothing more to do with each other." After this they return to the house and bathe and prepare things as previously related.

There are adjustments necessary within the family after the death of the father or the mother. If the wife has died, all her clothes must be given away to the Domar or Basor. A second wife should never wear the clothes of a deceased woman. However, she may wear the metallic jewellery and ornaments of the first wife, and they are usually given to her.

If the father should die his clothes should also be given away. The widow has to break her glass bangles and this is usually done at the place and the time of the funeral. They may be broken by a member of the family, or a Hindu *nai* may be called. The widow is not required to put away her metallic ornaments.

There is no trace of *sati* or widow burning among the Kols. We found none who had ever heard of a Kolin doing it. One man said: "We cannot get such faithful wives—they prefer to run away," and there was a hearty laugh.

In some parts of India the bodies of young children are sometimes buried under the floor of the house in which they lived but this custom does not prevail among the Kols. Children are buried in the regular *masan*, and not in a special place by themselves. If both mother and child die at the time of childbirth they are buried together in one grave. If they die on different days so that they cannot be buried together they are given separate burials.

Those dying abnormal deaths, by suicide, accident, or childbirth, are not treated differently from those dying in other ways. Kols are unlike most Hindus in this respect.

Sometimes grass plays a part in the funeral ceremonies, and in Rewa State we found that Kols used *urai* grass (*Vetiveria zizanioides*) at such a time. It was stated that at the time of bathing after the return from the funeral ground a bunch of *urai* grass should be held in the right hand and that it too should be bathed. At least the chief mourner should do this. During the following days and until the time of the funeral feast this same bunch of grass should be carefully washed every day. On the day of the funeral feast it is thrown into the tank or river.

An interesting explanation of the use of small plugs if gold put into holes bored in the front teeth came from the Rewa State. It was said that when one died and the body was cremated the teeth would not be consumed by the fire and the gold would still be in them Or even if the gold had melted out it would be in the ashes, and would be gathered with them and taken to the river. The throwing of gold into a river, particularly the Ganges, is a gift to the gods and pleases them and the spirit gets *aram*—rest—in the after life in *baikuntha*—the abode of *Vishnu*.

Tattoo marks are said to have a certain significance at the time of death. This applies to women as the men are not tattooed. If a woman has tattoo marks on her forearm, and also on her upper arm, the arms are so folded when she is placed in the grave that the two tattooed places touch each other. This is said to somehow afford protection, please the gods and help the spirit on its way.[1] See also pages 29 and 30.

The chief mourner should also keep a piece of iron about his person during the days of mourning, and possibly ever after. Sometimes, just before burial, this piece which is to act as a charm, is touched to the

[1] See Crooke, *Op. Cit.*, p. 298.

brow of the deceased seven times as the mourner encircles the body. It is then put into the clothes and carried about.

If a woman is carrying a *ghara* of water and sees a dead body she should at once throw out the water and return to get a fresh supply.

KOL CONCEPTION OF THE SOUL AFTER DEATH. It was noted that it is not a general belief among the Kols that the spirits of the dead return to trouble the family. The belief that the spirit of a pregnant woman becomes a *churel* is well known but even this is not consistently held. Further comments on this aspect will be found in a later section.[1]

Generally speaking, the Kols believe that the spirits of the good dead go to a place called *baikuntha* which in a general sense corresponds to a place of happiness, or paradise. The wicked may sometimes return as evil spirits—a male as a *bhut* and a female as a *churel*; but one must be rather wicked to be so severely punished. Others say that the spirits of the bad go to *narkunda*, the Hindu hell, a sort of well or pit in the lower regions.

The Kols know the doctrine of *samsara* or transmigration of souls, but they seem to have neither a clear idea of its details nor of its implications. While this belief is usually admitted when they are questioned and reflected in some of their practices, nevertheless the general conception seems to play but a minor part in their thinking of the present and the future. "From now on we have nothing to do with one another."

1 See Chapter IX : Churel.

CHAPTER VIII

RELIGION AND ATTENDANT FESTIVALS

Life apart from religion is unthinkable to the Kols. It has already been seen that their social activities are permeated with religion and magic. Nothing is done without reference to the all-pervading mysterious powers, for all of life's events may be traced to their activities, and it is fatal to be out of harmony with them. It is the duty of each individual as well as the whole community to keep the spirits contented and propitious so that they will aid them against the evils of life brought on by demons such as *bhuts*, *churels*, and the like. The Kols endow these spiritual beings with a form of personality; they have an objective existence, and are able to make or mar the future. Consequently, they cannot be ignored, and must be propitiated in divers ways.

The religious rites and tribal regulations of the Kols are all intended to strengthen a totalitarian conception of life. To their type of mind life cannot be broken up into compartments and there is thus no clear line of demarcation between economic, social and religious spheres. These three are really one, and their harmony and stability must be maintained, and to break it at one point is to break it as a whole. Anything which may seem to change the existing order of things is dreaded by people such as we are studying.

DIVINE ORDERS. The Kols of Central India hold that there are certain Divine Orders which ought to be respected and acknowledged, even though all are not implored. Here are some typical examples:

(1) Bhagawan—the Supreme One.
(2) Bhagavati—a mediator as Khermai and others.
(3) Shardamai of the "Seven Sisters."
(4) Kalimai—really one of the "Seven Sisters."

Another group:

(1) Bhagawan.
(2) Shivari—the Mother of all Kols.
(3) Shardamai of the "Seven Sisters."
(4) Khermai—a mediator.

Again:

(1) Bhagawan.
(2) Bhagavati—a mediator.

(3) Earthly King—"whoever he may be."

And a fourth:

(1) Bhagawan.
(2) Bhanmati—(meaning Bhagavati).
(3) Kalka of the "Seven Sisters."
(4) All others who are personally worshipped.

It has been noted that almost without exception the Kols speak of Bhagawan as the highest of all deities. The Supreme Deity of the Munda Tribes of Chota Nagpur is quite uniformly said to be Sing Bonga.[1] Crooke, in his *Tribes and Castes of the North West Provinces and Oudh* noted almost fifty years ago that the Kols knew nothing of Sing Bonga.

This is true of Central India to-day, for Kols have lost any recollection of this name as representing the Supreme Deity. Although Bhagawan is fairly consistently spoken of as the Supreme Being, nevertheless in the life of the Kols he is of small efficacy. He is not likely to pay much attention to Kols and no Kol priest knows how to approach him; only the Brahmins are said to have that ability. Kols have thus no exalted conception of Bhagawan. He is a passive distant Being influenced only by such mediators as Khermai and the like, and even then his actions are thought to be rather unstable and unpredictable. While Kols must without fail make offerings to *devatas* and *devis* yet they never make an offering directly to Bhagawan. If as a last resort an offering should be deemed advisable, a Kol may give a Brahmin a little money and ask him to make an offering and try to influence Bhagawan in his behalf. The very best Kols can do is to sing to Bhagawan. At such a time *bhagat* songs—songs of devotion—are used. Occasionally a *katha* is employed to invoke and praise Bhagawan: a Brahmin is called in and recites sacred stories (*kathas*). This, however, is infrequent among Kols and is practised mostly by higher castes. Again, the *hom* or fire offering, useful on all occasions, may be utilized, and at that time Bhagawan is invoked along with lesser deities. It is the ever-present *devis* who should be taken into account. The first step, according to Kols, is to please them. For example, Khermai, being a mediator between men and the great gods, can influence Bhagawan, but while the latter is more powerful than the *devis* and can overrule them, it is not often that he takes the trouble to do so.

Bhagawan is sometimes given the attributes of the lesser *devatas*

[1] Dalton, E. T., *Descriptive Ethnology of Bengal*, pp. 130, 132, 133, 141, etc.

and *devis*. For example, it is stated that he is able to send certain diseases such as smallpox and cholera. But while he may send them, it is of no use to ask him to banish them; for this a lesser deity like Khermai should be invoked. It is only if she fails, and if it seems necessary to avert further distress, that they will call to him and promise him that if he will save them they will send for a *pandit* and have a *katha* in the name of Bhagawan. It is our opinion that there is little trace, if any, of a higher conception of Bhagawan among the Kols of this area.

The contacts of the Kols with higher Hinduism is feeble and markedly inconsistent. Both Vishnuite and Sivaite elements are inextricably mixed, and while Rama, Krishna and other *avataras* of Vishnu are known and stories about them are related, they have nevertheless almost no significance in actual religious ceremonies. Again, while the phallic symbols characteristic of Sivaites are not often used by Kols, nor Sivaite temples frequented, nevertheless Kali, the wife of Siva, is propitiated. Taken as a whole, the Kol worship has in it but little of adoration. It is mostly a matter of propitiation. When asked why they do not worship in certain near-by Hindu temples, the answer has been that their fathers never worshipped there and why should they.

NATURE WORSHIP. In connection with the worship of the Supreme One, mention should be made of the relation of the Kols to the forces of nature, so often deified in Hindu thought. Primitive peoples all seem to have respect for the powers of the sky, air and earth; and while in the case of the Kols it appears to have lost its primitive expression, and become Hindu in ideology, it is nevertheless apparent in their thought.

The Sun. The Sun is usually thought of as a great God, a beneficent deity who is the source of all heat and light. It is stated that their forefathers worshipped the sun, and that they do also, but on examination this worship turns out to be very formal. The village shrine often faces the rising sun, but no image of the sun is ever made. He is often called *Suryanarayana*, Sun-God.

No disrespect should be shown to the sun. When going to the fields for a call of nature, the Kol never squats without first ascertaining where the sun is, and as far as possible keeps it always to his right. The back, the front, and especially the left hand should never be toward it at such times.

The Moon. Some Kols consider the moon a goddess, while others do not seem to regard it in the category of deity at all. They say there is nothing one does in relation to it. The moon is thought of as feminine and the sun as masculine, for the moon is cold and the sun is hot. There are a number of beliefs and superstitions concerning the moon. It is good luck to see the new moon before any stars are out in the sky. On seeing the new moon for the first time a Kol may either tear a corner off one of his garments and cast it toward the moon, or may hold up the garment toward the moon, saying: "Take these old clothes and give me new ones." It is usual at the same time to take worn-out pieces of cloth or just rags, and hang them on the tree near the house. This attracts the goddess of torn clothes, Chithra *devi*, who will bring good luck and in the course of time new garments.

The moon is thought to have no evil influences upon men folk and therefore is not feared by them. Women, however, are likely to be affected by the moon and as far as possible should avoid it. Pregnant women especially should not expose themselves to the moon as it is liable to cause a miscarriage or a deformed infant.

The time of an eclipse of either the sun or the moon is a time of special precaution and worship. The Kols say that the sun is devoured by a giant whom they call Dhrubh. The concept that a demon devours the sun is common all over India, but the usual Hindu concept is that it is swallowed by one named Rahu, the "looser or seizer." The Kol story goes that both the sun and the moon at one time borrowed something from Dhrubh, whom Kols call the brother of Indra. This debt must be repaid, and if at any time the sun or the moon is not able to pay on the debt, it is attacked by Dhrubh who begins to devour it. He never quite does so, however and vomits it up, as there is still money owing and payments must go on. Others say that Dhrubh is merely jealous of the moon because she is worshipped and adored while he is not. Therefore he attacks either the sun or the moon. One should bathe at the time of an eclipse. During such a time women should remain inside for it is a very dangerous season especially if they are with child. The men may go out to bathe, sing and beat the drums. Wicked spirits are abroad, and unless the women are protected by charms, they are liable to be attacked. After the release of the sun or moon, the women go out to bathe. The Nerbudda is the best place in Central India, but any tank or river will do if one cannot go so far. After bathing they should give some alms to Basors who will be waiting near by. They give to no others.

At home no food is prepared or eaten during the eclipse. Nothing cooked is left in the house, and all uncooked food should be carefully protected so as not to become a prey to the evil spirits. All the earthen vessels used in connection with food and water should be thrown out and new ones brought in. Metal vessels are not affected. Hindu influences are apparent.

Rivers. The Kols say that there are but two rivers in India which are really sacred, the Ganges and the Nerbudda. They put the Ganges in the first place. Like most Hindus, Kols believe that it is good to bathe in these rivers and that to do so will help to wash away sin and give one merit. Kols in the vicinity of Jubbulpore frequently go to the Nerbudda, but seldom to the Ganges.

GODS AND GODDESSES WORSHIPPED BY KOLS. The worship to which the Kols really give themselves is not that of the gods of the Hindu pantheon, nor the forces or the powers of nature, but rather of the village deities—*deotas* and *devis*—who are intimately connected with their daily life and outlook. The majority of these deities are female, and it is such deities that really count. They are termed "mothers," and many have *mai* meaning "mother" attached to their name. The male deities are called *babas*, "fathers"; or *deos*, "godlings."

The Kol Pantheon. Among Hindus the Supreme Being is worshipped as Vishnu by the Vaishnavas and as Siva by the Saivas. Others who worship the Supreme deity exclusively as a female principle are called Saktas. The wives of Vishnu or Siva may be worshipped as Lakshmi and Parvati, thus introducing the female principle. Nevertheless the *devi* is secondary to the *deva*. In the case of Sakti worship, the Devi is made supreme and the absolute Brahma from whom Brahma, Vishnu and Siva proceed, can do nothing without her activity. This form of religion is seen particularly in Tantra and Sakta Hinduism.

The goddess of the Saktas may be called by the general term "Devi," but is worshipped in many forms. Various aspects of her life or achievements are remembered under different names, and she even may assume the form of a male. The worship of Devi is usually associated with Siva, rather than Vishnu, and many of the concomitants of Saivitism are associated with her worship.

From the evidence that follows, which is largely from the lips of Kols, it would appear that the Devi principle is the main factor at work in the Kols' idea of deity. Khermai is occasionally given an all-inclusive aspect. Bhagavati is essentially Devi. She has "six sisters" who are really forms of herself.[1] Kols have never been

[1] "In all parts of South India the seven sisters are the most prominent among Dravidian deities." —Elmore, W. T., *Dravidian Gods in Modern Hinduism*, p. 19. He names the following as examples, though he notes their names vary from place to place: Poleramma, Ankamma, Muthyalamma, Dilli Polasi, Bangaramma, Mathamma and Renuka.

able to name for us just who the six are, but the following are among those included: Athabhuji, Bhanmati, Bindajali, Bindra Basni, Bindawasnimai, Chandni, Chandika, Kalimai, Kalka, Khermai, Maridevi, and Shardamai. It is not unlikely that others may be brought under the same principle, for Khermai acts as village watchman and protector, as well as guardian against spirits, disease, and death. In this latter aspect, she does the work of Bairam, Jognimai, Mahamai, Maridevi, Phulmatimai and Sitalamai.

The following list of Kol deities can hardly be arranged in the order of their importance to the Kol and therefore are listed alphabetically. Of course no one group has given all these names in any one list, and there is much overlapping. Lists made on the field have never agreed either as to the number or their order in importance. Sometimes we were assured that a certain deity was the foremost of all, yet a few miles away her name was not even mentioned. A few of the deities stand out in importance, and are discussed at greater length. No pretence is made of giving all the information available elsewhere about the gods and goddesses found in the Kol pantheon and no detailed comparative study has been attempted. What is related below is based upon what Kols have told us and presents their point of view:

Female Deities.

Alop
Anjanidevi
Asmanidevi (or mai)
Athabhuji
Bairam
Barmati
Bhagavati
Bhanmati
Bindajali
Bindra Basni
Bindawasnimai
Burimai
Chandika
Chandni
Chithra devi
Desh hari
Dhartimai
Hinglaj devi

Male Deities.

Baghdeo.
Bahanar Singh Deo.
Barandeo.
Barum baba.
Basdeo.
Bhainsokhar.
Bhaino.
Bhainsasor.
Bhuiyan.
Burhadeo.
Dulhadeo.
Gurdayal.
Gwalabansa baba.
Hardaul.
Khetrapal.
Mahabir.
Mansa deo.
Nanga baba.

Jalni
Joginimai
Jogni
Kalimai.
Kalka.
Karmasin.
Khermai.
Lorhadhar.
Mahamai.
Marhai.
Marhimai.
Paramjiyoti.
Phonamukhi.
Phulmatimai.
Raktpiyasi.
Shardamai.
Shivari.
Sitalamai.
Phul.
Sannyasi deo.

FEMALE DEITIES WORSHIPPED BY KOLS

Alop. This deity is not widely worshipped. She is able to disappear very suddenly and reappear just as suddenly elsewhere.

Asmani devi. "The heavenly one." This *devi* is the one who generally protects individual houses. She is particularly popular around Jubbulpore, but further north is not so often mentioned. Her shrine is found in connection with the house, and a white flag, or a white segment on a red flag, usually indicates her presence. Her favourite offering is a young female pig. She is usually worshipped just outside the house, although she may also be found within. The accompanying diagram shows a typical shrine to Asmani devi. She is frequently called Asmanimai.

Athabhuji. This is the goddess of eight hands. Kols are not clear about her, but probably this is a term for the wife of Siva, called Uma, Parvati, Durga, Kali and Bhavani.

Bairam. This deity is generally female, but sometimes is considered a male deity. She is usually kept outside the house, and seldom, if ever, within it. The Kols say that her chief work is to frighten away evil spirits—*bhuts*. As long as she is near the doorway, such will not dare to enter. The name may be related to the hero Bhairon, or may be a confusion with Barambaba.

Bhagavati. Really means "one who is a devotee"—a *bhagat*.

This is a very general term with Kols and usually refers to one of several. Khermai, Shardamai, and the like are frequently called Bhagavati.

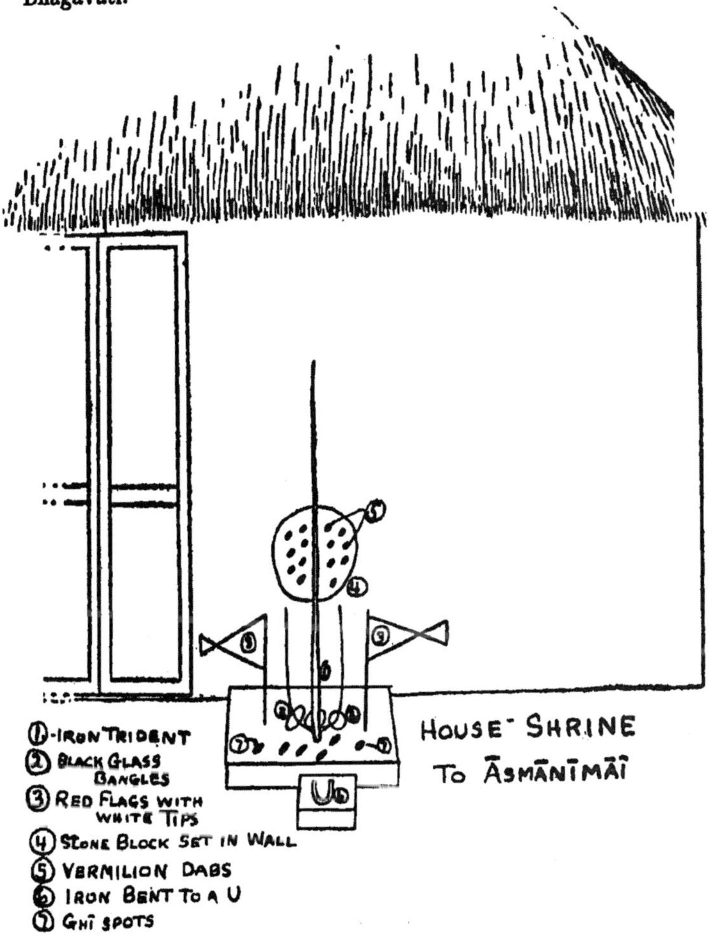

Fig. 25

Bindajali, *Bindra Basni*, *Bindawasnimai* are goddesses who had their origin in the Bind mountains, the modern Vindhyas. While not very important to the Kols of today, nevertheless they may represent the names of some of their deities in other days when they lived in the Vindhya mountains. It is not unlikely that they are forms of Kali.

Buri devi. "Bad Goddess." Sometimes this is made a male and called Bura Deo. It is probable that this is connected with the chief Gond deity, Buradeo. This deity is not widely worshipped among the Kols, but should a sacrifice be necessary she prefers a female kid of reddish colour.

Chandika. This deity is said to have one body and two mouths, one in the front and the other in the back, and is a form of Kali.

Chithra devi. Goddess of torn clothes. This deity is worshipped in connection with the new moon, when a piece of torn cloth should be offered her, good clothes held up, or some cloth tied to a Tamarind tree. In this manner she helps one to get new clothes.[1]

Dhartimai. The goddess of the earth. Worship and ceremonies in connection with this deity are observed at the time of ploughing and threshing, but only by the agricultural Kols. A *hom* offering is all that is usually given her. Probably she is related more closely to the Hindu pantheon than are those requiring a bloody offering.

Jalni. Some Kols claim that Jalni is the Creator of the universe. This may refer to Jalpati, the Hindu deity presiding over water. The Kols have the legend that before there was an earth all was water. Jalni, however, is not much worshipped by Kols.

Jogni devi. Frequently called Jognimai, is a goddess who particularly cares for children. The picture shows a shrine outside the home.[2] The pole above has black bangles and drops of *ghi* may be observed at the base. When children are ill, or in danger, or affected by the power of evil spirits, Jognimai should be propitiated. At the time of a smallpox epidemic, one of the parents offers her a cocoanut and pours water over her shrine, in order that she may not allow the smallpox to attack the children.

A Kol who worked on the railway claimed that it was Jognimai that caused the locomotives to run. He would often make an offering to her just before the locomotive started.

Kulimai. Kalimai is very popular among all the lower classes, and the Kols have also accepted her. While they do not give her the chief place, which is usually given to Shardamai, yet she is said to be one of the six sisters of Shardamai. It is not customary for Kols to have a shrine to her alone. When she is worshipped, it is at the village shrine along with the other deities such as Khermai, more generally worshipped by Kols of the village. Her colour is black, and black in a flag over a shrine indicates that she may be worshipped there. She should be offered darkish-coloured cocoanuts, or if animal sacrifices

1 See page 131.
2 See plate xxii.

A shrine to the Buffalo god Bhainsokhar, at Benda. The plant growing on the platform is the Tulasi.

Kol shrine to Khermai in

Shrine to Jogni devi beside

A Village shrine near Sihora. The Panda stands at the right. The shrine is at the base of a Nim tree.

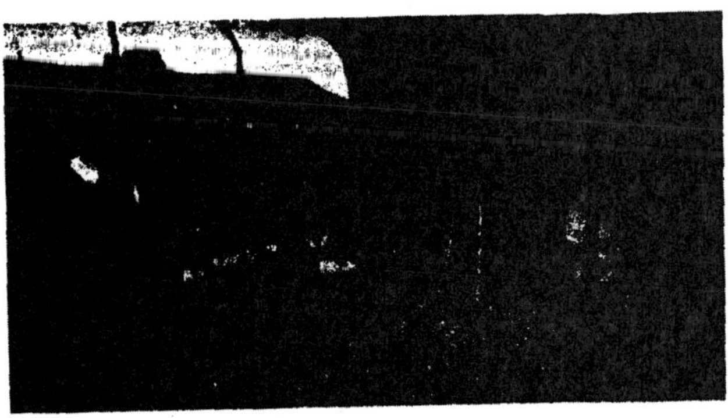

A closer view. Note the iron lash, Salagrama stone, flags and spiked sandals.

are made, the animal should be of a black colour. Black glass bangles will also be attached to her part of the shrine or found where she is worshipped. She likes the Tulasi plant and sometimes lives in it.

Occasionally she is a household goddess and is worshipped along with other household deities.

When the spirit of Kali possesses a worshipper, he can walk without discomfort or injury on spiked sandals.[1]

Kalka. Is one of Sharda's six sisters. She is seldom invoked, for according to Kols, when Shardamai or Kalimai are worshipped she is happy and pleased.

Khermai. This *devi* is probably the one most frequently worshipped by Kols. The Census Report classes her as the Earth Goddess[2] and Crooke[3] believes Khera to be the same as Khetrpal, the field guardian. Sometimes it would appear that the term included many kinds of deities such as Kali and Sitalamai. Her shrine is found in or near every Kol village, and she is always mentioned; it is also frequently claimed that she must be considered first, subsequently any others that one might choose. Sometimes she is called Bhagavati and is said to be the best mediator between men and Bhagawan, for if she is kept pleased and contented, one does not have to worry about Bhagawan.

Khermai's duties are manifold. She is the village watchman and protector. She wards off evil spirits and prevents their entry into the village. Sometimes her shrine is placed at the south of the village to ward off the evil spirits which so frequently come from that direction. In times of illness, she is invoked, and is thought to be intimately connected with disease; when one has smallpox she is worshipped in the person who is stricken. Cholera and smallpox are sometimes said to come directly from Bhagawan, and she is the best protector in case he sends them. On such occasions she should be given a libation of water and the village may be "tied" with her help.[4]

She is thought to help the Kols in all kinds of difficulties; she guards a man going on a journey; as he leaves, he may promise her an offering of a cocoanut which he will give if he returns safely. At set times she possesses her devotees, and through them reveals her will and answers their questions on problems confronting them. The sure test of her presence is the power to thrust an iron trident through the tongue or cheek.

1 See pp. 148, 160.
2 *Census of India*, 1911. X:1, p. 89.
3 Crooke, W., *Religion and Folklore of Northern India*, pp. 92, 93.
4 See Chapter IX, Tying the Village.

Khermai is offered many things: a few annas may be left at the shrine; cocoanuts are a favourite offering; *ghi*, *puris*, *balasa*, and *ganja* are forms of food and drugs which please her and are frequently placed before her shrine. She likes *sendur* marks here and there about the place where she is worshipped, and incense is welcomed. Lemons and limes are always acceptable and should be placed before her. They also prevent the evil spirits from molesting the place.

If the occasion is sufficiently serious, an animal sacrifice is made to Khermai. Apparently no particular colour is required, although in one centre it was said that should a chicken be offered, it should be white. She likes young female animals: pig, kid or lamb. These are later eaten at a ceremonial meal in connection with the shrine.

Khermai is best worshipped under a *nim* tree (*Melia azadirachta*), and her shrine is generally found there. If there is no *nim* tree available, a *pipal* (*Ficus religiosa*) or a *bel* (*Aegle marmelos*) tree will do. She is generally worshipped after sunset, although this is not always the rule, especially if there is an emergency In summer time when it is hot and dry, some *gharas* of water are kept at the shrine and people frequently pour water over the shrine to cool the *devi*.

If any danger threatens the village or an epidemic is near, some milk, liquor and powdered charcoal may be mixed and sprinkled about the village in her name. This is followed by an animal sacrifice and a ceremonial meal at the shrine. In case of smallpox, in addition to the regular offerings, she may be given a bath each day for ten days. Then a mixture of oil and turmeric powder is poured out before her.

Mahamai. "The Great Mother." This goddess is the same as Sitalamai, the goddess of smallpox and the name is an euphemistic title. Kols are not always clear concerning the relationship of the two and sometimes they have been named together. A red flag indicates the presence of this deity.

Marhai. Is said to be the goddess of death, but under this name at least, does not seem to be very important, and no satisfactory information can be given about her by the Kols. She is probably the same as Maridevi..

Maridevi. The goddess of epidemics, particularly of cholera and plague. By some informants she is said to be Khermai's elder sister. She is very powerful, and there is no better protector from these diseases than this goddess. In the Kaimur hills one group claimed that she was the most powerful of all the *devis* which they worshipped.

They said that she spreads and controls not only cholera and smallpox, but all sorts of diseases.

She should never be offered a chicken, because it is not valuable enough to please her. She desires a young goat or pig. The *hom* sacrifice is also pleasing to her and a cocoanut always is acceptable. Pots were noticed hung in trees, and it has been ascertained that these are for her to refresh herself on a hot day. In this way they hope to win her favour.

Phulmatimai. Is a sister of Sitalamai, goddess of smallpox, but causes a milder type of eruptive disease. An offering to Sitalamai is pleasing to her, and no further sacrifice need be offered.

Shardamai. Shardamai is generally placed at the head of their pantheon by nearly all Kols. Her name may be traced to the Sanskrit word *sarada* meaning autumnal. Her temple is near Maihar about 100 miles north of Jubbulpore, near the borders of Rewa State. It is situated on a steep hill which rises about five hundred feet above the surrounding plain, and can easily be seen to the west of the railway line. The spot is a very popular place of pilgrimage, both for Kols and other tribes and castes. A visit to this spot elicited much information about her and her worship. She has six sisters, according to informants, among them being found Kali, Kalki and Kalchi. In olden days animal sacrifices were made and the place ran with blood, but such are now prohibited by order of the authorities of Maihar State. Cocoanuts now represent the chief offering, but along with them *ghi*, *loban* (incense), *puris*, flowers, and the like are put before her. The hillside is literally covered with the shells of the cocoanuts broken before Shardamai. There are also images of other gods and goddesses under the same temple roof. These include Kali, the black goddess, wife of Siva; Narsingha, an incarnation of Vishnu; Bhagawan, the adorable one; Hanuman, the monkey god; Annapurna devi, here worshipped by the women desiring children; Chhatthi devi, worshipped on the sixth day after the child's birth, (and here the hair of the child's head is first shaved before her); Chandi devi, said to be a sister of Kali; Kotwali devi, the protector of the temple and the worshippers who come; and finally Kal Bhairo, said to be the son of Kali. In this strange company Shardamai is central and is *the* goddess of the whole.

While Shardamai dwells in Maihar and is localized as no other Kol deity, she is nevertheless also worshipped in the homes and at the village shrines. In some places a small earthen platform, about four feet square and raised some six inches above the ground, is sufficient. Upon this a trisul is stuck in the centre to represent the place of her worship. No image is found, but there are exceptions. In Rewa State it was said that she should be worshipped at least twice a year : two days before the *Dasara* festival (September-October) and eight days after Chaita (March-April).

While animal sacrifices are forbidden at the Maihar temple, they may still be offered at the village shrine.[1] One group said that a black kid was the only acceptable offering, while from others it was learned that chickens, lambs and suckling pigs may all be sacrificed. The usual vegetable offerings are likewise acceptable. She frequently possesses people and speaks through them.

Childless women, especially, should worship her and make offerings and sacrifices, so that she may speak to them through the *panda* and tell them what to do before they can expect children. Shardamai is therefore reverenced at this place by childless women. It is also claimed that she can restore sight and cause the blind to walk and is a general miracle worker.

During *Chaita*, the Hindu month corresponding to parts of March and April of the Christian calendar, there should be an evening fast to Shardamai covering nine days. Regular food may be taken only in the morning, and the evening meal should be limited to water, milk and water-nuts called *singhara* the Water-caltron (*Trapa bispinosa* or *natans*). On the ninth day the big offering to Shardamai must be made. Before anyone may partake of the meal on the ninth evening, a cocoanut[2] must first be broken before the village shrine and offered to her, and then the edible part distributed to those present. Thereafter regular meals may be taken. If possible someone from the village, or better yet several from the chief families should go to Maihar to worship. Their worship at Shardamai's temple and the worship at home will reinforce the bond of friendship which they must maintain.

Shivari or Sheori. Shivari is called the mother of all Kols and served Rama during his exile and search for Sita and has thus become deified. Shivari is nearly always listed by Kols, nevertheless actual worship of her is rare; but Kols talk of her temple somewhere in Rewa and also at Sheori-Narayan near Raipur, eastern Central Provinces. Stories concerning her are found in connection with the study of the origin of the Kols and in the chapter on legends.[3] She probably represents a tribal goddess.

Sitalamai. This name is a euphemistic title meaning the cool,

1 Kali worship is associated with animal sacrifice and Shardamai is probably equivalent to Durga in Hinduism.

2 Probably a relic of human sacrifice.

3 See pp. 8-10; also Chapter X.

the peaceful one, for she is the goddess of smallpox. The burning fever and high mortality are a terror to the village people. Any kind of kid is said to be acceptable to her, and a red flag usually marks her presence. This *devi* is mostly worshipped by Kol females, although both boys and girls go before her with vegetable and food offerings for five successive days. If men should be required to make the offering, on account of some home condition which prevents the women from going to the shrine, they must not be accompanied by any female relative, but must go alone. During an attack of the disease, the Kols suppose that the *devi* is actually dwelling in the person ill, and great care must be taken to keep her in a good humour. On no account should a Kol who dies of smallpox be cremated, as it is likely that the *devi* is still residing in him, and to burn his corpse would antagonize her.

This concludes the catalogue of the chief female deities worshipped by the Kols. In the future more information may be made available about the others not yet discussed at any length.

MALE DEITIES WORSHIPPED BY KOLS

Baghdeo. Baghdeo is the tiger god and is generally revered all through the jungle country of Central India. Certain of the tribes of this area have septs named after the tiger and it may be that there is a definite totemistic relationship. Russell and Hiralal[1] note that some of these primitive tribes such as Bhatia, Binjhwar, Kawar, Kharia, Kol, Korkus, Mowar, Rautia and Savara have septs relating to the tiger which may have totemistic implications. The Rautias, for example, are said to throw away their earthen pots on hearing of the death of a tiger. Other groups abstain from killing the tiger. In some cases the connection between taboos and totemism is very slight as Grigson has noted among the Hill Marias.[2] He also records[3] that the tiger was supplanted by the buffalo as the totem of one group "since tigers so far forgot themselves as to kill and eat some men of the phratry." Now they retaliate by joining the tiger beats! Among Gonds in general it appears that Bagh worship has become all but universal, and that this worship persists irrespective of clan, phratry or tribe. Since it is apparent that the worship of the tiger is largely confined to jungle areas, much of the worship is probably protective rather than totemistic. If there ever was a totemistic stage it is now long past and all but forgotten.

1 *Op. Cit.*
2 *The Maria Gonds of Bastar*, p. 239.
3 Page 241.

According to Kol legends tigers and Kols have been closely associated. This may refer to the jungle habitation of early Kols or it may have a totemistic aspect. Descent from the totem may be implied in the legend recorded on pages 41-42. But now the tiger and the Kol have separated and gone their own ways, this being symbolic of changes in the Kol way of living. The tiger is reverenced because he is feared. While Kols claim that they should never hunt the tiger nor assist in a beat, nevertheless this principle is often broken due to the temptation of money. This attitude may have a totemistic origin, but it also may be due to the fear that he will return evil for evil.

The tiger should be propitiated along with the household gods, but as a rule he is not included in them by people who live in areas where tigers are not to be expected. It is the Kol that lives in or near the jungle who fears the tiger. Baghdeo is offered a cocoanut, *chapatis* and other food. At the *Holi* season he should be given a chicken. The opinion is advanced that if this is overlooked Baghdeo may attack, kill, and eat male members of the family not sacrificing to him. It is claimed by these folks that he will never attack a woman or a girl. If he is pleased they may go into the mountains and jungle in search of wood and grass without fear of him. If he is met, he will pass them by, and should be respectfully spoken to. A Kol need not fear a tiger unless he has neglected his offerings to Baghdeo.

Bahanar Singh Deo is another of the Kol household gods and has the power to close the womb of the women folk and cause barrenness. In one centre it was said that women who desired children should come before him and sacrifice to him in preference to Shardamai. If Bahanar Singh should fail, then Shardamai may be tried. This *deo* is particularly fond of white offerings, and a white kid or chicken is preferred. This should be offered at the village shrine. At the time of offering the woman desiring children comes before the shrine with a pot of oil and *haldi*, into which she dips her right hand and somewhere about the shrine makes an impression of the whole of her hand. This attracts Bahanar Singh and helps him to identify the woman. The *panda* is there and cuts the animal, sprinkles the blood, and tells her what to do in order that her prayer may be granted. He may advise certain other offerings, and perhaps command that she abstain from certain foods, particularly rich ones, for a season.

Barum baba. Barum *baba* is quite often thought of as an evil spirit. In the Kaimur hills it is said that he always lives in *pipal* trees. No image or sign of his presence is made. The offerings are simply placed at the foot of the tree which he inhabits, and cocoanuts and *khichri* were mentioned as offerings. It was also asserted that he likes to have the sacred thread hung on the tree in which he is found. Animals are never sacrificed to him. One such tree, claimed to be the dwelling place of Barum *baba* was inspected, but there was no sign of offerings having been made there. As far as possible Kols avoid trees inhabited by him, particularly after dark.

In Rewa, Barum *baba* was said to be the spirit of a deceased Brahmin. Probably this is why the sacred thread is so acceptable to him as an offering and should be hung on the trees in which he resides.

Bas deo and Barum *deo* are probably the same in the thought of the Kol. These spirits prefer to live in the *bar* or Banyan tree, though they are reported as living in *pipal* trees as well. They are mostly thought of as vindictive and evil, but it is also said that they are somewhat afraid of people and that they try to please men if they can; it is good for man to get a vision of Bas *deo*.

Bhainsokhar, Bhaino, and *Bhainsasor* are all forms of the buffalo god or demon. Crooke has certain information in this connection.

> The Kols believe in Naga-era who occupies wells, tanks, and stagnant waters, the embodiment of malaria, and Garha-era, a water goddess, 'frequently and truly described as the cause of sickness, and propitiated with sacrifices to spare their victims' (from Dalton). Such spirits sometimes appear in the form of animals, like Bhainsasura, the buffalo demon akin to Mahishasura, with the same meaning, who gives its name to Mysore, the embodiment of death, like the black buffalo on which Yama, god of death, rides, which was slain by Durga, the life protecting goddess. They often show themselves in the shape of a turban which clings to the fisherman's hook and increases in size as he tries to drag it ashore or pulls him into the water—all impersonations of the vague awe and mystery of dark, still water pools. Hence they are special protectors of passengers at Ghats or fords.[1]

The Kols we interviewed are vague about this deity, but feel that the buffalo god is dangerous and ought to be propitiated. At Benda a shrine was found to him. A picture shows the white mound in the centre of a platform as his dwelling place.[2] The plants are *Tulasi*—the sacred basil.

Burha deo. This deity is probably the same as Bura *deo*, said to be the chief deity of the Gonds. While Kols know him, it appears that very little is actually done, other than that his name may be called at times of worship along with other lesser deities.

Dulha deo. The worship of Dulha *deo* or Dulha *baba* is widespread in Central India, and the Kols have much to do with him. He

1 Crooke, W., *Religion and Folklore of Northern India*, p. 60,

2 See plate xxii.

is the bridegroom deity. The general view is well summed up by Crooke:

> Strange, abnormal features of the scenery often become objects of veneration. In Mirzapur District there is a rock in the form of a hideous, grinning skull, with enormous teeth, known as Dantandeo, 'the demon with the teeth'. ....The same feeling is illustrated by the cult of Dulhadeo, 'the bridegroom deity', which is widely spread from the Central Provinces up to the hills which rise above the valley of the Ganges. He is one of the deified spirits of men suddenly slain before their desires were accomplished, and like others of his kind he should have become a Bhut or malignant spirit. But he is now generally regarded as a friendly household godling. Stone pillars and rocks are often associated with his tragic fate.......[1]

A Kol at Barela insisted that Dulha *deo* was the supreme deity, but generally speaking he is regarded by the Kols as a beneficent household god. He usually dwells within the house and a piece of stone placed in a notch in the wall and daubed with *sendur* indicates his presence. He is offered sacrifices at set seasons, but before each meal a little food should be put aside for him. If he is neglected and gets angry he may cause harm to the family. If he is to be venerated outside the house, a little mound of earth about eight inches high may be raised close to the wall of the house not far from the doorway. This is simply whitewashed and called Dulha *deo*.

Offerings made to him are much like those given to other deities. It is often said that he should never be offered a chicken. He prefers either a kid or suckling pig. His favourite time of worship is in the Hindu month of *Kunwar*, (September-October). This is the time his spirit possesses people and speaks through them.

In Rewa, Kols say that after the marriage festivities the families concerned must not eat without first making an offering to Dulha *deo*. The main offering should be a male pig, which is offered to him, then cooked before the shrine and eaten sacramentally. The bones and pieces that are left are buried in a hole in the floor of the house, for if they should be thrown out or exposed trouble would result.

Gwalbansa baba. This deity is another household god of the same type as Dulha *deo*. He is said to be the master of the house and is always worshipped within the dwelling. He is particularly propitiated at *Jawara* time when an animal offering, preferably a goat or pig, is sacrificed inside the house. The blood is sprinkled about the niche in the wall down near the floor which had been freshly plastered. Nothing whatsoever of the slain animal should be allowed to go out-

1 *Ibid*., pp. 100, 101.

side the house. The entrails and anything left over after the meal, such as bones, hair, skin and the like are thrown into a hole especially prepared for them. This hole is dug in the earthen floor not far from the place where Gwalbansa *baba* dwells. A bit of ashes may first be placed in the hole, then the leftovers, and on top a good layer of ashes; then the hole closed up again with earth and the spot plastered. Fevers and heart diseases are said to be the result if any part of the offering is carelessly exposed.

Hardaul baba is commonly worshipped by the Kols in connection with cholera. He is then offered a red chicken and cocoanuts. Crooke has noted the origin of this deity who is really a modern one.

> In Upper India the chief cholera godling is Hardaul, Hardiya, or Hardiha Lala, the second son of Bir Singh, Raja of Orchha in Central India, who in 1602 at the instigation of Salim, afterwards the Emperor Jahangir, slew the accomplished Abu-l-fazl, the historiographer of the reign of Akbar. Jhajhar Singh, the elder brother of Hardaul, suspecting that he was engaged in an intrigue with his wife, compelled her to poison him at a feast. His horses and dogs died with him, and, like the hero, became dangerous ghosts. When his body was cremated, a pole was set up to mark the place, and when his sister came to mourn him and flung her arms about the post, it split in pieces as a proof that he recognized her. His ghost continued to wander until he was deified and worshipped.[1]

Khetrapal, "field guardian," called Bhumiya sometimes, is another agricultural deity. He guards the fields and, during the growing season, an earthen pot is whitewashed, some black daubs are put upon it and it is placed upside down on the top of a pole in the field.

Mahabir. "The Great Hero." This is the name by which the Kols speak of Hanuman, "he with the great jaws"—the monkey god. *Langur* apes (*Semnopithecus entellus*), are very common through many parts of the Central Provinces and are highly respected and protected.

One group of Kols asserted that Mahabir is the greatest of the deities and that the sun is his shelter. Mahabir's favourite colour is red, and it is not uncommon over village India to see the figure of the monkey god smeared with *sendur*. Kols say that he likes red and that it not only increases his beauty, but also his wrath against the evils affecting human kind. When his wrath is thus aroused, he seeks to remove all the troubles and miseries of human beings. The red causes him to hate these things, and he can effectively act only when his wrath has been aroused by its presence.

1 *Ibid.*, pp. 125, 126.

He is given offerings of foods and vegetables and the *hom* offering is always acceptable. Because he is in the form of an animal, he should never be given an animal sacrifice. Among Hindus, Hanuman is also worshipped by the Vaishnavite sect which does not offer animal sacrifices. According to some Kols, Tuesday is the best day to offer Mahabir his sacrifices and these are offered only by men. The cocoanuts and foods offered and placed before him are, after prayer, taken up and distributed among the worshippers present. Some said that Mahabir is displeased if anyone should be worshipped before him. He has supreme control over all *devis* and *deotas*, and they have no power over him nor can they touch him. Therefore they worship him first. It was only one group that made this surprising claim.

Mansa deo. Mansa *deo* is also a household god, but is usually worshipped outside the house. A small platform of mud is raised by the wall just in front of the house, and on the wall some daubs (usually four) of *sendur* are put, and two small red flags are set up. Some ashes will often be found there and bangles, beads, and the like. If Mansa *deo* is not kept contented by the usual offerings of food and cocoanuts, he may attack the family. When he is happy, he wards off evil spirits.

Nanga baba. This word means "Naked Father," and the Barela Kols believe that he lives in the hills just above that town. He is greatly respected for his purity and plainness of life. His main task is that of stone sculpturing. Many of the oddities of geology about Barela are ascribed to him and his work, and some of the stones which he is said to have cut up, smoothed and flattened are used today for the building of bridges. Nanga *baba* fashioned them, they believe.

Sannyasi deo. This god is usually found associated with the village shrine. Probably he is the spirit of an ascetic of some kind, now elevated to the place of a *deota*. He is offered cocoanuts and tobacco, and protects people. The offering of tobacco probably confirms the conjecture that he was once a wandering *sadhu*. At the time of the *bawa* if he should enter and possess a devotee, the person possessed will reveal the presence of Sannyasi by taking up the iron tongs kept at the shrine and beating and pinching himself with them. To do this is a sure sign that Sannyasi *deo* has come and is truly present.

All of these deities are known to the masses of the people in Central India, and are propitiated from two points of view. This has been aptly described as "spirit scaring" and "spirit squaring."[1] If

1 Enthoven, R. E., *Folklore of Bombay*, p. 14.

the presence of the spirit is considered injurious to the interests of what is in hand, it should be driven away so that it may not interfere. The "spirit squaring" aspect is perhaps the more common in the case of the deities. They are to be kept happy, propitiated, and given a place to rest. If neglected, they become ill-disposed toward the village. Most of these deities are pleased with bloody sacrifices but one does not find, in this section, the orgies such as are prominent in the worship of the village gods of South India.[1]

THE VILLAGE PRIEST—THE PANDA. The religious life of the Kol is connected, as has been seen, with the lesser deities and evil spirits. Worship centres at the village shrine and is usually directed and controlled by the village priest. While the Brahmin priest may be called on occasions which require his presence, such as weddings, name-giving, Bhagawan worship or the like, he has nothing to do with the actual worship at the village shrine. His presence has a social validity rather than a religious one. The worship of the village *devis* is not reserved for a particular class. Any man who seems to have the proper credentials may become the village priest and is called a *panda*. The *panda* is usually a Kol, and while they respect the Baiga priests, the latter are usually called only for magical purposes; it is customary for a Kol *panda* to perform all that is necessary for the religious life of the community. It is usual to find but one recognized *panda* in a village, but every village does not necessarily have such a man. It may be necessary for one village to call a *panda* from another village. But the line of demarcation is so uncertain that, if such a priest is not able to come, any one of the elderly Kols may temporarily perform the function of a *panda*. The *pandas* do not confine themselves exclusively to their religious duties, and often they are found digging, cutting grass, breaking stones and performing all that the average Kol does.

In a certain sense the office is hereditary, although the son must prove his worth before he is recognized. It is usual to find that the officiating *panda's* father was the village priest before him, or a priest at some other village. The son is trained by the father, and at the time of the *bawa* when the father is possessed of the *devi*, the son is the assistant and keeps the shrine in order and the elements propitious as long as his father is in the trance. If the *panda* has no eligible son, it is the one whom "the *devi* selects" who becomes his successor. At any rate the son has to pass tests which will indicate whether or not he is the *devi's* choice.

1 Whitehead, Henry, *The Village Gods of South India.*

The Selection of the Panda. One old *panda* described to us how his son had been selected to be his successor and had even begun to assume some of the duties before the father had to give them up. When the old man wanted to know who would be his successor, he went with his son to the village shrine, and they prostrated themselves on the plastered courtyard before the *devi*. It was at *Jawara* time, when the *devis* are most active, and he told the *devi* (Khermai in this case) that he had a request to make of her; would she hear? He waited until he felt, by strange movings of his hair that she was present and listening, and then asked if she would have his son for her *panda*. He says that he became unconscious, and while in that state Khermai spoke through him to the people present to say that she was willing to have his son as her priest. When he came out of his trance he found that his son was also possessed of Khermai and that he was shaking and shivering and uttering the strange cries which are characteristic of one so enchanted. This was, he says, the confirmation of the *devi's* willingness to have him, and she had even then possessed him. From now on the son could not be considered as merely an assistant, for he was a *panda* who would soon take over all the work of the shrine. We did not see the son, who at the moment was working in the Cement factory at Kymore, digging up stone. But since that first time, the son had often been possessed of the *devis*, and on each occasion he had named the *devi* commanding him at that moment. He makes regular offerings to the *devis*.

If the *panda* has no sons, the selection is from a group of likely young men, or the community may simply join up with another village. A few weeks after the *panda's* death, the village elders gather in the evening at the shrine and begin to play the drum and sing songs of the *bhagat* type. As the evening wears on and the insistent throbbing of the drums becomes more strident, an emotional excitement spreads over some of them. It may centre on one of the players, or on another who is singing, or yet on another seated there. This is a manifestation of the presence of the *devi*, and those who feel the *bawa* coming upon them should go before the village shrine. It may be that one of those present is particularly affected; he may shout, scream, beat himself upon the ground, lash himself with a barbed iron lash to be found at the shrine, or he may put on the spiked sandals and jump about. Whoever thus shows that he is supremely possessed is marked out as the successor of the deceased *panda*.

If, however, the interested onlookers cannot agree that it is genuine, and if there should be more than one candidate in that state, there will have to be even more extreme tests. One of these is to thrust the point of an iron trident through the cheek or tongue or part of the skin of the neck, and ask the "candidate" to jump and run about with it in place. This is the final test, as it were, of the validity of the claim to be a Kol priest. Further on is a fuller description of the phenomenon of the *bawa*.[1]

Duties of the Priest. The duties of the priest are largely connected with the village shrine. He should keep it in order, offer the cocoanuts and animals, and perform the *hom* sacrifice. He is also the mouthpiece of the goddess. When possessed of the *devi* he is asked questions, and the answers that come from his mouth are not his, but are claimed to be the answers of the *devi* herself.

It is not infrequent that the *panda* is also expected to perform certain magical practices, although he is not as expert in these as the Baiga priest is believed to be. These practices are usually in connection with disease, but it may be any form of divination known to Kols. A child is ill, and the priest is asked for his help in healing the disease. The priest will go before the *devi* and vow to take no food for nine days, and after that to make a *jawara* offering. An earthen *ghara*, wheat and milk are given him. These he takes to the child's house and plants the wheat in the *ghara*. Sometimes this is done in his own house. The wheat is sprinkled daily with water and a little milk. It sprouts and grows, and in nine days, after being taken with ceremony to the village tank or a near-by stream, the earth is washed away. The wheat plants and the roots are then brought back to the house where the child is ill. If by this time the spirit causing the illness has not been satisfied, the wheat stalks and roots will surely satisfy her if left on the roof to dry. Like the stalks, the disease will dry up and disappear.

THE VILLAGE SHRINE. It was noted that each village has its central shrine. This, however, is not the only shrine in the village; there may also be other ones, but there is one which is recognized as the chief place of worship, and it is about this central shrine that the chief religious observances centre. The place of worship is a sanctuary of a god or goddess and not the place of public congregational worship. The pictures on plate xxiv show village shrines, and a ground plan in figure 26 is also given to show the disposition and arrangement of the various concomitants. Some shrines have more in them than others, and frequently a red *sendur* mark and cocoanut shells and ashes are the only sign that worship is carried on there. Hindu influences may be presumed.

1 See p. 159.

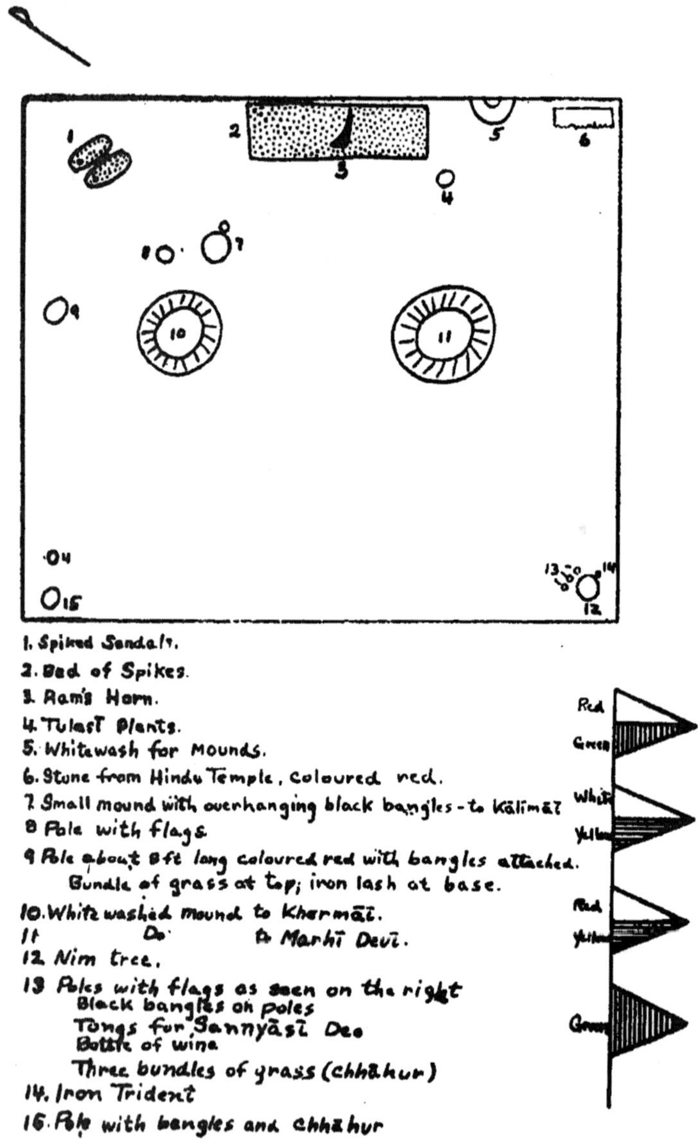
1
2
3
4
5
6
7
8
9
10
11
12
13
14
14
15
1. Spiked Sandals.
2. Bed of Spikes.
3. Ram's Horn.
4. Tulasī Plants.
5. Whitewash for Mounds.
6. Stone from Hindu Temple, coloured red.
7. Small mound with overhanging black bangles - to Kālimāī
8 Pole with flags
9 Pole about 8ft long coloured red with bangles attached.
Bundle of grass at top; iron lash at base.
10. Whitewashed mound to Khermāī.
11 Do to Marhī Devī.
12. Nim tree.
13 Poles with flags as seen on the right
Black bangles on poles
Tongs for Sannyāsī Deo
Bottle of wine
Three bundles of grass (chhāhur)
14. Iron Trident
15. Pole with bangles and chhāhur
Red
Green
White
Yellow
Red
Yellow
Green

Fig. 26

Only once did we find a Kol shrine with a roof. Usually shrines are just raised platforms of earth about the base of a tree, preferably a *nim* tree. The older and larger the tree the better.

Concomitants of Worship. The following items are usually found as component parts of the central village shrines.

1. *Flags* (*Jhanda*). Flags are an essential part of the village shrine. They are usually set up on bamboo poles which are in turn bound to the trunk of the *nim* tree. It is also not infrequent that these are placed high above in the tops of the tree where the flag waves over all. The flag makes it known, they say, that the deity is present, and the colours and colour combinations usually indicate which deities are likely to be found there. The flags also serve as an attraction to the godlings who may come and perch upon them. They also frighten away evil spirits. The bamboo pole is usually about fifteen feet long and may have from one to seven flags attached to it. The village pays for the purchase of these flags unless there is someone who wishes to gain merit by giving them to the shrine. The Kol *panda* who is in charge of the shrine and its properties, puts the flags on the pole and sets it in place. The flags themselves are from 18 to 24 inches in length and about six inches wide at the widest part.

In addition to these larger flags on the bamboo pole, there are always found smaller flags at the base of the tree or at the spot where the blood of the sacrifice is sprinkled. They are quite small and are brought by individuals or families who place them in position when the offering is made. These flags are usually red. When one seeks a boon from the goddess and makes a promise to give a sacrifice if the boon is granted, he should set up a red flag as a witness to his promise. A flag is set up by those going on a journey as a witness to the fact that they will make an offering when they return safely.

In general red is the favourite colour of the *devis*. There are some colours which are characteristic of certain *devis*. Kali likes black; Asmani likes white or red; Khermai is sometimes given green, though red is more common; yellow is for Sannyasi. This set-up lacks consistency, like much among the Kols, for some deny any particular significance and say that the flags are merely decorative. While the smaller flags may be set up at any time, it is usual that the larger flags are set up only once or maybe twice a year, *Chaita* and *Kunwar*, spring and fall, being the accepted times for new flags.

2. *Iron Tridents* (*Trisul*). These are found in varying sizes and numbers. There should be at least one long one with a very sharp point, see figure 25, and there are usually more. Smaller ones

are very common. The trident with the sharp point is used at the time the *panda* or another is possessed of Khermai, and is pierced through the tongue or cheek.

3. *Spiked Sandals* (*Kharau*). Every well-equipped shrine should have at least one pair of spiked sandals. These are made of pieces of wood in the shape of the sole of a shoe with sharp spikes driven through so that the person walking on them stands on the points. There is a wooden peg toward the front of each which fits between the big toe and the next and holds the sandal on the foot. These are generally used at the time of the trance. When the spirit of Kalimai possesses a man, it will be evidenced by his desire to put on these sandals and jump about in them.

4. *Iron Tongs* (*Chimta*). There is also another kind of iron instrument found in these shrines: iron tongs used for taking coals out of the fire. When Sannyasi *deo* comes upon a man he will take the tongs and beat himself with them. Hindu ascetics usually carry tongs.

5. *Iron Lash* (*Gurda*). This is a sort of magic chain made of iron links barbed with bits of steel. The handle by which it is grasped is also iron. During the *bawa*, if one is possessed (particularly by Bhuiyan *deo*), he will pick up this chain and lash himself till the blood comes. If some person, possessed of an evil spirit, is brought before the shrine, and the *panda* in his trance recognizes the reality of the spirit possession, he will attempt to cast out the spirit by lashing the unfortunate man.

6. *Iron Nails*. Some bits of iron or iron nails are usually found somewhere about the shrine. These serve a dual purpose: they are tests for Khermai, and one possessed of her can stick them into his flesh without pain or discomfort. They are also used to frighten away evil spirits who may make a disturbance, and are sometimes flung in their direction causing them to fly away.

7. *A Bed of Spikes* (*Palna*). Often a bed of spikes is found in connection with these shrines. This too is to test spirit possession. One possessed of Kali will seek to use the bed of spikes.

8. *A Ram's Horn* is sometimes found. It is lucky to have one and it protects the shrine.

9. *Clay Lamps* (*Dip*). Clay dishes into which oil is poured and wicks attached are also found at all shrines. Sweet oil and incense are mixed, and during the time of worship two or three of these are lighted and kept burning. The *panda* lights and cares for them.

10. *Ashes* (*Rakha*). A pile of ashes is always found somewhere about the shrine. This is a good protective device against evil spirits.

A shrine in the Kaimer Hills.

General view of Village shrines at Barela. Of the eight Kols may resort to only two: Mari Devi (left arrow) and Sitala Devi—Extreme right.

Shrine to Khermai and Asmani Devi at Benda Village.

If, during a worship period, a *bawa* does not come when it should be expected, ashes are sprinkled over the worshipper. Probably some demon is near, and the spirit of the *devi* will not enter as long as a *bhut* is about, and this will frighten him away. A person who is ill, or who is facing some danger, may come, make an offering, and sprinkle ashes over himself, saying the magical words "*ochha, ochha.*"

11. *A Grass Bundle* (*Chhahur*). This is the magic grass, and provides shade, shelter, and protection to *devis*. The *chhahur* is composed of stalks of wheat or some other sacred grass like *kans* (*Saccharum spontaneum*), *kusa* (*Poa cynosuroides*) or *urai* (*Vetivera zizanoides*) tied in a bundle to the end of a bamboo stick. These bits of grass are taken from thatch roofs of the houses in the village, usually one stalk from each house. Thus each house honours the deity and will therefore be protected. At times of smallpox or cholera this is a very effective procedure, and one or two stalks are brought from each house and tied together by the *panda* and set up. Each family which gives the grass is thus protected. Strings of red, yellow and black beads are usually hung about the *chhahur*. They give the household added protection as the *devis* are still more pleased.

12. *Flowers.* Marigold (*Tagetes erecta*), and *Tulasi* (*Ocymum sanctum*) plants are nearly always seen in connection with Kol shrines. The marigold is a sacred plant and is usually found in connection with Hindu worship, while *tulasi* plants are often found there too. At Kaimur, Kali lived in a *tulasi* plant and black bangles were hung upon it to indicate that fact.

13. *Bangles* (*Churi*). Bangles, being a feminine adornment, are always found at Kol shrines. These are usually red, yellow or black in colour, and they seem to be used with discrimination. They may be tied on a pole or on a *nim* tree, or fastened to some part of the furnishings of the shrine.

14. *Vermilion* (*Sendur*). Red lead is very necessary in worship. It was seen how it stimulated Mahabir into action. *Devis* like it, and it is also a devil scarer and helps to protect the shrine.

15. *Mounds* (*Pinda*). It is not infrequently found that there are one or more mounds raised on the mud platform to represent *devis* and to be their dwelling place. These are generally whitewashed once a week. At Kaimur, one was for Khermai and the other for Mari *devi*; at Benda Bhainsokhar was worshipped this way.

16. *Earthenware Vessels* (*Ghara*). These are not always found, but during the hot season are usually hung either in the tree or on a pole over the shrine. Sometimes liquor is kept in them. This is pleasing to the goddesses, especially Kali. Sometimes water is kept

in these vessels, and a tiny hole pierced in the bottom so that the water drops over the shrine. This is popular in warm weather when the *devi* should be cooled and the dripping water is pleasing to her.

17. *Tinsel* (*Tika*). Women often place a small round dot made of lac tinsel on the centre of their foreheads. It is usually of red colour. These bits of tinsel are used in the shrines as well, and are stuck on it here and there. The *devis* like them and they help to attract them to the shrine.

18. *Stone* (*Patthar*). Bits of stone, usually pieces rounded in the bed of streams and longish in shape, are often found somewhere about the shrine. This may be an imitation of the *Salagrama* stones found in connection with the worship of Vishnu. Sometimes they are of *lingam* type such as used in the worship of Siva.

This sums up the items usually found in Kol shrines. Probably no shrine we saw had all these components, though the Kaimur shrine came nearest to it. In addition to the above, there was at Kaimur an unusual feature. This was a flat stone which had apparently come from some ancient Hindu temple and on which two figures were carved. The *panda* of the shrine claimed that it was brought from Rewa and that the figures represented Sharda and Kalki. The stone must have weighed about eighty pounds, but, it was claimed, if a *hom* offering were performed when it was moved, it became very light and was easy to transport. It was coloured red with *sendur*. It will have been noticed how imperfectly anthropomorphized the godlings are, and that no special images are required.

The only Kol shrine which had brick walls and a roof was found on the outskirts of Katni. The room measured about five feet square inside, was four feet high, and had a flat roof. This was called the shrine of Khermai, although on the flat top Barmai was said to dwell. Also tongs were there for Sannyasi *deo*. The usual bundle of *kans* grass (*Saccharum spontaneum*) was on top of it.

The offerings, the lighting of the lights and the placing of the necessary parts, are all in the hands of the *panda*. It is not part of his work, however, to keep the shrine clean and properly plastered. This is the duty of the women of the village, and they take turns in doing it. The shrine is plastered at least once a week and cleaned oftener. The sweepings, including ashes, dust, bits of cocoanut shells and the like, are not swept to the ground beside the shrine, but are carefully put into a basket by the woman who is doing the work. If they should be thrown out upon the earth, evil will result, so they are carried to a stream or a tank and thrown into the water. They are sacred ashes, likened unto the ashes following a cremation and must be respected.

Worship at a Shrine. An account may here be given of the worship of the smallpox goddess as witnessed at a village shrine. The first hint of the matter was the beat of drums as a group approached the shrine. The instrument was a kettle-drum, hung about the neck of the drummer. Following the drummer came a young man with a brass tray filled with small *puris* and cocoanuts, carried on his shoulder. Beside him was a younger boy who was carrying two red flags, one of them rather large and on a long pole, and the other proportionately shorter. Both flags tapered to a point. Next came a woman apparently much perturbed, with dishevelled hair. Her head was partially covered by her *sari*. Close behind was her husband who seemed to be a rather elderly man, and with him was a small boy who appeared to be ill. It was not realized at first that this boy was the victim of smallpox. When they reached the shrine the drummer took his stand to one side and continued to beat his drum, while a woman came up and poured water over the shrine and the representations of Khermai and Asmani *devi*. As the drummer played, the woman with the dishevelled hair, who happened to be the mother of the lad, began to stretch herself repeatedly at full length before the shrine, and then, as it were, measured her length around and around the platform on which the shrine was situated. As she did this, she held a cocoanut in her right hand. She was then followed by her husband who rolled in the dust before the shrine until instructed by the *panda* to measure his length around the shrine as his wife was doing. Just before he came to the shrine his body had been anointed with *haldi* and oil, and this gathered much dust and dirt. The larger boy with the tray also went about the shrine as did the boy who had carried the flags. They did not, however, measure their lengths. An uncle from some other village joined them and each went around seven times in a clockwise direction. Except for the drumming, the measuring of their lengths about the shrine was done in silence. Only the adults actually measured their lengths.

When the proper number rounds had been completed, the group stopped at the steps of the platform in front of Kher *devi's* shrine. The tray of cocoanuts and *puris* was placed on the platform and the people ascended the steps and sat on the platform. The drummer seated himself and continued the beating of the drum, and the mother of the sick boy began to perform acts in which she appeared to be imploring the deity. She prostrated her head to the ground, then sat up and wildly swung her body, first from the upright position with a sweeping motion, to a position of prostrate petition. Except for the gentle drumming all this too was done in silence. She then poured water over the shrine and wiped it carefully with a rag. Asmani was washed as well. The *puris* were then put right beside the shrine in piles and the cocoanuts in front. The two flags carried by the boy were set up along with others which had accumulated at the shrine, the larger by Khermai and the smaller one by Asmanimai. Two or three of the cocoanuts were then broken and laid before the *devis*.

Another procession now started, this time around the shrine of Khermai only. It too went in a clockwise direction, not around the platform as a whole, but on the platform and around the *devi*. This time three rounds were made. The woman with the dishevelled hair and her husband both measured their lengths in this procession, but the others did not do so, they simply walked around. The group then gathered again in front of Khermai and the woman once more prostrated herself, although not as vigorously as before. In the meantime the drummer came down and sat beside a small hedge near the shrine. His wife spread out a piece of cloth in front of him, and the villagers proceeded to pour out their offerings of rice, wheat, *dal* and the like onto the cloth. It was said that this went to the drummer. At the same time individual members of the group on the platform were breaking the remaining cocoanuts into small pieces. These were distributed to everyone within sight. The *puris* were not distributed; that would be done later on.

The accompanying diagram shows the arrangement of this shrine and gives an idea of what was done. See figure 27 and plate xxv.

Offerings at the Shrines. Considerable mention has been made of the offerings presented at Kol shrines, but more should be added and the matter summarized.

The general tendency is toward offerings of cocoanuts and food rather than animals. This is partly due to economic reasons, but may also be due to the influence of the Vaishnavite sect of Hinduism.

The most common single offering is the *hom*, which is essentially a fire sacrifice. This must have been borrowed from the Hindus. Into the fire burning before the deity is dropped *ghi* and incense. Sometimes pieces of cocoanut, or seeds and drops of lime juice are added.

The cocoanut is universally offered, and it has been suggested that it is symbolic of human sacrifice and that the shell represents the human skull. As a rule Kols seem to have no knowledge of this point of view. At the temple of Shardamai and Maihar, the Brahmin priest told us the cocoanuts were symbolical of the head of a certain Alhandal who used to bathe Shardamai daily with water and finally sacrificed his own head to her. She was so pleased at this that she gave him the gift of immortality. According to Crooke, Alha and Udal were two Banaphar Rajput heroes engaged in a war between two Rajput clans. This was dated about 1165-1203 A.D.[1]

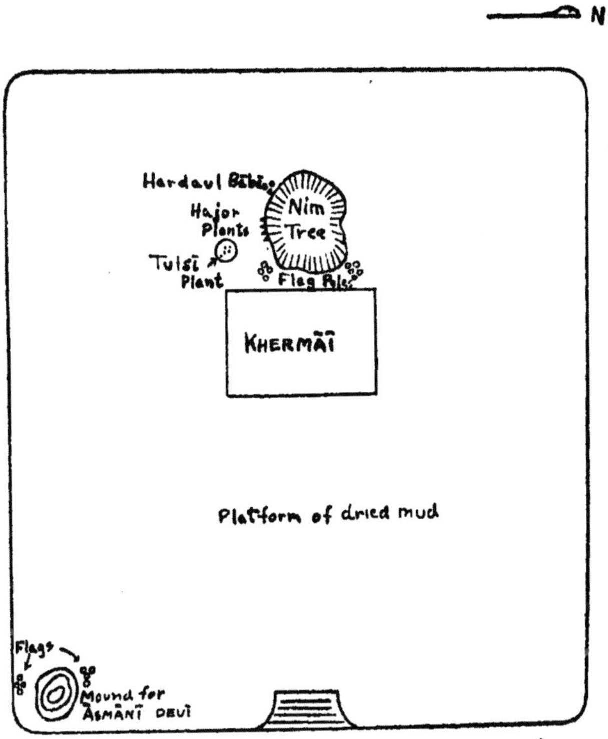

Fig. 27

Usually the cocoanut is first laid whole before the deity, and after the ceremonies have been performed and any invocations offered by the *panda*, the cocoanut is broken by hitting it on the ground or on a stone. It is always struck on the stone; not broken by being hit by a stone or other instrument. The shell is thrown aside and the edible portion placed before the deity. Pieces are distributed to each of the worshippers and onlookers, who then eat before her. A priest may break a cocoanut in the absence of the offerer, if the latter is not able to be present.

Lemons or limes are also offered. These please and attract the *devis*. They are also liked by demons and may attract them. Should

1 *Ibid.*, p. 258.

such seem to be the case, a piece of lemon may be thrown well away from the shrine. The evil spirit will go after it, forgetting all about what is going on at the shrine. Such spirits are easily outwitted in this manner.

Foods offered include almost all kinds cooked in *ghi*: *puris*, *khichri* and various sweets. *Ghi* itself is frequently put about.

Animals which make acceptable offerings include the chicken, goat, pig and sheep. The latter is very expensive and is not often resorted to. The mature goat or pig is almost never sacrificed—young ones are preferred by the *devis*. Usually a *devi* desires a female of th species offered, and a *deota* a male. The animal to be sacrificed is brought before the shrine, having been first washed and marked with *sendur*. Its throat is cut with an iron knife and the blood is sprinkled directly before the symbols, or at the foot of the tree where the little flags are located. Sometimes the animal is decapitated with a single blow, and only the head is taken on the platform, and blood from it dropped over the symbols. The animal is then cleaned, cooked and eaten beside the shrine, and the people partake of a ceremonial meal together. The bones and bits left over are carefully gathered and taken away, either by some low-caste Hindu who may be around, or by some Kol who takes them outside the village boundary and deposits them in a *nala* or place where water is likely to flow. The kid or suckling pig costs from one to three rupees each depending upon the size. Kols never raise pigs and so have to buy them. Goats, however, are often kept and are generally available. The kind and size of animal offered usually depends on the economic condition of the worshipper. It is also said that when a man desires to make an offering, he will pray that in a dream the kind of offering he should make may be revealed to him. A *panda's* advice is also sought.

Some deities are said to have particular preferences regarding the colour of the animal sacrificed. The Kols are far from consistent, but generally for Kali or Kalika, the colour should be black. Khermai generally prefers white and Marimai red. Most of the *devis* are not very discriminating.

Kols make these offerings in order to protect themselves from the troubles, diseases and miseries of life. Possibly they will lead the deities to be merciful. They are promised that if all goes well they will receive sacrifices and offerings regularly. If offered properly, these sacrifices are thought to bind the deity and practically force her to do as the worshipper desires. The people are thus psychologically confident of a good outcome. If the deities are kept pleased and happy in this way, all is well; but if they get angry, they will trouble the people who have neglected them.

THE HOME SHRINE. Shrines found at the homes are much simpler than the village shrines and are found either inside or just outside the house, or in both places. Those outside the house are placed in the front wall facing the courtyard, and the wall of the house is a part of the shrine. Sometimes a little hole is made in the wall to shelter the *devi* when it rains. These shrines may be dedicated to any of the *devis* mentioned in the preceding pages—Asmanimai, Kalimai, Khermai, Marimai and Shardamai being the most commonly worshipped outside the house. One finds flags above, and also below; the iron trident; black and other kinds of bangles; a *salagrama* stone; *sendur* marks and the like. Iron lashes and strings of beads are not uncommon.

The place reserved within the dwelling for the household goddess, or god is even simpler. There is a niche in the wall from four to six inches above the floor. Within the niche is found a *salagrama* stone or some iron symbol reddened with *sendur*. Vermilion is also daubed on the wall round the niche. The floor space immediately below the deity is plastered with cowdung. A small trident usually leans against the wall at one side of the shrine; there is a *dip* which is lighted at dusk, when the women of the house prostrate themselves before the shrine. As was noted, both kinds of shrines are usually found. If the house is just a hut of branches, and there is no earthen wall, symbols of the deities will be found on the floor in one of the corners. The house shrine is generally called *dewahar* or *dewala*.

DEVI POSSESSION. (*Bawa*). The phenomenon of spirit possession is fairly common among certain of the lower classes. The Kols also practise this. The trance occurs before the village shrine and is usually induced only at the time of the *Jawara* festivals, which come at the spring and autumnal equinox. It may be resorted to on other occasions if there seems to be a case of extreme necessity. The actual trance is induced partly by the singing and the beating of drums, at which Kols are so adept. The person seeking the *bawa* takes his place before the *devi* and after a period of concentration and emotion begins to tremble, then shout, beat himself upon the ground, and becomes in appearance a totally different person. During this time he will answer questions put to him by persons seeking guidance, who believe that it is not he that is answering them, but the spirit at that time resident in him. During this period, the one under the possession of the *devi* is practically insensible to pain, and very painful things may be resorted to without any apparent sensation on his part. Some drug may be partly responsible.

There are cerain tests as to whether a person is truly possessed of the *devi* or not. The following are tests Kols have given.

1. A trembling and jerking of the head and limbs.
2. A state of semi-consciousness. He is clearly not himself, but is able to recognize the people who stand about him and ask him questions.
3. The uttering of the magic words: "ochha, ochha." No meanings could be given for this, but it represents a gasping effort.[1]
4. The uttering of other unintelligible words and phrases.
5. The ability to walk and jump about on spiked sandals without evidence of pain or discomfort.
6. The lashing of the back with the iron lash until it is raw and bleeding.
7. The passing of the point of the trident through the tongue, cheek, or the skin of the neck and leaving it there from a half hour to two hours. During this time the person may move about, and if it is not through his tongue, may answer questions. This is said to be the supreme test. It is claimed that no sores or bleeding follow it and that it is treated by a mixture of ashes, *ghi*, *pan* and lime juice.

It is not held that all of these must concur to give adequate proof; and though often they do not go as far as really wounding themselves, the *bawa* is still regarded as a genuine one.

If two men, for instance, should be possessed at the same time by different *devis*, there may be a contest between those particular *devis* should there be any enmity between them. One may try to defeat the other, and the result is a fight between the men.

Kol women are also said to have the *bawa*, but with them this phenomenon is not nearly so common. It is taken as a sign that the deity is pleased with them.

During the time of the *bawa*, people come seeking guidance and help for their troubles: childless women ask what offerings they should give in order that they may bear children; domestic troubles are told and their solution asked for; illness, lack of work and the like, are all brought before the *devi*, and an answer is forthcoming.

Following is a description of a *bawa* seen by the author. It was a Domar *bawa*, not a Kol one, but Indians familiar with Kol *bawas* said that it was not essentially different. The *bawa* was performed under abnormal circumstances: it was not done before a regular shrine, but one improvised against a telephone pole.

The assistant first cleared a spot of grass making a bare area about two feet wide and three feet long. The one who was to perform then came and poured a little water over the spot, rubbed the earth

1 It may be connected with the name *OJHA* or "medicine man".

and smoothed it. This was to take the place of plastering. When this was done, he set in place the articles that were brought along for the ceremony. These included a cocoanut, some flowers, *sendur* powder, *ghi*, camphor balls, an iron ring, sweet oil, some bits of iron, a bottle of country liquor, and two limes. Some burning charcoal was brought from a house nearby. There was a group who had come to sing and play the drums. A song or two was sung while preparations were being made.

The *sendur* was mixed with *ghi* to form a paste, some of which was daubed on the pole immediately back of the cleared spot, also some on the *panda's* forehead and upper arms. On the left arm three daubs, and on the right arm two. A sort of trident was also marked on the telephone pole with the *sendur*. Next the coals were handed him, and were placed within the iron ring. The lamp with the sweet oil was lit, after a cotton wick had been rolled for it by hand. The bottle of country liquor was opened and some poured out to the left of the cocoanut which was leaning against the base of the pole. As he poured the *panda* muttered charms, held the lamp above the cocoanut for a few moments, then set it down before it. Next a few cloves were taken and after having been put to his lips, stuck into the ground about him and into his loin cloth. From the vessel containing *ghi* he took a few drops and let them fall on the glowing charcoal, which flamed up and gave off the incense of burning butter. He uttered the word "Ramchandra", and some other incantations, and more *ghi* was dropped on the fire. One of the limes was then cut with a knife into two pieces and placed to the right and the left of the burning *ghi* in the iron ring. The singing now began in real earnest. The camphor balls were next set afire and put on top of the cut limes. Everything was apparently ready for the coming of the *devi*. He turned around to the group and hailed them as if taking farewell, and with folded hands began to meditate, looking steadily upward at the electric light which had been fastened to the pole, for it was about eight p.m. As he did this, his assistant, who happened to be his brother, began angrily to address someone in the unseen world and looked toward the south as he called. Before long one could notice that the man's arms were beginning to quiver. The music became more strident and the man began to shake his head while his whole body swayed from side to side. He drew in his abdomen and stuck out his chest repeatedly. He picked up a rope lash and lashed his own back. Then the assistant with a loud tone and a hard look invoked Kali, saying, "*Kali Calcuttawali hajir ho*" : 'Kali of Calcutta be here'! Then it seemed that the spirit came upon him for the first time, as he began to jerk with great spasms, jumped up in a frenzy, screamed and shouted. The assistant then showed his brother a rupee and challenged Kali to show herself in her best possible form and then put the rupee beside the fire. This brought on a very wild period of shouting and falling to the earth and of beating himself with the lash. His tense face was that of another, and his eyes were glassy. He kept his tongue stuck out in imitation of Kali whose representations always show her with outstretched tongue. He also held out his hands as Kali does in her pictures. His writhings and tremblings now ceased, and he asked in a harsh voice if anyone wanted to ask advice of her, for he had become Kalimai. One of the Hindu women living on the compound came forward and asked why she had no children. She crawled up to him on hands and feet, and had her forehead on the ground. The goddess answered through the man possessed, that she had no issue because her mind was polluted, and charged her to worship her (Kali) or worship Bhagawan. He then took some ashes from the coals of the fire and throwing them upon her announced that she would have an issue within ten years.

A man came forward and asked the best method of worship. The answer was very indefinite: if he worshipped, he would be prosperous. Then he became very excited and swaying and looking fiercely at the questioner said in indignation: "You have come to test me, but haven't I done many things for you? Tell me the truth, haven't I done much for you?" The man became so excited that he was hissing and beating himself upon the ground, first with one shoulder then the other, and then in an up-right position, beating his arms. Another came and asked a question, but no attention was paid to him. A woman whose husband had disappeared came humbly crawling towards him. She wanted to know whether her husband was still living and if so where he was. The *devi* answered between broken breaths saying that the husband had left the woman at her own request and that she was thus to blame. The solution given was to "worship me daily for a month and a quarter, give your offerings daily at my temple in the Saddar for a month and a quarter, and for this period abstain from the use of salt in your food. Have your heart clean and you will get your desire." Another woman said that one of her relatives had gone to his country and had not yet returned. Would he come back? The reply was, "He is all right, but his heart has turned away from you. He will return in a few days."

The woman who had asked about her childlessness now asked what kind of an offering she should give to Kali. A wave of frenzy came upon the fellow and he said, "Offer an animal in my name; feed the *panchayat.*" He hissed some more, went through a great shaking and again added, "Don't you see my truth? You have called me to test my power, but I am showing you my glory." Turning to the spectators, he demanded if there was anyone else who had a request to make. The assistant then poured out before him on the ground some more of the country liquor. This greatly excited the man who screamed, jumped up and down, and after putting his mouth to the ground several times licked up the liquor in the madness of emotion. Then taking a bit of the lime he squeezed some out on the fire and said, "May all your desires be fulfilled."

The fellow then took up his knife and began to cut the end of the little finger on his right hand. We did not see any blood actually come out. There was more frenzy and hisses, and Kali left him; other goddesses and gods possessed him in turn, and he shouted out the name of the deities as they were coming upon him. He went through certain motions supposed to be characteristic of the deity but these could not always be detected as the scene shifted rapidly. The following deities came upon him in turn; Marhidevi, Hinlag devi, Phulmatimai, Bindabasini, Bhawani, Chausatt (64) Joginis (of Marble Rocks Hill), Sitalamai, Uddan Begni (goddess of Aeroplanes), Asmani-devi (which caused a further writhing), then a long burst of cruel laughter, and the name Manidas which, they said, was the god of the cemetery. More liquor was poured out, and fury again possessed the man. He was covered with perspiration. But the mood immediately changed, and he began to cry and sob like a child. Then rushing backwards and forwards and throwing himself writhing on the ground, he sat up with a triumphant look on his face, beat his arms with his fists and announced that he was Bir Pehalvan, the god of wrestling. Then last of all he changed back into Kali, and soon again made out that he was cutting his little finger, and held it over the fire as if to squeeze out some drops of blood—an offering to the bloody goddess. The musicians did not play all through the performance, but at this point they again took up their drumming and singing and shouted "*Kalimai ki jai*"—Hail to Kali. The chief character then took a bit of ashes and gave to his assistant, who sprinkled them over the singers, at which they shouted "Hail, Marhai Mata, Hail." The man now threw himself on his back and writhed again in seeming agony; then jumped up and forward to the elements; took up the iron ring, poured out *ghi* on the fire, which had been kept going by the assistant; poured some more liquor on the ground, removed the outer covering of the cocoanut and put the pieces in the fire; took the cocoanut in his hands and held it up in worship; then broke it upon a stone and separated the kernel, putting a bit of it in the fire. The juice of the remaining lime was squeezed out on the ground, the oil of the lamp was poured out, the knife was stuck into the ground and water sprinkled about seven times as he muttered incantations. Then with a shout he fell back exhausted, where he lay for several minutes before opening his eyes in a sort of stupefied manner. The pieces of cocoanut were then distributed to the singers and players. The man sat up, seemed normal again, and showed his hands, as if to say that the wounds were healed and no ill had befallen him. The group left and went to their homes. We heard later that they got thoroughly intoxicated and had a small pig for a feast. The whole performance lasted approximately an hour.

GODDESS SEPTS. Kols do not worship all the goddesses mentioned in the previous lists, but usually limit themselves to certain of them; they have a certain number which they call their own deities. Usually the son should worship the same number as the father worshipped, but not necessarily the same ones. By way of illustration, the following shows the reaction of five Kols who happened to be talking about this:

1. Three Deities: Shardamai, Kalimai and Barmatimai.
2. Three: Kalki, Phulmati and Sharda.
3. Said he too had three and named those in 2.
4. Four: Phonamuki, Athabhuji, Lorhadhar, Asmani.
5. Seemed much puzzled and said he worshipped several but no particular number.

TREES AND RELIGION. In another place more will be said about Kol beliefs concerning trees.[1] The chief trees thought of in connection with deities are noted here:

The *Nim* (*Melia azadirachta*) is the best tree for the Kol and is considered to be the home of Khermai, although other *devis* also like it.

The *Pipal* tree (*Ficus religiosa*) and the banyan tree (*Ficus indica*) are the home of Baran *deo* and other rather dangerous spirits. At Sehora a giant *danawa* lives in a *pipal* tree.

The Tamarind tree (*Tamarindus indicus*) is a favourite home of the *churel*, a particularly vicious spirit, but is also the abode of Chithra *devi*.

The Banyan tree also shelters Basdeo and Sannyasi.

1. See Chapter IX.

RELIGIOUS FESTIVALS OF THE KOLS. The chief religious festivals that Kols have interest in are the following :

Amavasya—"No moon day." Monthly.
Dasara—on the tenth (*dasa*) day of the month Kunwar.
Dewali—lamp festival, first day of Kartik, twenty days after Dasara.
Hareli—"greenery", during the monsoon time: Srawan.
Hariyari—a form of Hareli.
Holi—the spring equinoctial festival in the month of Phag at full moon.
Jawara—twice a year : just before Holi and again before Dasara.
Khajleniya—a portion of the Jawara festival and sometimes a synonym for it.
Khicheri—named but not clearly differentiated.
Marpak—in memory of the dead.
Nagpanchami—the snake festival in Srawan.
Naodurgan—a part of the Jawara festival.
Phag—the same as Holi.
Pusan—a festival known in Rewa.
Rakhi—"protector", the ceremony of amulet tying. In Sawan.
Ramnavami—Ram's birthday, 9th day of Chaita.
Sirwant—another name for the Rakhi festival.
Tija—another name for Khajleniya.

These festivals however, are not all of equal value, but as far as possible we have given a description of them and of how the Kols enter into the same. Hindu influences are apparent.

Amavasya. This is a monthly festival and is observed on the day when the moon is "new" that is, on the dark of the moon. It is only observed, however, by the more Hinduised Kols. As the new moon comes forth in its purity, all should be made ready to receive her. The women busy themselves in cleaning and plastering their houses, mending the holes or broken plaster, and making everything spick and span. The men may go to the Nerbudda to bathe. Among Hindus much attention is paid to Amavasya, and should it fall on Monday "it is sacred, people fast, bathe, make gifts to Brahmins, and worship the holy Fig tree."[1] In this connection the Kols will pluck off bits of their garments and throw them toward the moon, as described on previous pages.[2] The festival is apparently a Vedic one and needless

1 Crooke, W., *Religion & Folklore of Northern India*, p. 35.
2 See pp. 131, 136.

to say, Kols living away from strong Hindu influences do not pay particular attention to this, although it is known and mentioned.

Dasara is a very important Hindu festival and is celebrated on the tenth day of the Hindu month *Kunwar*—portions of September and October. In this case again, the Kols enter into it quite freely, yet it is not one of their important festivals. The Hindu legends connected with this day seem to indicate that it is a day to celebrate a victory and hold military displays.

Any observation among the Kols usually takes the form of a procession of men to the village boundary, carrying with them lights and torches, the procession being marked by the beating of drums and the singing of the men. From there they return home rejoicing as if from a victory, and are greeted by the women who have a feast ready.

It is also a semi-agricultural festival with some, as the wheat should not be sown till after *Dasara*. Ten days before *Dasara* wheat is sown in the houses. This is discussed in connection with the *Jawara* festival,[1] which seems to be the most important to the Kol and overlaps both *Dasara* and *Holi*.

Devali. This is the feast of lights and comes twenty days after *Dasara*, and is held on the new moon day (*Amavasya*) of the Hindu month *Kartik* (October-November). This too is predominantly a Hindu festival, and the Kols observance is largely by imitation. Hindus set out lights, and the illuminations, particularly in cities where it is well observed, are very beautiful. The Hindu believes that on this night the souls of the good dead return to visit their old haunts. So the houses are made ready—all is clean; old earthen lamps are thrown away and new ones replace them. The new ones should burn all night, and the family will stay up to receive the spirits of their deceased, not yet reborn.

Kols usually go no further than first burning a *diya* inside the house in front of the inner place of worship, invoking, they say, Shardamai, though the names of all the gods and goddesses known to them should be uttered before the shrine, as well as the names of their own sainted dead. Then the lamp is taken up and together with a few others is set on the doorstep to guide the spirit. If the Kol has any wealth, he may worship that too; but there is usually so little that they do not take it into account.

Haveli. The word literally means "greenery", and it appears that only the Hinduized Kols have much knowledge of it. Among

1 Page 169.

orthodox Hindus each passage of the sun from one constellation to another is marked by some kind of ceremony. The change after the sun has reached its most northern course coincides with the coming of the welcome monsoon rains, which turn the dry and dusty lands into a paradise of green. Russell and Hiralal also note that the Kurmis, an agricultural caste in the Central Provinces, keep this festival in the month of *Srawan* (July-August).[1]

Hariyari. This has been named to us by Kols and is probably very similar to, if not identical with, the *Hareli* festival. Crooke has a few words by way of information: "Bhuiyas, Kols, and Binds of the United Provinces also worship during the rainy season Haryari Devi, 'Mother of Greenery', by employing their Baiga priest to sacrifice chickens and to pour a libation of wine on the field after harvest or before the sowing season."[2]

Holi. This festival is usually called *Phag* by Kols as it occurs in the month of *Phagun* (February-March). It is essentially a spring festival, largely entered into and carried on by the lower castes. It marks the coming of spring, and the sympathetic magic in the ceremony tends to promote the fertility of crops and animals.

Kols who live in or near cities and towns observe this more than those isolated in villages. In Rewa a group of Kols claimed that they would not particularly observe it, but Kols near Jubbulpore said that those who remained behind in Rewa observed it much more fully than they who had left and come away.

Preparations for the *Phag* festival were watched in a Kol village close to Jubbulpore, and our enquiries were freely answered. The first part of the festival centres around a great bonfire which is arranged much as Hindu castes construct it. This should always be built outside the village and eastwards, towards the rising sun. If one Kol village cannot get up enough enthusiasm for a good celebration, they may join with another village in their preparations, or several villages may join together. The wood for the fire may be taken by force or stolen from its owners, and the owners are not supposed to make any protest.

The place chosen for the fire is first cleared and levelled. In the centre a hole is dug, into which the pole, around which the wood is to be stacked, will be inserted. Two pice, some *haldi* and a *supari* nut are dropped into the hole. The central pole should be of *andi* wood, the castor oil stalk (*Palma christi*), and around this the wood, brush and other inflammable materials are laid. The larger the pile the more

1 Russell and Hiralal, *Tribes and Castes*, Vol. IV. p. 84.
2 Crooke, W., *Op. Cit.*, p. 265.

successful the ceremony. Last of all the whole is covered with a layer of dry grass.

The time for the actual lighting is learned from the Hindu *pandit* who knows horoscopy and can tell it exactly. Theoretically the pile should be lighted at full moon, when the sun and the moon are exactly in opposition. This may occur before sunset, and if so, the pile should be lighted as soon as dusk has fallen. It was to be lighted in the case we investigated at 3 a.m. When the hour has come, all who take part in the festivities gather round the sacred pile with much laughing and vulgar jesting. A cocoanut is usually broken just as the fire is touched off. The fire is lit from burning cow dung cakes; and before touched off, it is carried by the *panda* seven times around the pile which is always kept to his right, so that he goes clockwise about it. The glowing cow dung cakes are then inserted into the wood and grass drawn over it, and the fire begins. One should never blow upon this fire to get it started. It should be fanned, but never blown from the mouth. Now the whole group will circumambulate the fire in a clockwise direction, throwing wheat or other gifts into it. Later on, as the fire dies down, some daring youths may jump over it or run through it. As the group goes about the fire, they shout: "*Hori ha, Hori mata*, take thou this wheat our *Hori mata*." *Hori* is used for *Holi*. Singing is kept up all night, and more wood may be thrown upon the fire.

With the lighting of the fire, the obscenity of this festival is loosened, and may be resorted to all night and the next day. Obscene songs of the *Kabiri* type in which the sexual act is described with appropriate gestures are sung. These are not directed against any particular individual, and no offense should be taken by anyone. A woman may snatch away a bit of the clothes of a man known to her, such as his cap or *pagri* or cloth flung over his shoulder. He must give her a present before he can recover it, and the hat should be filled with *gur* (raw sugar) and sweets before he can get it back. Sexual license is permitted at this time.

Certain prophecies about the coming harvest are made by observing the way the fire burns, the smoke rises, and how it is carried away by the wind.

On the day following liberties of all kinds are taken with people. Dust, mud, dirt, and water coloured red, are thrown over passers-by. Sugar garlands are exchanged and indecent remarks passed. *Kabiri* songs and others celebrating Krishna's love affairs are sung. The more shameless a lowcaste man can be, the more lustily he is cheered by his companions. There is no redress for those insulted on this occasion, as such acts are not considered really reprehensible if done during *Holi*.

Jawara. This is the most important of the festivals observed by the Kols and while linked to Hindu observances, is nevertheless probably a much more primitive affair than many Hindu ceremonies. The *Jawara* festival comes twice a year, in the Spring in the Hindu month of *Chaita* (March-April), and the Fall in the month of *Kunwar* (September-October). The former begins on the first day of the Hindu year in the month *Chaita*, and lasts for nine days ending on *Ramnavami* or the birthday of Rama. In the Fall it comes during the first nine days of *Kunwar* and ends just before *Dasara* on the tenth of *Kunwar*. The Fall festival comes just before the sowing of the winter crop of wheat, and the Spring festival comes just after it has been reaped.

The *Jawara* festival is entered into by the Kols with great enthusiasm, and it is during this period that the *bawa* or spirit possession is most common. During the nine days of the festival, singing, dancing and the beating of drums are kept up almost incessantly after nightfall.

It is called *Jawara* festival after the *juari* plant, a large millet, *Sorghum vulgare*. As this is not grown to a great extent in Central India, it is more usual to find that wheat rather than *jawar* is used in the ceremonies. On the first day of the nine days' celebration, a room or portion of a room is plastered and made ready for the sowings. A ceremonial bath should be taken first, and the one who plants the wheat should care for it the rest of the nine days. The wheat is then sown in small earthen vessels or sometimes in leaf dishes filled with earth, which is well-manured so that the wheat will grow nicely. It is watered daily and a few drops of milk are sprinkled over it in order to make it grow even better. The water should never be put on the plants directly from the hand, preferably the roots of a barley plant should be dipped into the water and thus it is sprinkled upon the growing plants. The vessels are kept indoors and probably not far from one of the household goddesses. It is said that all Kols do not sow this wheat, only those whose forefathers did so, or perhaps also those who have made some vow before a deity.

During the nine days of this celebration almost all the Kol deities are invoked and worshipped, and there is much singing before the village shrines, and *bawas* are common. The eighth night is the one most likely for a *bawa*, for that night all the people in the village are required to fast. During the nine days, the person caring for the wheat should fast in the evenings. The long stalks have sprung up by this time and are now ready to be taken out

22

The ninth day is the final day of the *Jawara* festival. The greenish-yellowish wheat can now be brought out and something foretold, in the case of the Fall festival, about the coming crop. If the wheat has grown nicely, in spite of the fact that it has been kept indoors, and in addition frequently covered by a basket, it is a sign that there will be a good crop of wheat. If the growth of the *jawara* is poor, the crop will likely be a poor one. The process appears to have an element of magic in it and is used as a method to secure good crops; for the earth is first well manured and then well cared for and watered. Frazer in his series, "The Golden Bough", has found a similar ritual elsewhere which he calls "The Garden of Adonis."[1]

The growing wheat cannot be taken out before the late afternoon. When the time comes to take it out, some animals are sacrificed at the village shrine, there is singing and dancing and probably there will be a *bawa* with Shardamai as the deity possessing the devotee. The procession is formed at the shrine, and the women carry the plants on their heads to the river or tank where the stalks are immersed. The men folk follow a short distance behind and loudly beat their drums to frighten away any evil influences. The women sing songs of the *bhagat* type and there may be some *bawas* as well, and the devotee has a trident stuck into his tongue or cheek. Upon reaching the place where the wheat will be "cooled", the women enter the water, and wash away the earth from the roots of the plants. The earthenware vessels are thrown away, and the stalks are retained. Most of them, though not all, are brought back and distributed to friends as a mark of goodwill. They receive from others as well as give. All enmities should be healed.

That evening there is a feast at the village shrine. The Kols gather by *kurhis* and the animals sacrificed are eaten along with other foods; there is more music and songs and perhaps some more *bawas*. Sometimes the animals are not sacrificed until the procession bringing the stalks of wheat, returns from the tank.

Khajleniya. This is another term for the Jawara festival and refers especially to the activities of the ninth day, and the part the women play in carrying the wheat stalks. It is therefore spoken of by some Kols as a woman's festival. Along with it there are certain activities for the children. Two sticks are set up to represent a man and a woman, and they dance about the sticks and sing some marriage songs. There is also a test of balance, and a long bamboo pole is placed on the ground, and the boys and girls try to see if they can

1. Fraser, J. G., *The Golden Bough*, Vol. I., p. 236 ff.

walk from one end to the other. In the evening the big meal is enjoyed by all alike.

Khichri or *Khichhrihai* is a simple festival, apparently one of fellowship when one should invite some friend to a meal and eat rice and *dal* which was boiled together. It comes several times a year.[1]

Marpak is a festival in memory of the dead. It has its Hindu influences and only the male members of the family go to a river where there is a Hindu *nai* and priest. The *nai* shaves their heads and beards and they go to the *ghat* to bathe. After this they visit the Brahmin who is sitting by the edge of the water. A few annas are given to him and holding up some water cupped in his hands, he mutters the name of the dead and recites some sacred texts. For the next few days whenever taking a bath or washing clothes, the Kol should do likewise and offer water in the name of his deceased. A leaf plate is put out either on the roof of the house or in a niche in the wall in front of the veranda. See plate xx. In this foods such as *puris*, *bhat*, *dal* and *bara* are put.

Nagpanchami. This is the worship of the serpent as symbolized particularly by the Cobra or *Nag*. This festival occurs on the fifth day of *Sawan* (July-August). Its institution is aptly described by Underhill :[2]

"This day celebrates the return of Krishna from the Yamuna after having overcome the big river snake Kaliya. Krishna had fallen into the river from a tree overhanging the bank, into which he had climbed to fetch a ball which had lodged there while he was playing with the herds people. His return with the snake was received with joy, the herdsmen offering Kaliya milk in gratitude for his not having harmed their favourite, Krishna..........

Another legend says that a man, ignorant of the festival, while ploughing on this day killed a nest of young snakes. The mother snake, in revenge, in the night bit the man and all his family, except one married daughter living in another village. Having killed all but this daughter, the mother snake set out for that village to kill her also. But the girl, knowing of the festival, had put out a dish of appetising food, which the snake tasted, and which gratified her so much that she not only refrained from killing the girl, but gave her a healing lotion to sprinkle on the bodies of the parents and other children, whereby they were all restored to life. After this, the festival became general."

1. Elwin also finds this festival among the Baigas and thinks they took it from the Gonds. He calls it a children's festival. The children beg rice and cook it by the riverside. *The Baigas*, p. 62.

2. Underhill, M. M., *The Hindu Religious Year*, p. 123.

Kols everywhere observe this festival. On the fourth day of *Sawan* or *Srawan* they should observe a fast which ends with a feast on the fifth day. On the morning of the fifth day Kols worship some symbol of *Nag* and put out saucers of milk near termite hills and other places where snakes have been seen or suspected. No digging or ploughing is done this day lest the snakes be disturbed or injured. Sometimes the women do no grinding or cutting. In the evening there is a big feast of "*puris, sewai, bara,* milk and sugar."

Naodurgan. Literally, "Nine Durgas." This refers to the *Jawara* festival noted above, and is especially connected with the one observed in the fall. Kols say it is observed in remembrance of the nine *devis*. Durga *devi* is the eldest and eight more accompany her. Hindus usually speak of this as *Naoratri* or Nine Nights.

Phag. This is the same as the *Holi* festival, which we have described.

Pusan. In Rewa it was said that this was held in the month of *Pus* (December-January). This may be a variation of the so called *Khichri* festival, for at this time Kols say they worship no particular *devi*, but have a feast with some friends.

Rakhi. "Protector." The full title of this festival is *Rakhibandhana*, "amulet tying." This ceremony is performed in the month of *Sawan* (July-August). This is probably the most unhealthful season of the year in the villages, a time when malaria is very common, and something must be done to ward off illness. A coloured cord decorated with tinsel is tied to the wrist; husbands should tie one on the wrists of the wife and the wife on the husband, sisters on the wrists of brothers and *vice versa*.

This festival is based upon the Hindu legend from the *Bhavishyottara Purana* in which the story is told of the earth, men and gods being under the power and tyranny of the great King Bali, who, by his devotion to Siva, had gained enough merit and power to rule. Before Vishnu became incarnated as the Dwarf Vamana and subsequently conquered him, it was necessary to have some kind of protection from this demon. Vishnu gave Indrani, the wife of Indra, a coloured silken thread which was tied by her about Indra's wrists, and thus he secured protection from Bali.

Ramnavami is the birthday of Rama and comes on the ninth day of the month of *Chaita* (March-April). This coincides with the ninth day of the spring *Jawara* festival, and is the Hinduised term a Kol may use to describe the doings that night. See under *Jawara*.

Sirwani. This is another name for the *Rakhi* festival. *Sirwani* comes from the word *Sravani*—severing of cords—and occurs in the month of *Srawan* or *Sawan* (July-August). This is really the Brahmanical name for *Rakhi* and refers to the removal of the old sacred thread and the gift of a new one. The festival was named only by the Kols at Kotmi, on the Southern border of Rewa.

Tija. This is often given by Kols and is the more common term for the *Khajleniya* festival noted above. It refers to the women's work on the ninth day and is thus essentially a woman's festival. In some places the words are put together: *Tija-Khajleniya.*

It should be observed that but few of the features in the more popular festivals observed by Kols may be traced directly to Hindu influence of a higher kind. Even where there are parallels, the worship is of a different nature, simpler and much more animistic.

AGRICULTURAL RITES. It will have been noted that some of the Kol festivals, *Jawara*, for example, are connected with agricultural magic. A few illustrations are given concerning the activities of the agricultural Kols at the time of planting, reaping and threshing.

Sowing. The sowing of crops is closely associated with the fall *Jawara* festival which precedes the sowing of the winter wheat, harvested in March and April. The second phase of *Jawara* comes in the spring at the close of the harvest. It was noted that the *Jawara* sowings at *Kunwar* give a forecast of the coming crops. The greater the number of plants the better the price, and the rootlets help one to judge the size of the crop.

At the actual time of ploughing the Kols have few, if any, ceremonies. A *hom* offering to *Dhartimai*—the goddess of earth, or Mother Earth—is made just before the ploughing begins.

During the growing season an earthenware pot, coloured white and dotted with black marks, is set upside down on a pole in the centre of the field. This is chiefly to avert the evil eye and to protect the crops, though some call it *Khetrapal* or *Bhumiya.* Its presence insures fertility.

Reaping. When the time to reap has come, the one who controls the harvest will take some curds with him to the field. From some heads of the still unreaped wheat or rice, a few grains are taken and mixed with the curds. The man then goes about the field scattering a bit of the curds and wheat here and there. This is said to be an act of propitiation as *Bura deo* is probably living in the field in some form or other, possibly as a snake, and some accident may result if he is not propitiated in this manner; it may be a serpent bite, or a cut from the sickle. This propitiation likewise helps to bring a good harvest. *Bura deo* may also be worshipped at some termite mound nearby, and a cocoanut offered him.

Threshing. Before the wheat is threshed, a threshing pole about which the cattle tread must be set up. A bundle of wheat heads, the first cut from the field, are tied together and placed at the top of at least one pole on the threshing floor. A string of beads and bangles is occasionally put with the bundle of wheat straw. The spirit of the wheat, who is thought of as being driven from her field, finds refuge here, and will have a chance to find a new dwelling place. The threshing may now begin and the animals tread the wheat as seen in plate x. It is then winnowed and the hot dry wind carries the chaff away. Before the grain is measured, there should be a *hom* offering made on cow dung cakes which are set alight, and *ghi* and pieces of cocoanut placed thereon. *Dhartimai* is very fond of this. When the offering has thus been made, the wheat is measured. The first measure is usually set aside for an offering at the shrine.

CHAPTER IX

MAGIC AND WITCHCRAFT

The Kols are fundamentally a primitive tribe, even though they have been for many years in contact with Hindu thought and life. It will be found therefore that they have outlooks which are properly termed animistic. This does not necessarily imply that their thought forms are simple and that a 'primitive' people have a 'primitive' outlook. Kol thought, though not philosophic, is complex and involved, and has behind it a long history. These beliefs are not limited to 'primitive' people either, but are shared with other groups living about them, and extend up into the very fabric of the thinking of intelligent Indians.

There are certain forces which are opposing this point of view, such as education, travel, books, and modern inventions, to say nothing of contacts with higher Hinduism and the political movements of the day. There are many ancient institutions such as caste, the authority of the Brahmins, and idolatry, which are being questioned at the present time; and these questionings have their repercussions among the villages and tend toward a sophisticated attitude toward many of the beliefs described below.

There are other forces which aid in the maintenance of animistic outlooks: ignorance of what is going on tends toward the *status quo*; women among the Kols are universally illiterate and are the stronghold of the old ways. Many a Kol says that he puts on charms for his wife's sake, but adds that he really does not believe that they do much good. Custom is another force very difficult to move. It is very strong over India and its persistence, in spite of knowledge to the contrary, is a thing which strikes an observer. Belief may change, but custom, though rationalized, remains as before.

A word of caution should be uttered concerning generalities in regard to animistic thought. There are few, if any, perfectly consistent generalizations which may be made concerning Kol beliefs and outlooks. For example, when the spirit world is described, one should not immediately conclude that *all* Kols enter into these concepts, any more than one should judge that all westerners regard the number thirteen with superstitious fear.

THE SPIRIT WORLD. To the average Kol all things animate and inanimate may be the abode of spirits of one sort or another.

Many of the daily occurrences can be traced to their activity. They are sometimes friendly, but it actually happens that they are more often unfriendly and do their best to injure and annoy human beings. The Kols have mentioned certain kinds of spirits with which they are familiar. A few Kols have claimed actual encounters with them, and yet others were not quite so certain of their existence.

The Bhut is commonly mentioned by the Kol, but the use of the term is frequently in a general sense. Ordinarily this is the spirit of one who has died a sudden or a tragic death. A *bhut* is always of the male gender. The spirit of a man killed by a train is sure to become a wandering *bhut*. So is the spirit of a murdered man, as well as one dying of a dread disease. The general belief is that it will remain in this form for twelve years until released. In a general sense, any man not taken up by Bhagawan after death becomes a wandering *bhut*. Another curious explanation was given. It was claimed that the expectation of life for a Kol is about thirty years, and for this period one must dwell on earth, whether in the body or in the spirit. If a person twenty years of age should die for any reason, his spirit will still have to stay upon the earth for another ten years, and will wander in the form of a *bhut*. A man living past thirty years of age will not become a *bhut* unless he meets a tragic end. The same group also related that during this unexpired period in which the spirit must wander upon the earth, the spirit of a very good man becomes a very evil *bhut*, while the spirit of a very bad man was a friendly and harmless *bhut*!

The *bhut* of a murdered man is certain to haunt the murderer's family and in the course of time is sure to destroy it. Murder thus means only more trouble and Kols should never resort to it. It is a fact that murders among Kols are very unusual. *Bhuts* as a rule never injure members of their own families and will even help them. Therefore the Kol holds that one should never fear the spirit of a loved one.

Bhuts and other spirits may enter a room as does the air which comes in everywhere; though the average Kol usually considers that they enter through some larger opening in the house, such as a door or a window. The lack of windows in Kol houses is partly due to this point of view.

The Churel is the spirit of a female who has died in distressing circumstances, especially if the death was caused by child bearing. The *churel* is of dreadful appearance, and her feet, if one would look at them, are turned backwards. She often attempts to seduce men and ruin them. As a rule her front is attractive but she is black and putrid behind. She often dwells in a palm tree. Certain Munda tribes, like the Bhuiyas, sometimes extract the fetus from a woman dying in pregnancy, and the two are buried on the opposite sides of a stream, as it is the theory that no spirit can cross water.[1] If the two should join they become witches. Kols do not practice this as far as we were able to learn, and no operation of this nature is performed. The woman is buried with the child still in her womb.

The Danawa is said by the Kols to be one of the most powerful of all spirits. He is likely related to the Vedic *Danava* who was connected with Vritra, one of the atmospheric demons. He lives in tall trees, and, if he can get the opportunity, attacks one at night, catching his victim round the throat and almost choking the unfortunate person to death. He is particularly met with in the Kaimur jungles.

The Jind, or more popularly *Jin*, according to the Kols, is the spirit of a Mohammedan, although it is usually considered one of the many kinds of spirits known to Mohammedans. Kols have a very bad opinion of *Jinds*, yet say that they know little about them, as they do not pay much attention to Kols but are out to injure Mohammedans.

The Kabbis is a lover of human blood. This demon has long teeth and sharp nails and attacks one ferociously. The nails are used to make deep cuts which let the blood flow and it is sucked or licked up by them. If the victim should struggle and give trouble, the demon will plunge his long teeth into the body and thus hold him while he drains out the man's life blood.

Matia is the demon of the whirlwind. It may destroy crops, bring up great storms and carry away roofs and thatch houses. During the warm season whirlwinds are common and one can trace their course by a cloud of dust reaching far up into the sky. Vultures soar about, looking for those whom *Matia* may destroy.

The Pret is the spirit of the deformed, the cripple, or the mentally defective. Males become *prets* and females are *pretins*. While Kols commonly mention them they usually do not believe them to be very dangerous, nor can they cause much trouble. Rather they should be pitied and fed, so sometimes food and water are placed out for them if they are suspected of being in the vicinity.

The Rakshasa is a terrible injurer and the very name of this demon is an euphemism, 'the preserver.' Most Kols have a great fear of a *rakshasa* and the report is that this kind is more commonly seen than any other and that they also suck blood if they can get a chance. They are usually about at night time and are very dangerous to women who are with child, and try to gain access to the house by

1. Crooke, W., *Religion and Folklore of Northern India*, p. 195.

entering into it in the form of a dog, a cat or an owl. They may assume almost any form and their bite is very poisonous. They can quickly change their shape and appearance. The female type, called *rakshasi* goes about in the likeness of a beautiful girl and seduces men. Nevertheless, this type of demon is easily fooled and if one is clever and does not lose his nerve he can outwit them.

Kols are also familiar with other kinds of spirits such as the *gayal*, the *pisach* and the *kogi*, but little seems to be known about them. The literature on tribes and castes is rich in spiritism and much might be compiled concerning spirits. The above represents the usual Kol point of view.

THE DWELLING PLACE OF SPIRITS. Kols believe that trees are the most likely place for spirits to dwell. The *banyan* tree seems to be the favourite place for the spirit, although it is said that the *churel* prefers a *nim* tree, particularly if broken or dead. It is claimed that the mango and the *bel* trees are not often inhabited by spirits. The tamarind tree is connected with the *jind*.

Spirits may also dwell in rocks and certain weird shapes in their appearance are probably due to the activity of some spirit living there.

Animals may become habitations for spirits, and some, like the *rakshasas*, freely enter into them. The graveyard and the burning grounds are sure to have some spirits dwelling near them and Kols avoid such places; or if they must pass by, go two by two. Such places should never be approached at night.

It was noted that spirits enter houses through doors and other openings. Doors are therefore generally surrounded by demon-scarers, and windows are never found. Evil spirits also enter and dwell in human beings, coming in through the mouth, eyes, ears or nose; so these points should be especially protected. They may also run up the legs or the arms and suitable bangles are worn to prevent this.

THE EVIL EYE: NAZAR. Men and women may also be possessed of an evil power to injure or distress one another. The evil eye, *nazar*, exerts a powerful and dangerous influence and is often evidenced by a squint or the loss of an eye. The person with an evil eye has an inherent power which may be transmitted through a mere glance, and this power strikes one as surely as a bullet. The very glance of such persons is particularly penetrating and it is not good to have any one gaze at you, for it may be that death is in the look. Children are particularly liable to be affected by the evil eye, and ill health and even death are often traced to this influence. A woman is more likely to have an evil eye than a man. Kols believe that Gond women should be avoided as far as possible for many of them are said to have an evil eye that is likely to affect children. A well-dressed person is more likely to be affected than a poorly dressed one, and to put on fine clothes is to attract attention and therefore invite danger.

The evil eye may also be directed against animals and plants; so a bad crop, or the illness or death of an animal, may be due to some one with an evil eye. Pumpkins are often trained to grow upon the roof of Kol houses and may be protected from the evil eye by white-washing an ordinary flat tile, making a cross in the centre with lamp-black, and putting upon the tile as many dots as there are pumpkins growing upon the roof. This will protect them and no pumpkin will rot. A rotted pumpkin is the sure sign of the activity of this mysterious force.

The time of eating is a particularly dangerous one from the point of view of the evil eye. No stranger should come into the presence of one who is taking his meal, and at that time he should turn his back on all people, including even the members of his own household. If one possessed of the evil eye should see the face of a person taking his food it may have a serious result. Therefore it is wise never to interrupt a man at his meals; this a stranger will never do. If accidentally confronted in this way, the eater should stop his meal and wait till the person has passed out of sight. To be seen in the act of putting on new clothes is also to expose oneself to the dangers of the evil eye, should such a person happen by.

WHAT THESE FORCES DO. We have seen something of the supernormal powers which the average Kol feels are all about him. What do these powers bring to pass? Some indication of this has been given already, but more may be stated. Diseases, particularly wasting diseases, are surely due to the presence of evil spirits or the spell of the evil eye. Any mysterious disease may be ascribed to these powers. Ill luck is also due to the attention of the forces named above. A man may be tripped up: it is the work of a spirit; he cuts his hand: a *bhut* directed the axe. We were told of a certain evil spirit dwelling in a banyan tree on the Great Deccan Road near Katni. He was particularly annoyed by cyclists: probably he could not get used to the march of civilization. This spirit was especially active at midday and midnight, and if a cyclist should fail to show respect, by not dismounting and walking by the tree at those particular hours, he was sure to be killed. It was commonly reported that several men had already lost their lives, and others had been injured because they failed to show deference. At any time of the day one who passes this place should get off his cycle, stop, ask permission of the spirit to pass by, then walk with his cycle and mount it again a few paces beyond.

PROTECTIVE MEASURES. Various kinds of devices are used by Kols to ward off the power and effectiveness of the evil eye and the spirit world. The protective remedies commonly employed are listed alphabetically.

Abuse. The abusive language and songs generally used at the time of the wedding have a prophylactic value. There is somehow resident in *gali* a power which protects the bride and groom from evil influences.

Ashes are commonly employed both on religious and social occasions. Immediately after birth the new-born babe is dusted with ashes. They are also scattered over the place of birth, lest the spirits get a portion of the afterbirth and use it against the child and the family. A magic circle of ashes is put around the bed of the mother and her new-born child. When the *nara*, the stump of the umbilical cord, falls off, it is buried in the floor of the house, and a fire which is kept burning over the spot constantly supplies fresh ashes.

Ashes are kept in shrines to frighten evil spirits away. A portion thrown into the air from time to time will be effective in doing this. A fleck of ashes in a child's mouth after feeding with milk keep *bhuts*, who are passionately fond of milk, at a safe distance from the child. The ashes from burnt cow dung cakes are especially useful as are the ashes of wood from the *bel* tree.

Bangles are a protection. The glass types are mostly decorative, but their colours are efficacious as certain colours repel demons. Kols believe that metal bangles are the most effective, particularly the copper and iron types. As *bhuts* may enter through the feet or hands, bangles on the wrists and ankles prevent that way of entry.

Beads about the neck of children are particularly defensive against the evil eye. They should be of bright colours and the Kols most often use a type made from lac. Blue beads about the necks of cattle help to protect them from the evil eye and all valuable animals should be so guarded. A unique charm noted in this connection, though not among the Kols, was that of old bicycle chains fastened about the necks of cattle.

Charcoal, because it is a form of ash and black in colour, is a devil-scarer. Mixed with milk and wine and spread in a circle, it forms an effective bar to evil spirits who dare not cross that line. Sometimes it is dropped into milk as it is brought home, in order to protect it from the milk-loving *bhuts*.

Colours are also an effective protection. Black is particularly valuable as a prophylactic from the evil eye. Hence lamp-black is put on the face just beneath the child's eye. This disguises and renders him less attractive, and as a result the evil eye will not linger on him. Black marks on a white-washed tile or earthen pot ward off the evil eye in the case of crops. Black also pleases Kali and she is glad to see it.

Red frightens off demons and red flags found above almost every shrine have a dual significance : they please the good spirits and frighten off the evil ones. The *sendur* (vermilion) put on the bride and groom is a protective at that vital time. Following the purification ceremony, six days after the birth of the child, the mother's feet are coloured red.

Yellow also protects and there are anointings with turmeric in oil at the times of birth, wedding and death. At such crises of the soul they keep away forces bent on evil.

White is also used : a white *pot*, or daub, placed on the side of the face, immediately in front of the ears, is said to be protective in the case of the child and wards off the evil eye.

Copper. Iron and copper bangles are common among the Kols and some say that of the two copper is to be preferred and is more effective ; it was offered to Hanumanji the monkey god, and is hence very sacred. On no account should this sacred metal be used for dishes nor *lotas*, especially if the *lota* is to be taken out for latrine purposes. To do this would insult Hanumanji and show disrespect to copper. The copper bangle is a very potent charm, and among Kols it is often found that children have a copper anklet on one foot and an iron one on the other. The same applies to the wrists. The little boxes frequently seen attached to strings about the neck, containing powerful protectives such as tiger's claws or *mantras* (written charms), are generally made of copper.

Incense and Smoke. Incense attracts good deities and, conversely, repels evil personalities. At the time of worship incense is thought of as having this dual function. The odour of burning *ghi* is very effectual in this respect. Smoke usually repels demons and if articles which cause an evil odour are dropped into the fire they are driven away. In the Kol birth chamber the baby is passed through smoke soon after birth, and for some days the air in the lying-in room is kept smoky by means of a fire smoldering somewhere within it.

Iron is, on the whole, probably the most common of protective metals; and while some put copper above iron, nevertheless in the case of the Kols, iron appears to be more widely used than copper. The use of iron takes many forms. A woman should always have a bit of iron about her as she is usually exposed to evil influences more than are the men folk. This may take the form of a bracelet, an anklet, a ring on the finger, or an iron ring about the neck. Again it may be just a piece of the metal tied somewhere in the garments or on a string about the waist. A sick man should always have iron about him to prevent further demonic influences during his period of helplessness. An iron key is a protective and even nails in shoes are useful in this respect. A piece of iron ought to be under the head as one sleeps and iron nails are often driven into the four corners of a wooden cot should the Kol sleep on one. In the case of children iron helps to repel the evil eye. At the wedding time the bridegroom carries iron about with him, and iron is found in the wedding booth.

Iron protects houses from the entry of evil spirits and makes their habitation there impossible. Therefore, when a house is built iron is buried under the floor, particularly near the threshold. Even though unseen by the human eye it will influence the demons and they fear to enter and abide in the house. Perhaps *bhuts* are thought of as still living in the stone age and dreading the new-fangled iron and its power to break the strongest things of which they know.

Lac, obtained from the gum of the *Khairwar* tree (*Acacia catechu*), and prepared in the form of bangles and beads, averts the evil eye and wards off spirits. This is variously coloured.

Lampblack is widely used for children and protects them from the evil eye. While it disguises them and renders them less attractive, it also has the practical purpose of protecting the eye from the glare of the sun. The lampblack, mixed with oil to make a paste, is placed just below the eyes and often gives the child a weird and unnatural appearance.

Leather is a very common devil-scarer throughout India and has its uses for the Kols, such as the custom of employing it in connection with the building of houses. For protection, in this instance, an old shoe will generally be found stuck somewhere about the wall which is being built. This is apparent in the picture appearing in connection with building customs.[1] If they can be afforded, leather shoes with nails in them are a double protection, and no Kol goes on a long journey without taking a pair of country shoes with him even though he seldom uses them. He will carry them hanging from a stick or in his hands.

1 See plate VIII.

Lemons and Limes are able to protect one by attracting the attention of the spirit so that he forgets his original evil intentions. So a lime may be carried about one, tied in the loin cloth. A spirit approaches the man, smells the lime and makes for it, and is so taken up with its 'find' that it forgets the man. If this should happen, the lime upon examination will be found to bear evidences of this attack : the juice will be drained away and the lime may even be split. At the time of worship a lime is sometimes cut and thrown as far as possible. Evil spirits hovering about the sacrifice will take after the lime and, fighting over it, will forget what is going on at the shrine. Limes are also pleasing to *devis* and when the *hom* sacrifice is made some lime juice is frequently squeezed into the fire.

Magic Circles. There are many forms of the magic circle and the shape does not always have to be circular. Any circular article like a bangle or a string of beads is a protection. At the time of the *bawa* an iron ring will often be found encircling the fire for the *hom* offering. The tying of the village with a mixture of charcoal, liquor and milk is an example of the use of the magic circle. Such a circle is put about the place of worship if demonic influence is feared. The circle of ashes round the bed of the mother and her new-born babe has been previously mentioned.

Magic Symbols and figures are also efficacious. Such are pictured upon the walls of the lying-in room and on the walls outside the door, and we have given reproductions of them.[1] Sometimes they are tattooed on the body, and the swastika and the *shasti* are the favourites. Symbols marked by the priest on the forehead are useful protective devices.

Mantras. There is also a great power resident in *mantras* or magic spells. Such *mantras* are very potent in driving off evil spirits. At one time *mantras* may have been Vedic texts, but now-a-days the term *mantra* "is extended to all magical forms of words, letters, sounds or any hocuspocus which bring good luck to the happy possessor of them and evil to his enemies, spirits, or casters of the evil eye. These are often inscribed on paper, the ink in which they are written is drunk, or they are kept in metal cases or inscribed on metal or other talismans."[2]

Some *mantras* which may be used against evil spirits and diseases are as follows :

1 See page 62.

2 Crooke, W., *Op. Cit.*, p. 299.

1. To cast out an evil spirit:

Kali, Kali, maha Kali; Brahma ki beti, dono hatha bajawe thali jaha dekho waha kali; teri shakti meri bhakti. Isi saihat bhut, churel, kabbis, jind, dono ko pakarai, na to dhobinke ghat nahawe.

Kali, Kali, great Kali; daughter of Brahma, who with both hands plays upon the brass plate; wherever one looks there she is. Her strength is my devotion. In this way bhut, churel, kabbis, jind, all are caught. If not, let her (Kali) go to the dhobi ghat and take a bath.

2. For fevers and the casting out of evil spirits:

Kalobharo ghungarwala, hatha karo, phulo ki mala chausath jogon sewa men chala, dekho dekhan. Nazar ka tala, raja praja dhawa tuhi sab ki dristi bande tuhi. Main puja pawa tuhi. Teri kiya sabi kuchha hohi. Sekhi Bharo mantra ki shakti. Phro mantra Ishwara wacha.

Kalo bharo, curly-headed, with garlands in your hands and with sixty-four goddesses at your service: look! Whoever has an evil eye, whether king or subject, control them all with but a glance. By worshipping you I get your spirit. Through me you can do everything. Let us see the power of Bharo charm. I cast a spell in Ishwara's (God's) name.

3. To cure fevers and drowsiness:

Ardha sisi huhu karib per pachhara, mukh more amukhari sisa, rahe sir men to Shivari ki ain.

By making a sound of *huhu* we overcome the spirit; with face turned, head diseased; by Shivari's name we say this.

4. To drive off fever, pain and bodily troubles:

Marhi, Marhi, mai pukari, tajo margut majh dhar. Usi murda ka dhuan, ka akshar dekha ko, bukhara, dard, na achha ho; to meri Mari na kahawe.

Marhi, Marhi, I call you. Thou who are in the heart of the cemetery. By merely looking at the smoke of that dead body drive out fever, pain and all that is not well; for if they do not depart then she is not my Marhi.

5. To bring a curse upon, or even to kill an enemy:

Chandi ke uppar Chandi awe. Muth phero nao. Khandi chakra uppar chakra dhawe. Nand masi ki kari age ari, na tak, cha tak, pherna sath muth pherayu, tin so sath. Sachhi meri Chandi.

Chandi after Chandi appears: with moving form and circle; wheel after wheel comes. We have waited for this month and the time is exact. Now go here, now go there, make sixty circles with this instrument (may be a knife is in the hand). Yea, three hundred and sixty circles. My Chandi is true.

6. For cure from illness:

Khermai, Khermai, Khermai, main pukharu. Teri dara yadi yeh achhi na kare to no kahawe sachhi meri Khermai. Washa khali na jai to dhobi ghat na hawe.

Khermai, Khermai, Khermai, I call to you. I am at your door. If you do not cure this one then you are not truly my Khermai. No, her words never fail, (but if you do not come) then better go to the dhobi ghat, and take your bath.

Probably no rational interpretation of these *mantras* is possible. The translations are more or less literal and no translation can really give the feeling put into them. They call upon the gods, plead with them, challenge them, threaten them. To tell one to go out and bathe where the *dhobis* wash clothes is an insult: no decent person would do such a thing. If the goddess can be angered she may accomplish the task just to prove that she is not what the speaker insinuates. The goddesses are made in the likeness of unstable and fickle persons and thus partake of human failings. When the *mantra* is properly recited it is thought to have an inherent power to force the deity to do what the one using the *mantra* desires. The above

24

examples are current among low caste Hindus and do not represent the more polished type to be found higher up.

Milk. The use of milk has been mentioned in connection with the magic circle. The good spirits like it and certain evil spirits are passionately fond of it. Milk is scattered over the ashes after the funeral pyre has burnt down. Milk propitiates Nag, the serpent god.

Names. Great care should be exercised in the selection and use of names, as they become a part of one's personality. A good name is also attractive to evil spirits, and if the spirits come to know that a certain child has such a name they may make an attack on the innocent thing. Therefore, call the child by an evil name such as 'fly', 'filth', 'one-eyed', and the spirits will not condescend to notice him. Such names protect in another manner as well. If one gets possession of the name of someone—his real name—he may, through the charms of black magic, work harm to the person concerned. Therefore the child's true name should never be known to people lest they should work ill with it. The use of magic on a false name is ineffective and no harm can come to one.

Noises of various types are demon-scarers for they dislike noise; hence the beating of drums, the occasional fireworks and other devices, by which loud noises are produced when necessary.

Nuts and Seeds of various kinds are useful. Many Kol children have a *ghata* nut (*Ziziphys xylopyrus?*) tied to a string which is hung somewhere about the person, often on the wrist. Mustard seeds are freely sprinkled about if spirits are expected, and, as in the case of limes, distract their attention. They are scattered round the place where a body is burnt. Black *urad* pulse (*Phaseolus radiatus*) is often used on similar occasions. The *supari* nut (*Areca catechu*) is placed below the sacred pole in the marriage booth and under the foundation stone of the house. These are in this manner protected from evil.

Salt has its magic use among the Kols. It has a preservative power, and this, together with its power over demons, accounts for its being scattered over the place where the dead have been cremated. It should not be put into the food during the period of mourning after a death in the home, and the chief mourner should not use it for a year.

Scape Animals. Among Kols there is a belief that an evil spirit resident in a man may be transferred to an animal and the man thus freed. It is not unusual to bring a man believed to be possessed of a spirit before the shrine together with a chicken or goat, usually the former. The *panda* invokes Khermai amid singing and drumming, or mostly drumming, and there may be a *bawa* along with it. Under these conditions the evil spirit is sternly addressed and in the name of Khermai is ordered to leave the person affected and enter the chicken. Upon being satisfied that the transaction has actually occurred there are now two or three ways of dealing with the chicken. The most common procedure is to sacrifice it to Khermai, and as the blood is sprinkled at the base of the shrine she is implored to conduct the evil spirit far away so that it may trouble them no more. The less common method is to take the chicken into the jungle, the further away the better, and loose it there, invoking Khermai to let the spirit be in the chicken as long as the latter lives; then when the chicken dies, never to allow the spirit to be able to find its way back to the village. If the chicken should return alive to the village it would mean that the spirit would also re-enter and harm someone.

Supa. The *supa* or winnowing fan is a great protective and has many magical uses. The new-born infant is laid in it and no evil spirit will dare touch him there. It is used in various wave ceremonies, notably during the wedding cycle. It is used to cast out demons and to detect demon possession.

Tattooing has its protective value and in an earlier section this was discussed. It was noted that it protected against disease and aided in the necessary household activities.

Threads, red or black in colour, are useful about the neck. This applies particularly to the child, but the adult often has one somewhere on his person. At *Rakshabandan* time the opposite sexes tie threads on members of the family. Threads are used in connection with the marriage of trees and a thread is wrapped seven times around the marriage pole. Threads are often knotted to afford further protection.

Thorns. Thorns afford great trouble to the spirits. They are put over the bodies of the deceased in the graves and are often put about the houses, where they serve the dual purpose of keeping off both beast and spirit. They are used in magical practices, so that when a jackal crosses the road a pile of thorns should be set up, a stone put in the centre, and with one's foot placed on the stone the jackal should be roundly cursed.

Trees and Plants. Any tree associated with the gods is holy and keeps away evil powers and influences. A *charpai* or cot of *nim* wood is very useful as it protects one when he is helpless in his sleep. Some *nim* (*Melia azadirachta*) should always be placed in the lying-

1. See pp. 29-31.

in room and about the door leading to it. Wood from the *bel* tree (*Aegle marmelos*) is useful if burned in the lying-in room and this is done for a period of six days after the child's birth, for this is a critical time from the point of view of evil influences. In Hindu thought *bel* is associated with the god Vishnu. The *tulasi* plant (*Ocymum sanctum*) is helpful in affording a safe delivery and a bit of it is laid over the abdomen of a woman expecting a child. Mango leaves, being lucky and everlasting, are uniformly used in connection with the wedding cycle. Ginger is a devil-scarer, and turmeric (*Curcuma longa*) with its yellow colour is used continually to afford protection. The *magrohan* of the wedding booth should have turmeric put into the hole in which it is placed. The same practice is observed when the umbilical cord is buried or the foundation of a house is laid.

Tying the Village. Tying the village and loosing the *devi* is a magic rite which is common among Kols and comes at set seasons. In Barela, for example, this festival is observed in connection with Mari *devi*, the goddess of cholera. It takes two forms and the observance is reported all over the Kol community.

The cholera *devi*, Marimai, must, if possible, be kept imprisoned in her shrine for a portion of the year, particularly during the cholera season. At Barela they say that she must be tied between *Baishaka* (April-May) and *Pus* (December-January). The rest of the year, say for the period of from three to four months, she may roam as she pleases. About the middle of *Pus* a *panda* cuts the cotton cord kept in the shrine. It is this cord that is supposed to imprison her, so when it is cut, she is no longer bound by it. Other *devis* are also considered to be loose at that season. Along in the month of *Baishaka*, the deity is brought back to the shrine by offerings and sacrifices, the magic thread is tied by the same *panda* that released the *devi* previously, and she is now considered bound. This is followed by a feast near the shrine to which only the men may come.

Along with this there is a second form of tying the village and the two are occasionally combined. In this case some water, wine, milk and powdered charcoal are brought to the shrine where a sacrifice is offered and the *devi* implored to let the magic ring about the village prevent the entrance into it of cholera or smallpox. The *panda* then mixes the ingredients mentioned above and the mixture is put into a glass bottle or into a tin with a tiny hole in the bottom. The men then proceed to tie the whole or a part of the village. If the whole is tied it is called *gaonbandh*, and if part, *tolabandh*. They proceed with drumming and singing and a line of the mixture is laid down, either from the tin or the bottle, around the whole or part of the village. The *hom* sacrifice should be made by each household, and following the whole procedure, animals may be sacrificed at the village shrine, and a feast enjoyed by all.

TESTS FOR EVIL SPIRITS. It was said by Kols that there are certain obvious evidences of spirit possession. Mental cases are attributed to evil spirits as are cases of paralysis and the like. If one acts irrationally it is taken for granted that he is possessed and efforts should be made to free him.

Sometimes it is not quite so easy to tell whether an evil spirit is really about, or whether he should be blamed for the misfortune under consideration. If a man has a disease which defies treatment, and if he is wasting away, it may be that he has an evil spirit working in him. To determine for certain there are some tests which may be made. Among them are the following:

On the floor of the room, in which the man lies ill, a circle made with wheat flour is marked out, and in the centre of the circle an earthenware lamp is placed. Grains of wheat and *urad* pulse are carefully counted and put in a particular position and sequence. The Baiga or *panda*, as the case may be, then pronounces some *mantras* over them and the room is left to the ill man for the rest of the night. In the morning the grains are counted again and their positions carefully checked, and the ring of flour is examined for any marks or indications of having been disturbed. If there are signs of a disturbance of any kind, or if there are missing grains, it is a sure proof that an evil spirit has been about and has meddled with those articles. Of course, it is difficult to believe that any disturbance could not have taken place with mice and rats everywhere in abundance.

A second method is based upon the use of limes. It will be recalled that spirits are very fond of this kind of fruit and greedily attack them. Several limes are therefore taken, and a large number of sharp needles stuck into each, perhaps as many as twenty-five. These limes are then placed in a position where a spirit, were it to come into the room, would be sure to notice them. In the morning these are again carefully examined, the needles pulled out, or the limes broken and the needles inspected. If there should be a drop of blood on any of the needles the spirit has been there. It would have seen the lime, snatched at it greedily without observing the needles imbedded in it and been pricked by their sharp points. Any formation of rust would be interpreted as blood and be the indication of the presence of a spirit.

MEETING A SPIRIT. Even though properly protected from spiritual forces one is still not immune from their attacks. If one should meet a spirit it is always proper to be very respectful in its presence and to try not to offend it in any way. If the *bhut* is addressed as one would address a gentleman he may behave like one. If one moves further on and the *bhut* insists on following, the person attended may, provided he is properly protected by charms, call out the name of Khermai three or four times in rapid succession. Her very name is so powerful that the evil spirit is helpless and goes away disgusted. But should the person not be properly protected by amulets and the like, he should not call upon Khermai.

If it should be necessary to pass the known dwelling place of a *bhut* or other spirit, the person should first stop and respectfully ask the spirit to let him pass safely. No person should be boastful in the presence of a spirit nor use the name of Khermai except as a last resort. The spirit should be addressed as "Maharaj" if a male, and if a female as "Mata". These respectful forms of address are pleasing to them and they will allow such people to pass without harm.

HOW SPIRITS MAY BE CAST OUT. Evil spirits may be cast out only by those who know the secret processes and *mantras* necessary, and such secrets are usually carefully guarded by the initiated. The *panda* is probably familiar with methods although not all of them would admit that they were, and a member of the Baiga tribe is *par excellence* the man. The *bawa* is usually associated with this ceremony.

The *supa* method, forms of which are described below, is the usual method of driving out an evil spirit. Again, the priest while possessed of the *devi* may order the family to perform certain rites, such as feeding the group, sacrificing at the shrine, abstaining from rich foods, and the like; or he may even beat the unfortunate being with his iron lash until the blood flows. This will surely frighten the demon away.

There is another form known to the Kols by the name of *jharna*, 'the sifting or winnowing'. A *supa* (winnowing fan), a *hansiya* (sickle) and a bit of *Kans* grass (*Saccharium spontaneum*) are made use of in this particular wave ceremony. The person on whom these will be used must have fasted for a period and have had *mantras* pronounced over him, then the above articles are one by one waved over him. The sickle, the grass and the winnowing fan are all symbolical of removing a spirit: the sickle, as it is first waved, symbolizes the cutting down of the spirit, the grass implies the work is done, and in the sifting it is like the chaff being driven away and lost. While the *supa* is being waved the Baiga blows, and thus the divine afflatus is communicated to the person.

There is also a magic way of warding off the evil eye and removing its power from one affected by it. A Baiga is called, who, after the usual preparations and offerings, takes a stick and dips it in *til* oil. This is lighted and held over a vessel filled with water, all being performed in the presence of the person suspected of being the victim of the evil eye. If drops of the burning oil fall into the water with a hissing sound the person affected at once begins to feel the influence of the evil eye passing from him. But if the hairs on his body begin to stand up and he begins to feel faint, it is a sure sign that something is wrong and that there is an evil spirit in the case, or that the power of the evil eye requires still stronger measures to remove it.

Kols also believe in, and practise, what may conveniently be called "cross-roads magic". The afflicted person is carried on a bed to the particular cross-roads where the ceremony is to be performed. He is set down in the centre and the friends who brought him make the offerings, which should be sacrificed in the same way as they would be at the village shrine. This may be done at any time of the day or night, but to be really effective it should not be witnessed by any stranger. If some one should approach while the sacrifices are being offered he will be warned away, for if he comes he may break the spell or may himself be affected. It is thought that the disease afflicting the person is loosed at the cross-roads and will attach itself to the first person who passes that way. For this reason Kols usually avoid cross-roads and if possible will pass by some other way. Sometimes a scape animal is released after the offerings are made, and it is believed that he will carry the disease away.

MEDICINES AND MAGIC. Among Kols illness and disease are often ascribed to the work of unfriendly spirits. Cholera and smallpox are particularly the work of the goddesses, and only through them can they be controlled. Other diseases are due to lesser evil spirits. In spite of this, there is also the attitude that in many cases illness is due to the foolishness of man, and that many types of illness can be cured by means of home remedies. Failing these, or any other explanation, the illness is looked upon as indeed the work of a spirit. There are many remedies in use by the Kols for the diseases which abound in India, and the remedies in common use among them are listed below.

Burns : charcoal dust is sprinkled over the burn from time to time. This should cake on it to be effective.

Chest Colds : mustard oil (from *Guizotia abyssinica*) is rubbed over the chest.

Colds : care should be observed regarding food. Only foods that give warmth to the body should be taken, such as grams, molasses, fish, and chicken curry.

Diarrhoea : the seeds of *mymri* (or *mamira*) are soaked in water and the solution given to the patient.

Eye Complaints : a solution containing onion juice and raw sugar (*gur*) from sugar cane, (*Saccharum officinarum*) is prepared which is called *bulni lal* due to its pinkish colour. The eye is washed in this solution.

Fever : a shrub known as *gataran* (*Caesalpinia bonducella*) is very useful for this. Some leaves and fruit from this plant should be boiled in water and the solution given to the person ill. If it is an ordinary fever, not due to an evil spirit, this should reduce it.

Leaves of the *nim* tree (*Melia azadirachta*) boiled in water is also an efficacious remedy in ordinary fevers.

Fractures : a broken bone should be fomented with hot *ghi* (clarified butter) and *haldi* (*Curcuma longa*), mixed together. Sometimes ordinary splints are applied, and when this is done leaves and portions of the skin of the *hajor* (*Cissus quadrangularis*) plant should be put under the splints.

Headaches : *hurhur* (*Celeome vissosa*) is ground and the juice extracted. This juice is put into the ears. The juice of the *bhelwa* nut (*Semecarpus anacardium*) is occasionally used. This is the marking nut and its juice causes a burn and a great deal of counter irritation, and leaves a scar that persists.

Itch : bits of the root and the bark of the *nim* tree are ground together and made into a paste which is applied to the affected parts.

Another remedy is oil from the seeds of the *Kanji* tree (*Pongamiaglabra*). This is rubbed on.

Malaria : malaria is not attributed to spirits; possibly it may be that it is too recent a phenomenon to have been considered as such. The leaves of the *nim* tree are boiled in water and administered.

There is a climbing creeper called *gurj* (*Menispermum glabrum*) which may be used for malaria. The wood and bark of this plant is ground up and put into water. A heated tile is dipped into the water and the solution is then taken. Following the taking of the *gurj* solution a lemon is cut in half and salted and peppered. The two halves are left on the roof over-night and should be sucked the next morning. Another report is that a good remedy for malaria is to grind together *golmirich* (black pepper), *long* (cloves), and *mitha lakri* (licorice). The paste is put into a bit of water and swallowed

Pain in the abdomen: this is relieved by rubbing a mixture of kerosene and mustard oil over the affected part.

Smallpox: there is no remedy for this, as it is due to a goddess and her will, but care should be taken that the patient takes only light foods during this period.

Snake bites: one should chew leaves of the *nim* tree. Crooke notes that "in Ahmednagar when a man is bitten by a snake he is taken to Bahiroba's temple, crushed Nim leaves mixed with chillies are administered, and the branches are waved over his head."[1]

Stomach trouble: for this the leaves of the *Babul* tree, (*Acacia arabica*) should be chewed and eaten.

Swellings: if it be the thighs that have swelled, *ghi* should be applied and rubbed in well. At the same time *Hing* paste (a variety of asafetida) should be applied to the nails of the leg affected.

Wounds: *chuna* (lime) is mixed with the juice of the *Kattha* tree (*Acacia catechu*) and the paste applied. The juice of this tree has good astringent qualities.

Fresh cow dung is very commonly applied, especially to the wounds of children.

The bark of the *Tinsa* tree (*Eugenia dalbergioides*) is ground into a paste and stops the bleeding from a wound.

For the wounds made by thrusting the iron trident through the tongue or cheek at the *jawara* season, the following mixture should be applied: Lime juice, some ground onion, *ghi*, wood ashes and *pan* leaves (*Piper betel*).

It is usual that each village has its *baid* or medicine man who suggests these simple remedies and advises what should be done. However, there may be no such person in the village, and even if there is such, the Kols have great faith in the Baiga, and may go to him.

1 Crooke, W., *Religion and Folk-lore of Northern India*, p. 410.

Kols, Baigas and Gonds live in close association under village conditions. The Baiga priest is revered by both Kols and Gonds, and it is asserted that he has a *deva* living within him which gives him insight as to what should be done. The Baiga, however, is more interested in the occult than he is in prescribing remedies, and if he believes the illness is due to a spirit, he performs over the ill person the *supa* ceremony. It is said that he takes a *supa* (winnowing fan) and places on it a little lamp (*diya*), *ghi* being used to make it burn. The Baiga sits before this and begins to mumble *mantras* and to concentrate on the fire. He calls the *devi* or *deva* when he feels that the time is ripe. When the *devi* arrives, the Baiga falls down in a trance, for the spirit has full possession of him and speaks through him to the people present, telling them just what they must do. This usually takes the form of the demand for some offering to be made either to the goddess speaking through the Baiga or to some other deity named by her, generally an animal: a chicken, goat or pig. As soon as the trance is over, the members of the household begin to take steps to fulfil the words spoken through the Baiga, for the man should start to mend as soon as the offerings are accomplished. If nothing is done, the *devi* will be angry, and the patient is almost sure to die. Should the man die in spite of the offerings, it is said that something was probably wrong with them and the *devi* was not pleased. This ceremony is termed by the Kols *totak vidha*, and requires the winnowing fan, the lamp burning in an earthen vessel, and the presence of the deity. For this service the Baiga charges a fee depending upon the capacity of the family to pay. The fee is decided on by the Baiga after careful inquiry and is said usually to be high. If it should not be paid, the *devi* is angered and the man may die. Sometimes, they say, the ceremony puts them in debt, hence they may hesitate to call in a Baiga.

Another form of the *supa* ceremony is this: the person from whom a spirit or a disease is to be cast is told to sit cross-legged on the ground, facing east. Those who cure come from that holy direction, made holy because the sun rises from there. Water is sprinkled on the *supa* cleansing it. The person is then fanned by the sorcerer, first from the front and then from the back. As he does this he repeats certain *mantras* supposed to be efficacious in driving evil away. The man is asked to move a few feet away from the *supa* lest it be not exactly the right spot, and the process is repeated.

The sickle is often used in casting out spirits and diseases. The person is asked to sit facing the east. Ashes from burnt cow dung are blown over him from the hand of the Baiga, and then the sickle is waved over and about his head. This will drive the demons away.

In a "yellow skin disease", probably a form of jaundice, the following procedure may be pursued: One should take some *til* oil and pour it into a brass *lota*. A sickle or knife is waved over this to frighten off any influences which might affect the magical powers resulting from the act to be performed. When it is believed that all the spirits have passed from the region of the cup, the sick man is asked to gaze into the oil and catch his reflection. If he can do this, the disease enters the oil in the cup and may be thrown out, no longer to work harm on the person concerned.

LUCK AND OMENS. There are auspicious and inauspicious days to be observed and taken into account. In the Hindu month there are five unlucky days which, however, vary from month to month; and the Kol, if he cares to, can find these out by consulting a *pandit*. Nothing new should be started on those days, nor a journey begun, nor any wedding preparations undertaken. Some days of the week are more auspicious than others. Kols believe the best days to be, in the order of their merit; Monday, Wednesday, Thursday and Saturday. Tuesday, Friday and Sunday are the least desirable, but these days are not really bad, it is usually added, but just inauspicious. On Sunday, for example, discussions should be avoided, as such are likely to become heated and quarrels ensue.

Omens should be taken into account, particularly when any new work is being started, as well as during the marriage preparations and at the beginning of a journey. Often a Kol sets forth on a trip to town and returns home not long after he has started. He probably came across some inauspicious happenings, and if the trip should be of a doubtful nature, and he does not quite understand its significance, he will be on the lookout for all kinds of omens. Kols have often promised to come to our stopping places and discuss matters with us, but they have failed to show up. The reason probably lay in the fact that they could not quite figure out why we wanted them, even though we thought we made it clear, and as they started out some omens presented themselves—omens which they probably would never have noted on ordinary occasions, and so they remained at home.

Among good omens the following may be named:

Passing four people seated together.
Meeting a Brahmin just as one starts out.
Passing a vessel filled with water or grain.
Observing a burning lamp by the wayside.
Seeing a woman carrying a healthy male child.

Opening his eyes in the morning and seeing a cow, or observing a cow before he gets up.

Coming across the roller bird (*Coracias indica*).

Bad omens include:

Meeting a person carrying an empty vessel of any kind.

Seeing some newly broken pots the first thing after stepping out of the house in the morning.

Meeting a *teli*, or member of the oil-making caste; but if he smiles so that his teeth are seen, it is all right.

Involuntary sneezing just as one is starting out anywhere.

Observing a dead body either being carried or just lying by the roadside, as in the case of an animal.

To see a jackal crossing the road from either direction.

To meet any deformed person.

To hear an ass braying or a dog howling.

To be startled by the sudden falling of a branch or tree.

The bark of a fox at night means a death in the village before dawn.

To see a crow sitting on the back of a pig or on a man's head.

SLEEP AND DREAMS. Animistic tribes and castes pay close attention to dreams. Kols believe that dreams are evidence that souls wander about over the earth during the hours that one is unconscious in sleep. The soul may then wander far and wide, but no one is ever really able to trace its movements. In a split second it can go great distances and is in no way limited by space. And yet, though the soul wanders about, it does not entirely sever its connection with the body, else the person dreaming would die. Kols believe that a thin thread something like a telegraph wire always connects the two. The soul, even though it is far from the body, is still conscious of what is going on at the house as long as this connection is not tampered with.

During the period when a soul is wandering here and there it may be attacked by an evil spirit. This attack is made known to the body through the thin thread, and the result is that the body talks, groans and shouts in its sleep, the intensity depending upon the seriousness of the attack. At such a time the person should be awakened, though not too suddenly, for this will force the soul to return and the possibility of its being injured will be avoided. If the sleeper should not be wakened, the spirit will return eventually, but will doubtless be injured, perhaps fatally.

A sleeper should never be awakened rudely or directly, for to do so is dangerous to him and may bring a curse upon the person awakening him. If it is found necessary to awaken another person a noise should be made from a distance and should gradually be increased. This gives the soul time to get back. Kols believe that if one dies in his sleep it may be due to the spirit being overcome by a demon and the thin cord connecting the two being broken. A man awakened suddenly may also collapse due to the fact that the one awakening him did so before the spirit had time to return to the body and his connections were cut off.

Dreams are good and bad, not merely in the sense of being pleasant or unpleasant, but their significance is either favourable or unfavourable. It is good to dream of elephants, Kols say, and of meeting relatives. Dances are welcomed as a part of a dream by some Kols, and others do not attach a good significance to them for they believe somewhat in opposites. Weeping, for example, is good for it means that happiness will come, and to dream of copper coins (the cheapest) is a sure sign that one will get silver ones. To dream of a death is also good, for it means that some one who is ill will soon be well. But it is bad to dream of a dead body or of wood or clay, for these things indicate that there will be a death in the family. Happy experiences in dreams may really mean that tragedies are ahead, and so to dream of a wedding or a hearty laugh is not good. While a dream of copper portends riches, to dream of gold or silver or jewels and ornaments, has the opposite significance. To dream of snakes or fish is also a bad omen.

We asked a number of Kols whether they ever dreamed that they were flying, but none ever had.[1] One said that he had often dreamed of riding a bicycle, though in actual life he had never ridden on one. Another Kol, working in a lime kiln, described a dream in which he went to the house of the superintendent of the kilns and when he entered he found everything he had ever wanted to eat all spread out on the table before him. He said that while in his dream it made him happy, he nevertheless knew that it probably meant that he would be hungry before long.

The gods and goddesses often reveal through dreams the kinds of gifts and sacrifices they would like Kols to give to them. If a *devi* should appear in a dream and demand a chicken or another animal, it would be necessary for the person to offer this. Sometimes the *devi* is asked at the shrine to reveal her will to the person in a dream.

1 Elwin records dreams of flying among the Baigas. *Op. Cit.*, p. 412.

Kols generally say that they, unlike the Hindus, are not particular about the direction of their head when they sleep. Inside their own houses they can make their couch in any direction. When they sleep outside, however, they should lie with their heads to the east. And yet, further questionings have revealed, that most Kols have a definite prejudice against sleeping with the head to the north, whether inside or outside the house. No doubt this is because the dead are placed in that position.

ANIMALS AND TREES. *Animals*. Among the Kols there is an exaggerated respect for the cow and it is said that she is the most sacred of all animals. To kill a cow is to commit a great sin, much worse even than killing a Brahmin. In the strictest sense it is murder, and anyone killing a cow even accidentally should make a pilgrimage to the Ganges and offer a gift to the river. On his return he is required to give a feast to the community. Kols as a rule are not rich in cattle and those they possess are a poor lot.

The palm squirrel (*Sciurus palmarum*), is very commonly found in the villages and frequents the houses of people. Kols have a great respect for this creature and some would even rank it above the cow, for, one said, to kill such an animal was as bad as killing a hundred Brahmins! Popular legend has it that when Rama was building his bridge from India to Ceylon in order to rescue Sita, these squirrels helped him by bringing dust on their tails. Rama was pleased with this act of devotion and stroked the backs of the squirrels and to this day the marks of his hands can be seen in the black strips on their backs. Any one who happens to kill a squirrel should give a feast. Boys will never shoot nor molest them.

The cat is likewise revered by Kols and is usually called *mai*, mother. In the ordinary sense Kols do not keep nor care for cats; they are just a part of the village and roam it freely in search of food while no one claims particular ownership. Sometimes they multiply to an alarming extent and in one village it was discovered that no chickens could be raised due to the presence of the cats who killed and ate the younger chickens. No effort was made to change this condition nor rid the village of the cats. That would be a breach of custom.

The dogs too are the general property of the village. To Indian villagers the dog is often an impure animal, but this is not true in the case of the Kols, for the touch of the dog is not defiling. He is a village watchman, and in a sense a custodian of their safety, as he gives the village warning should strangers approach. To slay him is to slay one's bodyguard. On the whole the dogs of an Indian village are a miserable lot and are a menace to the health of the people.

The tiger is another animal reverenced by Indian peasants and is very prominent in their folk belief, especially in areas where tigers roam. This is also shared by the Kols and as a jungle people they reverence him. A Kol should never take part in a beat to track down a tiger. If one should be met in the forest he should be addressed very respectfully. Certain parts of the tiger are useful as powerful charms. The whiskers, teeth and claws are prophylactics against the evil eye. To eat his flesh, particularly his heart, gives one the disposition of a tiger. To see a dead tiger is bad luck as his spirit may later harm the person observing him. If worshipped as Baghdeo[1] the tiger will not injure any one he meets in the forest nor molest the cattle. There is a story current among the Kols that in the distant past a tiger was born out of a Kol. During the years that followed they lived together peacefully in the forest, but after a time the tiger began to trouble Kols so that a separation was deemed advisable and since that time they have lived apart.[2]

The serpent is both feared and reverenced by Kols. It is usually the cobra which is adored, although Kols treat all serpents with respect. However, it is considered no great sin to slay a cobra, but it must not be done unless the cobra is stubborn and shows fight, particularly when in the house. If a cobra, or any other snake is found in a dwelling house it is addressed respectfully as *maharaj* and asked politely to leave. It may be helped out with a little judicious poking with a stick. If it goes out readily it is helped on its way and if all goes well is not molested further. If, however, the *nag* shows fight and does not appear willing to leave the house or courtyard it may be beaten and killed and its body burned. An offering should be made to its spirit after such an occasion. At the time of the festival of Nagpanchami[3] milk is set out for snakes, a common practice all over Central India.

The horse is an animal with which Rautiya Kols do not have much to do; as a rule they will not touch one, and its dung is absolutely taboo. Some of their traditions concerning horses are recorded on previous pages.[4]

The sacrificial animals are the chicken, goat, pig and sheep.

We could not find out much concerning the Kol idea of birds.

1 See pages 141-142.
2 See pages 41-42.
3 See pages 171-172.
4 See pages 34-35; also Chapter X.

The *galgal* or *maina* (*Acridotheres tristis*) is believed to be engaged, but not yet married, and is called a *brahmacharia*. He is never injured. Parrots are never molested, for some of them can speak and utter Ram! Ram! One legend, recorded in another place[1] has it that the *Sath Bhais* gave the Kols their gift of music.

Trees. Among the Kols trees are reverenced largely in connection with worship. The *nim* tree (*Melia azadirachta*) appears to be the favourite tree of the Kol tribe. It is the home of Khermai, the chief deity, and every Kol village or community has a *nim* tree under which the major shrine of the village is found. It has already been noted that this tree has certain magical protective powers and medicinal properties. Demons seldom, if ever, take up their dwelling in a growing *nim* tree, and it is considered healthful and safe to sleep under one.

The *pipal* tree (*Ficus religiosa*) and the banyan tree (*Ficus indica*) are also sacred to Kols and it is not infrequent that they put shrines under them. However, these trees are more liable to shelter evil spirits than is the *nim*, and Barandeo is often found in them. We were told about the growth of a certain *pipal* tree in one of the villages which we visited. It appears that Barandeo wanted to live on the veranda of that house so he saw to it that a *pipal* tree began to grow there. The leaves of this tree, however, were repeatedly eaten off by goats but still it grew. The people who lived there then realized that this must be the work of some deity and cared for it. As a result it grew and good luck came into the house. Kols will never destroy a young *pipal* tree even though they know that eventually it will destroy the building. Hutton, in writing about the survival of primitive belief, says the following in connection with the *pipal* tree:

> We may therefore continue to expect to find very ancient and primitive beliefs continuing under the guise of Hinduism. The sanctity of the fig tree, for instance is possibly to be associated with the beliefs of the Negrito inhabitants who appear to have formed the earliest population of India. It is possibly on account of its milk-like sap that the *ficus* is associated with the fertility cults in Africa, Italy and New Guinea as well as in Assam and in South India, and it is generally also connected with the spirits of the dead. This cult appears to be shared by the Andamese who are an approximately pure Negrito race, and perhaps the only race still surviving in the world comparatively unmixed in blood. At any rate they and their beliefs have probably been isolated for some 5000 years at least.[2]

As far as Kols are concerned the mango tree (*Mangifera indica*) and the *bel* tree (*Aegle marmelos*) are not commonly inhabited by either

1 See Chapter X.
2 *Census of India*, 1931, 1 : 1, p. 397.

spirits or goddesses. It has been noted that the mango branch plays an important part in wedding functions. It was also noted that in building the wedding booth Kols ought to use, if possible, wood from the *saleh* tree (*Boswellia serrata*) both for the main supports of the *marhwa* and for the sacred pole, the *magrohan*. The consensus of opinion is that for the latter the *saleh* is absolutely indispensable.

The *tulasi* plant (*Ocymum sanctum*) is found beside Kol shrines and in the courtyards of their houses. It should be watered daily and its leaves are said to have certain medicinal qualities, being especially effective in fevers. Tulasi was once a woman who engaged in religious austerities for a long time and at last dared to ask to become a wife of Vishnu. For this presumption Tulasi was cursed by Lakshmi the wife of Vishnu, and was turned into this plant. Vishnu comforted her by promising to be near her in the form of a *salagrama* stone. So they are often associated in worship and even in Kol shrines a *salagrama* stone is usually found close to the *tulasi* plant. The leaf is highly scented and a bit is often broken off by Kols and eaten with their food. During the evening hours it is worshipped by having a small *dip* lighted before it.

Dead trees are generally feared as the death of a tree is most certainly due to an evil spirit's influence and a *churel* often kills a tree to make a residence for herself.

MARRIAGE OF TREES. The Kols have a ceremony for the marriage of trees. The mango tree is the one usually married and this should be done at the time it first begins to bear fruit. Unless such a tree has been married no adult should eat of the fruit, although a child may do so. There are at least two methods of marrying trees, both of which require the Brahmin priest. In the first instance a mango tree should be married to a tamarind tree (*Tamarindus indicus*). This tree may be near at hand, or even some distance from the mango tree. The ceremony appears to consist in having a married couple wind a cotton thread coloured with *haldi* seven times around the tree. They should move about the tree in a clockwise direction and as they do this the Brahmin recites sacred texts. First the mango tree is wound then the tamarind; if they are close enough together the thread may be stretched from one to the other. It is not unusual to find a mango and a tamarind tree planted close by. Many of the features of the regular wedding are incorporated, and following the function there is a feast.

In the second instance a small wooden peg, variously coloured, takes the place of the tamarind tree. This may be made out of tamarind wood, although this does not seem to be essential. Stakes for this purpose may be purchased ready for use in the bazaars when the mango crop is about to ripen.

The peg is driven into the ground near the tree or trees which are to be married. One peg will do for a number of trees and it reduces the expense in connection with the ceremony. The Brahmin priest will stretch a thin yellow thread from the peg to each of the trees. The owner of the trees has some supplies on hand, said to include *til* oil, rice, *lawa* and *ghi*. Each person present is given a bit of these things which are put into a fire by the sacred pole at the signal of the priest, who says "swaha, swaha," as they are being cast in. The fire blazes up and gives off a scented smoke. The *pandit* (or even the *nai*), then ties, first of all, a bit of yellow cord around the wrist of the owner, and then on the wrist of each one present. The owner should give to everyone present a gift of uncooked rice, the amount varying according to his ability. This ceremony should be performed just before or after the time the tree bears its first fruits. A tree is married only once.

TANKS AND WELLS. There is a somewhat similar ceremony in the case of wells and tanks. In village India large earthen tanks are commonly used to store water. Water not so wedded will not be as potable as it ought to be. In the case of a tank there should be a pole set up in the centre of the pond. This is said to represent the male element, the husband of the spirit inhabiting the tank and guarding it. It may also correspond to the *magrohan*. An unmarried tank may be molested by evil spirits and the pole warns such away. No coherent account of a ritual in this connection could be obtained from the Kols.

Wells are "married" by putting a bit of *sendur* on the coping and the well is circumambulated seven times by a married couple. Another account was that a Brahmin is called who worships, says *mantras* and performs the *hom* sacrifiee. Following this he drinks a *lota* of water and others follow suit. This is sufficient to consecrate a well and make its waters sweet and wholesome.

MISCELLANEOUS BELIEFS. A number of other animistic beliefs may be mentioned here:

The man who commits suicide does a very foolish thing and it seldom occurs among Kols, for, they say, the police make a great fuss about a suicide, and there is much trouble as a result, and the whole community is hurt. But if committed, hanging from trees is the usual method resorted to. The soul of such a person cannot go to *baikuntha* (Vishnu's heaven), and is doomed to wander about homeless and fearful for at least twelve years. Usually such spirits are not dangerous, and some have said that after twelve years they go to Bhagawan or may be born into the world again.

Sometimes the woman may die in childbirth and the child be born alive. If so, it is thought very likely that the child owes its life to an evil spirit, who desires it for some evil purpose, and hence the child may really be a *bhut*. It is very difficult to get a wet nurse for such children and they usually do not survive very long.

We happened to be in a Kol village a few hours after an earthquake and we asked a group what caused the movement of the earth. Nearly all at once agreed that the earth shook because of *pap*, or sin. One or two though, began to think and said that the real reason was that the earth rested upon the heads of *Nag*—a many-headed serpent, and that once in twelve years he had to shift the earth from one head to another and that produced an earthquake. But when confronted with the obvious fact that an earthquake came oftener than once in twelve years they were puzzled and could not account for it. The latter explanation is the one frequently advanced among Hindus, but Kols were not very familiar with it.

Rain, so intimately connected with the welfare of forest people, may often be brought to pass by magical processes, and there are frequent instances of this among the tribes and castes of Central Provinces. In many of these rites nudity is an essential part, for moved by pity at their representation of poverty, Indra or some rain *deota* will grant refreshing showers. No trace of nudity practices was found among the Kols. The more sophisticated Kol believes that rain is sent only by Indra, the Vedic god of rain, and that it is only through a Brahmin that the gift of rain may be secured.

Some Kols use frogs in an attempt to bring the rains. Frogs and rains are intimately associated in their minds, for in the weeks that precede the coming of the monsoon, the frogs croak long and loudly, and it is thought that their calls bring the showers. So if the monsoon is delayed and there is a drouth, Kol boys will round up all the frogs they can. The larger they are the better for this purpose. A thread is tied round the leg of each frog and they are then dragged about the village. As they pass by houses the people living there come out and sprinkle a bit of water over them. The boys and their frogs finally end up at the village shrine and the latter are tied before the *devi*. It is said that the croaking of the frogs at the shrine will affect the *devi* resident there and she too will long for cooling showers, so she gets to work and uses her influence and power to help bring the rain to pass.

WITCHCRAFT. Magic, it has been seen, is very characteristic of the Kols and religion and magic are inextricably mixed, so that it is hard to say where one begins and the other leaves off. The Kol priest is sometimes learned in magic lore and may know the processes of black magic as well as white magic. Instances of white magic have been scattered throughout this study. And yet it is our belief that Kols are not over familiar with magic and witchcraft. Roy has a statement in his book on the Kharias which I feel is true of the Kols whom we have studied. The quotation follows:

> As we have said, the methods of mágic and witchcraft, practised in Chota-Nagpur and its adjoining territories inhabited by the Kharias, would appear to be generally common among Kharias as well as among their neighbours, both aboriginal and low-class Hindu. In fact, there are good reasons to believe that the methods of magic and witchcraft now practised in common by practitioners of the magic art among Hindu castes and Hinduised tribes of these parts as well as among the comparatively advanced aboriginal tribes such as the Oraons, the Mundas, the Santals, the Hos, and the Kharias, have been in great part derived from one main common source, probably the ancient Dravidian peoples of Mediterranean origin. Not that the pre-Dravidian tribes like the Kharias were altogether strangers to the art. In fact, the magic incantations even among the rudest aboriginal tribes have always been resorted to, and believed to work wonders: the occult powers of certain words, names and numbers, and even of animals and reptiles, and certain herbs, grains and other inanimate objects is dreaded.[1]

With Kols witchery and the evil eye go together and a woman is more likely to be a witch than a man. Gond women particularly, it was noted, should be suspected and kept at a distance. The true witch is not such through any power acquired by her, but is rather born a witch from the very beginning; the gift though, may be trained and the art developed. The witch's power frequently depends upon his or her control over the supernormal powers and spirits which are at beck and call and which can be sent out on missions of evil. We did not come across any actual witches. They were said to be found "in another village".

Witches are able to cast spells which reach far beyond the range of normal powers and are able to work havoc against whomsoever they are directed. It was found that these spells could be sent from Jubbulpore "even to Kewa"; that they travelled with great speed like an aeroplane, and that they would reach distant places within an hour or an hour and a half. If the spell should be directed against a particular person in a village it will fall somewhere in or near

1 Roy, S. C., *The Kharias*, p. 410.

that village. Wherever it alights it is bound to cause damage and this is a proof thát it has really arrived. From this point the spell is said to find its way to the person against whom it was directed.

There is no way of seeing spells travel towards one, and should they actually be discharged toward the intended victim harm is certain to result. Often the person gets information beforehand that his enemy is employing a witch to injure him, and he can then suitably protect himself and neither the spell nor any other agency employed by the witch can touch him.

Chapter X

FOLKLORE AND FABLES

It appears that on the whole the Kols of Central India are not particularly interested in fables and have but little folklore. The Kols pride themselves mostly on their music and song, and the stories which follow have not been easy to collect. No trace was found amongst them of bards or professional story-tellers. No doubt, however, there is much lore hidden away, but it is not obtained when it is directly asked for; the best account is usually found when the story incidentally comes up. Like most primitive people, the Kol knows more than he willingly reveals. The following stories were collected from Kols and represent stories current today.

The Origin of the Earth. Brahma is the creator in the Hindu Triad; associated with him are Siva, the destroyer, and Vishnu the preserver. Certain Kols indicated that it was Brahma whom they considered as the Creator of this world. In the beginning, everything was water, and there was not a bit of dry land anywhere. Brahma brought the earth into existence as follows. First he took the form of a fish and explored the depths of the primeval ocean. But a fish is handicapped in that it cannot carry anything. So Brahma became a tortoise and from some place beneath the primeval ocean, which he had explored as a fish, the Kols know not whence, Brahma got some mud which he put on his back and brought to the surface. It was from this mud that the earth was shaped.

This story bears a resemblance to the story of the Incarnations of Vishnu. The fish and the tortoise are the first and second respectively of the ten chief *avataras* of Vishṇu. But the content is quite different, especially in the case of the fish.

The Origin of Insects. Kols account for the presence of "insects" such as "snakes, scorpions and wasps" in the following way: Sankara was the greatest of all ascetics. He lived very simply without clothes and covered his body with ashes. The dirt from his body, when it fell to the earth, became alive, and so insects such as those named above came into being.

The Origin of People. The Kol story does not make clear how the first people came into existence, for they begin with a primitive couple. The man was named Baiju, which, they say, is the same as Bhil, and the woman was Shivari. These are the parents of all living races. The generation that came of this union is called Bhil, "because Baiju means Bhil." In the beginning, then, all were Bhils. This family has now separated into many races, and the present condition may be likened to a tree with one root, yet having many branches and leaves. These different branches were the result of the deeds and beliefs of individuals. For example, in the course of time among the Kols a certain *kurhi* began to keep pigs, and other Kols, such as Rautiyas would have nothing to do with such people. They are a different branch. Such events made distinctions within the Kol tribe. Other differences arose, and now the Kols are split up into many divisions, yet like the tree are all one. Baiju, it is believed, still lives as a god in a place in Rewa State called Baijnath. In his shrine a very large image of Shivari is also found. She is pictured as black and fat with a large gold ring in her nose. Of course Baiju's image is in this temple, and his brother Baijnath, but they are not together. There are also images to Bhagawanji and Mahadeoji. Many castes go there to worship, but they have respect only for the image of Bhagawanji and Mahadeoji, and not for Shivari and Baiju. Only the Kols know their worth and serve them.

This story illustrates the way Kols mix things together and also the distinction made by caste people between their gods and those of the Kols.

The name of Shivari often appears in connection with stories of the origin of the Kols. Previous note was made of this in connection with stories of origin.[1] Shivari is usually called the mother of all Kols and is linked to the story of Savari in the Ramayana, although it will be noted that the content is quite different. Once, when Rama, Lakshman, and Sita were on their way into the forest on their voluntary exile, it was discovered that they were in need of help. Savari also lived in the forest, and at once began to serve Rama. Savari, the Kols say, was particularly fond of a jungle plum called *Ber* (*Zizyphus jujuba*).[2] She knew that others would like them too, and she used to gather them and offer them to Rama and Lakshman. One day, however, she forgot what she was doing, and that the plums were not for herself, and as she picked them, she took a bite from each and dropped them into her basket. When she arrived at the *ashram* after this trip, she suddenly met Rama, who eagerly asked her for some

1 Also called Sheori. See pages 8, 9, 10, 42, 104, 140.

2 The *ber* is associated with the jungle and enters frequently into their stories. The Hindi word *Kol* is also used for the same fruit—the *Zizyphus jujuba*.

plums. She looked into her basket and saw the half-eaten plums, but was ashamed to tell him that she had forgotten him and had thought only of herself. So she did not offer the basket to Rama. Ramaji, however, was very persistent, and finally she had to present to him the basket filled with half-eaten *bers*. Rama asked Lakshman if he would eat some, but when he saw that they were already touched, he refused to do so. Rama, however, thought them fit to eat, and both he and Sita partook of them. He did not mind it as Lakshman seemed to do. Later on when Lakshman had been struck down by an arrow, he was revived only when he ate these plums. So he should have eaten them in the first place. Thus she served them faithfully for the period of their exile, and when they were preparing to leave the forest, Shivari asked for a boon. She asked for two things: First, for many descendants and secondly, for at least two pounds of grain daily for each, so that they might never starve, and clothes to cover the body. These boons were immediately granted, and so the Kols multiplied. There are today thousands of Kols, they relate, who are all clothed and fed due to the mercy of Bhagawan in the form of Rama.

The basis for the Kol stories related here and also at an earlier place, appears to be found in Valmiki's Ramayana Book III, Canto LXXV. The accounts nevertheless are very different and indicate the way a story is taken hold of and made quite different as it passes orally in legend and story. In the Ramayana Sita does not appear at all, as she has already been stolen away by the wicked demon King of Ceylon, Rawana, and Rama and his brother Lakshman were in search of her. In their journeyings they came to the edge of a great lake called Pampa where they found in a hermitage an aged female ascetic of whom they had heard before, named Savari. When they arrived, she reverently embraced the feet of the two brothers and confessed that it had been her life-long desire to get a vision of them. To her Rama was the greatest of heavenly beings, and now that she had seen him, she knew she could depart in peace to paradise. She had already been told of his expected coming to the hermitage, and in preparation for his visit, had collected the world-famous fruits of the hermitage for his comfort and sustenance. Rama requested the aged woman to show them the hermitage which was built up by the famous Matanga—a low-caste Chandala who had, by means of great austerities and asceticism, attempted to procure for himself the rank and status of a Brahmin. His works were great and would have to be rewarded, but to become a Brahmin was not possible in this world-order, and the gods tried to persuade him that his attempt was irrational. But he kept on and as he could not be made a Brahmin, he was eventually made a god. Long before the coming of Rama, Matanga had ascended into the heavens, and yet the flowers with which he had bedecked the altars had not withered nor decayed. Savari showed the friends all the wonders of the hermitage. After Rama had seen all, Savari told him that she was anxious to depart this world and join the ascetics above, whom she had served so long. So in the presence of Rama and Lakshman she entered into a fire and ascended into the sky, adorned, it is said, not in the ascetic garb of bark, deer skin and matted hair, but with glorious apparel garlanded for heaven. The whole sky was lighted by this splendour, and as a result of her life of simplicity and piety, she gained her reward above.

It will be noted that this story says nothing about boons nor descendants.

THE SPREAD OF MANKIND. The story runs that in the beginning Bhagawan created all men equal. There was neither high nor low, rich nor poor; all were contented and had the supply of every need. In the course of time Bhagawan conceived the plan of building a great fort called Bandhan to be located in Rewa. Many labourers were needed for this task, so Bhagawan sent Lakshman to find them. He went everywhere seeking workers but could find no one willing to do this hard work, for no one was in need of work. Moreover they said that they themselves would gladly employ labourers in their own projects if Bhagawan would only supply them. Thus it appeared to Lakshman that the people would not only do no work, but would also employ any labourers who were brought in; so, much disappointed, he returned to Bhagawan. Bhagawan too was disappointed, and began to think of what he should do. At last he conceived the idea of making all the people poor, for then, he reasoned, they should be glad to work. This he did, and after a time, when the people had experienced the pangs of poverty and want, he again sent Lakshman. Now this time he found that all were eager for employment and a daily wage. They were put to work and the fort was built as first planned. When the work was finished, Bhagawan had no further plan for them, and there were no wages forthcoming. Men were still poor, and in order to get work so that they might live, men began to move out over the face of the earth. They spread thus from Rewa everywhere, and the earth became peopled.

THE ORIGIN OF KOLS. There are several stories recorded elsewhere[1] concerning the origin of the Kols. This story may supplement them. While Rama was in exile in the forest, many of the gods took compassion on him and descended to the earth in human form in order to assist him. These gods called themselves Kolas. After the fourteen-year period of exile was over, Rama returned to his Kingdom and became King of Ayodhya. The Kolas went back to heaven—Indrapuri. The Kols of today are the descendants of the gods who were in the forest along with Rama. This proves the divine origin and nature of the Kols.

HOW THE KOLS LOST THEIR RIGHTS. From the beginning, the Kols enjoyed many rights, and in their prestige were second to none. Once Shivari was going on a journey. A man was hired to carry her luggage in a *kanwar*—two baskets attached to the ends of a bamboo pole slung over the shoulder. Thus they started off. After they had gone some distance, the man said to Shivari: "Why do you walk, when there in the field is a horse for you to ride upon?" This gave Shivari an idea. The horse was brought, but she could not get on it, and so she took an axe and began to chop at the horse's legs to shorten them. The man shouted: "What are you doing?" She replied: "I wish to prepare two pegs out of the horse's legs so that I may use them to mount the horse as he is too high for me." The man said: "Fool, you know nothing; you are spoiling the horse. Take this *kanwar* and I will show you how to ride a horse." So he gave to her the *kanwar* with her luggage within the baskets and jumping on the horse, he rode away. From that day on Shivari had to carry her own luggage everywhere, and her descendants became coolies. The man was really Bhagawan in the form of Ramachandraji, and took away from her the high privileges which were really hers, because she was so stupid. Thus Bhagawan deceived the Kols and cheated them of their rights, and ever since that time they have been burden bearers and coolies.

There are various stories about the horse and the dispossession of the Kols by others. A Brahmin was once ploughing a field, and a Kol happened to pass that way on horseback. The Kol was much interested as he had never witnessed ploughing before. He descended from his horse and after watching the process a while, wondered if he could also do it. To test himself he caught hold of the plough and attempted to use it. The Brahmin then jumped on the horse and rode away and was never seen again. So the Kol had to continue to plough the field and

1 See pages 4-10, 36, 37, 38, 39-40, 41-42.

has been ploughing ever since. It was really Bhagawan in the form of a Brahmin that deceived the foolish Kol, and Kols have never ridden horseback since that time.

DEPRIVED OF BREAD. In olden days Kols had plenty to eat, but they did not know how to eat their food properly. Instead of breaking their *chapatis* with their hands, they used axes upon them. This displeased Bhagawan, and he sent poverty amongst them, and Kols nowadays get their daily bread only after very hard labour.

There is another tradition linking the horse and bread together. The story goes as before that, when the Kols were first upon the earth, they had plenty to satisfy all their needs. They had horses to ride upon, plenty of wheat and *ghi* and fruits. They lived happily, acquired much wealth, and became the most powerful people in all the regions about. But they could not ride upon horses properly. They conceived the plan of shortening their horses' legs with axes, so that they would not have so much difficulty in mounting and would also not have to fall so far. They also began to chop up their *chapatis* with axes. When Bhagawan came to know of all this, he was very angry and took away the axes and all the horses. He gave the Kols sickles and commanded that thereafter they should never ride a horse and that they should work as labourers in reaping the harvests of others.

THE LOSS OF THE SACRED THREAD. In the beginning, the Kols were the highest of all peoples and wore the sacred thread, which is today the right of the twice-born castes only. But once for some reason, Bhagawan called the people together and put the Kols last, thus angering them greatly for they felt humiliated in the presence of all. In their anger and to show their disregard for the sacred thread, they tore them off and scattered them in all directions. These became attached to trees and bushes and at once began to grow and became *Amarbel* (*Cuscuta reflexa*), a greenish yellow parasitic plant now found in many parts of Central India. Any bit of it will attach itself to a tree or bush and grow easily. "Now," say the Kols, "we would challenge any Brahmin to do the same. Let them throw away their sacred threads. There was life in ours but theirs are dead."

HOW THE KOLS BECAME SEVEN FAMILIES. At first there was but one family of Kols, the descendants of Shivari. This family besought the favour of Bhagawan in prayers which were unselfish and which asked not for wealth or food. Bhagawan therefore blessed them and their number increased so greatly, above all other families on earth, so that there was no room for them to live together. So Bhagawan gave them permission to separate into seven groups, and thus the seven *kurhis* of the Kols arose. The groups named in this story are: (1) Thakuriya, (2) Mawasi, (3) Binjhwar, (4) Khairwar, (5) Khangar, (6) Pawai and (7) Kurha.

How the Kols came to be Popular. Sehai and Kuhai were two sisters who were very rich but lacked things to eat, being thus forced to gather the fruits of the forest in which they lived. One day Rama and Lakshman passed by their house. They were hungry and sought food from the sisters. The sisters had nothing but fruits to offer them, and Rama received these gladly, but Lakshman threw them away in anger. The brothers then departed on their quest, but not without the curse of the sisters upon Lakshman for his rudeness. In the course of a battle, while attempting to rescue Sita, Lakshman, was struck by an arrow and fell unconscious and no one was able to restore him. Then Rama remembered the curses of the sisters and sent a messenger to bring some of the rejected fruit. This was brought and forced into his mouth; as it touched his lips, he at once became well and regained the full use of his senses. Then Sehai (really Shivari) asked for a boon and Rama replied: "I am very much pleased with you; go and flourish in the world and increase the population of the world with many children." From that time the Kols have had large families and are found in every part of India. This is not unlike a story recorded earlier.[1]

Heroes among the Kols. Apart from the Kol woman Shivari, the Kols do not seem to have heroes or heroines in their legends. It is said that there is not even one hero among the Kols and the following story explains why that is and also explains the origin of their musical abilities.

Once Bhagawan called people together out of every community in order to bless them and give them a boon. Groups from everywhere set off to the place of *darshana* and among them were the Kols. Other groups reached the place where the boons were to be granted, but the Kols never arrived. It so happened that as they were proceeding on their way, the Kols heard the cry of the birds known as the *Sath Bhai* or Seven Sisters (*Crateropus canorus*). (The sarcasm of the story is to be found in the fact that these birds have a very unmusical cry, one which grates upon the ear). Hearing the cry *pay, pay, pay*

1 See pages 8-10.

of the *Sath Bhai*, and thinking this to be their boon, the Kols returned home. They took it that Bhagawan had given them the gift of musical expression, and from that time they became adept at the beating of drums and singing, for which they are famous all over India.

THE DOMESTICATION OF ANIMALS. After the creation of the earth Bhagawan peopled it with all kinds of animals. But the problem was, which one of them should be put to the plough in order that the ground might be tilled? First he tried the elephant, but he was too big and could not turn about in the field, and in addition he trampled down the ploughed earth. So he tried the camel next but it was not satisfactory either. Finally he created the oxen and tried them in the plough; they were just right and with them Bhagawan succeeded in turning up the soil. Then Bhagawan gave the cattle a gentle and kind nature so that man might have them with him and use the oxen to till the land. Thus they were domesticated.

WHERE AGRICULTURE STARTED. In the beginning certain peoples were created by Bhagawan specifically for the purpose of farming. These were the Kurmis, Lodhis, Kols and Gonds. It was with these groups that agriculture first started. But there are others who maintain that all people were of the jungle and that Bhagawan gave to them first the cattle which he had created; therefore they left living off fruits and roots and began to grow crops.

WHY WE HAVE A LITTLE FINGER. There is a story among Kols, that in the distant past when the Pandus and the Kurus fought in Hindustan, Shahadeo Pandu desired to see for himself just how one might become possessed of Shardamai. So he thought he would try an experiment. He brought before the goddess a cocoanut, some *sendur*, *ghi* and fire, and began to make a *hom* offering. As he was doing this, he suddenly became possessed of the *devi* and his fourth finger happened to rest in the *hom* fire. Being in the state of unconsciousness due to the *bawa* he did not notice this fact, and the tip of the finger began slowly to burn away. Ever since, man has had a little finger for it was shortened in the *hom* fire.

THE COMING OF DISEASES. There were once seven sisters in heaven, who were sent from there to the earth to live among men. As they left Bhagawan, they asked him for boons, for, they said, unless they had power of some kind no one would respect them nor would men worship them. It happened that each was granted a boon.

Khermai, called Bhagavati, chose the power of smallpox. If any one fails to please her, she appears in that person in the form of smallpox. Or, if not that, some other in the family will be with the pox, euphemistically called *mata*, "mother" She was given the power to remain in full control of the person for two and a half days, and during that time the sick person should be worshipped, for that really means the worshipping of Bhagavati; so men must respect and honour her for her power. Further honour must be shown by the whole family in the avoidance of certain foods such as pulses and *ghi*. No frying pan should be used, and the inmates of the house should not wear leather shoes.

THE KOLS AND MAHADEO (SIVA). The Kols have several stories in which they speak of a character which they call Baiju or Baijnath. One example has already been given. From some stories it appears that he is the husband of Shivari. Kols say that Baiju, under the name of Baijnath, and the god Mahadeo must always be worshipped together, but Baijnath should be worshipped first.

One story relates that Baijnath excelled all others in his devotion to Bhagawan, and when the time was right, he asked Bhagawan for a boon. He asked that at the time of worship, water might first be poured over him and then over Mahadeo. This was granted, and he used to worship Mahadeo and beat him with a stick five times a day.

A longer form of this story from another section of Central India is as follows: In this account Baijnath is spoken of as a Rautiya Kol, a farmer who worked daily in his fields. He had this peculiar characteristic, however, which was that as he went by a certain temple, he used to enter in and beat Mahadeo with a stick five times a day. The reason for this strange behaviour was known only to Baijnath. Once it happened that he was so busy in the fields that he forgot to beat the god and when he was almost home from work he recalled his omission. At once he decided to return to the dwelling place of Mahadeo, but on the way he found that, for some strange reason, the river was in spate, and would be very dangerous to cross. He decided to wait a bit, but there was no improvement in the river. The sun was about to set, and the day would be gone, so he decided to jump into the river and swim through it. He did this very dangerous thing and going to the temple gave Mahadeo five blows with the stick. On his return he had to swim the river again. Now Mahadeo, who saw all this, was afraid, for he realized that Baijnath was a man of purpose and would not be turned aside by dangers, so he decided that he must do something to please Baijnath. With this in mind Mahadeo waited till Baijnath arrived the next day intent on beating him. Greeting him he said: "Baijnath, I wish to give you a great boon. It is that people will worship you and pour water on you first and after that they will worship me. If they should fail to do this to you, they will have no fruit of their labours at all. So now that you have this *bardan* please give me release from this daily beating you are giving me." Hearing this, Baijnath was very happy and Mahadeo was beaten no more. So Kols always worship Baijnath first.[1]

How the Cat became a Household Pet. Once Mahadeo sent a cat to spy upon a certain home. He wanted to know whether there was a fire in there at that particular time. This cat had stayed with Mahadeo for a long time and, obeying his commands, she went to the house where she found the fire burning and milk nicely warmed beside it. There was also some freshly prepared butter on the floor. The cat tasted the butter and found it so delicious that she ate it all. Next she drank the milk, and feeling very comfortable, she curled up to sleep beside the cosy fire. She nevermore left the house, for she preferred it with its warmth, and butter and milk, to the treatment and food she had with Mahadeo. Since that time the cat has become a household animal, and it is a great sin to kill one, as it came directly from Mahadeo.

Why the Tiger fears the Red Dog. The wild dog, a red dog of India, (*Cyon dakhunensis*) is common in the wilder jungles of Central India. It is much feared by the animals of the forest, including the tiger, and tigers are sometimes killed by it. These dogs always hunt in packs containing often as many as thirty animals, and the pack does not give tongue, coming suddenly upon its prey.

The story goes that once Mahadeo quarrelled with Parvati his wife. He was so annoyed with her that he left home and went into voluntary exile in the forest. Parvati was sorry and wanted to get him back, but was too proud to humble herself before him. Finally she decided to frighten him and thus cause him to return. She was sure that if she could send a tiger after him to annoy him Mahadeo would surely fly to his home for safety. So she used her divine powers to make a tiger go to him, but in vain, for Mahadeo outwitted her, as

1 It is now established that Siva or Mahadeo worship is very ancient. Evidences of this are found in the Mohenjodaro civilization. A Census report notes that "Bhils, Savaias and the Korkus all trace their origin to Mahadeva, though it is possible that the tradition may be a latterly acquired Hindu Idea." (1931—I : 3 B. p. 63). Perhaps this story is a memory of a strife with groups who did trace their ancestry back to Mahadeo. The Kols frequently identify Baiju or Baijnath with the Bhils.

he was a god. He picked up some dry pieces of wood and threw them toward the tiger saying, "*Chhu, chhu*". The wood became the wild dogs of the Indian jungles, which do not fear the tiger and attack it in packs. These dogs attacked the tiger and with their tails spread urine in his eyes. This made the tiger blind and fearful and he hastened away.

Since that time Kols have held the tiger sacred because it is associated with the goddess Parvati; also the wild dog, because Mahadeo created it to protect himself. This also accounts for the fact that tigers today are afraid of the red dog. Neither the tiger, the jungle dog, nor any dog should be killed.

HOW ILL TEMPER BRINGS DISASTER, AND ITS CURE. Biran, a Kol, was the servant of a *raja* who possessed a very bad temper. This king constantly used bad language in the presence of everyone he met and annoyed Biran immensely. Once this *raja* gave a great feast to which many people were invited. Biran and his friend Dadul also came. After the food was taken, someone got something very bitter in his mouth, and was forced to spit it out on the costly rug, on which they were seated for their meal. This was seen by the *raja* who became very angry and used disgusting *gali*. Many people left, among them Biran and Dadul. The rainy season was about to come, but the rains were delayed. What was the matter? No one could tell, and week after week passed with no cooling drops. They did not know that it was all due to the ill temper of the *raja*.

The farmers felt that they must break up the ground so they might catch any rain that fell. Biran was ploughing along with others when his plough turned up a frog, and the frog cried out in his dismay. Bhagawan heard this, and thinking that the frog was very thirsty, sent rain upon the earth; the wickedness of the *raja* could no longer restrain its fall. But the *raja* was still angry and called for Biran and scolded him. Nevertheless his words had no more power to bring a curse upon the land.

"This story shows that magic can remove a curse," was the comment of the teller.

Chapter XI

MUSIC, SONGS, DANCE AND ART

The Kol people are passionately fond of music and song. It is not infrequent for them to sing, dance and beat the drum the whole night through. One of the reasons advanced for their living separate from Hindu villages is that it makes it possible for them to sing and play to their hearts' delight without being disturbed or disturbing anyone. The drums as played by the Kols beat with a particularly strident and penetrating note audible from long distances away. A real emotional release is connected with their music and the sense of rhythm felt throughout an evening with them can never be forgotten. The tones seem to pierce to the very marrow of one's being and make the body tingle. Great skill is required in playing the drum and for long periods the pace is kept up without a break. It takes practice, skill and strength to maintain this movement.

Musical Instruments. The Kols make no use of wind instruments nor do they often use the stringed type, although the *sarangi*, a one-stringed instrument, is sometimes seen. They limit themselves to various types of instruments of percussion of which four kinds are chiefly employed by them :

1. *The Dholak.* The *dholak* is the favourite instrument of Kols and, in comparison with other types of percussion instruments, it is by far the most frequently used. It is cylindrical in shape and is constructed by a hollowing process from a solid block of wood. Each end is covered with skin stretched out by leathern thongs attached to the shell. The tightening or loosening of the thongs by adjusting a round block of wood under them serves to give the drum its desired pitch. A mixture of wood ash and boiled rice is often applied to the leather to give it more resonance. Both hands are used in playing it, the beats of the two hands usually differing, producing a syncopated beat of a nature difficult to imitate. The illustrations[1] show *dholaks* and the accompanying text figure makes their construction clear. The diameters of each

Fig. 28. The Dholak

1 See plate XVIII.

end are about the same, being from nine to twelve inches; the length is generally from twenty to twenty-five inches.

2. *The Timakia or Nagariya.* This instrument is the kettle-drum and has only the one playing surface. The shell is made out of copper; brass, or iron sheets riveted together. Proper tension of the leather is produced by means of the leathern strap interlaced over the metal. The *timakias* used by Kols, seldom have a head more than twelve to fourteen inches in diameter. They are played along with the *dholak*, but unlike it, the hands are not used upon the leather; the drum is beaten upon by means of two sticks which are sometimes curved.

Various sizes of these two drums are in use, and when more than one is being played they must be tuned up beforehand. Their cost varies from Rs. 1-8-0 to Rs. 5-0-0. Drums are used on all singing occasions: dances, birth, marriage and religious worship. Women never play them for that is the preroga-tive of the men folk.

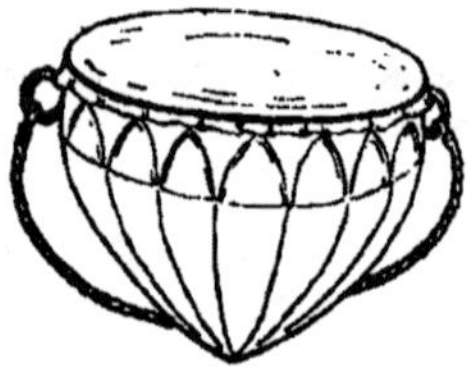

Fig. 29. The Timakia

3. *The Kartel or Kartal.* This is a form of the cymbal, being in reality a cluster of cymbals. A piece of wood twelve to fourteen inches long has built upon it cymbals of varying sizes, so adjusted that they may slide along the stick. The ends of the stick are held in the hands and the whole is shaken at various angles in order to produce modulations of tones. The beat must be exactly that of the drums, hence it is a very difficult instrument to play satisfactorily; but ex-pert players produce a most pleasing effect; in perfect resonance and rhythm.

4. *The Majira* or ordinary cymbals are of various sizes, but the type used by the Kols is usually about four inches in diameter and made of brass. One is held in each hand and they are mani-pulated so that there is modulation and variations of tone as well as perfect rhythm.

THE MAIN KINDS OF MELODY AND SONG. There are a number of types of songs sung by Kols, examples of which are found below. The main types and their chief characteristics will be briefly noted. The types vary both in rhythm and content.

1. *Dadar* or *Dadra*. This is by far the most common kind sung by Kols and is a well-known melody sung all over northern India. H. A. Popley in his book *The Music of India* says: "The *Ghazal* and the *Dadra* are two Hindustani melodies. They consist as a rule of *Antara* only, sung alike to a simple melody in syncopated time, which is known as Pashto."[1] Kols may sing this form on many occasions and at any time of the day and night, and its use is not limited as certain others are. It is used at the *Chhatthi* rejoicings when the women sing and dance on the sixth day after the birth of a child; it is used throughout the wedding cycle; and may even be used at times of religious worship. Sometimes the words are chaste and beautiful, and again a *dadra* song may contain abuse as is common at the times of weddings.[2]

2. *Bhagat*. This is predominantly the song of worship. Some Kols say it is used for the *devis* and *deotas* while *bhajans* are used for Bhagawan. This does not appear to be the actual practice however. The root of the word is from *bhakti* which means "passionate devotion," and a *bhagat* is generally sung before the gods and goddesses. It is sung when the *jawara* is sown. At times when men become controlled by the *devi* it is this type of song that helps to bring on the emotional excitement resulting in "possession". The words may apply to any occasion and the rhythm varies from the *dadra* and the *rai*.

3. *Bhajans* are religious songs, but are supposed to be addressed to the higher powers, and Bhagawan is generally mentioned. However we found an instance of a *bhajan* being addressed to Sharda.

4. *Rai*. This type implies songs of Krishna and Radha. There are various rhythms in use, but its content, as far as words are concerned, is frequently obscene. Like the two following types it is sung mostly at the *holi* season.

5. *Phag*. This is named from the month of Phagun for it is supposed to be sung only during that particular month, and may be called a spring song. Phagun is the eleventh month in the Hindu year and covers the last half of February and the first half of March. This corresponds with part of the *holi* season, and some say the *phag* type of song should be sung only during the last fifteen days of the season. The contents of the majority of *phag* songs are not respectable and it is very difficult to get one sung for an outsider; they are some-

1 *Op. Cit.*, p. 90.
2 Elwin calls the *Dadaria* the true forest songs of the Baigas. *The Baigas*, p. 438.

what reluctant to repeat them unless they are sung under emotional excitement.

6. *Kabiri*. This is another obscene type sung mostly at the *holi* season. It is said that the sexual act is described with obscene gestures. Kols say that it is called Kabiri as Kabirdas made and sang them. This is certainly a fiction. There may, however, be some Moslem influence in the songs, though this is open to doubt.[1]

7. *Dohari*. A type of song in which the verses are made up of two lines. The word comes from *doha* meaning a couplet. The full dohari has twelve couplets of two lines each.

8. There have been some other types and varieties of types named by Kols, but no information about them seems to be available and Kols themselves do not know the niceties of them. Among such may be mentioned Kotwerhai, Bhumhai, Kolhai (said to be a form of the *dadar*), Badhwa, Katili, Birha, Bihari, Chhauhar and Barahmasi. Examples of most of these kinds will be found below.

Those songs are sung by both men and women, though on certain occasions one of these groups may do the most of the singing. Women, for example, do all the singing on the sixth night after birth (*Chhatthi*); both sing at the time of wedding; at the periods of special religious worship it is generally the men who do the singing, although it is not unknown for the women to take a part.

KOL SONGS. Most of the songs sung by Kols are composed for special occasions, and the following songs are selected from a number collected by us in our visits among the Kols. They give an interesting insight into the Kol outlook on life. One finds the joys and sorrows of youth and love. An appreciation of nature is also evident, while many of the songs border on what many would consider indecent and questionable. Many songs centre about Ram and his victory over Rawana. Only a few of these are included. In Appendix III brief notations on certain of the songs will be found. The meanings of some of the songs are obscure and in many of them there are insinuations not easily grasped. In some cases only the composers, probably, know to what the songs allude and any translation is far from satisfactory. It is believed that the songs which follow are fairly typical of Kol songs in general. They are arranged topically in the main, though some songs fall into more than one classification. There are six divisions: 1. Songs of Nature; 2. Life: its Joys and Sorrows

1 How Kabir's name came to be associated with these songs is a mystery. Kabir's songs are highly respectable and well-thought of. See above page 46.

Kol Musicians with Dholaks and Timakia under a Nim tree in Rewa State.

3. Love and Intrigue; 4. Songs in Connection with Social Events; 5. Songs of Religion; 6. Some Miscellaneous Songs.

I. Songs of Nature

1. Morning. (*a*)

Suraja ke kirana karhi
Sagabana bana dholenge;
Pankshi bana bolenge,
Kaga bole angana.

When the sun's morning rays flash forth,
All the trees in the forest will quiver;
Then the birds will call in the forest,
And the crow will caw at your door.

2. Morning. (*b*)

Suraja ke kirana karha,
Chakahi piya milana bhaye;
Pankshi bana bolo gaye,
Kaga bole angana.

As the morning's first rays are drawn out,
Forth goes the Chakahi to its lover;
Then every bird called in the forest,
And the crow cawed loud at the door.

3. The Storm and Lonely Heart.

Purabadisha se uthi badariya,
Jaise kunjar ki rekha;
Nadai barse, nadai garje,
Jhare badal dhanray—
Kari re badariya ghumar ji ley.

From the East march the mighty clouds,
Like a line of elephants they move along:
They rumble and thunder
And pour forth terrifying streams—
And Oh, how they torment and afflict this heart—
Until he come!

4. Flowers and Music.

Tori angani phulana ki bahar re :
Bela bhi phule, chameli bhi phule,
Sab phulan men raja gulab re.
Tabala bhi baje, sarangi bhi baje,
Sab baja men raja sitar re !

Thy courtyard is the scene of abundant flowers :
The *bela* is blooming, the *chameli* is flowering,
Yet the king of them all is the rose.
The drums too are sounding, the *sarangi* resounding,
But the *sitar* is king of them all.

5. A Forest Song.

Age nadiya agam bahi hai,
Manai nawe jay.
Swami ke sandisawa ko le awe
Ko le jay ?

Before me flows a river of sickening depth ;
'Tis only crossed by boats.
Who shall bring my lord's message to me
And mine to him ?

II. Life : Its Joys and Sorrows.

1. Does Your Life Have Purpose ?

Ka karho jug men ayeke, aiso jiwan payke,
Merha mari, kukra mari, mirga mari ban se :
Aiso jiwan payke ?

With a life so precious you came into this world ;
Is it to kill a ram, or a cock, or a deer
With an arrow ?
Can this be the meaning of life ?

2. The Transitoriness of Life.

Sada turaiyan na phule,
Sada na Sawan hoy;
Sada piya na ran charen,
Sada na jihan koy;
Ek din marna sabhi ka hoy.

The gourd bears not blossoms forever,
The "green month" lingers not long;
Not often do husbands join battle,
And man does not live on perpetually:
One day each one must lie down.

3. The Need of Love amid Change.

Patta tute dar se,
Pawan lai gaye uraya,
Yari chhuti yara se,
Dukha kaise kahaun samujhaya?
Jiyara tu rahe sabai se pyar.

The leaf has dropped from the branch,
And the wind has blown it away,
The maid is torn from her lover,
And how may her grief be told?
O love everyone, my soul!

4. Sorrow Loosed upon the Life.

Maiya mori bairi bhai Rama Lachana:
Nadiya hoti sab kai bandhe,
Maiya mori bandhi na jai samudiya.
Chithiya hoti sab koi banche,
Maiya mori banchi na jai karmana.
Sampat hoi sab koi bante,
Maiya mori bati na jai bipatiya.

My mother is become my enemy
(Since she married me to such a one),
O Ram, O Lakshaman!
Rivers may be dammed,

But not this sea of pain
Loosed on me by my mother........
Any one can read a letter:
But, O mother, who can understand my luck?
Wealth may be shared by all:
But not this flood of sorrows
O mother, can be shared!

5. The Sorrows of Desertion.

Sona lena piya gaye,
Suna kara gaya desha;
Sona mila na piya mile,
Rukh bhaya sab kesh,
Yaha tan chola ka nahin biswas.

My lover left to buy me gold,
And all my world was gone;
Now neither have I gold nor lover,
And my hair has grayed with the years,
One cannot trust this body or life.

6. The Round of the Years, and yet—

Kaise karon, kahan janwa?
Umariya bhari ko harai;
Yaha tana ka pira bina banawali?

Asara bolai mora, shora bhaye bhari,
Bhadon me dara lagai, dekha andhiyari,
Kunwar karara hajara karo banawali;
Katika nahin aye shayama sawata sanghari,
Agahana agra suhana dukhai dukha bhari;
Maghai parai tusara deha dain dari.
Phaguna ma karau karana hajara banawali,
Chaita chakra chahara hara bhayahari,
Baishaka na lagai ankha bina banawali;
Jetha ma asa tanpaya tana jari,
Asara ban bolai mora shora bhari.

What to do? Where to go?
For my desire is urging me on.
Who can relieve this body's ache
But my dear husband?
For,
In Asara the peacock calls and sets the forest resounding.
In Bhadon upwards I look and fear the clouds and the darkness.
In Kunwar, O husband dear, a thousand times you have said "I am coming";
But now Katika has begun and still I long for your presence.
In this most auspicious Agahana I find my heartache unbroken;
In Magh with its mists and its cold I am lonesome and shivering in body.
O Companion, a thousand promises were made that in Phagun you'd surely be with me.
The wheel of Chaita is revolving: O come and remove my desire:
For without your presence, my dear, I have no sleep in Baishaka,
And if not, then in Jeth will this body burn as with fever:
......And in Asara again, they will hear the call of the peacock.........

III. Love and Intrigue.

1. The Call of Love.

Prita to aise ki jaise lota aou dora,
Apana gala phasaya ke pani lawata bora,
Pirati lagaya chhore na, jiyara hamara.

As the cord tied round the *lota* brings up water,
So is love;
Ah, tie the cord of thy love about me,
And never leave my soul again.

2. Admiration.

Kaun halwaiya ke khaye mithai?
Aur kaun baraï ke pan?

Aur kaun chail ki jiya marawaile kekha debabai dar?
Jiya marway men pahay kaya?

Ah sweetheart!
At which sweet-seller s shop did you take sweets?
And which *panwalla* gave you *pan*?
What lad will next be smitten by your beauty?
Whom now will you cause to be fined?

3. Unity and Rest.

Tala kahai purhaina se chala jala bich tu jaya,
Chirai chiragun pani na pawai kamala pata rahain jala chaya.
Dono jana rahi kamala gahachhaya.

The pond saith to the lotus:
"Go deep into my heart,
So the birds of the air may not reach me,
For your leaves shall ever protect me."
Thus shall they e'er be together:
The lotus covering the waters.

4. To a Doubting Husband.

Hansna mora subahu balam tum chinta na mane.
Jab mai raha barah baras
Kahi kahun najar nahin dugai,
Balam tum chinta na mane.

'Tis my nature to smile, dear husband,
Do not worry, mine own.
Since my twelfth year
Have these eyes never roamed;
Beloved, be not suspicious of me!

5. Yearning.

Kali daha ki machhari burawai utaraya,
Dhimarana jala umho bansi dora jaya,
Sakhi, inkar doha kahe sumujhaya.

In the depths of the ocean black
The fish go up and down.
When the water rises the *dhimar* casts his net:
Ah love! Need I explain?

6. The Refreshing Waters of Love.

Sakare mukha ka bawali lagata lambi dora,
Trisna kaise bujhai pani bina
Tarphai, jiyara hamara?
Aba pardeshi pani yan piawa.

The mouth of the well is narrow,
And its waters lie so deep.
How shall I quench this thirsty soul
Which pants for sweet waters?
O absent husband—give me of your drink!

7. The Satisfying Water of Love.

Sakara mukha ka bawali,
Siriya hai ratana joraya,
Utara utara pani piyo:
Jiyara kai tapana bujhawa......
Pani pa piye hai:
Jiyara nisocha.

The well's mouth is narrow,
Its steps are paved with gems,
Go down, ever down, then, drinking
Cool life's fierce fever......
Now have I tasted your waters:
And the pain of existence is gone.

8. A Challenge.

Hansa ke lagai tuma ari,
Nibaibe ko tuma jano balama.

Alas, your smiles have taken me to your bosom!
Now you yourself take charge of carrying on our love!

9. An Intrigue in the Home.

Ka dekh machari luriya karat hai?
Ka dekh bhamra lobhay?
Jal dekh machari luriya karat hai,
Phul dekh bhamra lobhay.
Ka mangai sari?
Ka mangai sarahaj?
Ka mangai ahaniya tumhar?
Sari to mangai phulon ka gajra,
Sarahaj lahra pator,
Ahaniya mangai sunne ki churiya,
Jo na rahe sansar.

Sari se sarahaj adhika piyari,
Sas Ganga jala pani.
Ab mat pita ki kiriya khaun:
Ab na jab sasurari!

What draws the fish? What tempts the bee?
Water the fish, and flowers the bee.
What wants your *sari*? (Sister-in-law)
Why beckons your *sarahaj*? (Brother-in-law's wife)
What does your *ahaniya* need? (Mistress, wife)
Your *sari* wants a wreath of flowers,
Your *sarahaj* looks for beautiful clothes,
And your *ahaniya* wants bangles,
Golden ones of matchless beauty.
Your *sarahaj* is dearer than your *sari*.
Your *sas* (Mother-in-law) is pure like Ganges water.
By My parents I swear:
I shall never henceforth
Go to my *sasur's* (Father-in-law) house!

IV. Songs of Social Life.

1. A Song of Birth-pangs.

Ghumara ghumara pira awai kou nahin janai,
Janai mori lahuri nandiya sasa to sowai mahaliya.
Nanda gajowari sasa ke dabai,
Chhanguriya raja ke pawaun pindariya.
Tumhari mahaliya kachhu shora jagaya nahi jagan.

Such birth-pangs and inner writhings as none ever
 dreamed, are upon me.
But only my little sister-in-law is aware of it all,
 And my mother-in-law in the palace peacefully
 sleeps!
And there sits my husband's sister:
 Massaging that woman—my mother-in-law!
 And the legs of that woman's king!
For in spite of all my groanings
 You waken not in your palace.

2. Congratulations for a Son.

Bhali khet jahan tilli upaji,
Gehun upaji nau sar.
Kokh bhali jahan lalan upaje,
Bajan badhaiya Ayodhya men.

Good earth is that which gives us sesame,
And wheat grows best in fields embanked.
Blest is the womb that gives good sons,
'Tis the occasion for the *badhawa* song;
For this was sung in Ayodhya (when Ram was born).

3. A Song for the Chhatthi Rejoicings.

Kajli ke bana phula phulai bara sundara phulai,
Nahi janau maliya ke sinche se,
Aur nahin janau kheta guna?
Jo woi charon phulawa pawanti to palana binauti,
Wohi men lalna jhulaunti jarawan ka jalaunti.

In the forests of Kajli the most beautiful flowers
 bloom.
To what this is due I know not:
 Is it the water from the gardener's hand?
 Or is it the virtue of the field itself?
If only thence I could get those fair flowers,
 I would form with them a sweet cradle:
 And in it rock my child,
 And all my neighbours should envy......

4. The Wedding Parties Likened to Warriors.

Purab disha se Purabiya, pakachim se chare Baghel.
Bajat awa barhon baja,
Ghumat awe tarawar.
Katni men hoi katal ki mar.

The *Purabiyas* march from the east,
From the west move forward the *Baghels.*
They come with beating drums,
Playing on twelve instruments,
Bravely they brandish swords,
In Katni they will fight and kill.

5. The Presence of The Bride.

Bagiya keti dura?
Awai mahaka bela ki?

How far to you garden of incense?
Whence cometh this fragrance of *bela*?

6. Marriage Song: At the Time of Building the Mandap.

Marawa garori ranga rasa men:
  Jo diwara naiyan mori basa men,
  Hon tori ranga rasa men.
Khamba garori ranga rasa men:
  Jo diwara naiyan mori basa men,
  Basa men hain tori ranga rasa men.
Kalas lipori ranga rasa men:
Chauka purori ranga rasa men:
  Jo diwara naiyan mori basa men,
  Basa men hain tori ranga rasa men.
Tel charhori ranga rasa men:
  Basa men hain tori ranga rasa men,
  Jo diwara naiyan more basa men.
Haldi charhi re ranga rasa men;
  Jo diwara naiyan more basa men,
  Hain tori ranga rasa men,
  Jo diwara naiyan more basa men.

The *marwa* is being built with great rejoicing :
Oh the brother-in-law is not friendly with me,
He is not under my power,
Nor the slave of my beauty and love.
The *khamba* is being fixed with great rejoicing :
Oh the brother-in-law does not respond to my love,
He is not the slave of my beauty and youth.
The *kalas* is being coloured with great enthusiasm :
The *chauka* is being marked with designs as well :
Yet the brother-in-law is not joking with me,
He is not the slave of my beauty and youth.
I the bride am anointed with oil, and joyful :
Yet the brother-in-law is cold toward me,
He never responds to my love.
Haldi is being smeared upon me with laughter :
Oh my brother-in-law does not respond to my love,
Will he ne'er be the slave of my beauty and youth,
Will he never respond to my yearnings?

7. Marriage Song : At the Time of Haldi Smearing.

Okho marawa kahe, bhaiya ham hain bare :
Oko marawa chale jajoman jaba to chokhi bhanwar pare.
Wo barhi kahe, bhaiya ham hain bare :
Oko kambha chale jajoman jabai,
To chokhi bhanware per barai.
Kumhar kahe, bhaiya ham hain bare :
Oke kalas chale jajoman jabai,
To chokhi bhanwar pare.
Nauwa kahe, bhaiya ham hain bare :
Oko chauka pure jajoman jabai,
To chokhi bhanwar pare,
Tiliya kahe, re ham hain bara :
Oko tel chale jajoman jabai,
To chokhi bhanwar pare.
Bahana kahe, bhaiya ham hain bare :
Oki bati chale re jajeman jabai,
To chokhi bhanwar pare.
Baniya kahe, re bhaiya ham hain bara :
Oki haldi chale jajo jabi,
To chokhi bhanwar pare.

Oho, saith the booth: sirs, I am chiefest of all;
 On account of me only can there be a good wedding.
Saith the carpenter: sirs, I am chiefest of all:
 On account of the wedding pole the wedding is good.
The potter says: brothers, I am chiefest of all:
 For without my water pot no marriage is truly made.
The barber speaks: sirs, it is I who am chief:
 For without my platform no wedding is likely.
Thus said the oilman: I am essential and chief,
 How can a marriage be performed without oil?
The carder replies: I am best of them all,
 For without my cotton wick no light can be had,
The merchant speaks: why sirs, it is all due to me:
 How could a marriage be celebrated without turmeric?

8. Wedding Song: When the Barat is Dining.

More ko kone wate aye more belakli,
More dulha ne wate aye, more belakli.
Belo deru je we matau jewe darbhajiya bhanji?
 More belakli.
Samthi ne wate aye, more belakli,
More daru jewe matjewe darbhajiya ki bhaji,
 More ke.
Kone newate aye, more belakli.

O beloved jasmin bower, who has now come to dine?
Thy bridegroom has now come to supper, O jasmin sweet.
Yet eateth he gram and the greens of the field,
O jasmin blossom.
With him have come his father and elders, dear jasmin,
They too eat of such common greens,
They have now come to dine, O jasmin sweet.

9. Teasing the Bridegroom's Party as they Arrive.

Man ke ekau na aye.
Bari bari muchan ke aye, man ke ekau na aye.

Bari Bari thondan ke aye, man ke ekau na aye
„ „ nakan „ „ „ „ „ „ „
We to pilawai pilwa aye „ „ „ „ „
Sabke ichaka bichaka aye „ „ „ „ „
Etc.

There is none that really appeals to my heart.
There came men with big moustaches:
  But none really appeals to my heart.
There also come men with big bellies:
  But they never appeal to my heart.
There now come men with great big noses:
  But none really appeals to my heart.
Strong and stout they come:
  But still they never appeal to my heart.
All sorts of men come on the scene:
  But none ever speaks to my heart.
Etc.

10. Marriage Song: For the Guests Who Have Come.

Sajnan aye more hinuana aye ao sajna ke lane.
Puiya pakai puriya ke jibiya more sajna na aye,
  Sajna na aye more hituwan aye, ne sajna ke lane, main.
Negruwa maraya geruwa dhulaiya more sagna na aye,
  More hit uana aye
Je sajnan ke lane main ne biriya lagai,
  Bira ke chabiya more sajna na aye, sajna na aye.
Sajna ke lane main ne choupare bichhaye,
  Chaupar ke khilaiya more sajna na aye.
Je sajnan ke lane main ne sijiya bichhai,
  Sijiya ke suwaiya more sajna na ae.
Je sajnan ke lane main ne jhula garaye,
Jhula ke jhulaiya more sajna na aye.
Sajna ke lane main ne randi bulwai,
Randi ke natchema more sajna na aye.

Everybody but my admirer and my lover came.
I cooked sweetmeats for my lover,
  But no eater ever came.
I filled the water pot for my lover,
  But he that was to bathe did not arrive

I prepared *pan* for him as well,
  But the eater of betel did not appear.
I spread a chess board for my lover,
  But no well-wisher came to play.
I made a bed for my lover,
  But no sleeper came to rest.
I tied a swing for him,
  But no lover ever came.
I called dancing girls for him to watch,
  But he that could make them dance did not arrive.

11. Marriage Song: At the Time of Circumambulation.

Ratan piyare ankhiyan sajna hans ke bolo re.
Jatan jatan se dhungata kholo nehan toro re,
  Ratan piyare ankhiyan sajna hans ke bolo re.
Jatan jatan se galua rijho neha na toro re,
  Ratan piyare ankhiyan sajna hans ke bolo re.
Jatan jatan chuliya kholo neha na toro re,
  Ratan piyare ankhiyan sajna hans ke bolo re.
Jatan jatan se chunri kholo re nema na kholo re,
  Ratan piyare ankhiyan sajna hans ke bolo re.
Jatan jatan se jubnan masko nehan toro re,
  Ratan piyare......
Jatan jatan se pidre masko nehan toro re,
  Ratan piyare......
Jatan jatan se koncha pak do nehan toro re,
  Ratan piyare, ankhiyan......

O husband of jewel-like eyes: only smile and speak.
Slowly and carefully remove the veil from my face,
  So that our love may never grow cold;
  O darling of jewel-like eyes only smile and speak.
Slowly put thy hand round my neck,
  So that our love may never grow cold,
  My darling of jewel-like eyes.
My darling of jewel-like eyes open thou
  My bodice with care,
  So that our love may never grow cold.
My lover of jewel-like eyes very slowly
  Disrobe me,
  So that our love may never grow cold.

My husband of beautiful eyes speak love,
  And slowly press my breasts,
  So that our love may never grow cold.
My lover of wonderful eyes; very slowly
  Press thou my thighs,
  So that our love may never grow cold.
My darling of beautiful eyes very gently
  Hold thou the calves of my legs,
  So that our love may never grow cold.
My lover of jewel-like eyes passionately
  Consummate all,
  So that our love may never grow cold,
  O husband of jewel-like eyes.

12. A Series of Coarse Impossibilities.

Sas kunwari bahu garabh men,
Sari sonth gur khay,
Dekhanhari ke lalna hoga,
Banjh piyane jay.

The mother-in-law is a spinster,
  Yet the daughter-in-law is pregnant;
Her sister gets dried ginger
  And date sugar to eat;
The woman who is a mere spectator
  Gives birth to an infant;
And the barren woman feeds the child
  From her breast.

13. The Bridegroom Likened to a Parrot.

Hare bansa ka pinjara wo ma suwana amola,
Tanga kaduma kai dari ma apana karata kilolu.
Sakhi samujhaiwali, batiya hamara.

A cage is made of green bamboos,
  And a priceless parrot within.
It is hung on a *kadam* branch,
  There he mutters and chirps and enjoys it.
O dearest one: what I am saying
  Is worth considering.

14. The Wife's Glory.

Bundawali are,
Bunda ke rale uchata gai,
Jota mari gai.

O fair one bedecked with that spot of vermilion,
If that be gone
Then shattered is all thy beauty.

15. A Warning Song.

Lakh gori lakh sanwari,
Lakh na chare pahar,
Bich dhar men gir pare,
Kaua gidh na khay.

Though her complexion be fair or dusky,
Though she climb hills *lakhs* of times,
Yet if she falls in the mid-stream of life,
Not even crows or vultures will touch her.

16. Marriage Song: For the Time of Parting.

Konnoki bangal bahinayan ban kajli lojawe lal?
Dulha ko bangal bahinayan ban kajli lojawe lal.
Hathi bhange ghora jam unt bicharo, unt bicharo,
Gutka khaye langa lugar samp jaye,
Gant gatili jariya jay tang utaye bichhu,
Jay, Mahadeo ko, jay.
Konnoki bangal bahinayan ban kajli lojawe lal?

What palanquin carrier will bear
  This sister of ours to Kajli forest?
Her husband's carriers will bear
  This sister of ours to Kajli forest.
He asked for an elephant—
  But was given a horse,
  And a camel was given him too.
If this potent be eaten
  All poisonous snakes will fly,
  And the scorpion will vanish

Leaving nothing behind;
They will go to the great Sivaji.
What palanquin bearer will carry
This sister of ours to Kajli forest?

V. Songs of Religion.

1. Religious Teaching: The Name of Ram.

Rama, Rama, saba kahai,
Dasharata kahai na koi:
Eka nama Dasharata ka lete
Koti janama phala hoy.
Ramu, Rama amola hai,
Damana bina bikaya.
Tulasi aise nama ko gahaka
Nahin karhaya.

Though all take the name of Ram,
And none the name of great Dasarath:
Yet the name of Dasarath, if breathed in prayer
Blesses through millions of births.
But the name of Ram—it is priceless,
And without price it is offered.
E'en then, saith Tulasi, there's no one,
No one ready to own his name.

2. Religious Teaching: Worship Ram Now.

Rama, Rama ki lutahai,
Lute ja pata luta.
Anta samaya pachhatawe pyare prana
Jo jaihain chhute.
Rama kai bhajana karau dina rata.

Ram, Ram, sounds and resounds,
And they who know his address should heed it.
When your life is past, dear friend,
And the time for repentance has vanished,
You'll rue it.
So now worship Ram day and night.

3. Religious Teaching : Kindness.

Mala pita ko lalana mare tiriya ko,
Larake kya karaho jaga men?
Aye ke aiso jiwana paye ke?
Parasa ke thali jewana baithe,
Murada mara ke ka karaho jaga men uyake?

Beating your parents and kicking your wife,
O lad, what's the gain in this world?
What will you get for such a life?
Sitting to eat at the funeral feast,
What in the world is the use of that?

4. Religious Teaching : Arrogance.

Prabhuji se garva kiya so hara.
Ban ki ghumachi lala badan muha,
Kara Prabhuji se gar garvakara so hara.
Garva kiya eka ban ki hiranaya,
Unhun ka nain bigara.
Garva kiya eka chaki chakha,
Unhun ka rain bigara.

He who lifts his heart against God is already defeated.
The *ghumachi* of the forest was vain and lofty,
So God gave its fruit a red face and black body,
And it was henceforward ashamed.
A deer in the forest thought against God,
And it was disfigured with blindness.
The Chakhi-Chakha birds were proud and vain,
Their nights were henceforward despoiled.

5. Religious Teaching : Vanity.

Na garbh karna dihiya se.
Garbh kiya Rama aur Lakshman,
Unhe dukh par gayo Sita haran se.
Garbh kiya Lanka ka Rawan,
Unhe dukh par gayo Lanka jare se.
Garbh kiya eka sadhu bairagi,
Unhe dukh par gaye dhuni hale se.

Garbh kiya eka jal ki machalaya,
Unhe dukh par gaye pani hale se.
Garbh kiya eka ban ki chiriya,
Inhe dukh par gaye pathara pare se.

Never be vain of thy handsome body.
Very proud were Ram and Lakshman,
So they suffered when they lost Sita.
And vain was Rawan of Lanka,
And mourned when his city was burned.
A *sadhu's* soul was lifted to vanity,
And his sacred fire went out forever.
A fish in the waters was sporting,
And was left when the pond dried up.
Then vain was a bird in the forest,
So hailstones ended his chirpings.

6. A Song to be Sung at the Phag Festival.

Kuan par kera lagawo sahjani,
Ghare chalo bundawari ko leke.
Utri mahanadi jhulani deke,
Mundari mora badala dewa yar.
Nadiya dudhan dhari bahi awe,
Kagada ka naiya bani chali dekhi.
Aguwa Phagun phagua khelaye rangrej ke sath.
Panch rupaya mardhi men,
Bar le Kashi men khel phag.
Hama ko holi khelan din jay.
Angam men tulasi kabirawa bola,
Ho Sitaram.
Kolin Kol kare jay tatiya deke.

O fair companion,
Let us set plantains by this well,
And go home with one who has this *bunda.*
The great river is crossed by a present of jewelry,
So give me back the ring, O my friend.
The river comes flowing down like a stream of milk;
Let us watch the paper boats
Bobbing in its currents.
In the month of *Phag* we'll play *phag* with the dyers.

O let us save five rupees for that:
Then we can go to Kashi and celebrate,
All day could be spent in *holi*.
In the courtyard the tulasi plant
Shouts "Sitaram"
Behind closed doors sport Kol and Kolin together.

7. A Song of Sharda Worship.

Kahan tor janam hoy Sharda,
Kahan liyo awatara?
Kaha na karu thapan,
Jhula motin ke har?

Kashi men mor janam bhayo,
Hinglas awatara;
Maihar karain thapana,
Jhula motin ke har.

Maihar ke Sharda gaye
Jogiya sapanay;
Mandir men mor mail bhaye,
Dhaja bhaye puran.

Man man ja Sharda,
Aba samaya nahi hai;
Age sal mandir daion putay,
Dhaja daion garway.

Oh Goddess Sharda, where were you born?
Where did you incarnate yourself?
Where should you be installed
Seated on a swing hung with ropes of pearl?

"I was born at Kashi,
At Hinglaj did I incarnate myself,
I should be installed at Maihar,
Seated there on the pearled swing."

When Sharda went to Maihar
They knew it in a dream.
"My temple is full of filth," quoth she,
"All my temple flags are old."

Ah Goddess Sharda, forgive us please,
We have no time just now;
Next year we'll wash your temple white,
New flags shall fly again.

8 Sharda's Marriage.

Sat bahin yahan dewi re Sharda,
Saton bahin kumwaron man.

Saton men kaun si lalarin?
Kaun karat hai byah?
Saton bahnon men Sharda lalari,
Bahi ka rachyon byah.
Dwij pare baka lagan dharodan,
Naumi ki baralon men.

Ai barat meli, ghumre hain tabala nisan;
Ai barat gaonre meli, baji lagi barat ke tabala;
Ai barat dware men meli,
Hoy lagi dwar ke char.

Isi gauna ke kaise ritiyan?
Dulhin dekhe barat!

Seven sisters are you *devis* all, O Sharda!
All seven are virgins.

Of all the seven who is the most beautiful?
Who now marries her?
Sharda is of all most beautiful,
And she is being wed.
Her *lagan* will be read on the moon's second day,
The *barat* will come on its ninth.

The procession is here! The *tabalas* beat!
The *barat* has reached the village:
  Hear the beat of the wedding drums!
The *barat* is at the very door;
  Everywhere folks meet and greet!

What sort of custom is this?
For the bride is watching the *barat*!

9. Ramayana Song: The Place of Ram and Sita

Kaune kuan khanai? Kaune bandhai bhita?
Kaune pali dharai? Kaune bhari jala nira?
Raja Dasarath kuan khanawai;
Raja Indra bandhawai bhita;
Sita pali dharawai,
Jalabhare Doshamata maya.
Kahan ma upajai chandana birawa?
Kahan belhari pana?
Kahan ma upajai Sita Janaki?
Kahan Shri Bhagawan?
Bana ke dali men chandana upajai;
Barai ke bangala pana.
Raja Janaka ke upajai Janaki,
Raja Dasarath ke Rama.
Kahe ko upaji Sita Janaki?
Kahe ko Shri Bhagawan?
Raja rachaika Sita Janaki:
Bhajai ka Raja Rama.

Who dug this well? Who made its walls?
Who first fixed its bars and drew its pure waters?
King Dasarath dug the well;
King Indra made its walls;
Dear Sita fixed the bars,
Mother Doshamata drew forth the first sweet drink.
O where does the sandal tree thrive?
And where do *belhari* leaves grow?
From whence does Sita spring forth?
How came the Lord God to be?
In the thickets are found the sandal tree;
In the *pan*-seller's house the luscious *pan*.
Sita was born in King Janaka's palace,
From King Dasarath's Ram came forth,
Why was Sita born?
Why came the Lord God to the world?
Janaki was born to build up the Kingdom:
Ram came forth to be worshipped.

10. A Song of Krishna: The Flute Player of Brindaban.

Brindabana ma baji muraliya,
Mohai tino loka;

Jo na mohaya loka,
Sakhi rahai kaun se loka?
Kanhai bajawai muraliya Kadama kai chhaha.

The flute was played in Brindaban,
Three worlds stood fascinated;
If anyone is not thereby entranced,
Then friend, who can he be?
For under the Kadam tree Kanhai is playing the flute.

VI. Miscellaneous Songs.

1. An Invocation at the Time of Song.

Dhulki men Ganesh,
Timki men hawa bhaiya Sharda.

May Ganesh dwell in my drum,
And Sharda give wind to my *timki*.

2. In Praise of the Drums.

Sumaro gaura Ganesh nita nayana mai Sharada.
Bije ke dholak baji san sutri ke dor,
Kas kas ke chura bane,
Bajawaiya na awe thaor.
Sharada mai tumhare sharan dholak baje,
Jamuna ke kinare khele gend Nandlal.

Always remember the fair Ganesh and Mother Sharda.
The *dholak* of *bije* wood is all ready,
Its strings have been tightly tuned;
So the players dare not approach.
O Mother Sharada, it is under your protection,
But Nandlal is playing ball on the edge of the Jamuna.

3. Of Forest Dwellers.

Gana bajana kya jano, jangal ke rahanewale?
Khana pakaenwa apa ke liye—khana pina,

Kya jano maya sukhi ke khanewale.
Garewa bharae apa ke liye—garewa ka ghalana,
Kya jano tumari ke pinewale.
Biriya banaewa apa ke liya—biriya ruchana,
Kya jano mayapalla ke khanewale.
Seja bichhaonwa apa ke liya—sejiya sona,
Kya jano gudri ke sonewale.

O dwellers in jungle, what do you know of singing and music?
I have cooked for you,—but how poor you make it out, for you have dry food always.
I have water ready for you,—but alas, will it please you? You who drink water from gourds?
Pan is ready too,—but you who use the leaves of the forest, can you enjoy this tender treat?
A bed is ready for you,—but tell me true:
How will you ever rest on such, O sleepers on rags!

DANCES. Dancing is found in connection with all happy occasions: births, weddings, feasts and festivals, but among the Kols it is only the women who dance. The men play and sing, but it is universally claimed that they never dance; it is considered effeminate to do so, for eunuchs dance, and since Kols are men they should not dance. In other groups among whom the Kols live, such as the Gonds and even the outcaste groups, the men-folk dance.

There is one main type of dance among Kols called by the same name as the songs that are sung with it: the *dadra*. There are various forms of this dance, differing somewhat in rhythm and also in movement. To the casual observer they look almost the same, but to the Kol there are real differences. The *purani chal* and the *shaitani* are forms of the *dadra*. The word *shaitani* is literally 'satanic' or 'devilish' and in this form the words sung are very abusive and suggestive. On the occasion of such a dance with its accompanying songs, youths and maidens often elope.

The famous *karma* dance of the Gonds, in which both men and women participate, is not danced by the Kols, though they know of it and have often watched it. Russell and Hiralal however, claim that the Kols dance it.[1]

1 *Op. Cit.*, Vol. III, p. 517.

Leaf Cup set in decorated niche in outer Wall.

Dancing is invariably accompanied by singing and drumming. Liquor is often consumed in connection with it, and in one place, when seeking to see a dance, we were told that they would give an exhibition only if we bought them some liquor. The intoxicated state also lends aid to elopement.

The *dadra* dance is the most popular and most Kol dances are purely *dadras*. On such an occasion the men first gather around in the evening and sing and play for an hour or so. Finally a few women, one to six in number, put on the dancing costume over their *saris*, for without this they will not dance. This costume consists of two pieces : a red and yellow *lahanga*, which is like a dress made of many folds and is tied at the top so that the bottom just sweeps the ground, leaving the feet barely visible. The head is covered with the second portion, the *chunariya*, a shawl made of the same material as the *lahanga*. The shawl is thrown over the head and is held by the left hand so that when the person is standing erect the face is covered. On the feet are *ghunghunis*, ankle bracelets, which make a jingling sound.

After putting on the dancing costume, which is usually done right before those present, the dancers go and stand facing the players. If there are several who are to dance they do not necessarily go at the same time, and when they get there they do not keep together in their movements. While one is standing the other may be whirling. The dancers usually stand for some minutes in silence in front of the players who are singing to them and coaxing them to begin their dance. Then the knee is slightly bowed and the dancer begins to whirl. If one starts this movement in a clockwise direction, that direction is apparently followed by all the dancers, and the other direction is not taken. On the other hand, if they begin with the counter-clockwise movement then that is retained for the evening. On the whole the clockwise movement is favoured and is mostly used, but it is said that there is no hard and fast rule about it. The dancer may turn a number of times, but there is no set number of turns, it must fit into the song. The whirling is not particularly rapid, nor is it done on the heel. Having completed the revolutions the dancer stops, facing the drummers and the male singers, and begins her song. The men cease from their singing, but accompany her on their drums. As the dancer sings she moves by slow steps first to the left and then to the right, but not more than four or five feet in either direction from the original position. As the feet move the legs are shaken so that the anklets make a jingling sound. As a rule the shawl is held closed by the left hand, but when bending over the left hand is kept free, and it is used along with the right hand to make certain movements with the fingers similar to snapping. The accompanying pictures, show something of the nature of the movements described.[1] The singing, which on this particular occasion was at the time of the *gauna*, was said to be *gali* or abuse. The women frequently started a song and sang two or three lines of the same, while the men remained silent except for their instruments. Then the men would answer in two or three lines and the women remain silent, though frequently making movements with the hands, or turning. Finally they all sang together. The men would frequently stop all of a sudden while a woman sang a solo which sometimes came from one and sometimes from the other dancer.

ART AND WORKMANSHIP. Our study of the Kols was disappointing in the results it yielded in the field of art, for we found practically no evidence of Kol art. Nothing which they make or draw or paint seems to be characteristic of them alone, and there is little they do in imitation. They do not ordinarily decorate their houses differently from their Hindu neighbours. Occasionally the doorways have a picture representing a peacock, as indicated on plate XX. The peacock motif was also found on the urns where wheat was stored. Certain non-Kol houses, however, sometimes had the same symbol. There is apparently no taboo connected with the peacock, and the work was said to be entirely decorative. At the *holi* season the walls of the house which face the courtyard are frequently decorated with various figures. Plate XXI gives an idea of how this is done, and the drawing on the wall contains representations of tigers, peacocks, birds, sunflowers, men, flowers in a pot, and a house. It was said that women and boys do this work, never the men.

Kols seem to be deficient in handiworks of any sort. They never make baskets, wooden dishes, *dholaks*, beads nor ornaments; they do no sewing, nor making of clothes nor embroidery work. The mattress makers, the Kathariyas, come the nearest to having a handicraft, but it is not generally practised even by them. Most Kols will mend clothes, if necessary, and this is mostly done by the men. There is the usual great need for handicrafts so sadly undeveloped in rural India. Occasionally they make their own beds and cots, and rope for them is obtained from the stalks of rice called *bagai*. Such ropes are also used for drawing water from the well. Sometimes they fashion their own grinding mills from flattish stones by a chipping process. The children have no toys with which to play and none are constructed for them by their parents. Boys sometimes make a very inferior type of bow and arrow with which to hunt birds.

1 See plate XIX.

Designs on the wall of a Kol House in Garha. The Figures represent a House, Sunflowers, Men, Tigers, Peacocks, Birds, Flowers and Trees. Dwelling Place of a Devi is at the lower right hand corner.

CHAPTER XII

LIFE STORIES OF LIVING KOLS

SUNNULAL: A KOL WHO STAYED IN HIS VILLAGE

I was born in the village of Kharara Ghat and was the youngest of five brothers. There were also three sisters in my family, which was a large one, as there are about fifty living relatives on my father's side alone. When I was about sixteen years of age my parents decided that I should be married and they found a girl for me in the village of Barela. My wife and I have lived happily together, and we have had two sons. My father died two years ago (in 1935). I have never had to leave Kharara Ghat in order to earn money. I have always seemed to be able to find things to do about the village and have earned enough to be well supplied with the things I need. One thing I do is to go into the forest and cut wood which I carry on my head to Jubbulpore. It is hard work, but it has to be done. My wife and sons also help out by gathering *tendu* leaves for the *biri* manufacturers. All of my five brothers live here in Barela. Together we control about fifteen acres of land which is rented from a *malguzar*. It is not all in one place, but in three or four places. We all do our share of work on this, and the income from the wheat and pulse is shared evenly by us. But all the money I make from selling wood, or grass, or *tendu* leaves I keep myself and we do not share it.

I have become one of the *panchayat* of this village and take a keen interest in the welfare of this village and our community. I would like you to put a school in our village. The nearest school is four miles away—too far for our small children to go even if we were sure they would be treated right if they were admitted. I can read a little and sign my name. I never went to school, but learned this from a man in Jubbulpore, who used to teach me after I had sold my wood. I even have bought some books.

I have no debts and do not drink any strong liquors. I have never been seriously ill, nor had any serious trouble in the family, nor have we suffered from the want of food and clothing. I have never had an accident either even though I have gone on hunting expeditions in charge of beaters. Very often some Europeans from Jubbulpore come out to our village which is close to good hunting places and I go with them and show them where they may find game.

I have tried to be an honest man and the police and government forest officers trust me and have just offered me the post of *Sarkari Mukaddam* (government headman) of my village. This is a very high honour for me for which my friends will respect me very much.

Bajranji : A Kol and a Famine[1]

I was born in Rewa, my *desh*, but I have no idea of the date of my birth nor of the names of my father or mother. When my parents left Rewa and came to Barela I was just an infant and didn't know much about what was going on. After three or four years my father died in Lunsar village while my mother died in Barela when I was thirty years old.

When my father died I did not get much property, but whatever I got was used up in feeding the people of the community at the time of his death, and later on more was spent on the ceremonial feast following my mother's death. At that time I had a few head of cattle, but soon after four of them were killed and eaten by tigers.

I have been married twice, and by my first wife had two children. The first child was a girl who is now married and who has children of her own. She is about twenty-one years old now. The second child was a boy who is now about twelve years of age. But when these children were about twelve and eight respectively their mother became very ill and died. Whatever money I had, all was spent on her for her recovery, but it was of no use. Then I married another wife and this cost me to a great extent the remaining money that I had. Between the two I spent all the money which I possessed, which was about Rs. 300/- in cash and I found myself moneyless.

When I was a boy I was very eager to learn, but it was very difficult for a Kol to think of studying with the Brahmins. The village school seemed reserved for them. So my parents could not send me and they didn't care much about my education, and though I couldn't study I made friends with an educated boy and he helped me and I finished the first Hindi book, but that too I have forgotten and cannot now read nor write.

When my mother died there were three of us: my sister, my brother and myself. Both my brother and sister have since died of plague here in Barela, but I was saved by God's grace. About eight years ago my brother died leaving his wife and children. I do not keep her with me in our home for I know that it would be hard on me and my wife and that if I keep her it would really mean that there will

1 See plate XXVI.

Bajranji—A Kol in Famine time.

Phaggu—A Kol who turned Back.

be two wives in my house and they will always fight and quarrel, which I don't like at all. And I can only support one wife.

I have a second wife, but only one. She helps me in my daily work and comes out with me into the fields and helps me dig and till the ground and together we earn about eight annas a day. At other times we work on the farm which we rent. We have about one acre and must give one-third of the produce to the *malguzar*. If the crops are good we get some benefit, but if they are not it is not worth the labour. I sow my fields in pulse, wheat and *kodo*. (*Paspalum scrobiculatum*). Often we get enough to eat for the whole year from our field. For about four to six months we eat *kodo* and then for three to four months we eat wheat and in this way provide for our food. This year (1937) our crops failed badly and we did not get much out of our field so we have to work as day labourers wherever we could get work. Farming brings us less return than daily coolie work, even though the latter is irregular. I have also taken a contract for a piece of ground where lac trees grow and pay rupees five a year for the privilege of collecting the lac. The contract is for twenty years and is made with the owner of the forest in Silgnor village. I also graze my cattle there, and after deducting my animal tax I get a profit of Rs. ten or twelve per year. I don't like to work as a coolie as we are often mistreated when under the authority of one man. I prefer to take or make a contract with people who are good farmers and thus go and work in their fields according to my own free choice and desire. Thus I am saved from all kinds of mistreatments which are meted out by owners or supervisors, and this, which is true of me, is true of all members of our Kol community. We would prefer to die of hunger than to have our liberty taken away and be treated as slaves.

Once when I was very young a great crisis befell our family. It was at the time when almost the whole of India suffered from a great famine (1899-1900). As my father was dead the support of the family fell upon the shoulders of my mother. Every morning and evening she used to cut grass wherever she could gather it and sell it to the people who could pay. She used to bring roots from the jungles and prepare a sort of bread for us out of them. She even brought the leaves of certain kinds of trees and made them do as vegetables in our rude food. Oh, it was a very hard time for us, but a mother's love and care saved us from that great famine. She used to work all day long; and though she seemed to be very old she worked like a young woman. Finally, after it was over she fell sick and died. She blessed us before she died. Her blessings are still with me and since then I have not suffered the want of anything. Now I have a *pakka* house and five children, two from the first wife and three from the second and we are living happily.

MOTIRAM : A KOL WHO BECAME A PROSPEROUS FARMER

I was born in Kotmi (in North East Central Provinces near Pendra). My grandfather came to Kotmi from a place in Rewa State and when he arrived here he had with him my father who was still just a boy. My father was a hard working man and when his father died he had to shift for himself and found work as a coolie wherever he could find employment. Finally he got together enough money to be able to purchase the right to farm a small bit of land. This land was obtained from the *malguzar* who was very kind to him. When I was still a very small boy and not long after we got this land my grandmother, who had lived to a ripe old age, died happily for she saw my father established on a piece of land he could call his own. My father had two brothers who also owned a share of the land and helped start the farming, but both of them died without issue, leaving the control of the land with us alone. As soon as I was old enough to work I would go out with my father to tend the cattle in the forests. Later on I went by myself. When I was about twenty years of age my father died, but I had been married before that and I began to control the land and care for it.

I am now quite independent and all along have never had to work as a coolie for another person. I am very proud of this fact. I even hire other people to work for me for I now have twenty-two acres of land with a good house of thick mud walls upon it and cattle sheds as well. I have about thirty animals : goats, cows and bullocks. I pay a yearly land tax to the *malguzar* of Rs. 9, and a tax on my carts and animals which amounts to Rs. 7 per year.

My family consists of four sons and one daughter. Two sons and one daughter are now married and live here in the same home with me. They help me care for the fields and crops. A younger son goes regularly to the Mission School in Kotmi and studies in the third Hindi class. I am glad that this son can get an education and I pay the regular fees for him. He is very clever, walks two miles to school and is very regular in his attendance.

Although I have always had money for our food and have never suffered that way, still we have suffered much through illnesses and death. We go often to the Mission dispensary in Kotmi for our medicines. My first wife died but not before giving birth to seven children, three of whom are now dead. They died of fevers and smallpox. I was married a second time and this wife has had but one child—the boy who is now going to school.

People around here count me one of the rich and well-to-do farmers of Kotmi, even though I am now only 35 years of age. I am now engaged in a controversy over a piece of land and the *panch* has not been able to settle it to my satisfaction. I have threatened to take the matter to court and I hope the *panch* will do the right thing.

PHAGGU : A KOL WHO RETURNED TO THE OLD PATHS[1]

My father was born in Barela and he held a few acres of land and farmed them and gained sufficient wealth to make us independent. He had nine children, five of them were boys and four were girls. Two of the sisters are now living, while two are dead. The time came when my father could not profitably farm his land so a Mohammedan of influence bought the field and father worked for him in the same field for forty or forty-five years. My elder brother is working as a factory coolie in Jubbulpore and I work as a coolie in Barela.

I too was born here in Barela. My father died when I was about thirty years of age. I did not get any share of my father's property, for when he died I was not at home but in Nagpur. I lived at home with my father for eighteen years and was then married. I started to school, but could not continue to study because the school master used to punish his students very much and once when he tried to punish me I tripped him up and he fell and hurt his head. I was then in the first Hindi. This was during the great famine.

By the grace of Narayan we did not die of hunger during this awful famine, for we had enough to eat, especially those first eighteen years when I never thought of hard work such as coolie work. When I was eighteen I took a rupee from father and set off for Nagpur and travelled without a ticket all the day. I would get off the train at every station and as the train started I used to get in another compartment. Thus I reached Balaghat and got a job in the Manganese mines where I worked for about ten years. I could not earn anything there except enough to feed me :

Jahan jao bhag,
Wahan lage Ag.
Age Age sab Sanichar ja raha hai
Tu kahan ja raha hai ?

1. See Frontispiece and plate XXVII.

Wherever thou goest
There a fire flares up.
You are haunted by Saturn (ill luck)
So where art thou going?

This verse sums up the story of my life.

When I was in Balaghat I did not marry. I left work there and went on foot to Sukari to see my sister and stayed there for eight years. In Gondia I kept a woman with me, but did not marry her, and had two children by her. From Sukari the four of us came by foot to Padriganj and from there bought tickets to return to Barela. We had but little money in hand, and although all our relatives were living together in Barela they would not take me back and I had to build a separate hut.

When I was ten or twelve years old I worked in the fort (Gun Carriage Factory, Jubbulpore) when its foundations were being built and for two years received four annas a day. Carrying dirt was my work at that time.

Just now, sir, I am very thin but before this I was very healthy and strong. Now I am working as a coolie and am settled here and hope never to leave Barela again. The woman I took to live with me in Gondia is still with me and altogether she has given birth to seven children, five of them having died, two when they were quite old. My son is sick and often has fits.

I have had a hard time in life. I have had no food and ate bread made of mango kernels and the flowers of the *semal* tree. And many other things which the ordinary man never eats. At the time of the great famine this was my lot. Rice was then four annas a seer, and we could not afford it. A few months ago I was very ill and we had no money so my wife had to get roots and leaves from the jungle. When I am sick I am not able to work and we all suffer. I am ashamed to ask for help from any one. Three years ago we were both very ill and we simply closed the door and remained inside. Our relatives didn't help us with either food or money, but both of us recovered.

I have a debt of about Rs. 4 or 5 but never in my life have I taken a large loan. I never drink wine except when invited to some wedding festivities. I am not in this habit and know that it is not good to drink liquor. I don't know the disadvantages of drink because I don't drink. Of course this I know, that if you are intoxicated then anyone may come, kick you and rob you of what you may have on your person. There is loss of money too. The same money can be used for children and in getting good food. I know nothing more than this.

Thus a Kol preaches to us a temperance sermon!

DHOLI: A LITERATE KOL AND MAGICAL PRACTICES[1]

We are two brothers and two sisters and our parents are still living and we live together happily. I am the younger son in the family. My elder brother lives separately. I was married when I was fourteen years old; now I am about twentyfour (1937). I started my school work when I was eight or nine. I did not have any trouble for two or three years when I was in school. My parents were very kind to me. I passed the first and second Hindi classes easily and happily. When I came into the third I could hardly study for three or four months, for I was bitten on the thigh by a dog. At once people began to give my parents advice as to what they should do and it was decided that a superstitious ceremony called *jharwana* should be performed. I was led around and forced to look into seven different wells and had *supas* waved over me. During this period some things like small bits of hair were found in the flour put out in a ring about the floor and this, it was said, showed that the dog was not a mad dog. After this was known my parents bought some medicines from a potter, Manawa Kumhar. After taking it I found blood in my urine and this lasted for eight days and I felt very ill. Then my parents gave me some curds and rice with sugar which seemed to make things even worse. My parents being ignorant and always listening to the advice of other people did not pay any attention to this new trouble but kept treating me for dog bite, saying that all my troubles were due to that. I was quite young and had no knowledge of these things and how I should take care of my health. I thought that I had lots of heat in my body and that is why I was suffering from these discharges of blood and hence I used to eat only those things supposed to cool my system. In spite of all this I did not stop my education and the reason for continuing was that I knew very well that I had become very weak physically and could never do hard coolie work, and therefore felt that I should study hard and pass my primary certificate exams, and then teach in some village school where I should get eight to ten rupees a month, which would be sufficient for my maintenance. That is why I kept paying but little attention to my health and kept on taking medicines and trying to work hard at school. The result was just the opposite because due to my bad health I failed in my

1 See plate XXVI.

certificate examination. And my disease increased so much that it seemed that I was useless to the life of the world. Ever since the time the dog bit me I was put to sorrow, trouble and all sorts of miseries. And up until now I could not get rid of my troubles and my disease is increasing and it seems that sooner or later it will cause my death. At the present time I am much disappointed in life. This world has become meaningless to me and everything seems to come to nothingness. At this time I seem to be absolutely unworthy of either heaven or hell. I pray that Bhagawan may never give such a mournful life to another.

With all these troubles and miseries of life I continued to study very labouriously. At least my classmates and teachers know of my hard study, or at least Bhagawan knows the heart of men and no one else. Fate! Thou art Wonderful!

HARLAL: A KOL STRUGGLING WITH THE NEW ORDER[1]

I was born in the month of *Srawan* (July-August), 1909 in the village of Burgi which is about 18 miles from Jubbulpore. My father was a railway worker and had a responsible position in the station at Burgi where he got Rs. 30/- per month which was later increased to Rs. 40/-. My grandfather came from our country Rewa, but both my father and I were born in Burgi. As time went on my father had trouble with the railway authorities and could not bear their ill treatment. In addition to this he was not granted leave when he wanted to attend marriages or festivals, so he finally resigned and came to live with an uncle who was living in Barela. I was the first born child and was about seven years old when we came to live in Barela.

At present we are two children; my sister and myself. My sister was born after we came to Barela. When my father retired from the railway and came to Burgi he had a lot of money, but at that time he was in the habit of drinking and it was all wasted in that way. Somehow, after it was all gone, he came to his senses and with the help of the *panch* and their influence he gave it up. With the little money that was left he made me learn the work of a carpenter and bought me about sixty rupees worth of tools which helped me get started. Through the help of those tools I was able to earn a daily wage and live nicely. I can make tables, chairs, and most anything that an ordinary carpenter can make.

As regards my education my father sent me to school, and I went for only a few days. Unfortunately the teacher began to punish me

1 See plate XXVII.

from the very first day and for two or three days he continued it, and so I thought that if this is all I am going to get in school every day then I had better stop, so I ran away from school. When my father discovered that I was not going he was very angry, and tried to compel me to go to school, but I ran away to Jubbulpore where I met another Kol who knew me and the family well and he cared for me for two days, and then brought me back to Barela. At this time I was about ten years of age. My father again and again advised me to go to school, but I never went again. Since that time I have regretted this very much, especially when I see some of my classmates (not Kols) who began their education along with me, and are now teachers in the same school in Barela. When they see me working as a coolie they laugh at my condition, but what can I do except put my head down in shame, for it was my own fault that I stayed away from school. I am able to read and write just a bit, but this is nothing compared to the education they have received. I really repent very much and curse my luck and fate.

When my father finally saw that I was not going to school and had no liking for it, he asked me to learn some trade and so I began to work along with him. Once he got angry with me during the working hours because I did not do just as he told me to do, and he punished me before other people ; and as this made me angry, I ran away from home again, and on leaving I stole Rs. 22/- from my father and went straight to Narsinghpur (about fifty miles from Jubbulpore). I reached the station in the evening and got down from the train and wanted to stop in a *dharmasala* for the night, but the railway porters would not let me out of the station premises without a ticket, for I had none, and for fear that the money I had would be snatched away from me by a ticket-collector or a thief I had it in my private parts. As I could get no place in Narsinghpur I went straight on to Itarsi (about 100 miles further) without a ticket.

I stayed a month in Itarsi searching for work, but could not find a thing to do and there were not many Kols there. I knew I must go back to Jubbulpore as I had only Rs. 10/- left and it would soon be gone and I would be far from help. So I returned to Jubbulpore and searched for work. Fortunately I got work as a *panka* puller in a bungalow for the period of five months and received Rs. 12/- a month. To my great surprise I learned that my father had reported my absence to the police station in Barela and before long some of the police in Jubbulpore caught me and taking me to the police station began to ask me about my parents and the reason I left home. I told them everything and later they sent me with a policeman back to Barela and my parents. My father asked me: "Harlal, did you bring any money with you?" I said, "Yes, I had money, but I spent it all." He did not say any more nor scold me, but asked me to live in the house and do coolie work along with them. But I did not like this and again left Barela and began to work again in the same bungalow where I was a *panka* puller and continued to work there for a whole year at Rs. 12/-.

Fortunately a big flood washed away the railway bridge over the Nerbudda river and there was much demand for workers to rebuild it. I went there and got a job and the railway authorities liked my work and were pleased by my skill and I was given the work of a blacksmith where I worked happily for six years.

During this time my father also was working steadily and was able to collect some money for my marriage as I was past the marriageable age. He called me back for the marriage and I had to return, because I too was anxious to get married and had some money saved up for it. But after my marriage I again left home and went back to my work on the railway, for by that time I was getting Rs. 19/- per month, which is a very good salary. I left my new wife with my parents. My father came to see me at my work, and walked the whole distance of forty miles and pleaded with me to go back to the house because they were all missing me a great deal. So I took six days leave and came back to Barela. When the people of my Kol community saw me they all began to give me advice, saying that half a *chapati* in your own home is better than a whole *chapati* in another place. So I listened to their advice and did not return to my work on the railway.

After a year at home there arose a great quarrel between my father and myself. My father began to ill treat me so that my wife and I left Barela and went to Kharara Ghat where my parent-in-laws and some other relatives were living. As there was much wood in the jungle about Kharara Ghat both of us began to cut wood and carry it to Jubbulpore to be sold there. But as time went on we became very hard up for money and we asked our parents and relatives to give us some money, but they absolutely refused, so we had to borrow money from a money-lender on security. We had some jewellery and ornaments, and with them as security we borrowed Rs. 100/- and with this we began to buy wood and collect it in a great heap near our village of Kharara Ghat. This we sold at a profit in Jubbulpore. In the meantime when my father thought I was well off he asked me for a loan of Rs. 25/- and as I had no cash at that time I had to refuse him saying that at present I had none. I also told him that I had borrowed money from others and had left the jewellery as security for that amount and that the money is being used in my trade of buying and selling wood. He got very angry at me for that and took away all the wood that I had, along with my bullock cart, and brought them to Barela. He not only took these things but also paid my debt at the money-lender's and took all our jewellery which I had left as security. So we became dependent upon him again, and our condition seemed helpless.

For two years both my wife and myself had a very hard time. We had no tools to work with, nor money, nor clothes, and also no heart to work anywhere. I borrowed Rs. 2/- but that amount was all spent for food. Later we took courage and again started to sell wood. We used to go out to the jungles together and I used to carry over a *maund* a day to Jubbulpore, a distance of eight miles each way. But this heavy work was too much for me and I became ill. For two more years we suffered very much. Father took away all that we had and so we were again without anything. After my health was recovered I again began to sell some wood and little by little I was able to carry greater loads to the city. By the money thus earned I was able to buy a few tools and by the third year we were again independent, and these tools are still (1937) helping me to retain my self respect and earn a living for my family.

At present I have learned to do many kinds of work: especially the work of a mason which I prefer above the others. I also do some carpentry work when it is available. I am able, when I work, to earn from eight annas to a rupee a day, and this is enough. But if there should be a long period without work we suffer.

I am still on bad terms with my father and while I am now living in Barela I am living in a separate house which I rent for eight annas a month. My sister is not yet married though she is about fourteen or fifteen years old. My first baby died when it was a month old but the next child, a son, is still living. I have only one wife. I don't want to keep two wives because they are no advantage and full of troubles.

MANBODHI : A CENTENARIAN KOL

I belong to the Shivari family of Kols and was born in Rewa State about 100 years ago. When I was born my father was working as a serf for some farmer. When I was about 25 years old my father died, but he had left Rewa State when I was but fifteen days old. My maternal uncle brought our family to Jubbulpore where we stayed a few weeks and then started on foot to Nagpur (about 200 miles).

In those days there was no road to Nagpur, but only a jungle pathway. We went to Nagpur because we heard that a road was to be started there which was going to Jubbulpore and they wanted Kols to do the work. We began to cut the forest from the Nagpur side and came toward Jubbulpore. But due to some *jadu tonha* (the spell of a magician) our Kols began to die and some of us were very much frightened. My father got permission to leave from the doctor and we came back to Jubbulpore another way, by the jungles of Mandala. Since that time we have lived here at Salivara (about six miles from Jubbulpore) where we have broken stones for the roads and done some other work if we have been able to find it.

I have seen two generations come and go and the men about us belong to the third. At present I am supervising work among the Kols of this place who break stones and they call me *Mukaddam* or the head of the village. My financial condition is much better than the other Kols here because I farm a piece of land and have some goats and cattle. I have a wife living with me but do not live in a house with mud walls, but in a *jhopri* or hut. Why? Because our forefathers lived this way and I too prefer this mode of living.

The above life stories are the simple annals of Kols with varying backgrounds, and are recorded as they told them. They omit many things that one might like to know about, but give an insight into what seems important to them. These stories were obtained only after long acquaintance and friendly contact.

The sketch of Sunnulal reveals a simple man who has stuck to his village with the opportunities it afforded and who has not attempted to break through his environment into the affairs of the outside world. As a result he is contented, and from the economic point of view has everything a village man thinks necessary. He has never had to meet the stresses and strains of an alien type of life.

Bajranji has vivid memories of the great famine and a mother's successful efforts to avert disaster. He shows the independent spirit of the Kol who would rather make a contract for work than take a daily wage and be bossed around.

Motiram, who lives in the "aboriginal belt" has also successfully maintained his independence and built up for himself a satisfactory economic situation. He respects himself and feels he can boss the *panch* and coerce it.

Phaggu is the sad story of a man who has wandered here and there and at the end has nothing to show for it. He is out of harmony with his group and lacks the support which would help him in times of difficulty.

Dholi is an example of a Kol who tried to rise above his environment and was pulled back into it and its superstition by ill health and worry. He feels his life is wasted and he sits around and mopes about it nearly all the time. Kols of his village laugh at him and say that is what education does to a man.

Harlal is a cheerful chap who ventures away from the home fires and again and again tries to become independent. But he is pulled back just as he seems to get there. He too is out of harmony with his group, but just the same he is so tied to them that he cannot leave them. Harlal's father talked a lot to us about him and calls him a disloyal son.

In the last story an old Kol dwells upon the days when the main roads were being built in the Central Province, and on superstitions in connection with it. He does not have much to say and while he claims that he is well off financially nevertheless he still prefers the crude hut as a dwelling.

Raha chhora kuraha chale, turata dhokha khaya.

Who leaves the road for a path, is soon astray.

CHAPTER XIII

THE ECONOMIC LIFE OF THE KOLS

The economic condition of the cultivators of the Central Provinces is not a very prosperous one. The following table is reproduced from the Census Report for 1931 and is for the average cultivator. It will be seen from the following pages that the Kols fall far below this meagre income.

Item	Normal	When crop is 25% below normal
Size of holding ..	Acres 21	
Value of gross crop outturn after deducting marketing expenses	Rupees 491	Rupees 369
Income from subsidiary sources	50	50
Total income ..	541	419
Cost of maintenances and clothing ..	214	214
Cultivating expenses ..	157	157
Rent ..	21	21
Total necessary expenses ..	392	392
Balance ..	149	27[1]

It is further noted that from this balance the worker must provide sums for funerals and marriages, repairs to buildings, journey costs, repayment on debt (the normal debt of the cultivator is said to be Rs. 227), interest charges, the cost of education for his children and the little luxuries such as *pan* and tobacco. These figures are worked out for a family which has an average of three surviving children. Not much can be done in normal years, to say nothing of bad years when actual deficits are expected and more money is borrowed.

As will be observed in the following pages, Kols are mostly day labourers and under village conditions the income of day labourers is very small. Usually no money is given; they are paid in kind. In villages near Katni it was found that the field labourer was paid three

1 *Census of India*, 1931, XII : 1, p. 60.

pounds of wheat for a day's work in the field. If a cash arrangement is entered into, the rate is 1½ annas for the same period of labour. In urban areas the situation is better. In 1911 the average wage was four annas a day. In 1921 it was six annas and ten years later it had increased to nine annas. It was our belief that seven years later wages had considerably fallen. Kol labourers in Jubbulpore industrial plants seldom received more than 5½ annas per day while for the same work in Katni and Maihar they received but four annas. As a rule women workers received about half the above.

It should be kept in mind that we have with the Kols the phenomenon of a primitive and backward people coming into the stream of rural and urban life. Many changes have occurred and many more will take place in the future.

ECONOMIC DEVELOPMENT. Kol people live together in groups, either in a section of the village or in a village of their own. Taking the village as a whole it would appear that they are economically well below the average. In certain places, however, they seem to be making a distinct advance as they continue to dwell there and develop a place for themselves in the life of the community. A resident of Barela, not himself a Kol, said that he had been watching them for many years. He said that twenty-five to thirty years ago they were very backward compared to their present condition. At that time they lived in grass huts, wore only loin cloths and in every respect were jungly, backward and inferior; but now the majority of Kols in Barela have houses with tiled roofs and thick mud walls, although the earlier type of dwelling is still occasionally found. This is indicated in Plate V. They now put on better clothing and in general their economic standard seems to be rising. In another place we found Kols putting tiles on their roofs which normally cost Rs. 20 per 1,000. These were being laid on top of the grass thatch. Country tile is more generally used and it costs from ten to twelve rupees to cover the house in this manner. Whenever the Kols are in contact with a somewhat higher culture and have a sense of security as regards lands and tenancy, they tend to make their houses much better than otherwise. Whenever we have asked groups why they have built and are living in such crude houses, they have told us that they do not know from one day to the next whether they will be staying there; and if they have to move on tomorrow they can easily pull up and leave. It is also said that this was the way their forefathers dwelt, and why should they do otherwise. Their employment is very uncertain and hence their houses are crude.

EDUCATION AND LITERACY. There does not seem to be any active interest in education on the part of the Kols. In most of the centres visited no Kol children were being sent to school. Of course many of the places were far from the nearest village school. In Barela, however, there is a good school, but of the 125 children of school age among the Kols only two were in this school. We asked the master about these children and he said they were below the average. There are six or seven Kols in Barela who have at one time been in school but not all of them have retained their literacy. Of this number one had read up to the seventh standard and we tried to get from him in writing some facts concerning the Kols, but his responses were very poor and did not give us the insight that we had hoped to get from him. In some places Kols say that they would send their children to school if there were such facilities at hand; but where they are actually at hand they do not take an active interest, and say they cannot afford to spend money on education. There are always one or two families, however, who seem to be interested and who make some attempt to educate their children in the primary schools. In Katni the Church Missionary Society has a school which is situated near one of the sections where Kols live and to which quite a number of Kols have gone at one time or another. There were, however, only sixteen on the list that had done credible work in the past eight years, three of whom had read through the fourth standard. In such schools there is no caste distinction, though in a few other places Kols told us that the schools made distinctions and that their children were not allowed to study with the caste children.

The Census reports reveal that as a group the Kols are among the most illiterate of the many castes and tribes. For India as a whole the report[1] shows that out of 122,695 Kols aged seven years and over there were only 301 literate persons: 290 men and 11 women. Seven of the men were reported as being literate in English. In the Central Provinces and Berar with 48,500 Hindu Kols and 10,813 Tribal Kols there were but 216 and 6 literates respectively. The proportion in the United Provinces is still less as out of 63,382 Kols only 79 were literate. The United Provinces Census Report[2] puts the Kols 89th in the order of literacy in a list of 93 tribes and castes. It is worked out in that Report that they are 0.24% literate as far as males are concerned and 0.01% for the females. In the Central India Agency out of 151,718 Kols there were 88 males and 50 females literate and two were literate in English. Outside of Rewa State it appears that

1 *Census of India*, 1931, I: 1, p. 460.
2 *Ibid.* XVIII: 2, literacy tables.

there are but three literate Kols in the Central India Agency[1]. It is a well known fact that the illiteracy of the lower groups is a source of much hardship to them as it leads to frauds of various kinds at their expense.

In respect of literacy the Kols do not compare favourably with other tribes and castes. The number of literates per thousand works out, in the case of Kol males, to just under five. For the Kayasths it is 607, the Brahmins 437, Oraons 35, Doms 16, Bhils 11 and Chamars 10. This figure of five in the case of the Kol is also lower, according to the report, than the figure of the Munda groups in Bihar and Orissa returned by the Census of 1931[2].

In the Central Provinces' Report a special subsidiary table of literacy of castes is given both for 1921 and 1931[3]. The average literacy for Central Provinces was 51 per mille in 1931: 93 per mille in the case of the males and 9 in the case of the females. The respective figures for 1921 were 42, 76 and 7, which would indicate some advances. On this table the Kols as a whole have a literacy of 4 per mille: for the males it is 7 and for the females nil. In 1921 the respective figures were 2 and 4. Taking all the groups listed, and there are seventy tribes and castes selected, there are only three who rank in literacy below the Kols of the Central Provinces: Wadder and Bhil with 3 each and Korku with 2, while two other tribes, Bharias and non-Christian Oraons, rank the same as the Kols with 4 per mille. The Kol thus ranks among the most illiterate groups of the provinces.

OCCUPATIONS OF THE KOLS. Census reports of the Central Provinces have interesting discussions of occupations. The report for 1931 shows that in the province as a whole 776 persons per 1,000 workers were engaged in the exploitation of animals and vegetables. Industry comes second with only 92 per 1,000. In the lists of occupations of selected groups we find the following of the Kol tribe:

Kol Tribe	Number per 1,000 earners engaged in each occupation
Agriculturalists	160
Field labourers, wood-cutters, etc.	560
Raisers of livestock, milkmen, herdsmen ..	17

1 *Ibid.* XX : 2, literacy tables.
2 *Ibid.* I : I, p. 342.
3 *Ibid.* XII : I, p. 290.

Kol Tribe		Number per 1,000 earners engaged in each occupation
Artisans and other workers	..	22
Labourers, boatmen, cartmen, *palki* bearers, etc.	..	19
Trade	..	12
Domestic service	..	11
Contractors, clerks, cashiers, etc. otherwise unspecified	..	17
Labourers, unspecified	..	157
Other occupations	..	27[1]

Our own investigations show that the Kols enter into the modern economic world more easily than other primitive tribes such as the Gonds. While there are scores of Gond villages in and around Jubbulpore, the Gonds are shy and retiring and are only seen in the town on bazaar days when they come to buy and exchange some of their forest produce. The Kols are not bad mixers, seem to like company, and have entered into the industrial life of the city quite readily. We did not find the Kols limited to any particular occupation. They are unusually good workers and wherever we went we found this fact mentioned about them. We found a few who are farmers and who hold small pieces of land from the *malguzar*. Others are farm workers and follow the crops; and during the time of the wheat harvest some Kol villages and *mahullas* are almost entirely deserted. Many of the Kols living in a town not far from Jubbulpore are road-workers, breaking the stone for the roadway and doing the required labour in repairing it. Others in Barela burn and sell charcoal; some Kols buy wood from the Gonds, cut it into convenient lengths and resell it in Jubbulpore. In Kharara Ghat, a purely Kol village about eight miles from Jubbulpore and quite inaccessible and isolated, the Kols seem independent, raising all their own food-stuffs and paying their *malguzari* rents by means of the proceeds from the sale of wood and of the leaves of the *tendu* plants (*Diosypros embryopteris, melanoxylon, montana, etc.*), used in the manufacture of country cigarettes or *biris*. No one in this village was said to be engaged in hard labour for others, known as coolie work. In other places we found indication that they can quite readily turn their hands to mechanical work. A few are so engaged in the factories in Jubbulpore. We watched Kols

1 *Ibid.*, p. 268.

Kols Buying wood from Gonds for resale in Jubbulpore.

A Cement Pit in the Kaimers. Most of the Labourers are Kols.

Kols Threshing and Winnowing their Wheat near Barela

prepare tiles in a workshop near Deori; a Barela Kol has taken up the work of a mason and bricklayer. In another family we found that members had been jungle postal-runners for three generations. In Sihora they said that their chief occupation was digging in the fields, though they also cut wood and sold grass; only one or two rented lands. At Katni we found that they were chiefly employed in the cement works, but would soon be going elsewhere, as the cement factories were in the process of closing down. In some of the villages about Katni they were found to be mostly labourers in the surrounding fields. At Kymore thousands are employed in the great cement factories; at Maihar they are mostly engaged in lime-kiln work. Near Rewa City they seem to be mostly serfs and labourers. Further north they grind sandstone for the glass works, and at Chunar in the United Provinces help to dig the rock out of the hillsides. We found a few literate Kols in Katni who had learned to read in the Church Mission School. One of these was a clerk in a warehouse at busy times of the year; the rest of the year he would do whatever he could find which often was nothing but coolie work.

THE SITUATION IN THE VILLAGES: *Land and Income*. In our visits to numerous villages we made enquiries as to the economic situation on the part of the Kols living there. A careful survey was made near Jubbulpore. Text figure 30 shows the area. Only a few Kols in the large group at Barela actually rent lands for farming purposes; either on shares or on straight rent. In Kharara Ghat the situation seems to be the opposite, for nearly every household there holds land from the *malguzar*. Money is earned on the side from the sale of wood, grass and *tendu* leaves for *biris*. In Barela a survey of thirty-nine families indicated that only three held lands, and that the total acreage so held was but 5¼ acres. Thirty families in Kharara Ghat hold 82 acres of land; in some cases taxes for the same are paid direct to the Government, while to the *malguzar* they say they pay Rs. 10 per *khandi* of wheat sown, this being considered as 1/3 the produce of the land.

Barela Kols do most of the coolie work on the roads near that place and also labour on the farms as occasion offers. All the able members of the family work and we found that on the average the family income was Rs. ten to twelve per month for this type of labour. One dealer in charcoal said that he cleared locally in Barela about Rs. 120 per year. Another Barela Kol has the custom of purchasing wood from the Gonds who bring it down from the hills near-by. This is bought for five pice, is then cut up into shorter lengths by himself

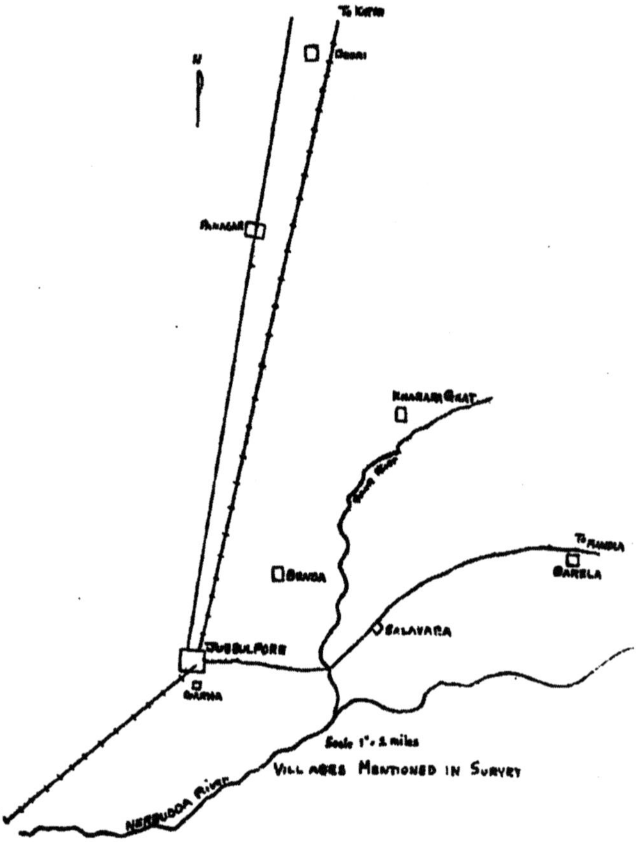

Fig. 30.

and family and is resold for ten pice, just double the amount he paid for it. Another Kol, acquainted with brick-laying and general repairing, earns twelve annas per day when work is available. A few in Barela deal in *tendu* leaves and sell the same to contractors from Jubbulpore. There was only one Kol in Barela whom the other Kols considered wealthy. "Wealthy" was defined as the possession of ornaments, animals, and some money. The rent for land about Barela varies considerably as it is not all of equal value. Two Kols, however, were paying at the rate of Rs. 4-10-0 per acre.

At Deori we found that the Kol colony was mostly employed in the tile factory where they are paid by piece work and receive

Rs. 4-8-0 per 1,000 tiles molded and put on the rack to harden. They told us that the average Kol worker would mold about 1,000 tiles per week.

In Panagar there are about 100 families of Kols. Some of them keep chickens and sell the few eggs they get in the local bazaar, or even take them to Jubbulpore on market days. Three or four own bullock carts. The rest of the community divide their time between working on the roads and doing coolie work in the fields when such work is available. This brings them from two to three annas per day. This work is far from steady, being largely seasonal.

In Benda village there are fifteen houses of Kols. Their main work is breaking stone for the metalled roads and preparing limestone for the kilns. They believe that by steady work they can make up to Rs. three per week, but the work is very hard and the hours are long. A few collect *tendu* leaves in season and when other work is slack they go out to the jungles and cut wood. They can earn from three to three and a half annas per day in that way. None of the Benda Kols does any farming.

At Salavara village on the Gaur River, we found that all were engaged in breaking stones for road metal. Their report seemed to indicate that they had to work harder for what they got than some other groups. They said it took them fifteen days to break a *saikara*—a stone measuring approximately 1,000 cubic feet—that two men were required and that they received Rs. 2-8-0 for the *saikara*. Five years ago, they said, they got Rs. 4/- for the same measure. They claim that the work is also harder now as they have to go further for suitable rock.

At Garha close to Jubbulpore, there is a fair-sized Kol community. The village is quite distinct from any other place and about 100 Kol families dwell there. Their occupations are various, and but few have steady work. This group consists mostly of coolies who get work wherever it is available or where the best wages are offered. Sawing wood is a common opening as they do not live far from the timber yards where all the sawing of planks is done by hand. During the wheat harvest they are nearly all away in the fields, leaving their houses empty for the few weeks of the harvesting season.

On a preliminary visit to Rewa State we went to a small Kol community not far from Rewa City. These Kols have considerable land for which they pay rental to a Mahratta landlord. What this group told us has been confirmed by many others, both in and out of Rewa State and seems to characterize the conditions of the Kols there. One informant told us that he was married about twelve years prviously, at which time he incurred a debt of Rs. fourteen for the expenses of the wedding. This was borrowed from a *Thakur* of a near-by village who appeared most glad to lend it to him. Ever since that day this *Thakur* has considered him as his serf, and he is supposed to go daily to him; and even though he has worked for the *Thakur* for the past twelve years he has not cleared the debt and does not believe that he ever will. He is virtually a slave of this man, is on call at any time, and must give him the first work until he no longer requires him. For each day's work the *Thakur* will give him 1½ *seers* of *chana* (usually *Dolichos lablab*) or perhaps the same amount of barley still in the head. Money was never given, nor rice or wheat. This group of Kols in Rewa was a very intelligent one on the whole, but indicated that Rewa State was not a place where one could get more than just the necessary food. As one expressed it: "In Rewa there is no stomach hunger, only money hunger." This appeared to be quite a common expression over a wide area. Food was available there, but no money for the other necessities of life nor for weddings, burials and the like.

In centres like Kymore and Katni where there are large cement works, the majority of the coolies employed in the many types of manual labour are Kols. The work is very hard and the wages are low: usually not more than four annas a day for males and three annas for female workers.

Kharara Ghat, the isolated Kol village, is perhaps as independent economically as any Kol group studied by us. It was previously noted that this village controls about eighty acres of land. They say that ordinarily they do not sell the farm products, rather keeping them for the use of the village as well as holding a small reserve for emergencies. The village contains about 135 adult persons and the land farmed takes care of their food. Money for other needs is gained in many ways: during the months of May and June the leaves of the *tendu* tree (*Diosypros melanoxylon*) are picked for use in the *biri* manufacture. The leaves are gathered in the early morning or the evenings, and in the heat of the day the people sit under the trees or on the verandas of their houses and arrange the leaves in bundles of one hundred each, tying them with fibre. These bundles are then sold to contractors at the rate of four annas per hundred bundles. Prices vary somewhat according to the quality and the demand. The Kharara Ghat folk claim that they earn from Rs. 400 to 500 per year from the sale of these leaves.

Kharara Ghat has other sources of income. The village is situated on a jungly section on the edge of the reserved forest. Wood is cut in this forest and carried to Jubbulpore where it is sold to customers among the military folks living on the Ridge. In this way three to four annas per trip are earned. The Kol who takes wood from the reserved forest must pay two pice for each load carried on his head out of the forest.

The cutting of grass during the rainy season is another source of income for this village and a good load of grass, such as may be carried on the head, will bring from three to four annas in Jubbulpore. Gardening would be possible along the banks of the river but they do not do any there. What gardening they do is limited to the manure pile where pumpkins and the like are allowed to grow. There is an occasional hunt with dogs and torches, mainly for hares which stand and watch the light and are either clubbed to death or caught by the dogs. There were no guns in the village, nor did they use the bow and arrow. Although they live right beside the river fishing is not common. Sometimes fish are cornered in shallow water and caught with strips of cloth.

In our visits to Kol villages we also went to numerous bazaars. The bazaar is usually a weekly feature and there is a definite rotation from village to village. In all our inspections we did not find anything for sale in the weekly bazaars which had been brought there by Kols. Any wood, grass, eggs or the like, which they do sell are sold privately to individuals.

Animals. Whenever possible Kols keep animals such as cows, bullocks, goats and chickens, but unless they are rather independent economically not many are found to own cattle. Out of twelve Kol families studied in Barela only four owned cattle: five bullocks, two cows and two calves. Most of the families had a few chickens. Dogs and cats are found in Kol villages but they do not seem to be owned by individuals, belonging rather to the whole village. No swine were kept in Barela, nor by any other Kol community which we studied. Some intimated that in the years that were past swine were kept but that they gave it up so as not to offend their Hindu neighbours. Kols never keep donkeys nor horses. One Kol in Barela wanted to purchase a pair of bullocks, and to do this went to a bazaar in Panagar a distance of twenty miles away, where he got one for eight rupees. A few days later he purchased another from a nearby Gond village and paid twelve rupees. Neither was a very good specimen.

The survey of Kharara Ghat indicated that there they owned 35 bullocks, 73 cows, 43 goats and about 200 chickens. In our investigations we found only one or two Kol families owning buffaloes; their cost and care is far too much for the average Kol. Eight out of the thirty families in Kharara Ghat owned neither goats nor cattle. If cattle are allowed to graze in the reserve forests the yearly payment is twelve annas for a bullock or a cow and six to eight annas for a goat. Young animals may graze without payment.

In Panagar and Deori chickens are the common possession and there are but a few who have goats and cattle. At Benda, with 15 houses of Kols, there are six head of cattle and five goats. They cannot raise chickens there as they are plagued with cats, both domestic and from the jungle, which makes this impossible. Cats are regarded as sacred animals and are called "mothers" and may not be killed[1]. The villages which are largely made up of people employed in industrial enterprises are found to have few animals. The more agricultural type of village has more cattle; but those who consider that they are here today and gone tomorrow do not have many animals. In the Kol *mahallas* about Jubbulpore the number of cattle is not large. Nowhere did we find a Kol who owned a horse. As was seen[2] they have a tradition that causes them to consider a horse something that should not be touched.

Taxes. Direct taxes are paid by very few Kols, for unless he actually owns his land the taxes are not paid directly. Those who take land on shares from the *malguzar* pay him one-third of the crop as his rent; in other cases a certain sum per *khandi* of seed sown is agreed upon. Some Kols about Barela told us they paid seven rupees for 1½ acres of *malguzari* land and another of the same place fourteen rupees for three acres of the same. The houses in which the Kols of Barela live are built on *malguzari* land. When a new house is put up they pay the *malguzar* two to three rupees depending on the size of the house and report that subsequently no further land rent is asked for. As long as the buildings are occupied by that man, and kept in good repair the land on which it stands can be controlled by the builder. In other places there seems to be a yearly tax for houses; on the municipal land in Jubbulpore it was two rupees per house per year; at Garha, near the edge of Jubbulpore town limits the landowner asked one rupee per house per year. This amount seems to be the general rate or tax to *malguzars* for the houses or huts in which they live. In the industrial settlements they are given rent-free land on which they may erect their huts when they live on the property of the company employing them.

1 See page 198.
2 See pages 34-35; 210, 211.

When the reserved forests are used there are certain fees that the Kols must pay. In Katni, along the Great Deccan Road, we found that the area of the house was considered for assessing the tax, and that the rate there was annas four per one hundred square feet of land area. In addition to this each family had to pay four annas per year for "sanitation". The standard rates for grazing cattle near Katni are as follows: buffalo Rs. 2-8-0 per year; cattle 0-12-0 to 1-4-0; goats 0-8-0 and to the shepherd who took them out daily annas four per head per year.

Debt. Debt does not seem to be as heavy a burden upon Kols in British India as it is upon their Hindu neighbours. The normal debt of the Indian cultivator has been estimated to be well over two hundred rupees. The surveys we made among the Kols seem to indicate that most of them will be found to have small debts of one kind or another, but that it is not the heavy burden that is so often found in village India; also that the Kol *panchayats* or councils are active in discouraging indebtedness. Out of eleven Kol families questioned in Barela six indicated that they were in debt. The highest debt was Rs. 16/- and the total of the six amounted to only Rs. 42/-. This is much lower than one would expect. Debts were mostly acquired for clothes and marriages. They were made in the Barela bazaar and interest on them was paid at the rate of two pice per rupee per month, which is an interest rate of 37½%. On the other hand one Kol family reported that they made loans to farmers and others on good security and that they had about Rs. 300/- loaned out in that manner.

It was sometimes the custom, in order to avoid debt at the time of marriage on the part of some poor family, for members of the village to subscribe one rupee per family to help defray the expenses. This was considered as a loan which would be paid back later without interest charges if the family was able. The heads of the Kharara Ghat families were questioned about debt. It was found that only three were really involved: one owed fifty rupees incurred by the purchase of a field and a wedding in the family; another ten rupees, also for a wedding and a third fifteen rupees for the same reason. In some other places such as Panagar and Deori, debt was found to be more common, and in Panagar the Kols who farmed land would often take as a loan an amount up to one-third of the expected produce of their lands. Usually the respective *panchayats* watch the matter of the indebtedness of the community quite closely and in some places money may not be borrowed without its consent. In the industrial and city centres indebtedness is quite common, much more so than under village conditions. Almost every time we were in the Kol sections in and close to Jubbulpore we met Pathan money-lenders who were there to collect what they could of interest due to them. It appears that as Kols come into close contact with city life, their natural hesitation to acquire a debt is broken down, and money is taken as a loan which they have practically no expectation of being able to repay.

It should also not be overlooked that in some sections there is a state of perpetual debt on the part of the Kol villager. Money is not exactly borrowed—it is rather a gift which cannot be paid back, but which means a life-long obligation of service to the giver. This is particularly true of conditions in Rewa State and the more backward parts of the Central Provinces.

GAMBLING AND BEGGING. Some enquiries were also made concerning gambling. The *panchayat* allows it on certain festival days such as *Dewali* when all groups gamble, and also it is allowed occasionally in private. The gambling is not for large stakes and most communities seem to avoid it. At present the most popular form of gambling found mostly near cities is said to be with the use of playing cards. Under village conditions a block of wood is taken and on the six sides numbers are marked. These blocks are thrown somewhat in the manner of dice. Coins are also thrown, singly and in combination.

There are not many beggars among the Kols and we came across nothing of this type although the Census Report indicated that some were returned as "beggars, vagrants and prostitutes". When we made our enquiries they indicated that they felt a responsibility for those of their own group who were in need, and that they tried to care for such during the period of their dependency.

We did not find that they made use of co-operative societies, although in the case of Barela, there was one which they might have used. As far as we were able to observe no active interest was taken in politics, and none of the village Kols reported as ever having cast a ballot. It is otherwise with the Kols in Jubbulpore, for the Congress party has been very active and all who have been eligible have been recorded under its banner.

From many enquiries it is clear that among themselves, apart from the *panchayat*, they have no clubs nor associations of any kind.

From the above survey of the economic conditions existing among the Kols it will have been seen that they are among the poor and dispossessed of the land. As a group they rank toward the bottom of the economic level; and in spite of their being such good workers it appears that there is but little chance for them to earn, in even a moderate way, enough to lift themselves from the pit in which they rest. Their burdens are many and their ignorance is great. And yet they do not worry much; and they have a saying to the effect that, "when there is food in the house why should one go out and labour?"

CHAPTER XIV

THE KOL TRIBE IN TRANSITION

It is rather difficult to compare the Kols of today with the Kols of an earlier period. There is no material old enough and complete enough to show the changes that are occurring in Kol life and thought. The best single account of the Kols of Central India is found in Mr. William Crooke's Volumes on *The Tribes and Castes of the N. W. Provinces and Oudh*. This was written some fifty-five years ago, and while it contains something that may be used in a comparative way it is not full enough. Russell and Hiralal's book which is about thirty years old is not specific enough and is based more on general Munda customs than it is on actual Kols in Central India. And yet to use Crooke's account as a criterion of conditions among the Kols of Central India some fifty years ago would not be quite fair, as his account is based largely on the Kols in the southern edge of the United Provinces. Thus he is talking of the Northern Kols. Our investigations have been mainly among the Southern Kols, but we have checked our materials in Rewa State, the centre of Kol distribution. The fairly consistent account of the main outlines of Kol life and experience has led us to believe that we have a fairly accurate account of things as they are today. Nevertheless one senses a great unexplored world of belief, custom and outlook of which but the edge has been touched. No anthropologist would claim finality for any study such as this.

From our discussions with Kols and observations and comparisons there have clearly been changes among them in the economic, social and religious spheres of life.

ECONOMIC CHANGES. The striking thing from the economic angle is that this tribe, a jungle people originally, is moving away from the forests, first into agricultural centres where they earn their livelihood as farm coolies or tenant farmers, and then on into the industrial world as the factory coolie.

The further the Kols have moved from their jungle life the more industrialized they have become. Kols in Jubbulpore are nearly all engaged in factory work, or some other form of industrial work such as sawyers, and those yet further from Rewa are in manganese mines. There are still large groups of Kols who are agricultural serfs and others who follow the wheat crop at the harvesting seasons. Along with other members of the family able to work they leave their rude huts and then return three or four months later with a bit of money with which to buy clothes and the like. Some of the women accompany them, though not the children, and when they return at the end of the season there are a large number of infants which have been born to them in the fields as they have worked.

There are three strata among the Kols of today. From the economic view the factory coolies are better off. While wages are not high they are higher than can be won in agricultural or forest work and the income is steady. As forest people and agricultural serfs they may have enough to eat, but no money for anything else. Factory work brings three to four times the wage of the Kol who works away in the villages, and lasts the year round. Everywhere it is said that the Kols are the best group of workmen among those employed and often they are the main workers throughout a factory where unskilled labour is needed. As they are working in the factories they are also learning trades, and fifty years from now it may be found that Kols have taken up many trades and have made good. There is no occupational restriction as with many Hindu castes.

As the economic level is raised there is usually found a definite improvement in living conditions. Bad as the factory lines are they are much better than the rude huts of the jungle Kols. A Kol in Katni has built for himself a brick house of a very respectable appearance. In order to supplement their farm earnings the agricultural Kols still practise on the side their primitive occupations of wood and grass cutting. The industrial Kols are not able to do this, for they must work daily in the factory unless it happens to be closed on Sunday. On that day it will be found that a few Kols have gone out where wood may be cut and each brings back a load to the factory lines. This is cut for their own use and is not for sale.

Wherever Kols have been settled for some years they have told us how they first came and lived in grass huts and how gradually, as they became sure of their place there and as work became fairly regular and certain, that they have put up better living quarters and finally have built good mud houses with tiled roofs. More is owned by them than they ever had before. They possess livestock and there may be considerable amounts invested in jewellery.

Judging from the pictures in books like Crooke, Russell and Hiralal and Roy's work on the Mundas and other related tribes, the Kols of today in Central India cover their persons with clothes much more completely than the earlier pictures represent. Today one finds but little exposure of the breasts by Kol women, and in the presence of men they usually cover their heads with their *saris*. It was difficult to get, for the anthropometric data, photographs of Kol women with their heads uncovered.

SOCIAL CHANGES. In the social realm there are certain important changes which may be noted and yet there is a persistence in the older ways. This is characteristic of much of Indian life. Even fifty years ago the Brahmin priest was called for some Kol weddings and some other groups did not call him. The same holds true today, though now-a-days to call the *pandit* is the "right" thing to do, and those who do not call him, but manage things themselves, are looked down upon. Outside of the marriage cycle the Brahmin priest is nowhere else absolutely essential to Kol life, though occasional use is made of him at the name-giving ceremony and the throwing of ashes into the rivers Ganges or Nerbudda.

It appears that there is a definite hardening of the social divisions within the Kol tribe. The Kols are apparently forming a miniature caste system within the tribe somewhat modelled after Hindu caste. These groups are endogamous and interdining is forbidden and in general they take the form of true castes[1] If a Kol is asked about his race, he will probably not answer Kol, but give the subcaste: Rautiya, Thakuriya or another. Kols are very particular about their sub-divisions, and while there is some evidence available to show a desire to break down these distinctions, the main interest seems to be in their preservation. The system seems to be hardening and more firmly entrenched than ever. In discussing this, one Kol gathering said that they were trying to discourage this group consciousness and they were encouraging (1) intermarriage and (2) interdining. They felt that this was the proper order. As yet, however, to their knowledge, no actual cases of intermarriage or interdining had occurred.

HINDUIZATION. The process of Hinduization is essentially a social phenomenon. Considerable attention has been paid to Hindu influence in passing and the matter may be summed up here. Throughout the centuries and up till the present time there has been a persistent movement of primitive tribes into Hinduism. They have not come by conversion but by absorption. The term Hindu is very elastic and it often happens that a member of one of these primitive races does not know whether he is a Hindu or not. There has been no

1 Blunt, in *The Caste System of Northern India*, states that there are three characteristics of a caste: Heredity, Endogamy, and restrictions on Commensality. (pp. 1-2).

PLATE XXIX

Kols migrating North following the Wheat Harvest.

exact criterion of Hinduization, and the Census reports from year to year, while attempting to distinguish between members of primitive tribes who are Hindu and those who are followers of Tribal Religions, are not to be relied upon.

In its contact with more primitive religions Hinduism has steadily absorbed their beliefs and practices and has made them its own. All over Central India, Hinduism in the villages is hardly to be distinguished from the 'animism' of the primitive tribes. There may be a different terminology, the 'Hindu' may give the name of a Hindu deity as his god or goddess, but his worship of it is akin to the worship of the primitive people about him. The Census of 1931 made the surprising returns of tribal religion by a Bania, four Brahmins, three Gossins, three Kurmis, and a few others. These came from backward tracts and had been living among primitive peoples and worshipping their gods. Outside of. this tract they would have called themselves Hindus.

No really satisfactory attempts have been made to determine whether a tribe or caste is truly Hindu or how far Hinduization has progressed. The Census Report of the United Provinces for 1931[1] presents criteria to determine whether or not a man is a Hindu and comments that if these tests are to be accepted they reveal almost no movement toward Hinduism in the past twenty years.

It would appear that the Hinduization of the primitive tribes will eventually lead to their becoming a part of the Hindu social system and then being integrated into its lower strata and becoming regarded by Hindus as outcastes or scheduled classes. This seems to have widely occurred in the United Provinces where tribes have not been able to isolate themselves in mountain and forests and have thus been thrown into close contact with Hinduism. It was previously noted that this same fact is also true of Chota Nagpur, where, in spite of a strong Munda environment, some groups from this racial stock are now classed as untouchables and must be counted along with them.

At the present time, the Kols, though Hinduized to a considerable extent, are not yet counted among the outcaste and scheduled groups except in the United Provinces and their Hindu neighbours in Central India do not consider them unclean. In Central Provinces there are the Gandas and the Pankas, aboriginal peoples who have lost their identity and who have become recognized throughout the Provinces by the Hindus as untouchables. Throughout the years the gradual cultural changes and stratification have brought them to the lower strata of Hindu society.

1 *Census of India* 1931 : XVIII : pp. 516—517.

It has been noted that one of the evidences of the tribal groups becoming Hinduized was the abandonment of forest life and migratory methods of cultivation and the settling down in villages. This the Kols seem to have done in a large part of Central India. Today they generally live in small hamlets of their own, and oftener than not these are attached to larger villages. They appear to have totally abandoned *Bewar* cultivation, the method of burning off some of the jungle, planting seeds in the scratched ashes, and moving on to some newly burnt place the following year. The Government has either stopped this altogether, or limited the area in which this can be done. Most of the primitive tribes used to practise this. Even now though they live in villages there is still considerable seasonal migration. The villages near Jubbulpore are almost deserted in late March and April when the wheat is being harvested throughout the Nerbudda Valley. On our way to Rewa State at the end of April we passed hundreds of Kols along the Old Deccan road returning northwards to their homes in Rewa. They had their wives and new-born children with them, and were carrying their meagre possessions slung on the ends of bamboo poles across the shoulders. See plate XXIX.

The Kols do not admit that they are abandoning their tribal gods, or that they are accepting higher Hindu deities. As we have seen, they know very little of these higher deities other than their name, but feel that they have always known them. The actual worship of the Kol centres around the more primitive type of animistic ideology, modified, no doubt, by years of contact with other groups.

There is a real question whether the word "Hinduization" is really an accurate one to describe the process. The movement is not a one-way process. Mundas *are* becoming "Hinduized", but Hinduism itself owes much to more primitive religions for it has constantly borrowed from them and unconsciously absorbed many of their concepts and practices. The religious life of the Kol is much akin to the villager who calls himself a Hindu. Yet both are very unlike the "Aryan religion". For example, is the burning of the dead a Munda or a Hindu phenomenon? Generally it is thought of as a Hindu way of disposing of the dead, and it is overlooked that some Hindu sects bury their dead. But the earliest accounts of the Mundas show that they, too, did both[1].

CONCLUDING REMARKS. The Kols of today have been strongly influenced by Hinduism, but seemingly have not come much into contact with other faiths. It has been noted that they are found

1 Dalton, E. T., *Descriptive Ethnology of Bengal.*

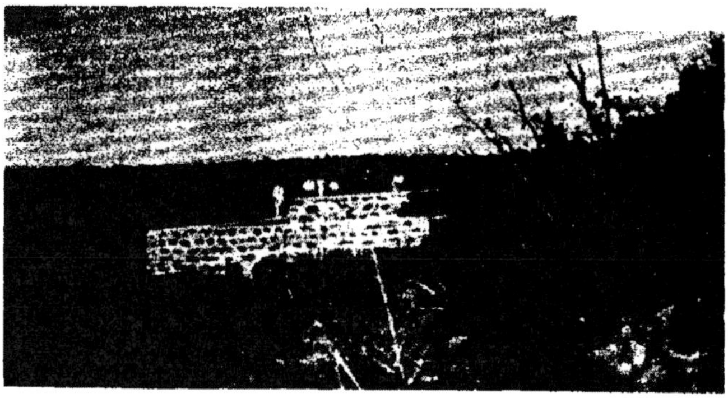

Kol Temple in process of construction near Katni. An attempt to gain recognition.

Closer view of the uncompleted Structure. Funds for finishing the work were not forthcoming.

FRONTISPIECE :

Phaggu and Family.

among the most illiterate of the land. Up till now Christian Missions have started no work among them and there has been no attempt from any quarter to give them adequate facilities and opportunities whereby they may make some cultural advancement. There is great need for the improvement of their social and economic environment.

It would be wrong, however, to assume that the Kols are indifferent or that their aspirations are dormant. There are stirrings among them, which, unfortunately, have been taken advantage of by unscrupulous people. They are seeking for religious recognition, and we have traced two attempts, one near Jubbulpore, and the other near Katni, to erect Kol "temples" In both cases wide appeals were circulated and fairly large sums of money collected. In the first case not a single stone was laid and some thousands of rupees were swindled. Near Katni they had got as far as the foundation and plinth when the funds gave out.[1] We were accompanied by five Kols to this project about which they were very enthusiastic. Our interest in it stimulated them greatly. They complained that nobody cared for Kols and that Hindus thought of them as coolies who had no self-respect; so they wanted to show the world that they are really worthy of recognition. They were very self-conscious about this matter. It was said that if they can only reveal their real spirit and show that they are truly interested in religious things, then Hindus must respect them and no longer despise them. They showed a pathetic eagerness for this recognition and were pleased with our visit. They made the claim that so far, not one person outside their own community, had shown the least concern for their welfare, and that in spite of their conscientious and earnest work, no one recognized nor knew them.

As a tribe the Kols are self-respecting and industrious. They are cheerful in disposition and greatly enjoy social fellowship. We found them open-hearted and ready to answer questions when once their confidence had been gained. Like most primitive tribes they are honest and trustworthy. That they have deep emotional feelings can be seen from their music and songs. They enjoy nothing better than a long evening of song and drum. We found but little evidence of their disobedience to the rules of the tribal codes of morality.

Taken all in all the Kols are a lovable people and as one comes into intimate contact with them he feels that much ought to be done to alleviate many of the difficulties and handicaps under which they bravely carry on.

In their case it is difficult to make recommendations for the future. For years Kols have been gradually losing their identity as an

1 See plate XXVIII.

aboriginal tribe. They are becoming assimilated into the caste system of the Hindus, and like others before them, may one day have to take their place as a caste or a series of castes, and would most likely find their place among the groups considered unclean. Their society as a whole will then be integrated into Hinduism and their future will be bound up with the Hindu system.

In the years to come the Kols will probably maintain many things found in their present culture, for example, their love for music and the *dholak*. Without the long evenings of song, life would take on an added drabness for them. And yet, their Hindu neighbours often bring pressure upon them to stop their drumming.

It would hardly do to set apart a definite area for the Kols. There is no place where they predominate in a manner to make this possible. Their nature is a roving one, they would not take kindly to a reservation, and one would not keep them together nor preserve their tribal life any more than many of the reservations for American Indians have done.

The Kols suffer from the exploiter[1]. More might be done for them in cooperative schemes, but there again the area is too large for any single scheme embracing the tribe as a whole. Schemes ought to be framed that would, in selected areas, take in other tribal groups as well.

Possibly much could be done for the tribe if their illiteracy could be reduced. The type of education provided for village India is not suitable for the villager, to say nothing of the Kol tribe. Their lack of education leaves them at the mercy of exploiters, and even though they are in the majority, still they have no influence in local bodies. Formal education is not enough. Along with the three Rs. which have their real value, something on the lines of modern handicraft project should be introduced, but should be radically modified to meet the needs of the Kols. Tribal interests and skills should be worked into any curriculum set up. Such schemes should not be left in the hands of local bodies, who, far too often, have no genuine concern for the aboriginal, but should be the direct concern of the Provincial Government.

Much of the Indian Penal Code cannot be applied to primitive tribes. Where lawyers cannot be consulted the groups get along with a minimum of trouble to the authorities. The tribal life is regulated

1 Verrier Elwin, in "The Aboriginals" (Oxford Pamphlets on Indian Affairs No. 14) says "If you want to help the aboriginal, do not try to reform him : reform the lawyer, the doctor, the schoolmaster, the official, the merchant, with whom he has to deal. Until that is done it is far better to leave the aboriginals alone. p. 31.

by the *panchayat*. The *panch* should be encouraged and strengthened, and more recognition given to it. Kols seldom go to court and where the *panchayats* are given the serious attention they deserve, the tribe will be greatly benefited and the tribal sanctions and customs upheld.

The aboriginal tribes of India, the Kols included, deserve all the help and consideration that can be given them. Their presence in the land is far too often ignored or forgotten. They are not vocal and are easily overlooked. Yet they form an important part of the human life of India—life which should be protected, cherished and exalted.

APPENDIX I

TERMS OF RELATIONSHIP AMONG KOLS

Some investigations were made into the kinship nomenclature of the Kols to see what index it might afford as to the structure of Kol society. Unfortunately materials sent out were not returned and so no widespread investigation was possible. Below will be found a chart prepared from the responses of two different groups of Kols. There are variations and discrepancies in the two lists, but they may form the basis of a further investigation along this line.

LIST OF KINSHIP TERMS

English term of Relationship.	*Responses.* I.	II.
I. Speaker's own generation :		
Brother ..	Bhāiyā	Bhāī.
Elder brother ..	Baṛe bhāī	Bhāī.
Eldest brother ..	Jeṭhe bhāī	Bhāī.
Youngest brother ..	Saphale bhāī	Bhāī.
Father's elder brother's son ..	Bhāī	Bhāī.
Father's younger brother's son ..	Maphale bhāī	Bhāī.
Father's elder sister's son ..	Bhāī	Bhāī.
Father's younger sister's son ..	Bhāī	Bhāī.
Mother's sister's son ..	Bhāī	Bhāī.
Mother's elder sister's son ..	Bhāī	Bhāī.
Mother's younger sister's son ..	Bhāī	Bhāī.
Mother's elder brother's son ..	Bhāī	Bhāī.
Mother's younger brother's son ..	Bhāī	Bhāī.
Husband's elder sister's husband ..	Bahanoī	Nandoī.
Husband's elder brother ..	Jeṭha	Jeṭha.
Husband's younger brother ..	Dewar	Dewar.
Wife's elder sister's husband ..	Sāṛhū bhāī	Sāṛhū bhāī.
Husband's younger sister's husband ..	Sāṛhū bhāī	Loara bahanoī
(Man's) Elder sister's husband ..	Bahanoī	Nandoī.
(Woman's) Elder sister's husband ..	Bhāī	Sāṛhū bhāī.
(Man's) Younger sister's husband ..	Bahanoī	Nandoī.
(Woman's) Younger sister's husband ..	Sāṛhū bhāī	Sāṛū bhāī.
Wife's younger brother ..	Sār	Sār.
Wife's elder brother ..	Sār	Sār.
Mother's sister's son ..	Bhāī	Bhāī.
Wife's elder sister's husband ..	Sāṛhū	Sāṛhū bhāī.
Husband ..	Mard	Adamī.
Son's wife's father ..	Sasur	Samdhī.
Daughter's husband's father ..	Sasur	Samdhī.
Wife ..	Mehrāk	Lugāī.

Husband's elder brother's wife .	Sār	Bahin.
Eldest sister .	Baṛī bahin	Bahin.
Elder sister .	Maphali bahin	Bahin.
Youngest sister .	Bāiyā	Bahin.
Younger sister .	Saphali bahin	Bahin.
Mother's elder brother's daughter .	Bahin	Bahin.
Mother's younger brother's daughter .	Bahin	Bahin.
Mother's elder sister's daughter .	Bahin	Bahin.
Mother's younger sister's daughter .	Bāiyā	Bahin.
Husband's elder sister .	Phuā	Nand.
Husband's younger sister .	Phūā	Nand.
Husband's younger brother's wife .	Bhaujī	Dewarāṇī.
Husband's elder brother's wife .	Bhaujī	Dewarāṇī.
Wife's elder brother's wife .	Sarhaj	Sarhaj.
Wife's younger brother's wife .	Sarhaj	Sarhaj.
Father's elder sister's daughter .	Bahin	Bahin.
Father's younger sister's daughter .	Bahin	Bahin.
Father's elder brother's daughter .	Bahin	Bahin.
Father's younger brother's daughter .	Bahin	Bahin.
Wife's elder sister .	Sārī	Sārī.
Wife's younger sister .	Sārī	Sārī.
Younger brother's wife .	Bayāhū	Bahū.
Elder brother's wife .	Bhaujī	Bhaujī.
Son's wife's mother .	Sās	Samdhīn.
Daughter's husband's mother .	Samdhīn	Samdhīn.

II. Generation next above the speaker

Father .	Dādā	Dādā.
Father's elder brother .	Kākā	Baṛā dādā
Father's eldest brother .	Baṛā dādā	Baṛā dādā
Mother's elder sister's husband .	Mausiyā	Baṛā dādā
Father's youngest brother .	Kākā	Kākā.
Father's younger brother .	Kākā	Kākā.
Step-father .	Dādā	Kākā.
Mother's younger sister's husband .	Mausiyā	Mausiyā.
Father's elder sister's husband .	Phūphā	Phūphā.
Father's younger sister's husband .	Phūphā	Phūphā.
Mother's elder brother .	Māmā	Māmā.
Mother's younger brother .	Māmā	Māmā.
Husband's father .	Bābā	Sasur.
Wife's father .	Sasūr	Sasur.
Mother .	Didi	Bāu.
Stepmother .	Māyābha Māhatirī	Kākī.
Father's elder brother's wife .	Kākī	Baṛī bāu.
Father's elder sister .	Phūā	Phūā.
Father's younger brother's wife .	Kākī	Kākī.
Father's sister .	Phūā	Phūā.
Father's younger sister .	Phūā	Phūā.

Mother's elder sister	.. Mausī	Baṛī bāu.
Mother's elder brother's wife	.. Main	Main.
Mother's brother's wife	.. Main	Main.
Mother's younger sister	.. Mausri	Mausrī.
Wife's mother	.. Sās	Sās (Ammā).
Husband's mother	.. Didi	Sās (Amma).

III. Generation next below the speaker :

Son	.. Dādū	Betāwā.
Elder brother's son	.. Dādū	Betāwā.
Wife's elder sister's son	.. Dādū	Betāwā.
Husband's elder brother's son	.. Dādū	Betāwā.
Wife's younger sister's son	.. Dādū	Betāwā.
Husband's younger brother's son	.. Dādū	Betāwā.
Husband's younger sister's son	.. Dādū	Betāwā.
(Woman's) Elder brother's son	.. Bhatījā	Betāwā.
(Woman's) Younger brother's son	.. Bhatijā	Betāwā.
(Man's) Elder sister's son	.. Dādū	Betāwā.
(Man's) Younger sister's son	.. Dādū	Betāwā.
Husband's younger sister's son	.. Dādū	Laṛkā betāwā.
Wife's younger brother's son	.. Bhatījā	Betāwā.
(Woman's) Elder sister's son	.. Bhatījā	Betāwā.
Daughter's husband	.. Dāmād	Dāmād (Bābbu).
(Man's) Elder brother's daughter	.. Bhatījī	Biṭiyā.
Husband's elder daughter's husband	.. Pāhunā dāmād	Nandoī.
(Woman's) Elder brother's daughter	.. Bhatījī	Biṭiyā.
Husband's younger sister's daughter	.. Bhatījī	Biṭiyā.
(Man's) Elder sister's daughter	.. Bhānjī	Biṭiyā.
(Woman's) Elder sister's daughter	.. Bhatījī	Biṭiyā.
Husband's Elder sister's daughter	.. Bhatījī	Biṭiyā.
(Man's) Younger sister's daughter	.. Bhatījī	Bhanj
Wife's elder brother's daughter	.. Bhatījī	Bhanjī (Biṭiyā).
Wife's younger brother's daughter	.. Bhatījī	Biṭiyā.
(Woman's) Younger sister's daughter	.. Bhatījī	Biṭiyā.
(Man's) Younger brother's daughter	.. Bhatījī	Biṭiyā.
Wife's younger sister's daughter	.. Bhatījī	Biṭiyā.
Son's wife	.. Bahū	Bahū.

IV. Third generation from the speaker :

Son's son	.. Nātī	Nātī.
Daughter's son	.. Nātī	Nātī.
Son's daughter's husband	.. Nātpāhunā	Nātidāmād.
Daughter's daughter's husband	.. Nātpāhunā	Nand dāmād.
Sister's son's daughter's husband	.. Nātpāhunā	Dāmād.
Sister's son's son	. Bhānjā	Nātī.
Sister's daughter's son	.. Bhānjā	Nātī.
Son's daughter	.. Nātina	Nātina.
Daughter's daughter	.. Nātina	Nātina.

Sister's son's daughter	Pāntī	Nātina.
Sister's daughter's daughter	Nātina	Nātina.

The above may be compared with the list given in the Central Provinces Census Report, 1911, page 146. This list, however, does not refer to Kols in particular, being terms in general use in the area.

Males		*Females*	
Maternal uncle	Māmā	Maternal Uncle's wife	Māmī or Main.
Paternal uncle	Kākā or Chāchā	Paternal uncle's wife	Kākī or Chāchī.
Father's sister's husband	Phūphā	Father's sister	Phūphī or Phūā.
Mother's sister's husband	Mausiā	Mother's sister	Mausī.
Father's father	Ājā	Father's mother	Ajī.
Mother's father	Nānā	Mother's mother	Nānī.
Elder brother	Dādā	Elder sister	Didi or Jiji.
Husband's elder brother	Jeṭh	Elder brother's wife	Bhavaj or Bhaujī.
Husband's younger brother	Dewār	Younger brother's wife	Bhaihau.
Elder sister's husband	Jija or Bhauwā		
Sister's husband	Bahnoī	Husband's younger brother's wife	Dewarānī.
Wife's brother	Sālā		
Husband's sister's husband	Nandoī	Husband's sister	Nānād.
Wife's sister's husband	Sāṛhū	Wife's sister	Sālī.
Brother's son	Bhatījā	Wife's elder sister	Jiṭh sās.
Sister's son	Bhānej or Bhānjā	Wife's brother's wife	Sarhaj.
Son of husband's elder brother	Jiṭhaut	Brother's daughter	Bhatijī or Banchī.
Wife's brother's son	Sarput	Wife's brother's daughter	Sarputin.

Appendix II

LIST OF KOL NAMES: MALE AND FEMALE

The numoer following the name indicates the number of times that particular name was found.

I. Names of Men:

Agurnū
Ajwā
Arjun
Āshram

Bābādīn
Bābūlāl (3)
Bahdanwālā
Bajrangī (3)
Baldī
Bālirām
Bandsūdhāri (2)
Bansau
Bakrū (2)
Barlāl (2)
Bathuā
Batihā
Bhaddī (2)
Bhaddhū
Bhaiyālāl (2)
Bharōsā (4)
Bhōka
Bhujiā
Bhūpat
Bhūra (2)
Biśewar
Biśnāth
Bisrām (3)
Bisrāmnāo
Bōddhī
Bōrā
Borsākī
Brindāban
Buddhū (2)

Chaita (2)
Chaitrām
Chakōdi
Chakōrī

Chamrū
Chandāmī
Chandin
Cherko
Chindwādī
Chunīlāl
Chhangā
Chhannū
Chhoṭā
Chhoṭālāl (2)
Chhutai

Dādu
Dafaiwālā
Dāmilāl
Daśarā
Desain
Devī (2)
Devidīn
Dhōlī
Dhunkā
Diman
Durgī
Dwārkā Praśād

Gabarū
Ganesh
Garībā
Gautiyā
Ghanesham
Gullū

Hajra
Hajrai
Halkī
Harlāl
Horlāl
Hukumā

Jagadhāri.
Jagadīn.
Jagdeo.
Jaggā.
Jailāl.
Jāmālin
Jari.
Jeman.
Jeṭhū.
Jhāllā.
Jhennā.
Jīban.
Jātawālā.
Jhuniā.

Kairā.
Kalkū.
Kallū (3)
Kammā
Kandhāī.
Kandlāl.
Kangai.
Kapuriā.
Khamenā.
Khetdāiyā.
Khimiyā.
Kolārī.
Kourī.
Kulhāiā.

Mahādeo (3)
Mahādevī.
Mahāṅgū (2)
Mahāṅgunwā.
Mallā.
Makkhī.
Mangal (3)
Manglā.
Manitolliā.

Markā
Matukdhāri
Mehiā
Mihālāl
Mohan
Mori
Muliā
Mullāiā
Mulu
Munīlāl
Murālī
Murī (2)

Nandilāl
Nannū
Namiyā
Narbud
Nauhuldi
Nunhū
Nunsarwale

Pachmā
Pachokī
Pacholā
Pāgal (2)
Pakīre Pardesī
Pancham (2)
Pansan
Parśadī
Phaggū (3)
Phragū
Piyārilāl
Pusan
Pusiā

Rājā
Rāmadīn (3)
Rāmāvatār (2)
Rāmcharan
Rāmdās
Rāmdhāri
Rāmlāl (2)
Rāmnāth.

Rāmphal.
Rāmparśād (3)
Rāmśaraṇ.

Sādhulāl.
Sādhuwā.
Sahain.
S'amśera.
Sepāl.
Sōnā.
S'ripraśād.
Subhai.
Sukhrām.
Sukkhā (3)
Summan.

Ṭhākurdīn.

Unjiyā.

Viālā.

Total men 205

II. Names of Women :

Baurini
Buddhiā

Jaghī
Joghārī

Maikī
Maitī
Muliā
Muṇgī (2)
Phuliabāī.

Ramiā.
Rāmkālī.
Ratanī.

Ṣandī.
Śemanī.
Sukhbārī (3)
Sumantī.
Sundarī (2)
Suniā (2)

Total women 23

Appendix III

NOTES ON POETRY IN CHAPTER XI

I. Songs of Nature.

1. A *dohārī* from Katni. The theme of love is also set forth. The crow is symbolical of an ordinary human being.

2. The chakahī-chakā (or Chakhī-chakvā) (*casarca rutila*) birds are a pair supposed to be under an eternal curse. During the day they may stay together and sport in the river, but when night comes they must be separated and stay apart from one another. A *dohārī* from Katni.

3. A *dādrā* from Imalhapur village.

4. A *dohārī* from Katni.
Belā : a kind of jasmin. *Chameli* : a creeper of the jasmin type.
Sarangī : a one-stringed country violin.
Sitār : an instrument usually having seven strings.

5. A *birhā* or forest song. This is sung as one walks through the forest and no musical instrument is used to accompany it. The woman is anxious about her husband whom she calls her lord.

II. Life: its Joys and Sorrows.

1. This song is a *rāī* from Sihora.

2. The 'green month' is *Sāwan*, which corresponds to the last half of July and the first half of August. The rains by this time have set in well and the heat-scorched landscape has been transformed. It is of the *dādrā* type of song and comes from Barela.

3. A *dādrā* from Katni.

4. A wedding *dohārī* from the village of Salavara. This song and others like it are used to tease the bridegroom. Here the girl is said to protest the choice of a mate for her.

5. A *dādrā* from Katni.

6. Called '*bārāhmāsi*.' 'A twelve-month song.' Sung by women who have to stay at home while their husbands go afar for work. This song is from Katni and comes from a woman. There are only ten of the Hindi months named here: Sāwan and Pūs are omitted by the singer, probably by error. The Hindi months are as follows—

Asārā	..	June-July.
Sāwan	..	July-August (omitted in the poem).
Bhādon	..	August-September.
Kunwār	..	September-October.
Kātika	..	October-November.
Agahana	..	November-December.
Pūs	..	December-January (omitted above).
Māgha	..	January-February.

Phāgun	..	February-March.
Chaita	..	March-April.
Baishāka	..	April-May.
Jeṭh	..	May-June.

III. Love and Intrigue.

1. A *dādrā* from Katni. The *loṭā* is a brass vessel used for carrying liquids. A cord is frequently tied about its neck and it is lowered into a well in order to bring up water. See note on 6, 7 below.

2. A *kāṭili* from Imalhapur. This is a teasing song and in this case the *kaṭili* is addressed to a young maid of beauty. The *pānwāllā* prepares and sells the *pān*, a mixture of betel nut, lime and tobacco wrapped in Piper leaves (*Piper betel*).

3. A *dādrā* from Katni.

4. A *dādrā* sung at the wedding season: from Jubbulpore. The suspicious husband is assured that his wife's smiles and blushes are innocent, and are directed to no other man. The first line should be repeated four times.

5. A *dādār* from Katni. The *dhīmar* is a member of the fisherman caste, but is used in another sense.

6, 7. These are both *dādrās* from Katni. The symbolism of these two songs is perhaps obvious. Sexual matters are referred to by the men as entering a house, as a lotus on a pond or in terms of getting water from the well.

8. A *rāī* from Katni.

9. A *biyā*, or wedding song; sung at the time of the circumambulation of the sacred post. From Salavara. The terms of relationship are noted in the text of the translation. The intrigue is rather complicated and it is evident that the mother-in-law, who ought to be on her guard, is a simpleton and does not realize what is going on. The symbolism is apparent.

IV. Songs of Social Events.

1. This song is called *chhauhar* as it is sung on the sixth night after the birth of a child. The woman complains that the in-laws care nothing for her birth-pangs. Given by women near Katni.

2. A *badhwā*, a song sung by women when a male child is born. The song is kept up for long periods and is repeated again and again. It is essentially a song of congratulation. Ayodhya was the place of Ram's birth. This song given by women near Katni.

3. Another *chhauhar* or sixth-night song from Katni. A Kajali forest (dense—black as *kajal*) is one inhabited by elephants. The swing has a sexual symbolism.

4. A *dādrā* from Imalhapur. The *Pūrabiyās* are dwellers in the eastern parts. There is a Purbiya subdivision of Chamars. (Briggs, *op. cit.* page 24). The *Baghels* are men of Baghelkhand.

5. A *rāī* from Katni.

6. A marriage *dādrā* from Barela and sung as a teasing song. *Marawā* or *marhwā*: the wedding booth.

Khambā : the sacred post.
Kalas : The water pot.
Chauka : The small raised platform under the booth.
Haldī : Turmeric (*Circuma longa*).

7. This is a wedding song from Barela. The headings indicate the time the song is sung.

8. The important guests are teased by being told that they are being fed with food fit only for animals.

9. Another song with a sting. Sung in connection with the arrival of the bridegroom's party. From Salavara.

10, 11. From Barela.

12. A marriage *dādrā* from Barela. The whole is a coarse series of jesting absurdities: the unmarried woman can hardly have a daughter-in-law, and yet the latter is pregnant. It is, however, her sister who is fed the food given to women in confinement, and a woman who is a mere spectator to all this suddenly gives birth to the child which a barren woman takes and suckles.

13. A wedding *dādrā* from Katni. The *kadam* tree is the *Nauclea orientalis*. In wedding imagery the bridegroom is frequently likened to a parrot.

14. A *rāī* from Katni. The spot of vermilion denotes a living husband.

15. A wedding song from Barela in which the bride is teased and warned to be careful. A lakh is 100,000.

16. From Barela. The *barāt* is being teased. Kajlī forest is a forest frequented by elephants. A *guṭkā* is a magic ball prepared by devotees which, when eaten, is supposed to make one invisible. Here it makes others disappear

V. Songs of Religion.

1. *Dādrās* from the vicinity of Katni. These are examples of numerous songs of this nature which were collected and translated but are not reproduced here. It is likely that most of the songs centering about Rām and his experiences in search of Sītā are borrowed as in their actual worship Rām is seldom taken into account by Kols. Daṣarath was the father of Rām.

3. From Sihora: a *rāī*.

4. A *dohāri* from Imalhapur. The *ghumachī* is said to be a fruit of reddish colour with black spots upon it. It is probably the *ghunghachī* (*Abrus Precatorius*.) For *chakhī-chakvā* birds see notes on 1 : 2.

5. This has references to the Rāmāyaṇa story. A *dohārī* from Imalhapur.

6. A song for the *phāg* season, composed in Garha. *Phāg* and *holī* refer to the same season. A *bunda* is a dot or decoration on the forehead to enhance a woman's beauty. Kashi is the holy city of Benares.

7. A *bhajan* called *sumaran*—'song of remembrance'. Hinglās: or Kailās, the holy mount of Siva in the Himalayas. Maihar: a town and state about 100 miles north of Jubbulpore. It is the seat of the main temple dedicated to Shārdā *devī*.

8. A *bhagat* from Jubbulpore. *Lagan*: the wedding horoscope. *Barāt*: the party which comes to the girl's house bringing the groom with

them. *Tabalās*: drums. But the procedure is irregular for the goddess is spying on the procession of the men-folk.

9. A *bihārī*, a song used at seasons of enjoyment and happiness. From Katni. Dasarath: the father of Rām.

Sītā: the chaste wife of Rām.

Doshmātā: a name for the wife of Indra.

Belhārī leaves are used for *pān*.

Rām and Bhagawān are often used interchangeably.

10. A *dādrā* from Katni. Kānhāī is another name for Kṛishṇa, one of the incarnations of Vishṇu and famous for his flute playing. His name is usually associated with the Jamunā river and the city of Brindāban.

VI. Miscellaneous.

1. A *rāī* from Jubbulpore. Ganesh is the god of wisdom, son of Siva and is distinguished by his elephant face. *Timkī*: kettle drum.

2. A *rāī* from Sihora. The *dholak* is the common type of Indian drum.

3. A *dādrā* from Katni, sung by women.

Appendix IV.

A Glossary of Tribes and Castes mentioned in this book and found in the Central Provinces. Based on Russell and Hiralal.

Ahīr	The professional caste of herdsmen.
Bahna	The occupational caste of cotton cleaners.
Baigā	There is a Baigā tribe, once said to be of Dravidian origin, although Munda affinities would seem to class them with the latter. Their priests are believed to possess great power.
Bani	See Baniā.
Baniā	The occupational caste of bankers, money lenders and grocers.
Banjāra	A caste of carriers and drivers of pack-bullocks.
Baraī	The caste of growers and sellers of betel-vine leaf.
Baṛhaī	The occupational caste of carpenters.
Bāri	A caste generally working as household servants and makers of leaf-plates.
Basor	The occupational caste of bamboo workers.
Bhangī	Low caste sweepers. Synonym for Mehtar.
Bhāriā	See Bhūiyā.
Bhīl	An important primitive Mūṇḍā tribe of Khandesh, Central India and Rajputana.
Bhīlālā	A caste of mixed origin, probably from alliances between Rājpūts and Bhīls.
Bhoi	A primitive tribe.
Bhūiyā	An important Mūṇḍā tribe confined largely to Chota Nagpur.
Bhūmiā	Same as Bhūiyā.
Binjhwār	A caste supposedly formed from a Dravidian tribe, though more likely a branch of the Mūṇḍās.
Brāhmin	The highest of the four castes. In general usage a Brāhmin and a priest are synonymous.
Chamār	The occupational caste of leather workers.
Chaṇḍāla	An outcast, supposedly originating as a child of a female Brāhmin and a male S'ūdra.
Chatrī	A common synonym for a Rajput.
Dahāit	A mixed caste of village watchmen.
Darzī	The occupational caste of tailors.
Dhīmar	The caste of fishermen and *pālkī*-bearers.
Dhobī	The professional caste of washermen.
Dom	An aboriginal tribe of north India now reduced to servitude and classed as untouchable.
Domaṛ	A caste related to the Doms and Basors.
Gānda	A servile caste of village drudges, watchmen, and musicians.
Gaolī	A name of the Ahīr or herdsmen caste.
Ghāsiā	A low caste, possibly of Dravidian origin, which cuts grass, tends horses and acts as musicians.
Goṇḍ	Probably the most important of the primitive forest tribes of India and supposedly of Dravidian origin. There are about 2,500,000 in Central Provinces.

Gowārī	The herdsmen of the Maratha country corresponding to the Ahīrs.
Halbā	A caste of cultivators and farm servants.
Jain	A religious group.
Julāha	A group of Mohammedan weavers.
Kāchhī	A cultivating caste. Growers of vegetables and irrigated crops requiring intensive cultivation.
Kalār	An occupational caste of distillers and sellers of fermented liquor.
Karchulī	A clan of Rājpūts; formerly a ruling race in the Jubbulpore country.
Kawar	A primitive tribe, possibly of Mūṇḍā origin, found in the Chhattisgarh area.
Kāyasth	The caste of writers and village accountants.
Kewat	Fishermen, boatmen, gram-parchers and cultivators.
Khairā	A Mūṇḍā tribe found in north-east Central Provinces.
Khangār	A low caste of village watchmen and field labourers.
Khatī	A caste of blacksmiths.
Khond	A Dravidian tribe.
Korī	A weaving caste.
Korku	A Mūṇḍā tribe of south-west Central Provinces. To a great extent this tribe has maintained its Mūṇḍā type of language.
Koshti	Weavers of silk and fine cotton cloth.
Kotwār	Caste of village watchmen.
Kshatriya	The second of the four traditional castes.
Kumbā	See Kumhār.
Kumhār	The occupational caste of potters.
Kunbī	The main agricultural caste in the Maratha country.
Kurmī	The representative cultivating caste of central and northern India.
Lodhī	An important agricultural caste.
Lohār	The occupational caste of blacksmiths and iron-workers.
Maharā	The low caste of menials, labourers and village watchmen of the Maratha country.
Mālī	The functional caste of vegetable and flower gardeners.
Mārāthā	The military caste of southern India.
Mariās	The Mariā Goṇḍs; a branch of the great Goṇḍ race found principally in Bastar State.
Mawārī	A subcaste of Dahāit.
Mehra	A synonym for Mahār.
Mūṇḍā	A tribe in Bihar. A general term for primitive people of Mon-Khmer affinities.
Nāī	The occupational caste of barbers.
Nishāda	A primitive people mentioned in Hindu scripture.
Orāoñs	A Mūṇḍā tribe of Chota Nāgpur with members in Central Provinces.
Panka	A Dravidian caste of weavers and labourers.
Pansārī	Growers and sellers of the *pān* leaf. A synonym for Baraī.
Pardhān	A branch of the Goṇḍ tribe which acts as priests and ministrels.
Parwār	A subcaste of Baniā.
Pāṭhān	A Mohammedan money-lender, usually from Afghanistan.
Rāj Goṇḍs	The landholding subdivision of the Goṇḍ tribe.

Rājpūt	Representatives of the Kshatriya or warrior caste.
Satnāmī	A religious movement among the Chamārs of the Central Provinces resulting in a new group.
Savar	A primitive tribe of Mūṇḍā origin.
Sonār	The occupational caste of goldsmiths and silversmiths.
S'ūdra	The fourth of the four traditional castes.
Sunār	See Sonār.
Sutār	Synonym for Barhaī.
Telī	The occupational caste of oil-pressers and sellers.
Thākur	A common title for the Rājpūt.
Vaisha	The third of the four traditional castes. Merchants.

Appendix V

BIBLIOGRAPHY

Balfour, Edward — *Cyclopædia of India*, London, 1885.

Bean, R. B. — *The Races of Man*. New York, The University Society, 1942.

Blunt, E. A. H. — *The Caste System of Northern India*. London, Humphrey Milford, Oxford University Press, 1931.

Briggs, G. W. — *The Chamars*. London, Humphrey Milford, Oxford University Press, 1920.

Bonnerjea, B. — *De Hevesey on Munda and Finno-Ugrian Linguistics and Easter Island Scripts*. American Anthropologist, Vol. 38, No. 1, pages 148, 149.

Buxton, L. H. Dudley — *The Peoples of Asia*. London, Kegan Paul, 1925.

Census of India Reports — General and Provincial.

Chakladar, H. C. — *Problems of the Racial Composition of the Indian Peoples*. Man in India, Vol. XVI, pages 99-134.

Chandra, Ramprasad — *The Indo Aryan Races*. Rajshahi, 1916.

Crooke, William — *Kol, Kolarian*. Hasting's Encyclopædia of Religion and Ethics, Vol. VII, p. 754.

Munda. Hasting's Encyclopædia of Religion and Ethics, Vol. IX, p. 1.

Religion and Folklore of Northern India. London, Oxford University Press, 1926.

Things Indian. London, John Murray, 1906.

Tribes and Castes of the North West Provinces and Oudh. Four Vols., Calcutta, 1896.

Dalton, Col. E. T. — *Descriptive Ethnology of Bengal*. Calcutta, 1872.

The Kols of Chota Nagpur. Journal of the Asiatic Society of Bengal, Vol. XXXV, part I, pp. 155ff, 1866.

Davids, T. W. Rhys — *Buddhist India*. New York, G. Putnam, 1903.

Davidson, D. S. — *The Question of Relationship Between the Cultures of Australia and Terra del Fuego*.

Dixon, Ronald B. — *The Racial History of Man*. New York, Charles Scribner's Sons, 1923.

Dubois, Abbe J. A. — *Hindu Manners, Customs and Ceremonies*. London, Humphrey Milford, Oxford University Press, edition of 1924.

Dutt, Nripendra K. — *Origin and Growth of Caste in India*. London, K. Paul, Trench, Trubener Co., 1931.

Eickstedt, Egon Frh. Von — *Ranssengeschichta von Indien mit besondered Berucksichtigung Von Mysore*. Zeits f Morph u Anthropol, XXXII, 1933.

Elmore, Wilber T. — *Dravidian Gods in Modern Hinduism*. Hamilton, New York, 1915.

Elwin, Verrier — *Leaves from the Jungle*. London, John Murray, 1936.

The Baiga, London, John Murray, 1939.

Enthoven, R. E. *Tribes and Castes of Bombay.* Three Vols. Bombay, 1920.
Folklore of Bombay. Bombay, 1924.

Forsythe, Capt. J. *The Highlands of Central India.* London, Chapman and Hall, 1871.

Fraser, Sir. J. *The Golden Bough.* Vol. I. New York, The Macmillan Co., 1906 and 1935.

Ghurye, G. S. *Caste and Race in India.* London, Kegan Paul, Trench, Trubener Co., 1932.

Gopinatha Rao, T. A. *Elements of Hindu Iconography.* Madras, The Law Printing House, 2 Vols. 1914.

Grierson, Sir G. A. *Bihar Peasant Life.* Patna, Government Printing Office, 1926.

Griffith, R. J. H. Translation of the *Ramayana.*

Grigson, W. V. *The Maria Gonds of Bastar.* London, Humphrey Milford, Oxford University Press, 1938.

Guha, B. S. *An Outline of the Racial Ethnology of India.* Reprint from *An Outline of the Field Sciences of India*, pages 125-140, Calcutta, Indian Science Congress, 1937.

Progress of Anthropology in India During the Past Twenty-five Years. Reprint from *Progress of Science in India During the Past Twenty-five Years*, pages 300-335, Calcutta, Indian Science Congress, 1938.

Census of India, 1931, Vol. 1, Part 3. Delhi, Government of India Press, 1935.

Hadden, A. C. *The Races of Man.* London, Cambridge University Press, 1924.

Hiralal Rai Bahadur *The Aborigines of Central India.* Man in India, II, pp. 14-38, 1922.

Hislop, S. *Papers Relating to the Aboriginal Tribes of the Central Provinces.* Nagpur, 1866.

Hodson, T. C. *The Primitive Culture of India.* London, Royal Asiatic Society, 1922.

Hoffman, J. and Van Emelen, A. *Hore.* Encyclopædia Mundarica, Orissa, Superintendent of Government Printing, 1930-1935. Set not complete. Up to 1935 A to O published.

Hume, R. E. *The Thirteen Principal Upanishads.* London, Humphrey Milford, Oxford University Press, 1930.

Huntington, E. *The Character of Races.* New York, Scribner's, 1924.

Hutton, J. H. *Census of India*, 1931. Vol. I, parts 1-3. Delhi, Superintendent of Government Printing, 1933-1935.

Mon and Munda in India and Beyond. Proceedings National Institute of Sciences, India, Vol. I, pages 101-106, 1935.

The Sema Nagas. London, Macmillan and Company, 1921.

Kraemer, H. *The Christian Message in a non-Christian World.* New York, Harpers, 1938.

Kroeber, A. L. *Anthropology.* Harcourt Brace & Co., 1923.

Lacy, W. G. *Census of India*, 1931. Vol. VII, parts 1 and 2. Patna, Government Printing Office, 1933.

Law, B. C. *Ancient Indian Tribes.* Lahore, 1926.

Lowie, R. H. *Primitive Society*, New York, Boni and Liveright, 1925.

Luard, C. F. *The Ethnographic Survey of Central India.* Indore, 1909.

Macdonell, A. A. *India's Past.* Oxford, Clarendon Press, 1927.

Macdonell, A. A., and Keith, A. B. *A Vedic Index of Names and Subjects.* London, Two Volumes, 1912.

Macdonell, A. R. *Lecture on Comparative Religion.* Calcutta, Calcutta University Press, 1925.

Mackay, Ernest *The Indus Civilization.* London, Lovet, Dickenson and Thompson, 1935.

Majumdar, B. C. *The Aborigines of the Highlands of Central India.* Calcutta, University of Calcutta Press, 1927.

Martin, E. O. *The Gods of India.* London, J. M. Dent and Sons, 1914.

Marshall, Sir John *Mohenjo-daro and the Indus Civilization.* Vol. I, Text. London, Arthur Probsthain, 1931.

Mitra, P. *Cultural Affinities Between India and Polynesia.* Man in India, XI, pages 217-242; and XII, pages 30-43.

Monier-Williams, M. *Brahmanism and Hinduism.* London, 1891.

Muir, J. *Sanskrit Texts.* London, 1868.

Murray *New English Dictionary.* Art. Coolie.

Nelson, A. E. *Jubbulpore Gazetteer,* Allahabad, 1909.

O'Malley, L. S. S. *Popular Hinduism.* New York, Macmillan & Co., 1935.

Peake, H. and Fluere, H. J. *Priests and Kings.* London, Humphrey Milford, Oxford University Press

Popley, H. A. *The Music of India.* Calcutta, Association Press, 1921.

Rahmann, Von Rudolf *Gottheiten der Primitivstamme in Nordostlichen Vorderindien.* Anthropos, Vol. 31, pages 37-96. 1936.

Rangachariya, V. *Pre-Mussalman India.* Vol. II. Madras, Indian Publishing House, 1937.

Rawlinson, H. G. *India, a Short Cultural History.* London, D. Appleton-Century Co., 1938.

Rapson, E. J. (Ed.) *Cambridge History of India.* Vol. I. Cambridge University Press, 1922.

Risley, Sir H. H. *The People of India.* Calcutta, Thacker Spink & Co., 1915.

The Tribes and Castes of Bengal. Two Vols., Calcutta, Bengal Secretariat Press, 1891.

Rose, H. H. *Tribes and Castes of the Panjab and North West Frontier Province.* Three Vols:, Lahore, 1911-1919.

Roy, Sarat Chandra *The Birhors.* Ranchi, Man in India Office, 1925.

The Hill Bhuiyas of Orissa. Ranchi, 1935.

The Kharias. Two Vols. Ranchi, 1937.

The Mundas and Their Country. Ranchi, 1912.

The Oraons of Chota Nagpur. Ranchi, 1915.

Oraon Religion and Customs. Ranchi, 1930.

Russell, R. V., and Hiralal, Rai Bahadur *The Tribes and Castes of Central Provinces.* London, Macmillan & Co., 1916.

Saletore, B. A. *The Wild Tribes in Indian History.* Lahore, Panjab Sanskrit Book Depot, 1935.

Sewell, R. B. S., and Guha, B. S. *Mohenjo-daro and Indus Civilization.* II, 1931.

Shoobert, W. H. *Census of India.* 1931, Vol. XII, parts 1 and 2. Nagpur, 1933.

Slater, G. *The Dravidian Element in Indian Culture.* London, Ernest Benn, Ltd., 1924.

Sleeman, W. H. *Rambles and Recollections of an Indian Official.* London, Oxford Press, 1915.

Smith, V. A. *The Early History of India.* London, Oxford University Press, 1915.

Thurston, E. *Castes and Tribes of Southern India.* Seven Vols. Madras, 1909.

Underhill, M. M. *The Hindu Religious Year.* Calcutta, Association Press, 1921.

Uxbond, F. A. *Munda-Magyar-Maori—An Indian Link Between the Antipodes.* London, Luzac, 1938.

Various *Anthropological Society of Bombay, Jubilee Volume.* Bombay, Fort Press, 1938.

Venkatachar, S. C. *Census of India,* 1931, Vol. XX, parts 1 and 2, Delhi, 1933.

History of Tribal Migrations in Central India. Census, 1931, XX, Vol. I, pages 267-297.

Viswanatha, S. V. *Racial Synthesis in Hindu Culture.* London, Kegan Paul, Trench, Trubener & Co., 1928.

Wallis W. D. *An Introduction to Anthropology.* New York, Harper's Brothers, 1926.

Whitehead, Henry *The Village Gods of South India.* London, Oxford University Press, 1921.

Wilkins, W. J. *Hindu Mythology.* Calcutta, Thacker Spink & Co., 1882.

Wissler, C. *An Introduction to Social Anthropology.* New York, Henry Holt & Co., 1929.

GLOSSARY OF VERNACULAR TERMS

Agahān	The eighth Hindu month: November-December.
Ajwāyan	The dill plant, *Anethum graveolens.*
Amarbel	A parasitic plant, the common dodder, *Cuscuta reflexa.*
Amāvāsya	The festival of the new moon.
Anāsa	From the Sanskrit: 'noseless.'
Andī	The castor-oil plant: *Palma christi.*
Anna (ānā)	A coin of the value of one pence or two cents. There are sixteen annas to the rupee.
Antara	The second section of the northern Indian type of melody.
Ārām	Rest.
Āryā	A member of the Aryan race.
Aṣāṛa	The third Hindu month: June-July.
Āshram	A hermitage; place of retreat and meditation.
Asura	A demon.
Atharvaveda	One of the revealed scriptures of the Hindus.
Avatāra	A manifestation (sometimes called incarnation), of the Hindu god Vishnu.
Bābā	Father. The term often applied to an ascetic.
Babūl	The tree *Acacia arabica.*
Badhāwā	The song of congratulation sung by the women at the time a male child is born.
Bagāi	Rice straw from which ropes are made.
Baghelkhaṇḍ	The northern part of the peninsula of India which borders the Ganges valley.
Bahnoī	Sister's husband.
Baid	The dispenser of village remedies.
Baikūnṭha	The abode of Vishṇu.
Baishākh	The first month of the Hindu year: April-May.
Baṛ	The sacred banyan tree. *Ficus indica.*
Barā	A food made with black pulse.
Bārahmāsi	'Twelve months': used of a song covering the months of the year.
Baṛāin	An earthenware pot.
Barāt	The procession of men bringing the bridegroom for the wedding ceremonies.
Baṛdān	A boon given by a god.
Baṛī	'Elder' as in *baṛī rānī*; first; big.
Barkhī (Barsī)	The feast observed on the first anniversary of a death in the family.
Barti	Blessing.
Batāsā	A sugar-like sweet.
Bāwa (often bhāwa)	The state of spirit-possession, trance.
Bel	The tree *Aegle marmelos.*

Ber	A fruit from the tree *Zizyphus jujuba.*
Bewar	The custom of burning jungle and planting seeds in the ashes. Next year the tribe moves onward and burns another area.
Bhādon	The fifth month of the Hindu year: August-September.
Bhāgal	Elopement; running away.
Bhagat	A kind of song sung before a village shrine.
Bhagawān	Literally, 'the Adorable One'; a name of deity. Frequently applied to Rāma.
Bhajan	A song addressed to deity, usually to Rāma or Bhagawān, according to Kols.
Bhakta	One following the way of *Bhakti.*
Bhakti	Passionate devotion to deity.
Bhanwar	Circumambulation of the wedding pole.
Bhāt	Cooked rice; rice ready to eat.
Bhelwā	The nut from the tree *Semecarpus anacardum.*
Bhū	The earth; ground.
Bhūmi	Of the earth or the ground.
Bhūt	An evil spirit or ghost.
Bidā or Bidāi	Farewell. A part of the wedding cycle. Leave taking.
Bihārī	A kind of song used at times of enjoyment and happiness.
Biluī	The feast observed by women on the sixth night after the birth of a child.
Birhā	A forest song sung without the help of an instrument. A song of separation.
Biṛī	The country cigarette.
Biwāh	Marriage.
Brahmā	The Creator in the Hindu triad.
Brahmachāriā	The period of life lived as a bachelor.
Brāhmaṇa	A portion of the sacred scriptures of the Hindus.
Brān	A food used in the wedding ceremony. Prepared at both houses and mixed in the wedding booth.
Chaita	The last month of the Hindu year: March-April.
Chanā	Pulse, usually *Dolichos lablab.*
Chandan	The sandal wood tree, *Santalum album.*
Chāṇwal	Uncooked rice.
Chāpātī	An unleavened bread made of whole wheat flour.
Chaṛ	The tree *Buchanania latifola.*
Charī	The presentation of gifts at the time of marriage.
Chārpāī	A rude cot with rope bottom.
Chaṭāī	A bamboo screen.
Chaṭnī	A condiment generally highly seasoned.
Chaudharī Chamār	A headman from the caste of leather workers.
Chauk	An area marked off by lines; usually square.
Chhāhur	A bundle of grass, often consisting of a piece from the roof of each dwelling place, put on a pole and set in the village shrine.
Chhaṛībardār	The assistant to the head of the village council.
Chhatarī	Umbrella.

Chhaṭṭhī	The sixth-day celebration. A woman's festival observed on the sixth day after a birth.
Chhattrī	A member of the second caste. A Kshatariya.
Chhauhar	A kind of song sung on the sixth night after the birth of a child.
Chhoṭi (f.)	Small.
Chimṭā	Fire-tongs.
Chitā	The cremation spot, pyre.
Choṭī	The tuft of hair left at the top of the head by orthodox Hindus.
Chūlhā	An earthen fireplace where food is cooked.
Chūṇā	Lime.
Chūnāriyā	The coloured dancing shawl.
Churel	The evil spirit of a deceased female.
Chūṛī	Bangles such as worn by women. Usually glass.
Chuṭiyā	See *choṭī*.
Daba (Dūba)	The grass, *agrestis linearis*, Koen; *Cynodon dactylon*, Royle.
Dādrā or dādar	A particular kind of song with a syncopated rhythm. Also the name of a dance.
Dahī	Curds.
Dahīṇgar	An earthenware vessel in which curds are brought to the engagement ceremonies.
Dāī	Mid-wife.
Dāl	A pulse; split pea.
Dān	Charity.
Dānawa	A kind of evil spirit.
Dārchīnī	Cinnamon.
Darśana	A heavenly visitation; a vision.
Dāsa	A slave; servant.
Daśarā	Hindu festival observed in the Fall.
Dasyu	Peoples; nations.
Daśwī	The mourning period of ten days.
Daurī	A small basket.
Ḍaunā or ḍonā	A leaf-plate; a cup made of leaves.
Ḍaunā rakhnā	To put out food for the deceased.
Deotā	Godling.
Desh	Country; habitation.
Deva	A god.
Devatā	Godling.
Devī	A goddess.
Dewāhar or dewāla	The shrine in or by the house.
Dewālī	A Hindu festival coming in the Fall.
Dhan	Wealth; property.
Dharam	Duty; virtue; religion.
Dharamśālā	A rest house for travellers.
Dholak	The common form of drum used by Kols.
Dinpānī	The funeral feast at the end of the period of mourning.
Dīp	A small earthenware lamp.
Diyā	Same as *dīp*.

Dohārī	A song in which the verses are in couplets.
Donā	See *daunā*.
Durgā	One of the names for the wife of Siva.
Dūta	A messenger or angel.
Gaiṇtī	A country pick.
Galgal	The *mainā* bird : *Acridotheres tristis*.
Gālī	Abuse ; curses.
Gandā (*gendā*)	The marigold plant.
Gānjā	A narcotic drug : from the hemp-plant.
Gaonbandh	Tying the whole village to protect against evil.
Gār	Maker ; digger.
Gārnā	To bury in the earth.
Gaunā	The return of the groom to his own home his bride with him.
Gaundā	The gift of alms ; often a cow.
Gayāl	A particular kind of evil spirit.
Gendā	See *gandā*.
Gharā	An earthenware vessel for carrying water and other liquids.
Ghāṭ	A landing place. A bathing place. Used as a name for the place of burning or burial. (*Ghāṭ*).
Ghaṭā	A nut from the plant *Ziziphys xylopyrus*.
Ghazal	A kind of song.
Ghī	Clarified butter.
Ghunghunis	Anklets worn while dancing.
Gobar	Fresh cow dung.
Godnā	Tattoo.
Godnārī	One who tattoos.
Gol mirch	Pepper.
Got	See *gotra*.
Gotra	Literally, 'race', 'family' ; usually used as a name for an exogamous section of a caste. Among Kols exogamy is not implied in their use of this term.
Gūlar	A kind of fig tree, *Ficus glomerata*.
Guṛ	Raw sugar.
Gurda	An iron lash.
Haldī	Turmeric. Yellow colour from *Curcuma longa*.
Hansiyā	The country sickle.
Hareli	The 'greenery' festival, occurring in the rainy season.
Hariyāri	A Hindu festival.
Holī	The spring festival of the Hindus.
Hom	The fire sacrifice or burnt offering.
Hōṛō	Man.
Hukkā	A pipe used in smoking tobacco.
Hurhur	Ginger root, *Cleoma viseosa*.
Ilāchī	Cardamon, *Elettaria cardamomum*.
Imli	The tamarind tree, *Tamarindus indica*.
Indra	The Vedic God of rain.
Ishwara	A name for God.
Jādū ṭonhā	A magical spell.

Jāman	Fruit from the *Eugenia jambolana.*
Janmāsā or Janwāsā	The tarrying-place of the bridegroom and his party durin their stay at the bride's village
Jawārā	One of the most important of the Kol festivals. Associated with sowing season.
Jeṭha	The second Hindu month: May-June. The eldest; feminine form *Jeṭhi.*
Jhaṇḍā	Flag.
Jhāṛnā	To sweep; to exorcise.
Jhopṛī	A rude hut.
Jind	The spirit of a deceased Mohammedan.
Jīrā	Cummin seed, *Cuminum cyminum.*
Juār	The millet *Sorghum vulgare.*
Kabbīs	An evil spirit said to suck blood.
Kabīrī	A particular type of song, often obscene.
Kachhā or kachchā	Unripe; not strong; temporary.
Kājra	Lamp-black.
Kālī	A goddess, the wife of S'iva.
Kalśa	An earthenware vessel.
Kaṉkan	Coloured beads strung on an iron wire.
Kaṉs	The grass *Saccharum spontaneum.*
Kaṉwar	A bamboo pole with a basket slung from the ends.
Karma	The postulate that one reaps according as he sows and that the events of the present life were determined by the deeds of the previous ones.
Kartāl	A cluster of cymbals.
Kārtika	The seventh Hindu month: October-November.
Kaṛowār (Kaṛwā)	Oil from the mustard plant *Brassica juncea.*
Kathā	A sacred story sung at time of worship.
Kaṭhautā	A wooden dish used by a group of Kols.
Kaṭhotā	See *Kaṭhautā.*
Kathrī	Mattress, quilt.
Kaṭīlī	A teasing song
Khaḍga	A sword.
Khair	Gum from the *Acacia catechu.*
Khairwār	The tree *Acacia catechu.*
Khajleniā	A religious festival.
Khajūr	The wild date palm *Phoenix sylvestris.*
Khanḍī	A measure of grain. Varies, but around Jubbulpore is about two hundred pounds.
Khaṛaū	Spiked sandals.
Kharī	Ashes remaining after cremation, chalk.
Kārīghaṭ	The place at the river where the ashes are thrown.
Khaskhas	Poppy seed.
Khaṭiyā	A rude country cot.
Khichṛī	A food made of rice and pulse boiled together.
Khīr	Rice boiled in milk.
Khodnā	To dig.

Khurpī	An iron weeder used by gardners.
Kodāli	Mattock.
Kodo	The grain *Paspalum scrobiculatum*.
Kogī	A kind of evil spirit.
Kos	A rough measure of distance. About two miles.
Krishṇa	One of the incarnations of Vishṇu.
Kuli	Tamil word for coolie.
Kumhṛā	Gourd; pumpkin.
Kuṉwār	The sixth Hindu month: September-October.
Kuṛhā	A black earthenware dish.
Kuṛhī	Literally a 'share', or 'family'. Kols use this term for their subdivisions.
Kurset	The common night-jar bird: *Caprimulgus asiaticus*.
Kuś	The grass *Poa cynosuroides*.
Kusum tel	Oil from *Sleichera trijuga*.
Laḍḍū	Balls made of whole wheat flour.
Lagan	The directions for the wedding as drawn up by the priest.
Lahakaur	Food prepared for the bridegroom.
Lahangā	The coloured dancing dress.
Lahasun	Garlic.
Lāī	Puffed or parched rice.
Lakshmi	The wife of Vishṇu.
Lakshmaṇ	The brother of Rāma.
Lāṭhī	A bamboo staff.
Lāwā	Food prepared at the *mangarmāṭī* ceremony for use in the marriage ceremonies.
Lepnā	To plaster with a mixture of cow dung and mud.
Lingam stone	The stone used in connection with Saivite shrines and temples.
Lohān	Incense.
Long	Cloves.
Loṛhā	The stone roller used to grind spices.
Loṭā	A drinking vessel, usually of brass.
Māgha	The tenth month of the Hindus: January-February.
Magrohān	The sacred wedding pole at the centre of the wedding booth.
Mahābhārata	One of the epics of the Hindus dealing with the heroic age.
Mahābrāhmin	The funeral priest.
Mahādeo	A name for S'iva.
Mahallā	A section of town usually reserved for the lower classes.
Mahārāj	May mean 'sir' or 'great king'.
Mahāsabhā	A general gathering.
Mahāta	Leader; head of the village council.
Mahūā	The tree *Bassia latifolia*.
Māī	Mother.
Majīrā	Cymbals.
Mālguzār	A landlord.
Mānḍāp	The wedding booth.
Manḍil	A small raised platform.
Mangarmāṭī	A part of the wedding cycle. Lucky earth ceremony. The Betrothal-earth.

Māngnā	To beg; to ask.
Mantra	A magic spell: written or oral.
Manu	The ancient law giver of the Hindus.
Marghaṭ	The place of burial.
Maṛhwā	The wedding booth.
Maṛki	An earthenware pot used in the wedding cycle.
Marpake	A festival in connection with the dead.
Masān	The burial place.
Mashāl	A lighted torch set on the end of a stick.
Mātā	Mother.
Matia	The whirlwind demon.
Maund (Man)	A measure of weight of about eighty pounds.
Maur	The wedding crown worn by the bridegroom.
Māyā	The Hindu doctrine of illusion.
Melā	A religious gathering on some festival day.
Mukaddam	Head man of a village.
Muṇdan	The ceremony of first hair-cutting.
Muni	An ascetic; a holy man.
Murdyāghāṭ	The cremation place.
Mūsar	Threshing flail.
Nāī	Barber.
Nāg	Snake: usually the cobra.
Nāgpañchamī	The festival when snakes are worshipped.
Nagāriyā	The kettle drum.
Nalā	A water course, but usually dry.
Naodurgāṇ	A Hindu religious festival.
Nārā	The umbilical cord.
Narkuṇda	Hell.
Nāriyal	Cocoanut.
Nazar	The evil eye.
Nerbuddā	The sacred river of Central India.
Nim	The tree *Melia azadirachta*.
Nimār	A district in south-western Central Provinces.
Pagṛī	The cloth tied around the head for protection.
Pakkā	Ripe; mature; firm; settled.
Palāsa	The tree *Butea frondosa*.
Pālkī	A litter; sedan carried by bearers.
Pālnā	Bed of spikes.
Pān	A concoction used for chewing and made of areca nut, lime, tobacco and piper leaves.
Pañch	Five. The village council.
Pañchāyat	The village council.
Paṇḍā	The Kol priest.
Paṇḍit	A wise man. The Brahmin priest.
Paṇkhā	Fan.
Pāp	Sin.
Paramātmā	The Supreme Spirit.
Pardā	Curtain; screen.
Pārvatī	A name for the wife of S'iva.
Pasni	The first-feeding with solid food.

Patthar	Stone.
Paṭel	A landlord.
Phāg	The festival coming in the spring; *holī*. A type of song sung at this season.
Phāgun	The eleventh Hindu month: February-March.
Phāoṛā	Mattock.
Phūphā	Father's sister's husband.
Phūphī	Father's sister.
Phūphū	Father's sister.
Pice (Paisā)	A coin valued about ¼ pence and ½ cent. There are four pice to the anna.
Piṇḍā	Mounds in which a goddess may reside.
Pīpal	The sacred tree *Ficus religosia.*
Pīṛā (piṛhā)	A low stool.
Piśācha	A particular kind of demon.
Pret	Another kind of evil spirit.
Pūjā	Worship.
Purāṇas	Part of the Hindu scriptures.
Pūrī	A pancake-like food fried in clarified butter.
Purānī chāl	A type of the *dādrā* dance.
Purusha	One of the names applied to God.
Pūs	The ninth Hindu month: December-January.
Pūsān	A festival falling in the month of *Pūs*.
Rāī	Mustard. A type of questionable song.
Rāj	Kingdom.
Rājā	King.
Rājkumār	Prince.
Rājpūt	Warrior and landholding caste.
Rākhi	The festival of 'protection'.
Rākshasa	A very powerful demon.
Rāma	The name of one of the descents of Vishṇu, hero of the epic poem Rāmāyaṇa.
Rāman (Raunā)	Bringing the bride to live permanently in the husband's house.
Rāmāyaṇa	The epic poem relating the adventures of Rāma and Sītā.
Rāmnavami	A Hindu festival on Rāma's birthday.
Rānī	Queen.
Raunā	See *rāman*.
Rāwat	Prince.
Ṛigveda	A revealed scripture of the Hindus.
Ṛishi	A hermit; devotee.
Rupee (Rs.) (Rūpiyā)	A coin valued about one shilling four pence or thirty-five cents.
Sādhu	An ascetic; holy man.
Sādhunī	A female ascetic.
Sādī	A general term for the wedding, but specifically the part of the ceremony performed on the second night.
Sāg	A green vegetable.
Saikarā	A measure of stone, about 1000 cubic feet.
Sāl	The tree *Sheora robusta.*

Salām (Salaam)	Greeting.
Sālagrāma	A stone used in connection with Vishṇu worship.
Sāleh	The tree *Boswellia serrata*, essential wood for the wedding pole.
Saṃsāra	The Hindu doctrine of transmigration.
Sār (sārā)	Brother-in-law.
S'āradā	Pertaining to autumn.
Sarahaj	Brother-in-law's wife.
Sārangī	A one-stringed musical instrument.
Sāṛī	The woman's dress.
Sarsoṉ	Mustard oil from the *Brassica juncea*.
Sās	Mother-in-law.
Sasur	Father-in-law.
Sāth Bhāī	Birds which go about in groups of seven, popularly called the seven brothers. *Cratcropus canorus.*
Satī	Literally 'the faithful wife'. The woman who burns herself upon her husband's funeral pyre.
Sāwan	The fourth Hindu month: July-August.
Seer (ser)	Two pounds as a measure of weight; also a liquid measure of about a quart.
Semal	The cotton tree *Bombax malabaricum.*
Seṉdūr	Red lead. Usually mixed with oil to form a red paste and used in many ceremonies. Vermilion.
Shaitānī	Satanic. The name of a dance.
Sil	The flat grindstone on which condiments are ground.
Siṉghārā	The water caltrop, *Trapa bispinosa* or *natans*.
Sirānā	Headside. The act of throwing ashes into the river in order to bring rest to the dead.
Sirwant	A Hindu festival.
Sītā	The wife of Rāma. Stolen by the demon king of Ceylon.
Sitār	A musical instrument generally having seven strings.
S'iva	The third member of the Hindu triad; the destroyer.
S'rāwan	See *Sāwan*.
S'ubha	Auspicious.
Sūpa	The winnowing basket or fan.
Supārī nut	Used in making *pān*, the *Areca catechu*.
Swāhā	Burnt to ashes, hence accepted.
Swasā	Helper.
Swasāhā	Self-help. Probably a corruption of *swastha*, 'self-reliant,' 'independent.'
Tablā	A drum.
Tahsīl	A subdivision of a district or state.
Ṭakkā	A coin valued at two pice. Half penny; two cents.
Ṭaṭarī	The bamboo sling on which the corpse is transported to the cemetery.
Ṭaṭī	A bamboo screen.
Tel	Oil
Teṉdū	Leaves used for the covering of country cigarettes from the *Diosypros embryopteris, melanoxylon, montana,* etc.

Ṭhākur	A master; a landholder; usually a member of the second or warrior caste; a Kshatriya.
Thālī	A brass tray.
Til or tillī	The *Sesamum indicum* from which sweet oil is manufactured.
Tījā	A religious festival; particularly observed by women.
Ṭīk	The tuft of hair left on the head by orthodox Hindus.
Ṭīkā	A mark or marks made on the forehead or face with vermilion or other colours. Sometimes the *ṭīkā* is of lac and is pasted on.
Ṭimakiā	The kettle drum.
Ṭimkī (ṭamkī)	Another term for the kettle drum.
Ṭolābandh	The tying of a portion of a village to protect it from the entrance of evil spirits.
Ṭōpī	Hat; headgear.
Ṭoṭak vidha	A magical charm.
Triśūl	The trident.
Tulasī	The sacred plant *Ocymum sanctum*.
Umā	A name for the wife of S'iva.
Upanishad	The wisdom literature of the Hindus.
Urai	The grass *Vetiveria zizanioides*.
Urad	The black pulse *Phaseolus radiatus*.
Vindhya	A range of mountains in Central India, running from south-west to north-east.
Vishṇu	The second member of the Hindu triad, the preserver.
Yama	The Hindu god of death who dwells in the south.
Yogī	An ascetic; a devotee.
Zamīndār	A landlord.

APPENDIX VII

ANTHROPOMETRIC

In April 1938, by an arrangement with Dr. B. S. Guha, of the department of Anthropology of the Zoological Survey of India, a trained worker, Dr. B. K. Chatterji, came to Jubbulpore and during the course of some two weeks we made the usual measurements on 150 Kols : 127 men and 23 women. In the tables following the men are divided into two groups depending whether they belonged to the Rautiya or the Thakuriya subdivision.

The statistical results which follow were kindly compiled by Dr. C. Chandra Sekar, head of the Statistical Laboratory, Indian Statistical Institute. Dr. Chatterji is also working out a detailed analysis which at the date of printing is not ready for publication and inclusion here. However, it is hoped that this will appear separately later on and will give a full analysis of the measurements together with his observations on racial likenesses and affinities to other groups.

No detailed comparison with other groups is made here, nor are any theories of racial relationship advanced in respect to these measurements. They are recorded for the use of any who may find them helpful in making wider generalizations in relation to other anthropological data.

In addition to the tables the following general observations are taken from our notes :

1. *Skin Colour, (Von Luschan Scale).*

(1) Men :

Colour No.	No.
23	2
24	5
25	31
26	56
27	8
28	13
29	12
	127

(2) Women :

Colour No.	No.
21	2
22	1
23	2
24	2
25	7
26	7
27	—
28	1
29	1
	23

2. *Eye Colour*

Men :

Black	48
Dark Brown	47
Medium Brown	32
	127

(2) Women :

Black	15
Dark Brown	3
Medium Brown	5
	23

3. *Eye Shape*

(1) Men:

Oblique	19
Slightly oblique	47
Straight	20
Not recorded	41
	127

(2) Women:

Oblique	5
Slightly oblique	3
Straight	3
Not recorded	12
	23

Epicanthic fold noted in two cases, both men.

4. *Mongoloid appearances*

(1) Men:

Slightly mongoloid	2
Mongoloid	26 or 22%

(2) Women:

Slightly mongoloid	1
Mongoloid	7 or 35%

5. *Hair Colour*

Both men and women:

Black	56
Dark Brown	94

6. *Hair Texture*

Curly	Nil
Wavy	4%
Straight	73%
Straight and rather coarse	23%

7. *Lips.*

Very thick	13 %
Thick	78 %
Medium	4.5%
Thin	4.5%

Lower lip generally thicker than upper.

TABLE I.

Statististical analysis of Anthropometric Measurements of 95 Adult Male Rautiyas

Measurement in mm.	Mean	Probable error of mean ±	Standard deviation	Probable error of standard deviation ±	Coefficient of Variation	Probable error of variation ±
1. Stature	1599.66	5.38	77.72	3.80	4.9	.24
2. Height up to Tragion	1477.25	3.68	53.77	2.60	3.6	.18
3. Auricular height						
4. Max. head length	182.20	.58	8.45	.41	4.6	.23
5. Max. head breadth	137.35	.29	4.23	.21	3.1	.15
6. Min. Frontal breadth	101.75	.27	3.96	.19	3.9	.19
7. Max. Bizygomatic breadth	131.13	.29	4.16	.20	3.2	.16
8. Bigonial breadth	98.81	.33	4.82	.24	4.9	.24
9. Interorbital breadth	29.76	.23	3.30	.16	11.1	.54
10. Orbito nasal breadth	101.33	.41	5.93	.29	5.9	.29
11. Orbito nasal arc	117.13	.41	5.95	.29	5.1	.25
12. Nasal length	47.29	.25	3.66	.18	7.7	.38
13. Nasal breadth	37.00	.20	2.85	.14	7.7	.38
14. Nasal height or depth	16.96	.12	1.77	09	10.4	.51
15. Upper facial length	57.45	.30	4.40	.22	7.7	.38
16. Total facial length	113.38	.53	7.66	.37	6.8	.33
17. Hor. circm. of the head	526.08	.94	13.63	.67	2.6	.13
18. Sagittal arc	336.22	.88	12.70	.62.	3.8	.19
19. Transverse arc	318.02	.82	11.81	.50	3.7	.18

TABLE II

Statistical Analysis of Anthropometric Measurements of 23 adult female Rautiyas

Measurement in mm.	Mean	Probable error of mean ±	Standard deviation	Probable error of standard deviation ±	Coefficient of variation	Probable error of variation ±
1. Stature	1490.80	6.78	48.21	4.7[illegible]	3.2	.31
2. Height up to Tragion	1362.20	7.05	50.10	4.98	3.7	.37
3. Auricular Ht.						
4. Max head length	174.65	.92	6.56	.65	3.8	.38
5. Max head breadth	133.39	1.01	7.17	.71	5.4	.54
6. Minimum frontal breadth	98.57	.46	3.24	.32	3.3	.33
7. Max. Bizygomatic breadth	124.74	.72	5.12	.51	4.1	.41
8. Bigonial breadth	96.22	1.18	8.41	.84	8.7	.87
9. Interorbital breadth	29.35	.23	1.63	.16	5.6	.56
10. Orbito nasal breadth	99.04	.50	3.58	.36	3.6	.36
11. Orbito nasal arc	114.70	.43	3.03	.30	2.6	.26
12. Nasal length	44.30	.55	3.90	.39		.88
13. Nasal breadth	34.00	.25	1.79	.18	5.3	.53
14. Nasal height or depth	15.39	.22	1.58	.16	10.3	1.02
15. Upper facial length	55.04	.72	5.15	.51	9.4	.93
16. Total facial length	105.61	.82	5.82	.58	5.5	.55
17. Hor. circm. of the head	517.70	1.93	13.74	1.37	2.7	.27
18. Sagittal arc	317.36	1.50	10.45	1.06	3.3	.33
19. Transverse arc	306.13	1.73	12.31	1.22	4.0	.40

TABLE III

Statistical Analysis of Anthropometric Measurements of thirty-three adult male Thakuriyas

Measurement in mm.	Mean	Probable error of mean ±	Standard deviation	Probable error of standard deviation ±	Coefficient of Variation	Probable error of Variation ±
1. Stature	1613.21	5.26	44.83	3.72	2.8	.23
2. Height up to Tragion	1483.72	5.48	46.00	3.88	3.1	.26
3. Auricular Ht.						
4. Max. head length	183.55	.59	5.03	.42	2.7	.22
5. Max. head breadth	139.67	.64	5.47	.45	3.9	.32
6. Minimum frontal breadth	103.85	.43	3.62	.30	3.5	.29
7. Max. Bizygomatic breadth	131.55	.43	3.63	.30	2.8	.23
8. Bigonial breadth	98.88	.51	4.33	.36	4.4	.37
9. Interorbital breadth	29.52	.27	2.28	.19	7.7	.64
10. Orbito nasal breadth	102.21	.41.	3.50	.29	3.4	.28
11. Orbito nasal arc	118.85	.42	3.55	.29	3.0	.25
12. Nasal length	48.70	.38	3.21	.27	6.5	.54
13. Nasal breadth	37.73	.24	2.02	.17	5.4	.45
14. Nasal height or depth	17.45	.27	2.32	.19	13.3	1.10
15. Upper facial length	59.81	.48	4.01	.34	6.7	.56
16. Total facial length	115.33	.70	5.99	.50	5.20	.43
17. Hor. cirm of the head	528.91	1.53	12.99	1.08	2.5	.21
18. Saggital arc	339.91	1.23	10.48	.87	3.1	.26
19. Transverse arc	322.85	1.35	11.48	.95	3.6	.30

TABLE IV

INDICES

Index	Mean	Probable error of mean ±	Standard deviation	Probable error of standard deviation ±	Coefficient of Variation	Probable error of Variation ±
1. Ninety-five adult Rautiya Males—						
Cephalic	75.55	.31	4.45	.22	5.80	.20
Nasal	78.78	.64	9.29	.45	11.79	.58
Facial	86.53	.42	6.14	.30	7.10	.35
2. Twenty-three Rautiya Females—						
Cephalic	76.44	.61	4.34	.43	5.68	.56
Nasal	77.33	1.12	7.07	.79	10.31	1.03
Facial	84.79	.78	5.58	.55	6.58	.65
3. Thirty-three adult Thakuriya Males—						
Cephalic	76.13	.38	3.22	.27	4.23	.35
Nasal	77.82	.79	6.69	.56	8.60	.71
Facial	87.73	.58	4.94	.41	5.63	.47

INDEX

C

L

M

N

U

V

W

Y

Z